ARBITRATION OF TRUST DISPUTES

ELGAR ARBITRATION LAW AND PRACTICE

The Elgar Arbitration Law and Practice series is a library of works by leading practitioners and scholars covering key areas of commercial and investment arbitration. The titles in the series are analytical in approach, highlighting and unpicking the legal issues that are most critical and relevant to practice. Designed to be detailed, focussed reference works, the books in this series aim to offer an authoritative statement on the legal and procedural framework in both established and emerging areas of arbitral practice. The series will include texts covering the rules of specific arbitral bodies and national arbitration laws, regional approaches to commercial and investment arbitration, as well as sector-specific arbitration.

Titles in the series include:

International Commercial Arbitration and the Brussels I Regulation
Louise Hauberg Wilhelmsen

Investment Arbitration in Central and Eastern Europe
Law and Practice
Edited by Csongor Nagy

International Arbitration and EU Law
Edited by José Rafael Mata Dona and Nikos Lavranos

Arbitration of Trust Disputes
Lucas Clover Alcolea

ARBITRATION OF TRUST DISPUTES

LUCAS CLOVER ALCOLEA

Lecturer, Faculty of Law, University of Otago, New Zealand

ELGAR ARBITRATION LAW AND PRACTICE

Edward Elgar
PUBLISHING

Cheltenham, UK • Northampton, MA, USA

Published by
Edward Elgar Publishing Limited
The Lypiatts
15 Lansdown Road
Cheltenham
Glos GL50 2JA
UK

Edward Elgar Publishing, Inc.
William Pratt House
9 Dewey Court
Northampton
Massachusetts 01060
USA

A catalogue record for this book
is available from the British Library

Library of Congress Control Number: 2022932829

This book is available electronically in the **Elgar**online
Law subject collection
http://dx.doi.org/10.4337/9781802201321

Printed on elemental chlorine free (ECF)
recycled paper containing 30% Post-Consumer Waste

ISBN 978 1 80220 131 4 (cased)
ISBN 978 1 80220 132 1 (eBook)

Printed and bound in the USA

'Tradidi quod et accepi' (I Cor. 15:3)

CONTENTS

EXTENDED CONTENTS

ACKNOWLEDGEMENTS

As with all things in life, this book would not have been possible without the help and support of numerous individuals over the years.

Firstly, I would like to thank Professor Fabien Gélinas of the Faculty of Law, McGill University, who has been very supportive of my work over the years and without whose comments, assistance and funding it would not have been possible to complete this work. I am particularly appreciative of his enthusiasm for a work with a very 'English' approach despite being some 5,000km away from the Royal Courts of Justice. In a similar vein, I would like to thank all the members of my supervision committee over the years, Professor Kirsten Anker, Professor Yaëll Emerich and Professor Lionel Smith, whose comments and feedback proved invaluable in refining my work into something I could be proud of. I would also like to thank the various anonymous peer reviewers, whose feedback, whether positive or negative, has proved invaluable.

Secondly, I would like to thank my parents (and family) who formed me into the person I am today and who, more than anything, taught me that '*Principium sapientiae timor Domini*' (Proverbs 9:10). I would also like to highlight their patience in supporting my very roundabout trajectory into the labour market. In the same way, I need to thank my friends, both from the UK and those I have met here, without whose companionship I would long ago have lost my sanity in Montreal's freezing winters and boiling summers.

Thirdly, I would like to thank all the staff of the Faculty of Law and the Nahum Gelber Law Library, without whose work and outstanding resources no student at the Faculty of Law would be able to complete their work.

Fourthly, I would like to thank God and the Holy Family, without whose help I could do nothing. Similarly, I would like to thank my late Godmother, Angela, who, despite our very different traditions, was never anything less than understanding and without whom I would never have completed the most important journey of my life.

Last, but far from least, I would like to thank the entire team at Edward Elgar, not only for having faith in the value of my work but also for their assistance and support during this entire process. I would also like to thank those who have endorsed the book, Professor Nicola Peart, Professor S.I. Strong, and Sophie Nappert for their vote of confidence in my work.

TABLE OF CASES

TABLE OF LEGISLATION

Statutes, treaties, rules and practice directions

1

INTRODUCTION TO THE *ARBITRATION OF TRUST DISPUTES*

A. THE CONTEXT OF TRUST ARBITRATION

Over the last century, arbitration has established itself as one of the most popular means for resolving commercial disputes[1] and has even penetrated fields of law traditionally reserved for the courts, such as antitrust/competition law, company law and even tax law.[2] However, despite offering several clear advantages over court proceedings such as greater enforceability, the ability to choose one's judge, neutrality, confidentiality and speed,[3] it has not made any great inroads into trust disputes.[4] This is all the more surprising considering that at least one major arbitral body, the American Arbitration Association, has created specialist rules for the arbitration of trust and will disputes.[5] Equally the International Chamber of Commerce, whilst not having specialist **1.001**

1 Gary Born, *International Commercial Arbitration* (2nd edn, Kluwer Law International 2014) 93–97; '2015 International Arbitration Survey: Improvements and Innovations in International Arbitration' (Queen Mary University of London 2015) 5.

2 See generally Loukas A Mistelis, *Arbitrability: International & Comparative Perspectives*, vol 19 (Kluwer Law International 2009) pt II.

3 Nigel Blackaby and others, *Redfern and Hunter on International Arbitration* (5th edn, Oxford University Press 2009) 28–31; Philippe Fouchard and Berthold Goldman, *Fouchard, Gaillard, Goldman on International Commercial Arbitration* (Kluwer Law International BV 1999) 1–4; Jacob Grierson and Annet van Hooft, *Arbitrating under the 2012 ICC Rules* (Kluwer Law International 2012) 23–28.

4 See generally Georg von Segesser, 'Arbitration of Trust Disputes' (2017) 35 ASA Bulletin 10; L Cohen and J Poole, 'Trust Arbitration – Is It Desirable and Does It Work?' (2012) 18 Trusts & Trustees 324; Nicholas Le Poidevin, 'Arbitration and Trusts: Can It Be Done?' (2012) 18 Trusts & Trustees 307; Bridget A Logstrom, 'Arbitration in Estate and Trust Disputes: Friend or Foe' (2004) 30 ACTEC J. 266.

5 American Arbitration Association – Wills and Trusts Arbitration Rules and Mediation Procedures 2012.

rules, did create a model clause for trust disputes in 2008[6] and recently released a revised version.[7] Moreover, many academics and practitioners believe that the use of arbitration in trust disputes would be beneficial through, for example, reducing costs, minimising adverse publicity and increasing enforceability.[8] Recent years have also seen a wave of jurisdictions enacting statutes which permit trust arbitration, including New Zealand,[9] Switzerland,[10] the Dubai International Financial Centre,[11] Guernsey[12] and the Bahamas.[13]

1.002 There appear to be several reasons for the relative lack of enthusiasm for arbitration amongst trust law practitioners. The first of these is that it is unclear whether trust disputes are valid subject matter for arbitral proceedings, i.e. whether they are arbitrable at all. This is for two interrelated reasons. Firstly, there is a line of case law in testamentary and trust matters which prohibits the exclusion (ouster) of the court's jurisdiction whether by arbitration or other means. Secondly, there is an argument that court supervision is part of the trust's irreducible core and thus cannot be excluded without doing violence to the very nature of the trust.

1.003 The second reason for the lack of enthusiasm is that even if the subject matter of trust disputes is arbitrable, there are a number of legal issues about how arbitration agreements with regard to trust matters can bind all the relevant parties, for example the trustee, the settlor, the beneficiaries, any protectors or enforcers and so on. As a preliminary point, it must be noted that to come within the scope of the Arbitration Act 1996 any means of binding such individuals must constitute an 'agreement to submit to arbitration present or future disputes (whether they are contractual or not)'.[14] The usual way of demonstrat-

6 BW Boesch, 'The ICC Initiative' (2012) 18 Trusts & Trustees 316; cf 'Model Arbitration Clause for Trusts' in 2012 Rules of Arbitration of Liechtenstein 28.

7 'ICC Arbitration Clause for Trust Disputes and Explanatory Note' (*ICC – International Chamber of Commerce*) <https://iccwbo.org/publication/icc-arbitration-clause-trust-disputes-explanatory-note/> accessed 5 December 2019.

8 SI Strong, 'Arbitration of Internal Trust Disputes: The Next Frontier for International Commercial Arbitration?' (2019) 20 ICCA Congress Series; von Segesser (n 4); SI Strong and Tony Molloy (eds), *Arbitration of Trust Disputes: Issues in National and International Law* (Oxford University Press 2016); 'Review of the Law of Trusts: A Trusts Act for New Zealand' (New Zealand Law Commission 2013) 130, 197–199; Boesch (n 6); 'Arbitration of Trust Disputes' (Trust Law Committee 2011).

9 Trusts Act 2019 ss 142–148.

10 'Revision of the Swiss International Arbitration Law' [2020] Homburger Bulletin <https://media.homburger.ch/karmarun/image/upload/homburger/rJV2uF1RU-Revision_of_the_Swiss_International_Arbitration_Law.pdf>.

11 Ss 30–32; Schedule 2 DIFC Trust Law 2018.

12 Trusts (Guernsey) Law, 2007 s 63.

13 Bahamas Trustee Act s 91A–C.

14 Arbitration Act 1996 s 6.

ing such agreement would be to have the parties sign an arbitration agreement, as happened in several Australian trust arbitration cases.[15] However in trust arbitration situations, it will often not be possible to have the parties sign an agreement because, *inter alia*, the beneficiaries are members of a class; they do not know about the existence of the trust;[16] they are minors or in some other way incapable of giving consent; or they refuse to do so. Moreover, a contractual solution is in any event not ideal because it gives rise to a personal and not a real right so that a successor to the contract, for example a successor trustee, a descendent of a beneficiary and so on, might not be bound to it.

English law does provide for some means of binding third parties or non-signatories to arbitration clauses, for example agency, novation, assignment, merger,[17] but they are all essentially contractual in nature. Consequently, it is hard to predict what the approach of the courts would be when dealing with trust deeds and trust relationships, which are generally held not to be contractual.[18] This has not deterred scholars and practitioners from proposing several solutions which will be briefly outlined below. **1.004**

The first approach used to justify the binding force of arbitration agreements with regard to trusts is unique to England and Wales, and jurisdictions with similar arbitration statutes.[19] It is based upon a particular interpretation of s 82(2) of the Arbitration Act 1996. This section describes a party as including 'any person claiming under or through a party to the agreement', and as beneficiaries can be said to claim under or through the settlor they are parties to the arbitration agreement according to the Act and can, therefore, be forced to arbitrate their claims.[20] However, the validity of this interpretation of the Act has not been tried in the courts, and several authors doubt whether beneficiaries to a trust are caught by s 82(2) on the basis that such an interpretation **1.005**

15 *Rinehart v Welker* [2012] NSWCA 95 (Court of Appeal, New South Wales); *Hancock Prospecting Pty Ltd v Rinehart* [2017] FCAFC 170 (Federal Court of Australia); *Fitzpatrick v Emerald Grain Pty Ltd* [2017] WASC 206 (Supreme Court of Western Australia).

16 This might happen deliberately in order to prevent unwanted claims or family disputes or where the trust is a will trust and does not come into effect prior to the settler's death.

17 Stavros Brekoulakis, Julian Lew and Loukas Mistelis (eds), *The Evolution and Future of International Arbitration* (Wolters Kluwer 2016) 194–195.

18 *Baker v JE Clark & Co (Transport) Uk Ltd* [2006] Court of Appeal of England and Wales A3/2005/1939, EWCA Civ 464 [17–20]; Paul Matthews, 'Capacity to Create a Trust: The Onshore Problem, and the Offshore Solutions' (2002) 6 Edinburgh Law Review 176; Ming Wai Lau, *The Economic Structure of Trusts: Towards a Property-Based Approach* (Oxford University Press 2011); Alastair Hudson, 'The Trust as an Equitable Response', *Staff seminar paper* (2002).

19 (Australia) International Arbitration Act 1974 s 7(4); (Singapore) International Arbitration Act s 6(5)(a).

20 Cohen and Poole (n 4).

strains the language of the statute and the section more likely refers to assignees than beneficiaries.[21]

1.006 The second approach to the issue of lack of consent to an arbitration clause in a trust is to include a clause whereby a beneficiary who refuses to arbitrate forfeits their rights under the trust.[22] However, such clauses run the risk of being held to be invalid, or being narrowly interpreted,[23] on the basis of the *in terrorem* rule in several jurisdictions, including England and Wales,[24] Australia[25] and Canada,[26] unless the beneficiaries' right accrues to someone else (the technical term for this is a 'gift over').[27]

1.007 The third approach is closely related to the second, but whereas forfeiture clauses act as a condition subsequent, i.e. failure to comply with them deprives the person concerned of an existing legal right, [28] this approach would lay down that as a condition of receiving any right under the trust beneficiaries would have to agree to arbitrate any disputes arising out of the trust. In other words, no right exists unless and until the condition is complied with by the beneficiary. Trustees, protectors, enforcers and any similar officeholders would likewise be required to agree to the arbitration clause as a condition for receiving any fee for their work, reimbursement of their expenses and so on. The use of a condition precedent is not novel in Commonwealth arbitration law, with *Scott v Avery* clauses having a long historical pedigree, and it is also the approach that was adopted by the 2008 ICC Trust Arbitration Clause, although not by the updated 2018 clause. The benefit of such clauses is that the

21 Tony Molloy QC & Toby Graham, 'Arbitration of Trust Disputes' (2012) 18:4 Trusts and Trustees 279 at 282–286; cf Lord Mustill and Stewart C Boyd QC, *Commercial Arbitration. 2001 Companion* (2nd edn, Butterworths 2001) 145–149, note although Lord Mustill and Stewart C Boyd QC, *Commercial Arbitration in England* (2nd edn, Butterworths 1989) 136 makes an analogy between trusts and agency, this is clearly only in the context of contracts with third parties and thus external trust disputes; but see *Rinehart v Hancock Prospecting Pty Ltd, Rinehart v Rinehart* [2019] HCA 13 where the Australian High Courts set out a very broad interpretation of this sub-section.

22 Jonathan Blattmachr, 'Reducing Estate and Trust Litigation Through Disclosure, In Terrorem Clauses, Mediation and Arbitration' (2008) 9 Cardozo Journal of Conflict Resolution 237.

23 *AN v Barclays Private Bank and Trust (Cayman) Limited and others* (2006) 9 ITELR 630 (Cayman Islands Grand Court).

24 David J Hayton and others (eds), *Underhill and Hayton Law Relating to Trusts and Trustees* (19th edn, LexisNexis 2016) para 11.87.

25 Peter G Lawson, 'The Rule Against "In Terrorem" Conditions: What Is It? Where Did It Come From? Do We Really Need It?' (2005–2006) 25 Estates, Trusts and Pensions Journal 71 at 79.

26 ibid at 84–89.

27 *Leon & Anr v Lim Beng Chye* [1953] Privy Council Appeal No. 33; *In the Matter of the Estate of PQR, Deceased* [2014] SC (Bda) 95 Civ; Peter G Lawson, 'The Rule Against "In Terrorem" Conditions: What Is It? Where Did It Come from? Do We Really Need It?' (2005) 25 Estates, Trusts & Pensions Journal 71, 89–92; Hayton and others (n 24) para 11.87.

28 Daniel Greenberg and William Allen Jowitt, *Jowitt's Dictionary of English Law* (Sweet & Maxwell 2010) 500.

courts are more reluctant to interfere with them than conditions subsequent; for example they apply a more liberal test of certainty,[29] thereby improving the chances of them being upheld. Moreover, the courts likely cannot relieve their effect.[30]

The third approach has to do with the necessity to ensure that unborn, minor, incapable and unascertained beneficiaries are represented.[31] Although there are means to represent such beneficiaries in litigation,[32] it is unclear how these could be transposed to arbitral proceedings. Failure to ensure that the rights of such beneficiaries are protected is likely to lead to uncertainty in the continuing administration of the trust and enforceability problems on public policy grounds such as a breach of the rules of natural justice or a violation of the Art 6(1) European Convention on Human Rights (ECHR) right to a fair trial.[33] However, it is, of course, open to the settlor to provide for such representation in the trust deed, perhaps by appointing a person to act in such beneficiaries' interests.[34] **1.008**

Fourthly, there are more general issues that arise with regards to Art 6(1) of the ECHR. For example, where the specific conditions for a waiver of Art 6(1) have not been met then trust arbitration may amount to a violation of that article as, *inter alia*, it will not be public nor will the tribunal be a body established by law.[35] This will not be an issue where the violation can be remediated by subsequent Art 6(1) compliant proceedings, namely the ability to challenge the award in court. However, the grounds of challenge should not be too narrow, as is often the case, or such proceedings will not remedy the Art 6(1) violation.[36] Further issues arise where the provisions for appointment of the arbitral tribunal create a situation of inequality between the parties. This might happen where there is one trustee but several beneficiaries, so the former **1.009**

---

29 Hayton and others (n 24) paras 8.95–8.97; Lynton Tucker and others, *Lewin on Trusts* (19th edn, Sweet & Maxwell/Thomson Reuters 2015) para 4-039.

30 *AN v Barclays Private Bank and Trust (Cayman) Limited and others* (n 23) paras 108–115; *Lucius Henry Cary Lord Viscount Falkland, Son and Heir of Edw Cary, an Infant, by his Guardian v James Bertie and Elizabeth his Wife, Sir William Whitlock, John Grout, and others* (1696) 23 ER 814, 333.

31 David Hayton, Paul Matthews and Charles Mitchell, *Underhill and Hayton: Law Relating to Trusts and Trustees* (19th edn, RELX (UK) Limited 2016) at para 11.84.

32 See e.g. Rule 19.7 of the English and Welsh Civil Procedure Rules.

33 'Arbitration of Trust Disputes' (n 8); Lucas Clover Alcolea, 'Trust Arbitration and the European Convention on Human Rights' (2018) 24 Trusts & Trustees 976.

34 Lynton Tucker, Nicholas Le Poidevin QC and James Brightwell, *Lewin on Trusts* (19th edn, Sweet & Maxwell 2015) at para 27-277.

35 See generally Clover Alcolea (n 33).

36 ibid at 981–982

can easily agree on an arbitrator whereas the latter cannot,[37] or where a party lacks the financial resources to bring a claim and cannot receive legal aid for the arbitral proceedings.[38] It should be noted, however, that none of these issues are necessarily insurmountable. They merely require careful drafting on the part of the settler.[39]

1.010 Fifthly, it is often said that one of the major attractions of arbitration is the easy enforceability of arbitral awards worldwide under the New York Convention (NYC),[40] which has over 160 contracting states,[41] by contrast to state court judgements, which do not benefit from a similar wide-ranging convention or treaty.[42] However, under Art I(3) of the NYC, signatory states were able to sign, accede to or ratify the convention subject to a reservation that they would apply it only to differences arising from legal relationships which were considered commercial under their national law. Approximately fifty states have made such a reservation to date.[43] It is *prima facie* difficult to see how trusts which are not settled for commercial or financial services purposes could be classified as 'commercial'. Consequently, it is likely that in many states arbitral awards rendered in trust disputes would not benefit from the provisions of the NYC.[44] Another serious issue for trust arbitration is whether the trusts comply with the writing requirement in Art II(1)–(2) of the Convention, as although the clause will obviously be in writing the beneficiaries will not have signed it, nor will their consent be contained in an exchange of documents. Instead, it is likely that the beneficiaries' consent will be merely tacit or arise by implication due to their conduct, and thus a strict interpretation of the writing requirement might lead to such clauses being unenforceable under the NYC.

1.011 Even if the NYC was held to apply to arbitral awards arising out of trust disputes, such awards would still be vulnerable to the possibility of non-enforcement on the grounds listed in Art V – in particular, that trusts will often involve parties who are not legally capable of giving their consent to arbi-

37 ibid 980.

38 ibid.

39 ibid 984; cf for suggested drafting points, Lawrence Cohen and Joanna Poole, 'Trust Arbitration – Is It Desirable and Does It Work?' (2012) 18:4 Trusts and Trustees 324 at 330–331.

40 Nigel Blackaby, Constantine Partasides QC, Alan Redfern and Martin Hunter, *Redfern and Hunter on International Arbitration* (6th edn, Oxford University Press 2015) at para 1.211.

41 'Contracting States' (*New York Arbitration Convention*) <http://www.newyorkconvention.org/countries> accessed 1 August 2021.

42 Hague Convention of 30 June 2005 on Choice of Court Agreements; cf Convention of 2 July 2019 on the Recognition and Enforcement of Judgments in Civil or Commercial Matters. Note however that it has yet to enter into force.

43 'Contracting States' (n 41).

44 Huai Yuan Chia, 'Keeping Trusts Out of Court: Toward Arbitrating Trust Disputes in Singapore' (2014) 27 New York International Law Review 1, 6.

tration, i.e. minors, unborn and incapable beneficiaries, and this is a ground for refusing to enforce an award under Art V(1)(a) of the Convention. A further problem that arises is if these parties have not been represented in the arbitration, it is at least arguable that Art V(1)(b) applies. These issues are effectively co-existent with the Art 6(1) ECHR matters but approach the subject from a different angle, that of arbitral procedural law as opposed to human rights law. Equally with regard to the issue of arbitrability discussed above, if trust disputes are not arbitrable in the country where recognition and enforcement is sought, then Art V(2)(a) applies, and the court may decline to recognise or enforce the award. However, several courts have held that they have a discretion to recognise and enforce an award even if one of the Art V grounds exists.[45] Any such discretionary enforcement is, however, by its very nature, likely to be determined on a case-by-case basis. The consequence of the above is that arbitral awards rendered in trust disputes, at least in some jurisdictions, might be no more enforceable than court decrees, thereby arguably removing one of the main attractions of arbitration.

Lastly, trusts raise a complex choice of law problems. Although the Hague Trusts Convention[46] has adopted the principle of party autonomy for trusts,[47] complications arise regarding whether transnational law can be applied,[48] the role of the *lex situs* where immovable property is concerned[49] and whether certain types of trusts offend against public policy.[50] Moreover, some trust scholars have argued that the principle of party autonomy does not sit comfortably with trusts law or at least does not make as much sense as it does for contract law.[51] The lack of enthusiasm for trust arbitration discussed above is, therefore, entirely understandable if unfortunate. **1.012**

45 *Dallah Real Estate and Tourism Holding Company v The Ministry of Religious Affairs, Government of Pakistan* [2010] UKSC 46; *Pacific China Holdings Ltd v Grand Pacific Holdings Limited* Court of Appeal of the British Virgin Islands HCVAP 2010/007; *Thai-Lao Lignite (Thailand) Co, Ltd et al. v Government of the Lao People's Democratic Republic* (2011) XXXVI Yearbook: Commercial Arbitration 2011 491 (United States District Court, Southern District of New York); *Paklito Investment Limited v Klockner East Asia Limited* [1993] HKLR 39.

46 Convention of 1 July 1985 on the Law Applicable to Trusts and on their Recognition.

47 ibid Arts 6–7; Jonathan M Harris, *The Hague Trusts Convention: Scope, Application and Preliminary Issues* (Hart 2002) 166.

48 Harris (n 47) 185–186; Alfred von Overbeck, 'Explanatory Report by Alfred von Overbeck' (Hague Conference on Private International Law 1985) para 64.

49 Harris (n 47) 171–175.

50 David J Hayton (ed), *The International Trust* (Jordans 2011) 177.

51 Lionel Smith, 'Give the People What They Want? The Onshoring of the Offshore' (2018) 103 Iowa Law Review 2155, 2164.

B. THE STRUCTURE AND SCOPE OF THIS BOOK

1.013 Having set the scene for this work, and trust arbitration more generally, it is now possible to briefly outline the limitations and structure of this book. Firstly, this book will only deal with express trusts for the benefit of an individual or individuals; it does not deal with private purpose trusts, charitable trusts or (what are informally called) commercial trusts. Secondly, it primarily focuses on English law although it looks at other legal systems where relevant, and this explains some of the earlier limitations: for example, it does not look at private purpose trusts because, outside of very narrow and controverted exceptions, these do not exist in English law. Thirdly, it only addresses internal trust disputes. Unfortunately, this is a surprisingly difficult term to define: one must make do with a negative definition. External trust disputes were defined in *In Re Earl of Stratford*, decd as 'cases in which there is some issue between the trustees on behalf of the trust as a whole and the outside world'.[52] Internal trust disputes would therefore be all disputes which do not fall into this category. The New Zealand Trusts Act 2019 is one of the few statutes globally which makes provisions for trust arbitration but does not define internal trust dispute as it applies not just to disputes but also to non-contentious matters, it therefore uses the term 'matter' rather than 'dispute'. It defines an 'internal matter' as [a] 'matter to which the parties are a trustee and 1 or more beneficiaries, or a trustee and 1 or more other trustees, of the trust'.[53] Although this definition would appear to be more on point by directly defining what an internal matter, or dispute, is, rather than by defining it indirectly with reference to external trust disputes, it also poses new problems. For example, what happens if the dispute involves protectors or enforcers? According to the literal wording of the definition such a dispute would not be an internal matter but an external one. The case is the same for disputes involving the settlor, as a result this work will adopt the definition provided by *Re Earl of Stratford* instead of applying a modified version of the statutory New Zealand definition.

1.014 As regards the structure of the book, in line with its fundamentally practical nature, it is organised chronologically in the order of when a particular issue is likely to arise for an individual considering trust arbitration. For example, the first issue that such an individual encounters when considering trust arbitration is whether trust disputes can be arbitrated at all (arbitrability), next is the issue of how to bind individuals to a trust arbitration clause, then there are due process issues and so on.

52 *In Re Earl of Stratford, decd* (1978) 3 WLR 223, 227.

53 Trusts Act 2019 s 142.

2

(IN-)ARBITRABILITY

A. INTRODUCTION

This chapter will begin by briefly looking at the concept of arbitrability in general, before turning to specific arbitrability issues which arise in the context of trust arbitration disputes. These include the intertwined issues of the irreducible core of the trust and the supervisory jurisdiction of the court, the doctrine against ouster of the court's jurisdiction and finally a possible mismatch between the remedies which a court and an arbitral tribunal can grant in trust disputes. **2.001**

B. ARBITRABILITY: A GENERAL INTRODUCTION

2.002 The term 'arbitrability' is at its simplest, self-explanatory. It refers to the question of 'What is arbitrable and what is not'.[1] However, the use of this term in the literature is counterintuitive. For example, it is generally accepted that there are two types of arbitrability issues: subjective and objective.[2] However, rather than referring to these as 'subjective and objective inarbitrability', scholars will use the terms 'subjective and objective arbitrability' to mean different reasons why a particular dispute cannot be arbitrated.[3] In the interests of avoiding confusion by contradicting the literature, this work will also use the term in this way, notwithstanding its counterintuitive nature. Having addressed the use of the term in the literature, it is now possible to proceed to its definitions.

2.003 Subjective arbitrability relates fundamentally to a situation where a party 'is unable to refer disputes to arbitration on account of its status or function',[4] and is generally encountered with regard to states, state-owned enterprises and other public bodies.[5] Objective arbitrability, on the other hand, relates to 'circumstances in which the subject matter of the dispute is not capable of settlement by arbitration'.[6] Examples where objective arbitrability issues are likely to arise include criminal matters, employment disputes and insolvency proceedings.[7] The concept of subjective arbitrability is rejected by some authors,[8] who consider it rather to be an issue of capacity.[9]

2.004 A further complication is that the issues which arise in the context of trust disputes do not necessarily neatly fit into either category, nor can they always be considered as issues of capacity. For example, whilst the doctrine against ouster of the court's jurisdiction as well as the doctrine of the irreducible core of the

---

1 Loukas A Mistelis, *Arbitrability: International & Comparative Perspectives*, vol 19 (Kluwer Law International 2009) 48.

2 Julian DM Lew and others (eds), *Arbitration in England: With Chapters on Scotland and Ireland* (Kluwer Law International 2013) 399–400; Philippe Fouchard and Berthold Goldman, *Fouchard, Gaillard, Goldman on International Commercial Arbitration* (Kluwer Law International BV 1999) paras 532–623.

3 Fouchard and Goldman (n 2) paras 532–534, 559; Karl-Heinz Böckstiegel, 'Public Policy and Arbitrability' (1987) Comparative Arbitration Practice and Public Policy in Arbitration, Volume 3 ICCA Congress Series 177, 180–183.

4 Stavros Brekoulakis, Julian Lew and Loukas Mistelis (eds), *The Evolution and Future of International Arbitration* (Wolters Kluwer 2016), 400.

5 ibid; Fouchard and Goldman (n 2) para 533.

6 Lew and others (n 2) 400.

7 ibid 405–411.

8 Jean-François Poudret and others, *Comparative Law of International Arbitration* (2nd edn, Sweet & Maxwell 2007) para 3.4.1.1.

9 ibid.

trust clearly relate to whether trust disputes can be arbitrated at all, the issues raised by certain types of parties would appear to be clearly subjective but may not relate to capacity. For example, in a case which involves an otherwise legally capable party who would receive legal aid if the case was before the courts but cannot for arbitration and therefore cannot afford to raise the dispute, the issue is one of due process rather than objective arbitrability or capacity.

Equally, where a party seeks to enforce an arbitration clause against a minor or **2.005**
legally incapable person in an otherwise arbitrable matter, the issue is not just one of capacity (could and did they consent to the arbitration clause), but also involves due process: who will represent them in the arbitration? These due process concerns are also arbitrability concerns, as a court which is approached by a party in such a case who seeks to restrain an arbitration or set aside a mandatory stay of litigation, will have to decide whether to require arbitration of the grievance at hand or not. In other words, in the case of trust disputes, and indeed to some extent in all cases involving both non-commercial and natural persons, due process concerns are elevated to the level of arbitrability concerns.

It can be seen then that trust disputes raise serious difficulties of categorisation **2.006**
as regards arbitrability. Arguably, this results from the fact that they do not necessarily involve sophisticated commercial parties and, thus, it is not possible to adopt the usual *laissez-faire* approach of the courts and commentators regarding arbitrability. In consequence, there are two possible paths this book could follow, it could engage in a detailed analysis of the categorisation of the various arbitrability issues which arise in trust disputes, or it could adopt a more pragmatic and flexible approach by addressing the consequences of the various arbitrability, capacity and jurisdiction issues without explicitly categorising them.

The latter approach would appear to be more in line with the aim of this book, **2.007**
which is to address the practical problems of arbitrating trust disputes, given that ultimately all the various categories of arbitrability or unenforceability lead to the same result: the arbitrators cannot resolve the dispute.[10] Of course, one must apply this conclusion with a degree of nuance, as the issue may only arise with regard to one and not all of the parties so that the arbitrator can hear claims against or by one party but not others. The practical effect, however, is the same: arbitration cannot be used to resolve the dispute as regards certain or all the involved parties. Moreover, English law itself appears to reject overly

10 Böckstiegel (n 3) 181–183.

strict categorisation of arbitrability, as English writers, and even more so English courts, have spent very little time considering the matter.[11]

2.008 Consequently, this chapter will only address the 'objective arbitrability' issues raised by the arbitration of trust disputes, namely the doctrine against permitting ouster of the court's jurisdiction and the irreducible core. Issues of 'subjective arbitrability' or capacity as well as jurisdiction will be addressed in the chapters regarding unborn, minor, incapable and unascertained beneficiaries as well as the New York Convention.

C. ARBITRABILITY IN STATUTE

2.009 The English Arbitration Act 1996 lays out as one of its general principles in s 1(b) that 'parties should be free to agree how their disputes are resolved, subject only to such safeguards as are necessary in the public interest'.[12] Although the wording does not mention arbitrability *per se*, the DAC (Departmental Advisory Committee) report on the draft bill states:

> In some cases … the public interest will make inroads on complete party autonomy, in much the same way as there are limitations on freedom of contract. Some matters are simply not susceptible of this form of dispute resolution (e.g. certain cases concerning status or many family matters) while other considerations (such as consumer protection) may require the imposition of different rights and obligations.[13]

2.010 It would seem then that, as is the case more generally, arbitrability under the 1996 Act is inextricably intertwined with the public interest and thereby public policy. However, it is worth noting that *Mustill and Boyd* does not view this section as addressing the question of arbitrability but, perhaps as a result, is 'unable to suggest any circumstances in which the reservation in general principle (b) would have any practical effect'.[14] Patten LJ cites this view with approval in *Fulham Football Club*,[15] but as discussed above, the DAC report views it as referring to arbitrability and other authors also presuppose this.[16] Consequently, it would seem that the better view is that s 1(b) lays down as

11 See generally Lew and others (n 2) 399–412.

12 Arbitration Act 1996 s 1(b); cf Hong Kong Arbitration Ordinance s 3(2)(a).

13 'Report on the English Arbitration Bill' (UK Departmental Advisory Committee on Arbitration Law 1996) para 19.

14 Michael J Mustill, *Commercial Arbitration: 2001 Companion Volume to the Second Edition* (Butterworths 2001) 27.

15 *Fulham Football Club (1987) Ltd v Richards and another* [2012] Ch 333 (Court of Appeal).

16 Lew and others (n 2) 399.

a general principle a limitation on the arbitrability of certain disputes when this is necessary in the public interest.

2.011 The situation is clearer in other jurisdictions, such as New Zealand and Singapore, where the relevant arbitration statute explicitly regulates the matter of arbitrability. For example, s 10 of the New Zealand Arbitration Act provides that:

> (1) Any dispute which the parties have agreed to submit to arbitration under an arbitration agreement may be determined by arbitration unless the arbitration agreement is contrary to public policy or, under any other law, such a dispute is not capable of determination by arbitration.
> (2) The fact that an enactment confers jurisdiction in respect of any matter on the High Court or the District Court but does not refer to the determination of that matter by arbitration does not, of itself, indicate that a dispute about that matter is not capable of determination by arbitration.[17]

2.012 The provisions of the Singapore International Arbitration Act are to very similar effect,[18] and go even further in recognising the links between arbitrability and public policy as they are simply entitled 'Public policy and arbitrability'.[19] On the other hand neither the Australian International Act 1974 nor the Hong Kong Arbitration Ordinance explicitly refer to the term 'arbitrability' and there is therefore significant variety among Commonwealth statutes on the matter.

2.013 The English Arbitration Act does not, however, provide any guidance as to when the limitation in s 1(b) might come into effect, and s 81 provides that any common law rules regarding 'matters which are not capable of settlement by arbitration' are to be left intact.[20] As can be seen above, even those jurisdictions which do regulate the matter explicitly provide sparse guidance on the issue of 'arbitrability' or 'public policy': thus the English Act is certainly not alone in doing this. As a result, arbitrability is in general governed by case law,[21] and as the courts will 'approach arbitrability on a case-by-case basis … it is difficult to single out any particular "class" of civil dispute that is uniformly and absolutely non-arbitrable'.[22] The English courts have, in general, adopted a broad

17 Arbitration Act 1996 (NZ) s 10.

18 International Arbitration Act s 11.

19 ibid.

20 Arbitration Act 1996 s 81.

21 *Tomolugen Holdings Ltd and another v Silica Investors Ltd and other appeals* [2015] SGCA 57 (Singapore Court of Appeal) [75].

22 Lew and others (n 2) 400.

approach to arbitrability, holding that issues such as competition law, IP rights and shareholder disputes are, at least *inter-partes*, arbitrable.[23] *Fulham Football Club*, which involved an unfair prejudice action under s 994 of the Companies Act 2006, is an illustrative case, with Longmore LJ stating, 'To the extent therefore that public policy has a part to play it can only be as a "safeguard ... necessary in the public interest". This is a demanding test...'[24]

2.014 Similarly, the Singapore Court of Appeal, in dealing with a minority shareholder oppression action, held that even if the arbitral tribunal could not grant particular statutory remedies 'there is nothing to preclude the underlying dispute from being resolved by an arbitral tribunal, with the parties remaining free to apply to the court for the grant of any specific relief which might be beyond the power of the arbitral tribunal to award'.[25] In consequence, the court stated that although this process would cause 'some, perhaps even substantial, inconvenience ...This would be regrettable; but inconvenience is not the threshold that justifies refusing a stay of court proceedings on the basis that the subject matter of the dispute is non-arbitrable'.[26] Although known for being arbitration friendly, the picture is more nuanced in Australia,[27] and thus unsurprisingly it would appear that there is no consensus over the exact scope of the arbitrability exception among Commonwealth jurisdictions.

D. ARBITRABILITY IN THE CONTEXT OF TRUST DISPUTES

2.015 As there are three main arguments in the literature for why trust disputes are not capable of settlement by arbitration, this section will be divided into three main parts. The first part will look at the issue of ousting the jurisdiction of the court; the second will look at the closely related doctrine of the irreducible core of the trust; and the third will examine the issue of the alleged limitations on the remedies which arbitral tribunals can grant or enforce and the effect some argue this has on the arbitrability of trust disputes.

---

23 ibid 399–411. The situation is the same in Singapore, see Loukas Mistelis and Laurence Shore (eds), *Arbitration Law and Practice in Asia* (Juris 2020) 603–606.

24 *Fulham Football Club (1987) Ltd v Richards and another* (n 15) paras 98–99.

25 *Tomolugen Holdings Ltd and another v Silica Investors Ltd and other appeals* (n 21) para 100.

26 ibid 105.

27 Luke Nottage and James Morrison, 'Accessing and Assessing Australia's International Arbitration Act' (2017) 34 Journal of International Arbitration 984–988.

1. Ousting the jurisdiction of the court

This section will firstly look at the development of the rule against ousting the jurisdiction of the court by arbitration over time, tracing its evolution from its genesis to the modern day, and then analyse those cases which consider the rule against ousting the jurisdiction of the court in trust and testamentary cases. The aim of looking at matters in this order is to set the trust and testamentary cases in their proper context and demonstrate that they do not exist in isolation from the rest of the jurisprudence on ouster but rather form an integral part of it. **2.016**

(a) Ousting the jurisdiction of the court and arbitration

The origins of the rule on ousting the jurisdiction of the court at common law can be traced back to the 1746 case of *Kill v Hollister*,[28] where it was held that 'Action on a policy of insurance lies, though the policy says the matter shall be referred in case of a loss or dispute ... [as] the agreement of the parties cannot oust this court'.[29] The first case using the modern formulation of the rule appears to be the 1789 case of *Street v Rigby*,[30] which provided 'that the jurisdiction of a Court is not ousted by an agreement of the parties to refer a question to arbitration'.[31] The principle was again affirmed in the 1799 case of *Thompson v Charnock*,[32] which provided that 'it [has] been decided again and again that an agreement to refer all matters in difference to arbitration is not sufficient to oust the Courts of Law or Equity of their jurisdiction'.[33] **2.017**

It should be noted, however, that the above cases did not mean that arbitration was impossible; rather, as had been done since the mid-1600s,[34] parties could embody arbitration agreements or awards in a 'rule of court' if they wanted them to exclude court jurisdiction to hear the case.[35] Another advantage of the 'rule of court' procedure was that 'acting contrary to such a rule was a contempt of court, and rendered the defaulting party liable to attachment'.[36] **2.018**

28 *Kill v Hollister* 1 (1746) Wills KB 129 (King's Bench).

29 ibid.

30 *Street v Rigby* 1 (1789) Ves Jun Supp 665 (Chancery).

31 ibid.

32 *Thompson v Charnock* 8 (1799) TR 139 (King's Bench).

33 ibid.

34 Hon TF Bathurst, 'The History of the Law of Commercial Arbitration' (Francis Forbes Society Australian Legal History Tutorials, Woolloomooloo, 18 October 2018) para 48.

35 *Mitchell v Harris* 2 (1789–1817) Ves Jun 769 (Chancery).

36 Bathurst (n 34) para 48.

2.019 The situation changed in the mid-19th century with the decision of *Scott v Avery*,[37] which involved an ingenious piece of drafting that provided that no cause of action would arise until a dispute had been arbitrated, that is to say, that arbitration was a condition precedent to litigation.[38] This was held not to oust the jurisdiction of the court, as there being no cause of action the court had no jurisdiction at all, and thus there was no ouster.[39] The practical effect, however, was the same as ouster because 'the Court will stay litigation brought in respect of a matter agreed to be referred … [and] he cannot successfully bring an action on his claim'[40] except by arbitration. Although this is not entirely clear it would also seem that it would usually be impossible to set aside the award, as, if the award was set aside, it never existed, and if it never existed then no cause of action ever existed.[41] Presumably, in such cases the matter would simply have to be sent back to arbitration again. The courts were only willing to interfere on very limited and exceptional grounds such as where the entire agreement had been repudiated or where the arbitrator did not act with impartiality.[42] The consequence of such difficulties was that the UK parliament eventually legislated for judicial discretion to dispense with *Scott v Avery* clauses in 1934.[43]

2.020 *Scott v Avery* is an important case as it demonstrates that the 'no ouster of the court's jurisdiction' argument is not as strong as is often assumed. The courts were and, so far as *Scott v Avery* is still good law, remain[44] willing to allow parties to oust their jurisdiction via clever drafting, and the legislature did not see fit to correct this allegedly egregious breach of public policy for over half a century. The case, therefore, seems to significantly undermine arguments that arbitration agreements were, or are, against public policy because they oust the jurisdiction of the courts.

2.021 At roughly the same time as *Scott v Avery*, in 1854 the Common law procedure Act provided for judges to have the discretion to stay a case pending an arbitration,[45] and thereby oust their own jurisdiction. As with *Scott v Avery*,

---

37 *Scott v Avery* V (1856) HLC 809.

38 Bathurst (n 34) para 55.

39 *Scott v Avery* (n 37) 853–854.

40 'Report on Commercial Arbitration' (Law Reform Commission of New South Wales 1967) 27 paras 4.2.2–4.2.3.

41 See re revocability ibid 4.2.3.

42 HK Lucke, 'Arbitration Clauses in South Australia' (1975) 5 Adelaide Law Review 244, 248.

43 ibid 249.

44 *B v S* [2011] EWHC 691 (Comm).

45 Common Law Procedure Act 1854 22, s XI.

two years later, this statute marked a sea change in the law as 'prior to [it] the Court could not refuse to settle any such dispute which was brought before it, because it not only had the jurisdiction but also the duty to decide that dispute if called upon so to do'.[46] This provision was subsequently re-enacted in the 1889 Arbitration Act.[47]

The 1854 Act provided for the, now infamous, stated case procedure in section V, which granted arbitrators the discretion to ask for an opinion of the court regarding their award. Section IV provided for a judge to direct such a case to be stated where a question of law was 'fit to be decided by the Court, or upon a Question of Fact fit to be decided by a Jury' with the consent of the parties. The 1889 Act updated this procedure in various sections, the most important of which, s 19, provided that 'Any referee, arbitrator, or umpire may at any stage of the proceedings under a reference, and shall, if so directed by the Court or a judge, state in the form of a special case for the opinion of the Court any questions of law arising in the course of the reference'. In other words, the procedure for a stated case on questions of law became mandatory. **2.022**

The case of *Czarnikow v Roth, Schmidt and Company*[48] interpreted s 19 as applying even to *Scott v Avery* clauses, thereby significantly reducing the degree of ouster such clauses caused and reasserting the importance of the Court's supervisory jurisdiction. In that case, the rules of the Refined Sugar Association required that members include in their contracts a *Scott v Avery* clause which excluded the stated case procedure. The court held that 'To hold that … the agreement not to apply for a special case is not to oust the jurisdiction of the Court … is in effect to decide that the [Arbitral] Tribunal is entitled to be a law unto itself, and free to administer any law, or no law, as it pleases. I cannot but think that this is against public policy'.[49] The court justified the stated case procedure on the basis that it was necessary so that the 'Courts may insure the proper administration of the law by inferior tribunals … There must be no Alsatia in England where the King's writ does not run'.[50] **2.023**

The importance of the stated case procedure and *Czarnikow* lies in its qualification of the court ouster via arbitration including by *Scott v Avery* clauses. It, therefore, demonstrates that the courts and legislatures' forbearance of such **2.024**

46 Francis Russell, *Russell on the Power and Duty of an Arbitrator and the Law of Submission and Awards, with an Appendix of Forms, Precedents and Statutes* (Stevens and Sons 1935) 84.

47 ibid 83–84.

48 *Czarnikow v Roth, Schmidt and Company* (1922) 2 KB 478 (Court of Appeal).

49 ibid 486.

50 ibid 488.

clauses does not undermine the view of arbitration clauses being an unjustified ouster of court jurisdiction in as clear-cut a fashion as was previously thought. It also represents a qualification of *Scott v Avery* and a reassertion of the Court's rights to supervise the administration of justice regardless of the forum chosen. On the other hand, *Scott v Avery* clauses remained good law, and thus, as noted before, the rule against ouster of the Court's jurisdiction is far from an absolute one and remained in effect, albeit in a significantly weakened form.

2.025 The stated case procedure was provided for again in the Arbitration Act 1950,[51] which consolidated the Arbitration Acts from 1889 to 1934[52] and survived the Arbitration Act 1975 as well. Amongst other things, this latter act finally provided for a mandatory stay of court proceedings by the court, thereby enforcing the UK's obligations under Art II of the New York Convention (NYC) as well as refusal of enforcement of arbitral awards only on the grounds provided by Art V of the NYC.[53] The Arbitration Act 1979 also eliminated the stated case procedure, replacing it instead with a preliminary determination and an appeal on points of law to the High Court.[54]

2.026 The grounds of appeal allowed under the 1979 Act were more limited than those of the stated case procedure, as either the consent of all the parties was required or the leave of the court, which would not be granted, 'unless … the determination of the question of law … could substantially affect the rights of one … of the parties to the arbitration agreement'.[55] Section 2 provided for a 'Determination of preliminary point of law by [the] court',[56] although this was only permitted where 'the determination of the application might produce substantial savings in costs to the parties',[57] and it was one upon which the court would likely have granted leave for an appeal on a point of law.[58] Moreover, s 3 of the Act provided that this right of appeal could be excluded by the parties, although s 4 provided that the effect of this over admiralty, insurance or commodity matters was limited.

2.027 The exact interpretation of s 1 of the 1979 Act led to one of the leading cases in English arbitration law, *Pioneer Shipping Ltd v BTP Tioxide Ltd (The Nema)*.[59]

51 Arbitration Act 1950 s 21.

52 Arbitration Act 1950.

53 United Nations Convention on the Recognition and Enforcement of Foreign Arbitral Awards 1958.

54 Arbitration Act 1979 s 2.

55 ibid 1(4).

56 ibid 2.

57 ibid 2(2)(a).

58 ibid 2(2)(b).

59 *Pioneer Shipping Ltd v BTP Tioxide Ltd (The Nema)* 1982 AC 724 HL(E) (House of Lords).

The issue was that the section could be interpreted in two ways, '(1) that the court would give leave where there was a real and substantially arguable point of law or (2) [that] it was much more restrictive'.[60] At first instance, the judge adopted the former approach, but the Court of Appeal overturned this,[61] with a particularly forthright opinion to that end being espoused by Lord Denning. The decision of the Court of Appeal was distinguished as *obiter dicta* and criticised by Lord Goff,[62] something that was particularly surprising given his expertise in commercial matters,[63] and the decision came before the House of Lords. The House of Lords endorsed the approach of Lord Denning, which provided that 'the judge should have accepted the decision of the arbitrator as final unless it was shown "either (i) that the arbitrator misdirected himself in point of law or (ii) that the decision was such that no reasonable arbitrator could reach"'.[64]

Lord Diplock further noted that the act contained indications 'of a parliamentary intention to give effect to the turn of the tide in favour of finality in arbitral awards ...'.[65] He also noted[66] that s 3 reversed the public policy against exclusion agreements as laid down in *Czarnikow*.[67] The 1979 Act as interpreted by *The Nema* represents a clear example of how public policy can change over time, with the view that arbitration or exclusion agreements were contrary to public policy now being firmly confined to the history books. **2.028**

The 1996 Arbitration Act provides further demonstration of the change in public policy, with further restrictions placed on the appeal procedure. Leave to appeal would now only be granted if the 'determination of the question [would] substantially affect the rights of one or more of the parties'[68] and only where 'the question [was] one the tribunal was asked to determine'.[69] Moreover, there was a further restriction in that the decision of the tribunal had to obviously be wrong or the issue had to be one of general public impor- **2.029**

60 The Right Hon The Lord Thomas of Cwmgiedd, 'Developing Commercial Law through the Courts: Rebalancing the Relationship between the Courts and Arbitration' (The Bailii Lecture, London, 9 March 2016) para 19.

61 *Pioneer Shipping Ltd v BTP Tioxide Ltd (The Nema)* [1980].

62 *Schiffahrtsagentur Hamburg Middle East Line GmbH v Virtue Shipping Corpn* (1981) 2 All ER 887, 892–894.

63 Alison Ross, 'Lord Goff 1926–2016' (*Global Arbitration Review*) <https://globalarbitrationreview.com/article/1067645/lord-goff-1926-2016> accessed 3 August 2019; The Lord Thomas of Cwmgiedd (n 60) para 19.

64 *Pioneer Shipping Ltd v BTP Tioxide Ltd (The Nema)* (n 59) 738–739.

65 ibid 739–740.

66 ibid 740–741.

67 *Czarnikow v Roth, Schmidt and Company* (n 48).

68 Arbitration Act 1996 s 69(3)(a).

69 ibid 69(3)(b).

tance, and the tribunal's decision had to be open to 'serious doubt'.[70] However, even if all these conditions were met, the court could still not grant leave to appeal unless 'it is just and proper in all the circumstances for the court to determine the question'.[71] Clearly then it is only in the rarest of cases that an appeal would be successfully brought, and as regards appeals on points of law the ability to exclude this was now extended to all types of cases including admiralty, insurance and commodity matters.

2.030 It is clear that taken together the 1979 and 1996 Arbitration Acts, as well as the case law that has been developed by the courts regarding them, represents a complete change of English public policy towards an expansive pro-arbitration approach. As noted by Lord Thomas of Cwmgiedd, the 1996 Act marked the apparent triumph of those who believed that 'the well-established approach of allowing courts to intervene to correct and develop the law was out of step with other arbitration centres … It [made] London a less attractive prospect for dispute resolution'.[72] The initial scepticism of English Courts and practitioners towards arbitration has not, however, been completely eliminated. Some have questioned whether the 1996 Act went too far in the degree to which it permitted ouster of the Court's jurisdiction as regards arbitration agreements.[73] Moreover, the Act still allows parties to appeal on legal matters as long as they have not contracted out of this provision[74] and as the provisions for parties to challenge awards on the grounds of serious irregularity[75] or jurisdiction[76] are both mandatory,[77] it is not possible to completely contract out of court supervision as is the case in Switzerland, for example.[78]

2.031 It is important to note however that the above interpretation of the history of English arbitration is not accepted by all scholars; several have argued that in actual fact the English courts were traditionally supportive of arbitration.[79] Their thesis has two main strands: firstly they argue that English judges often

---

70 ibid 69(c).

71 ibid 69(d).

72 The Lord Thomas of Cwmgiedd (n 60) para 18.

73 The Lord Thomas of Cwmgiedd (n 60).

74 S 69 Arbitration Act 1996.

75 S 68 Arbitration Act 1996.

76 S 67 Arbitration Act 1996.

77 Schedule 1 Arbitration Act 1996.

78 Art 192 PILA.

79 Stavros Brekoulakis, 'The Historical Treatment of Arbitration under English Law and the Development of the Policy Favouring Arbitration' (2019) 39 Oxford Journal of Legal Studies 124; Chantal Stebbings, *Law Reporting in Britain* (Hambledon Continuum 2003) 133–168; The matter was also put to the author in commentary on his work.

referred cases to arbitration or even acted as arbitrators themselves;[80] and, secondly, they argue that cases such as *Kill v Hollister* were misreported.[81] As an initial point it should be noted that it does not matter for the purposes of this work whether the English and Commonwealth courts were actually hostile to arbitration, as has been stated in several decisions of the House of Lords[82] as well as in the decisions of other Commonwealth courts[83] and commentators,[84] or whether the courts were merely less supportive of arbitration than they are today. Either approach suffices to validate the comments made above regarding the history of English arbitration, as well as the conclusions made regarding ouster clauses below. It is therefore only necessary for this work to prove that the English courts were at least less supportive of arbitration in the past than they are now. This view cannot, and indeed has not, been seriously contested for the following reasons.

Firstly, it is clear that (subject to the statutory reforms discussed earlier) the English and Commonwealth courts traditionally retained close control over the arbitral process,[85] moreover there were broad grounds for setting aside awards,[86] and a party could revoke an arbitrator's authority at any time prior to his rendering the award,[87] although for it to be effective the arbitrator must have had notice of it prior to rendering the award.[88] **2.032**

Secondly, even assuming *Kill v Hollister* was misreported, neither *Street v Rigby* nor *Thompson v Charnock* have been so impugned, and both cases set forth the rule against ouster in similar terms. The same goes for *Scott v Avery* and *Czarnikow*, which, as discussed above, examined the matter in detail and **2.033**

80 Henry Horwitz and James Oldham, 'John Locke, Lord Mansfield, and Arbitration During the Eighteenth Century' (1993) 36 The Historical Journal 137.

81 Stebbings (n 79) 133–168.

82 *Scott v Avery* (n 37); *Bremer Vulkan Schiffbau und Maschinenfabrik v South India Shipping Corporation Ltd* [1981] AC 909 (House of Lords).

83 *Uber Technologies Inc v Heller* 2020 SCC 16 [205–208]; *Seidel v TELUS Communications Inc* [2011] SCC [89–102; 160; 170]; *Paper Products Pty Ltd v Tomlinsons (Rochdale Limited; Nigel Watts and David Murphy* [1993] FCA 346 [12].

84 Ernest G Lorenzen, 'Commercial Arbitration. International and Interstate Aspects' (1934) 43 The Yale Law Journal 716, 716–718; G Ellenbogen, 'English Arbitration Practice' (1952) 17 Law and Contemporary Problems 656, 658; Johan Steyn, 'Arbitration and the Courts: Arbitration Systems in England and Wales' (1980) 35 Arbitration Journal 9, 9–10; 'Improving the Arbitration Act 1996' (New Zealand Law Commission 2001) Preliminary Paper 34 para 43; Chief Justice Robert S French, 'International Commercial Dispute Resolution and the Place of Judicial Power' (International Commercial Law and Arbitration Conference, Sydney, Australia, 22 August 2013) 8–11; Robert MacDougall, 'Courts and ADR: A Symbiotic Relationship' (LEADR & IAMA Conference, Sydney, Australia, 7 September 2015) paras 10–13.

85 Shown for example by the stated case procedure, see Russell (n 46) 177–181.

86 *Award and Arbitrament* (1667) 21 English Reports 864, 866–867.

87 *Vynior's Case* (1572) 77 597, 597–601.

88 *Vivion against Wilde* (1609) 123 English Reports.

clearly restated the rule against ouster. Indeed, the principle against ouster of the court's jurisdiction has been independently restated in many cases, including *Pickering v Cape Town Railway Co*,[89] *Elliott v The Royal Exchange Assurance Company*[90] and *Mulkern v Runtz, Farquharson v Morgan*.[91] The House of Lords also confirmed that the rule was the same in Scotland in the case of *Tancred Arrol & Co v Steel Company of Scotland*.[92] Turning to the Commonwealth, one finds cases in Canada,[93] Australia[94] and New Zealand[95] which also restate the rule against ouster of the court's jurisdiction. Lastly, the leading arbitration monograph at the time clearly stated, 'In one sense ... such an agreement may be said not to be binding, for it cannot be pleaded in bar to an action in respect of the matters intended to be referred, and so does not oust the jurisdiction of the court'.[96] This is not to say that the court could not exercise its discretion not to hear a case subject to arbitration,[97] but there was no obligation to stay such proceedings, as is now common globally.

2.034 The relationship between the discretionary nature of the stay of proceedings subject to an arbitration clause and the doctrine against ouster of the court's jurisdiction is explained in the case of *Doleman & Sons v Ossett Corporation*[98] where the court stated that:

> If the Court has refused to stay an action, or if the defendant has abstained from asking it to do so, the Court has seisin of the dispute, and it is by its decision, and by its decision alone that the rights of the parties are settled … There cannot be two tribunals each with the jurisdiction to insist on deciding the rights of the parties and to compel them to accept its decision. To my mind this is clearly involved in the proposition that the Courts will not allow their jurisdiction to be ousted. Their jurisdiction is to hear and decide the matters of the action, and for a private tribunal to take that decision out of their hands, and decide the questions itself, is a clear ouster of jurisdiction.[99]

---

89 *Pickering v Cape Town Railway Co* [1865] LR 1 Eq 84.

90 *Elliott v Royal Exchange Assurance Co* (1867) 2 LR Exch 237.

91 *Mulkern and Runtz v Lord* (1879) 4 App Cas 182 HL.

92 *Tancred, Arrol & Co v The Steel Co of Scotland Ltd* (1890) 15 App Cas 125 HL.

93 *Vidal v William Robinson Company* (1923) 33 305.

94 *Murphy v Benson* [1942] NSWStRp 66.

95 *United Insurance Company Limited v Arthur* [1928] NZGazLawRp.

96 Francis Russell, *A Treatise on the Power and Duty of an Arbitrator, and the Law of Submissions and Awards; with an Appendix of Forms, and of the Statutes Relating to Arbitration* (Philadelphia: T & J W Johnson 1849) 67 <http://archive.org/details/powerdutyofarbit00russ> accessed 28 February 2021.

97 ibid; *Waters v Taylor* (1708) 33 English Reports 658.

98 *Doleman & Sons v Ossett Corporation* (1912) 3 KB 257.

99 *Doleman & Sons v Ossett Corpn* 3 KB 257 CA, 269.

The alternative to a stay of proceedings was for a party to bring an action for damages for the breach of the arbitration agreement, but as the court goes on to note: **2.035**

> the remedy in damages must be an ineffective remedy in cases where the arbitration had not been actually entered into, for it would seem difficult to prove any damages other than nominal. In the case of an arbitration pending, which was rendered abortive by the action, substantial damages might perhaps be proved, because it would be open to the jury to give damages commensurate with the costs to which the plaintiff had been uselessly put in the arbitration.[100]

Thirdly, commentators on the Acts and judges interpreting them have consistently mentioned the changing, and more supportive, relationship between the courts and arbitration brought about by their reforms.[101] In consequence, it is safe to say that the historical basis upon which this work proceeds is a sound one, and as we have traced the development of the law regarding arbitration and ouster clauses to the modern day, it is now possible to consider the operation of ouster clauses in testamentary or trust provisions below. **2.036**

(b) Ouster clauses in testamentary or trust provisions

The first case to deal with ouster clauses and trust deeds is not, as is often supposed,[102] *Re Raven*[103] but the earlier Irish case of *Massy v Rogers*.[104] The case concerned the estate of a Mr GHM Baker who provided what is likely the first trust arbitration clause in Commonwealth trust law in his will,[105] buttressed by a forfeiture clause for those who brought a dispute before the courts.[106] The dispute came before the Irish Courts which held, on the authority of *Scott* **2.037**

---

100 *Doleman & Sons v Ossett Corporation* (n 98) 268.

101 Ellenbogen (n 84); Reuben Clark and Dieter G Lange, 'Recent Changes in English Arbitration Practice Widen Opportunities for More Effective International Arbitrations' (1980) 35 The Business Lawyer 1621; Michael Kerr, 'Arbitration and the Courts: The Uncitral Model Law' (1985) 34 International and Comparative Law Quarterly 1; Roy Goode, 'Arbitration – Should the Courts Get Involved?' 2 Judicial Studies Institute Journal 33; Lord Hacking, 'The Story of the Arbitration Act 1979' (2010) 76 Arbitration 125; *Bremer Vulkan Schiffbau und Maschinenfabrik v South India Shipping Corporation Ltd* (n 82); *Pioneer Shipping Ltd v BTP Tioxide Ltd (The Nema)* (n 59); *Paper Products Pty Ltd v Tomlinsons (Rochdale Limited; Nigel Watts and David Murphy* (n 83); *Pathak v Tourism Transport Ltd* (2002) 3 NZLR 681; *Seidel v TELUS Communications Inc* (n 83).

102 Nicholas Le Poidevin, 'Arbitration and Trusts: Can It Be Done?' (2012) 18 Trusts & Trustees 307, 311; Toby Graham, 'The Problems with Compulsory Arbitration of Trust Disputes' (2014) 20 Trusts & Trustees 20, 25; Tony Molloy and Toby Graham, 'Arbitration of Trust and Estate Disputes' (2012) 18 Trusts & Trustees 279, 288; Andrew Holden, 'The Arbitration of Trust Disputes: Theoretical Problems and Practical Possibilities' (2015) 21 Trusts & Trustees 546, 548.

103 *In Re Raven* (1915) 1 Ch 673 (High Court).

104 *Massy v Rogers* XI (1883) LRI 409 (Irish High Court).

105 ibid 412.

106 ibid.

v Avery, that parties could not oust the jurisdiction of the courts but could agree on the determination of damages or the time or mode of payment via arbitration, with an award being a condition precedent to any action on the contract.[107]

2.038 The most interesting aspect of this case is its reference to contractual arbitration cases, and its application of the rule laid down in those cases, e.g. *Scott v Avery*, as regards ousting the jurisdiction of the court. The court does not state that there is a special public policy regarding testamentary dispositions and ousting the jurisdiction of the court but rather contents itself with applying the principle laid down in *Scott v Avery*.[108] Consequently, one can deduce that the rule for both contractual and testamentary arbitration clauses is the same, with the result that as contracting parties are now allowed to oust the jurisdiction of the court via arbitration so are testators. Indeed, this conclusion would seem to align with the statement of the court that 'What the parties to a contract cannot be permitted to effect by stipulation cannot, in my opinion, be effected by a testator in his will'.[109] In consequence, it would seem that the inverse is, *mutatis mutandis*, also true so that as contracting parties are now allowed to provide for arbitration in their contract so is a testator in his will.

2.039 The next important case is *In Re Raven*,[110] where a testator had provided for several charitable legacies and as there was a dispute regarding which charity was intended to receive one of the bequests the matter came before the courts.[111]

2.040 The court held that the provision for the trustees to decide the matter was invalid, essentially on the grounds that it was repugnant for the testator to grant a particular right whilst at the same time stating that a dispute regarding that right should not be resolved by the courts.[112] This argument is clearly an archaic one, as it is now accepted that there is no 'logical inconsistency'[113] between granting rights under a trust or in a will and providing for those rights to be enforced only in arbitration and not the courts.[114] Instead, the repugnancy doctrine should now be seen as being 'concerned with clauses which prevent

107 ibid 416–417.

108 ibid 416–417.

109 ibid 417.

110 *In Re Raven* (n 103).

111 ibid 673.

112 ibid 677.

113 Matthew Conaglen, 'The Enforceability of Arbitration Clauses in Trusts' (2015) 74 The Cambridge Law Journal 450, 466.

114 ibid 466–467.

enforcement of rights which have purportedly been granted, rather than with preventing enforcement through the courts of such rights'.[115] The court also rejected the testator's clause on the ground of public policy and referred to the case of *Massy v Rogers*. Again, one can state that the evolution of the public policy in English law as regards arbitration means that this argument is no longer applicable.

The next important case regarding ouster and testamentary dispositions or trusts is *In Re Wynn*,[116] which adopted the reasoning of *In Re Raven* to hold that testamentary arbitration clauses were both repugnant to the benefits conferred under them and contrary to public policy.[117] As both of these arguments have been discredited, the case does not add anything new to the discussion. **2.041**

The next case which is of interest to us is the Scottish House of Lords case of *Board of Management for the Dundee General Hospitals v Bell's Trustees*,[118] which was another situation where there was a dispute over the provision in a will for a charitable legacy to be paid, in this case to the Dundee Royal Infirmary. The trustees had to be satisfied that the Dundee hospital had not come under the control of the state or local authority either directly or indirectly in order to pay it the bequest.[119] The court held that there was no issue with the clause and upheld the trustee's decision refusing to pay out the bequest. The decision might seem odd considering the cases previously discussed, but it is worth noting, firstly, that it was a Scottish case with the result that it did not consider any English cases, and, secondly, the clause itself was peculiarly worded. As the court itself noted, 'The trustees, as a condition of refusing payment, had not to be satisfied positively that the infirmary had been taken over by or placed under the control of the State … The right to receive the legacy was contingent on the trustees' state of mind, the absence of state of doubt…'.[120] **2.042**

It would seem, therefore, that the clause was a condition precedent and not a condition subsequent. Consequently, as with *Scott v Avery*, the court was willing to give effect to such a clause notwithstanding the fact that it ousted their jurisdiction. That said, the court could still intervene as regards such clauses if the trustees did not consider the proper question, did not really consider it, or 'perversely shut their eyes to the facts'.[121] **2.043**

---

115 ibid 467.

116 *In Re Wynn, Decd* (1952) 1 Ch 271 (High Court).

117 ibid 278–279.

118 *Board of Management for Dundee General Hospitals v Bell's Trustees* [1952] SC (HL) 78 (House of Lords).

119 ibid 79.

120 ibid 84.

121 ibid 92.

2.044 The case of *In re Tuck's Settlement Trusts*[122] concerned the estate of Sir Alfred Tuck who wished to ensure that his successors remained Jewish.[123] In consequence, he made various provisions regarding the need for beneficiaries to the settlements he set up to marry an approved wife, who would either be Jewish by blood or have been brought up in and never departed from the Jewish faith, and, of course, the beneficiaries themselves were not to leave the Jewish faith.

2.045 The most important clause for our purposes is that which followed the clause regarding the 'approved wife' and which provided that where there was a dispute or doubt the decision of either the Chief Rabbi of the Portuguese or Anglo-German community was to be conclusive.[124] There is a clear parallel between this clause and those of earlier cases such as *Massy, In Re Raven* and *In Re Wynn*, but the clause, in this case, would seem to be more restricted, leaving only certain specific matters to be decided by a Chief Rabbi. Lord Denning rejected the argument that *In Re Raven* and *In Re Wynn* rendered the clause invalid and held that the case law on the subject should be reconsidered in the light of *Dundee General Hospitals*. Lord Denning further stated that if contracting parties could allow a dispute or doubt to be settled by a third party, there was no reason why testators should not also be able to do so and thus upheld the clause.[125]

2.046 The most recent case to consider ouster is *AN v Barclays Private Bank and Trust (Cayman) Limited*,[126] which is a landmark case with regard to no contest or forfeiture clauses. The key issue for our purposes is the court's statement that 'it [would not] matter for these purposes whether the trusts contain … internal machinery for controlling a defaulting trustee … [there] can be no justification for a complete prohibition against access to the courts'.[127]

2.047 One interpretation of Smellie CJ's statement is that beneficiaries must always have a right to go to court, even an alternative justice mechanism such as arbitration cannot displace this right, and thus arbitration clauses in trust deeds cannot oust the jurisdiction of the courts. As the court analysed cases such as *Re Raven* and *Re Wynn* such an interpretation is plausible. However, there are also clear differences between the internal mechanism of removing trustees through a vote and the quasi-judicial process of arbitration. In the latter case

---

122 *In re Tuck's Settlement Trusts* (1978) 2 WLR 411 (Court of Appeal).

123 ibid 413–415.

124 ibid 415.

125 ibid 417–418.

126 *AN v Barclays Private Bank and Trust (Cayman) Limited and others* (2006) 9 ITELR 630 (Cayman Islands Grand Court).

127 ibid 666.

the beneficiaries can still hold the trustees, and any other power holders, to account through an adjudication of the process by impartial third parties whose decision will be supervised and enforced by the courts. This would appear to satisfy Smellie CJ's requirement of accountability because 'effective accountability does not mean that the trustees can be accountable only to a court rather than to some other body which has power to enquire into the trustees' administration of the fund and to require them to abide by the terms of the trust instrument'.[128]

It is therefore submitted that there is a sufficient difference between arbitration and the internal mechanism provided for in *AN v Barclays Private Bank and Trust (Cayman) Limited*[129] so that the decision does not pose an obstacle to the arbitration of trust disputes. **2.048**

2. The irreducible core of the trust

The idea of the irreducible core of the trust was first explicitly stated by David Hayton in an article published in 1996,[130] in which he stated, 'The beneficiaries' right to enforce the trust and make the trustees account for their conduct with the correlative duties of the trustees to the beneficiaries are at the core of the trust.'[131] This received judicial approval in the English case of *Armitage v Nurse and others*,[132] where the judge concluded that 'If the beneficiaries have no rights enforceable against the trustees there are no trusts.'[133] David Hayton's statement in his article, as well as the statement in *Armitage v Nurse*, have subsequently been widely approved of in the main practitioner texts such as *Underhill & Hayton*[134] as well as *Lewin*[135] and numerous law reform reports.[136] **2.049**

The issue that the idea of the irreducible core of the trust poses for the arbitration of trust disputes is that part of this irreducible core is often held to be a degree of supervision by the court and the enforcement by the beneficiaries of their rights through a judicial mechanism, i.e. the court system. For example, **2.050**

---

128 David Fox, 'Non-Excludable Trustee Duties' (2011) 17 Trusts & Trustees 17, 24.

129 *AN v Barclays Private Bank and Trust (Cayman) Limited and others* (n 126).

130 AJ Oakley (ed.), *Trends in Contemporary Trust Law* (Clarendon Press 1996) 47–62.

131 ibid at 47.

132 *Armitage v Nurse* [1998] Ch 241 (Court of Appeal).

133 ibid 253.

134 David J Hayton, *Law Relating to Trusts and Trustees* (LexisNexis 2016) para 48.61.

135 Lynton Tucker, *Lewin on Trusts* (Sweet & Maxwell 2012) para 39-130.

136 'The Duties, Office and Powers of a Trustee' (New Zealand Law Commission 2011) 26 para 1.17; 'Trust Law: General Proposals' (Law Reform Commission of Ireland 2008) 92 paras 4.23–5.02; 'Trustee Exemption Clauses' (Law Commission of England and Wales 2006) 301 paras 2.13–2.16.

in the seminal case of *Morice v Bishop of Durham*[137] the court stated, 'it is a maxim that the execution of a trust shall be under the control of the court, it must be of such a nature that it can be under that control, so that the administration of it can be reviewed by the court, or, if the trustee dies, the court itself can execute the trust'.[138]

2.051 The more recent privy council case of *Schmidt v Rosewood Trust Ltd*[139] confirmed this, with the Board stating that 'It is fundamental to the law of trusts that the court has jurisdiction to supervise and if appropriate intervene in the administration of a trust …'.[140] The Privy Council restated this several years later in *Crociani v Crociani*,[141] explaining that:

> In the case of a trust, unlike a contract, the court has an inherent jurisdiction to supervise the administration of the trust … [it] is clear that the court does have a power to supervise the administration of trusts, primarily to protect the interests of beneficiaries, which represents a clear and, for present purposes, significant distinction between trusts and contracts.[142]

2.052 In recent years the concept of the irreducible core has evolved with the emergence of an idea of 'mandatory' and 'default' rules (or rather duties imposed on the trustees).[143] The former cannot be overridden by the provisions of the trust; the latter can but will apply if the terms of the trust do not provide otherwise. The concept of mandatory and default rules in the trust context would appear to have first been developed by the American Uniform Trust Code in 2000[144] and was recently implemented in the revised 2019 New Zealand Trust Law Act. Examples of mandatory duties imposed on the trustees include a duty to know the terms of the trust,[145] a duty to act in accordance with the terms of the trust,[146] a duty to act honestly and in good faith,[147] and a duty to act for the benefit of the beneficiaries (or in the case of purpose trusts to further

137 *Morice v Bishop of Durham* 10 (1805) Ves 522 (High Court).

138 ibid 529.

139 *Schmidt v Rosewood Trust Ltd* (2003) 2 AC 709 (Judicial Committee of the Privy Council).

140 ibid 724.

141 *Crociani v Crociani* [2014] UKPC 40 (Judicial Committee of the Privy Council).

142 ibid 35–36.

143 'Review of the Law of Trusts: A Trusts Act for New Zealand' (New Zealand Law Commission 2013) 130 197–199; BW Boesch, 'The ICC Initiative' (2012) 18 Trusts & Trustees 316.

144 John H Langbein, 'Mandatory Rules in the Law of Trusts' (2004) 98 Northwestern University Law Review 1105; Uniform Trust Code s 105.

145 Trusts Act 2019 s 23.

146 ibid 24.

147 ibid 25.

the specified purpose).[148] Examples of default duties include a duty of care,[149] a duty not to exercise a power for one's own benefit,[150] a duty to avoid conflicts of interest,[151] and a duty not to profit. [152]

In the context of trust arbitration, the relevance of the idea of the irreducible core being composed only of 'mandatory' as opposed to 'default rules' is that trust arbitration of issues which were only default clearly does not impact on the irreducible core as the settlor would be free to exclude these duties altogether. However, in practice this caveat is (even if one assumes that other Commonwealth legal systems outside New Zealand accept the concept of mandatory and default rules) unlikely to be of much comfort to anyone considering trust arbitration. This is for two main reasons. Firstly, disputes may encompass both mandatory and default trustee duties: what is an arbitral tribunal supposed to do in such a case? Hiving out the arbitrable part of the dispute from the non-arbitrable part is unlikely to be practicable or efficient, and it is inevitable that any such attempts would lead to further disputes or challenges against any award which is rendered. Secondly, if a settlor was to provide in an arbitration clause that only disputes regarding default duties could be arbitrated, disputes about what duties are involved in a dispute would inevitably arise. It would be simple for a party to allege, genuinely or otherwise, that a dispute involved mandatory and not default duties and should not therefore be arbitrated. To this would be added the uncertainty of whether the court would recognise the concept of mandatory or default duties at all. **2.053**

The consequence of the above is that while recent discussions about 'mandatory' and 'default' rules in the context of the irreducible core are interesting, they are of limited relevance to trust arbitration. If trust arbitration is going to be practical it is necessary to show that it does not violate the irreducible core at all, without getting into convoluted discussions about whether there are mandatory and default rules in the law of trusts and whether trust arbitration does or does not violate either class of rules. **2.054**

(a) Does the arbitration of internal trust disputes violate the principle of the irreducible core of the trust?

If one takes the above statements from courts literally, then enforcing arbitration clauses in a trust deed would violate the irreducible core of a trust because an arbitral tribunal is not a court; and even if courts retain some supervision **2.055**

---

148 ibid 26.
149 ibid 31.
150 ibid.
151 ibid 34.
152 ibid 36.

over the arbitral process, such supervision is extremely limited as compared to the powers they could exercise directly in trust litigation matters. However, it is submitted that this view is incorrect for several reasons.

2.056 Firstly, 'The supervisory jurisdiction of the court is not ousted. It continues to have the supervisory role conferred upon it by the relevant legislation'.[153] It is true that the degree of supervision which a court exercises over an arbitration is no doubt less than its supervisory jurisdiction over trusts generally, but it remains a fact that it does exercise some power of supervision. For example, a court can set aside awards where the tribunal lacks jurisdiction or has committed a serious irregularity, and can even hear appeals on points of law where this had not been excluded by agreement.[154] This jurisdiction is not much narrower than the court's jurisdiction over trustees who have been made the arbiters of a particular matter, as in *Dundee General Hospitals* or *In re Tuck's Settlement Trusts*, and thus *prima facie* would seem to be sufficiently broad to avoid violating the principle of the irreducible core.

2.057 Secondly, as argued by David Fox, 'there is nothing in the concept of the irreducible core that necessarily precludes compulsory arbitration. The principle is that the trustee must be sufficiently accountable so that his status as the non-beneficial owner of the assets vested in him is practically real.'[155] There is no reason in principle why arbitration cannot ensure accountability over trusts as effectively as the courts. The alternative view, that only courts can ensure effective accountability, is rooted in antiquated and formalistic views of the justice system generally, and of arbitration in particular.

2.058 However, although the arbitration of trust disputes does not, *ipso facto*, violate the irreducible core of the trust, that principle does impose some restrictions. Namely, it is submitted that it would not be possible to contract out of all court supervision over the arbitral process. This is at any rate not permitted under the Arbitration Act 1996,[156] and it is unclear whether 'settling' a trust abroad which still had links to England would be sufficient to exclude the jurisdiction of the English courts over the matter, notwithstanding any attempt to exclude court supervision.[157]

---

153 *Rinehart v Welker* [2012] NSWCA 95 (Court of Appeal, New South Wales) para 175; cf *Fitzpatrick v Emerald Grain Pty Ltd* [2017] WASC 206 (Supreme Court of Western Australia) para 96.

154 Arbitration Act 1996 ss 67–69.

155 Fox (n 128) 24.

156 The provisions for challenge of the arbitral award found in ss 66–68 and ss 70–71 are listed as mandatory provisions in Schedule 1 to the Act.

157 For example in Switzerland under Art 192 of the Private International Law Act.

Thirdly, if the procedure for selecting or constituting the arbitral tribunal was procedurally unfair, for example by appointing arbitrators that were not impartial, by unduly restricting the ability of a party to appoint arbitrators or to plead their case, such a clause would likely fall foul of the irreducible core. However, this restriction is unlikely to have much importance in practice as such restrictions would, in any event, fall foul of public policy in the arbitral context and thus be unenforceable. **2.059**

Fourthly, where a particular dispute necessitates the granting of remedies which an arbitral tribunal cannot grant, the doctrine of the irreducible core might make inroads into the 'exclusivity' of the arbitral process either by allowing the courts to grant the remedy or by requiring the matter to be settled by litigation and not arbitration. The issue will be analysed in depth in the next section. **2.060**

3. Issues regarding the remedies an arbitral tribunal can grant as opposed to a state court

One important argument that has been made against the arbitrability of trust disputes, as well as other 'sensitive' types of disputes such as insolvency or shareholder disputes, is that as an arbitral tribunal appears to lack the power to grant certain remedies which courts possess, or to effectively enforce them, such disputes should not be considered arbitrable.[158] This section will explore this argument in two parts. Firstly, it will consider the general approach of the courts to this argument and then it will look at the specific issues that might arise in the context of trust arbitration. **2.061**

(a) Jurisprudence of the courts regarding the 'remedies' objection to arbitrability

The view that because, in relation to a particular matter, an arbitral tribunal cannot grant the same remedies as a court, that matter should be held to be inarbitrable is not new and was argued by counsel in several cases. In the cases of *Societe Commerciale De Reassurance v Eras (International) Limited*[159] and *Wealands v CLC Contractors Ltd*,[160] the issue was that arbitrators might lack the power to grant a claim for contribution under the Civil Liability (Contribution) Act 1978. In both cases, the court rejected the disapplication of an automatic stay of court proceedings, on the grounds that even if the arbitral tribunal did lack the power to grant a claim for contribution, this was merely **2.062**

158 *Rinehart v Welker* (n 153) paras 225–227; *Silica Investors Limited v Tomolugen Holdings Limited and others* [2014] SGHC 11 (Singapore High Court).

159 *Societe Commerciale de Reassurance v Eras International Ltd (formerly Eras (UK))* (1992) 1 Lloyd's Rep 570 (Court of Appeal).

160 *Wealands v CLC Contractors Ltd* [1999] CLC 1821 (Court of Appeal).

'the consequence of the parties having agreed to submit their disputes to arbitration'.[161] Similarly, in the more recent case of *Fulham Football Club*, which concerned an unfair prejudice petition by a shareholder, Patten LJ rejected the argument, stating, 'these jurisdictional limitations ... are no more than the practical consequences of choosing that method of dispute resolution'.[162] The same holds for Singapore, where the Court of Appeal has stated that, 'We are unable to agree [with the first instance judge] that jurisdictional limitations on an arbitral tribunal's ability to grant relief are relevant to the question of arbitrability'.[163]

2.063 As the issue regarding inarbitrability due to restrictions on the remedies which can be granted is fairly open and shut, this then leads to the question of what happens in disputes where a party needs or wants a remedy which an arbitral tribunal cannot give. It should be noted that in England this problem should arise relatively rarely, as s 48(1) of the Arbitration Act 1996 allows the parties to agree on the powers which can be exercised by the tribunal regarding remedies. Furthermore, the DAC commentary clarifies that 'there is nothing to restrict such remedies to those available at court'.[164] Consequently, parties could agree on an arbitral tribunal granting remedies which would not be available if the matter was brought before a court. The outer limit of party autonomy in such cases, as also in general, is that tribunals cannot grant remedies contrary to public policy. In those cases where the issue arises, usually because the parties have not provided the required remedy in the arbitration agreement, it would appear that the courts are willing to exercise their powers in order to prevent the arbitration agreement from being frustrated. For example, Patten LJ stated in *Fulham Football Club* that in such cases the matter could be brought before the court either to lift the automatic stay of litigation or to seek relief from the court.[165] In similar words, the Singapore Court of Appeal in *Silica*[166] stated that the parties could apply to the 'court for the grant of any specific relief which might be beyond the power of the arbitral tribunal to award'.[167] As regards findings by the arbitral tribunal, 'the parties would be bound by such findings and would, at least as a general rule, be prevented from re-litigating those matters before the court'.[168]

161 ibid 1828.

162 *Fulham Football Club (1987) Ltd v Richards and another* (n 15) para 84.

163 *Tomolugen Holdings Ltd and another v Silica Investors Ltd and other appeals* (n 21) para 97.

164 'Report on the English Arbitration Bill' (n 13) para 234.

165 *Fulham Football Club (1987) Ltd v Richards and another* (n 15) para 83.

166 *Tomolugen Holdings Ltd and another v Silica Investors Ltd and other appeals* (n 21).

167 ibid 100.

168 ibid.

A practical example of how the court will deal with a tribunal allegedly granting a remedy beyond its powers can be found in the case of *Sterling v Rand*.[169] That case concerned a property dispute which was brought before the London Beth Din, a Jewish tribunal, for a binding arbitration under the Arbitration Act 1996. The Beth Din rendered a decision in which they ordered that the property be transferred to the claimant; the defendant did not comply, and so the claimant sought to enforce the award under s 66 of the Act. One of the grounds of defence raised by the claimant was that the Beth Din did not have jurisdiction to order specific performance of the contract, i.e. ordering that the property be transferred to the claimant. The court rejected this argument, holding that as s 48, which lists the default powers which an arbitral tribunal possesses, was not a mandatory section of the Act and the parties had chosen Jewish procedural law to govern the proceedings, which allowed for such powers, the Beth Din possessed the power to transfer the property.[170] **2.064**

In consequence of the above, it would seem that parties who wish to have a London seated arbitration could get around any potential arbitrability issues regarding an arbitrator's lack of powers by applying the procedural law of a jurisdiction which granted arbitrators all potentially necessary powers. An example of such a law would be New Zealand law, as s 12 of the New Zealand Arbitration Act 1996 provides that '(1) An arbitration agreement, unless otherwise agreed by the parties, is deemed to provide that an arbitral tribunal— (a) may award any remedy or relief that could have been ordered by the High Court if the dispute had been the subject of civil proceedings in that court: …'.[171] Section 32 of the 2018 DIFC Trust law is similarly worded with the addition of a carve out for situations where the parties provide otherwise in the trust deed, thus making it beneficial for parties to not so provide, as the default position would seem to be that the tribunal would have all the same powers as the court.[172] **2.065**

The court also stated that it 'would have been willing to find that the court had jurisdiction under section 66 transferring the Property even if the Beth Din lacked powers to make such an order'.[173] However, as the court itself recognised, 'this would be a somewhat unusual situation since (on the presumed basis) the award would be open to challenge on grounds of the tribunal's lack of power and the absence of power may give rise to other good reasons for **2.066**

169 *Sterling v Rand & Anor* [2019] EWHC 2560 (Ch).

170 ibid 58.

171 Arbitration Act 1996 (NZ) s 12(1)(a).

172 DIFC Trust Law s 32.

173 *Sterling v Rand & Anor* (n 169) para 60.

refusing enforcement as a matter of discretion'.[174] If one combines these statements with those made in *Fulham Football Club* and *Silica*, it would seem that the courts would be willing to enforce an arbitral award even if the tribunal did not possess the powers to grant a particular remedy and, if necessary, would supplement the tribunal's powers with their own. If the parties have agreed that the tribunal should have power to grant the remedy in question, no particular difficulties should arise. However, if they have not done so, it would, as noted above, be open to one of the parties to challenge the award for serious irregularity under s 68(2)(b).

2.067 It should be noted that challenges to arbitral awards under s 68 are subject to a high bar as the section 'is really designed as a long stop, only available in extreme cases where the tribunal has gone so wrong in its conduct of the arbitration that justice calls out for it to be corrected'.[175] This is in keeping with 'A major purpose of the new Act [which] was to reduce drastically the extent of intervention of courts in the arbitral process'.[176] It is for this reason that s 68 defines a serious irregularity as one which 'has caused or will cause substantial injustice to the applicant'.[177] Thus the mere fact that an arbitral tribunal exceeded its powers would not be sufficient to bring it within the scope of s 68(2)(b). Examples of such excesses of power include where 'in conflict with an agreement in writing of the parties under section 37, the tribunal appointed an expert to report to it [or]... where an arbitration agreement expressly permitted only the award of simple interest and the arbitrators ... awarded compound interest'.[178]

2.068 In summary, it is fair to say that a party seeking to challenge an award under s 68, therefore, faces an uphill battle, something which is confirmed by the very few successful reported cases. In consequence, it is suggested that, except in extreme cases, this section is unlikely to be harmful to trust arbitration disputes where the tribunal awards a remedy which is usually reserved for the courts, even if the parties have not explicitly provided for this. If a tribunal wishes to act *in abundantio cautio*, however, it can often achieve the same result as a potentially *ultra vires* remedy through less controversial means. For example, in the context of trustee removal and vesting orders, Bathurst CJ stated in *Rinehart v Welker* that 'An arbitrator could give effect to a claim for removal by

174 ibid.

175 'Report on the English Arbitration Bill' (n 13) para 280.

176 *Lesotho Highlands Development Authority v Impregilo SpA and others* [2005] UKHL 43 [26].

177 Arbitration Act 1996 s 68(2).

178 *Lesotho Highlands Development Authority v Impregilo SpA and others* (n 176) para 29.

ordering the trustee to resign, to appoint a new trustee and to convey the trust property to that person. Such an award could be enforced as a judgment'.[179]

Having now looked at the issue of arbitrability and remedies, in general, the next section will consider the specific public policy and statutory problems which arise in the context of trust arbitration. **2.069**

(b) The 'remedies' argument against arbitrability in the context of trust arbitration

This section will firstly provide a brief overview of the most important powers which a court has in trust law matters and then explore the specific issues which arise with regards to an arbitral tribunal exercising certain powers in trust disputes. **2.070**

(i) Remedies which a court can grant in relation to trusts and trustees

Compensation due to breach of trust

If a trustee has 'fail[ed] to carry out his obligations under the terms of the trust, the rules of equity or statute'[180] either by 'doing something contrary to those obligations, or … neglecting to do something which he ought to have done'[181] he has committed a breach of trust and must compensate the beneficiaries.[182] The type of compensation required from the trustee depends on the nature of the breach, for example if he has misapplied or misappropriated trust funds 'he must either restore the trust property in specie or pay a money substitute'.[183] On the other hand, if he has breached some other duty, he may be ordered to pay reparation by the court.[184] It is important to note that all these remedies are personal, against only the trustee or trustees, and thus may be useless when the trustee is insolvent or where for some reason it is impossible to get at his assets.[185] Fortunately, however, equity also developed a category of proprietary remedies which beneficiaries can assert even against innocent third parties, and these will be discussed next. **2.071**

179 *Rinehart v Welker* (n 153) para 175.

180 DWM Waters, Mark R Gillen and Lionel D Smith, *Waters' Law of Trusts in Canada* (4th edn, Carswell 2012) 1270.

181 ibid.

182 David J Hayton et al., eds, *Underhill and Hayton Law Relating to Trusts and Trustees* (19th edn, LexisNexis 2016) para 87.1.

183 ibid.

184 ibid.

185 Waters, Gillen and Smith (n 180) 1334.

Proprietary remedies available due to a breach of trust

2.072 If a trustee commits a breach of trust which results in trust property falling into the hands of a third party then, unless he can prove that he acquired a legal interest in the property in good faith, for value and without notice of the breach, this property will be subject to a trust which requires the third party to hand the property over to the trustees.[186] Similarly, if the trustee has made an unauthorised disposition of property, for example if they have profited from selling trust property, then the proceeds of that disposition will themselves become trust property.[187] Such remedies have several obvious advantages over personal remedies, they grant the beneficiaries priority over unsecured creditors of an insolvent trustee, final orders recognising proprietary rights can be enforced even if the trustees cannot be found, and proprietary rights carry with them any increase in the value of the property.[188]

Removal of trustees

2.073 The court can remove trustees in Commonwealth jurisdictions either under its common law power,[189] or under various statutory powers.[190] As trustees are so essential to the running of a trust and as bad trustees can cause many problems by depleting the trust fund either through maliciousness or incompetence, the power to remove trustees is clearly an important one.

Variation, rectification and rescission of trusts

2.074 Although all of these terms involve changing the terms of the trust in some way, in the case of rescission by winding it up altogether, their use, extent and consequences are very different. It is for this reason that each will be dealt with separately below.

Statutory variations of trusts

2.075 The first variation of trusts statute was the English Variation of Trusts Act 1958, which gave the courts very wide powers under s 1 to vary or revoke trusts. English courts had possessed similar, albeit perhaps not as broad, powers until the 1954 House of Lords decision of *Chapman v Chapman*.[191] That decision held that, as it was the duty of the court to ensure that a trust was executed it couldn't alter a trust merely because it was beneficial for an infant beneficiary, rather it was required to hold trustees and beneficiaries to the provisions in the

---

186 ibid 1334–1335.

187 ibid.

188 ibid 1337.

189 See for example *Uvedale contra Ettrick* (1682) 2 Chan Cas 130.

190 In England and Wales this is s 41 of the Trustee Act 1925; in New South Wales it is s 70 of the Trustee Act 1925 and there are similar provisions in most Commonwealth jurisdictions

191 [1954] 1 All ER 798.

trust deed. The statute effectively reversed this decision of the House of Lords and similar statutes were passed throughout the Commonwealth,[192] though not in Singapore.[193] The importance of legislation that allows for the varying of trusts is that it allows the correction of any errors made in the trust deed as well as omissions, for example where family circumstances change, or new tax rules make the structure of the trust unfavourable.[194] Its importance is even greater given the courts limited power to make such changes under the common law doctrines of rectification and rescission, which will be discussed below.

Rectification and rescission

Rectification aims to '... [put] the record straight. In the case of a voluntary settlement, rectification involves bringing the trust into line with the true intentions of the settlor ...'.[195] The mistake may be that the wording of the instrument is not what was intended or where the legal effect of that wording was not intended.[196] This might be because the settlor misunderstood the consequences of their actions or for other reasons.[197] Unlike with the statutory power, however, there must have been some mistake[198], and thus a mere change in circumstances is not enough to justify rectification. Rescission similarly arises where there is a mistake, but unlike rectification, its effect is to '[restore] the status quo'[199] and effectively 'unwind' the trust. **2.076**

Vesting orders

In the case of the original trustees of a trust the 'trust property is vested [in them] by virtue of the complete construction of the trust at the outset';[200] however, this is not the case for subsequent trustees, and thus they obtain no legal or equitable right *ex-officio*.[201] Instead, the trust property must be specifically vested in them, for example by deed or other transfer from the prior trustees. The situation has, however, been remedied by statute so that trust **2.077**

192 For example s 63A of the Victoria Trustees Act 1958; The Ontario Variation of Trusts Act 1959; The Isle of Man Variation of Trusts Act 1961; s 58 British Virgin Islands Trusts Ordinance 1961; ss 47–48 Bermuda Trusts Act 1975; s 47 Jersey Trust Act 1984.

193 Michael Hwang SC and Nicholas Thio, 'Why Does Singapore Not Have a Variation of Trusts Act?' (2011) 23 Singapore Academy of Law Journal 58–73

194 See The Law Reform Commission of Irelands, *Report on the Variation of Trusts* (2000) LRC 63 at paras 1.11–1.19.

195 *Allnut & Anor v Wilding & Ors* [2007] EWCA Civ 412 [11].

196 Tucker L and others, *Lewin on Trusts* (19th edn, Sweet & Maxwell/Thomson Reuters 2015) 1354.

197 Hayton et al. (n 182) at 384.

198 Tucker and others (n 196) 1354; Hayton et al. (n 182) 384.

199 Tucker and others (n 196) 1354.

200 Hayton, *Law Relating to Trusts and Trustees* (n 134) 1047.

201 Hayton et al. (n 182) 1047–1048.

property automatically vests in the trustees in a broad range of situations,[202] and where this is not the case the court has power to issue a vesting order which will vest the property.[203]

Relief of trustees from liability

2.078 The title of this section is perhaps a little misleading as when we speak of liability we are not speaking of any and all liability which a trustee may accrue, but rather of liability for a breach of trust.[204] The power is clearly an important one as, among other things, trustees may be reluctant to act where there is no possibility to relieve them from liability, and it is related to the courts' supervisory jurisdiction, meaning that many of the same issues arise.

Re Beddoe *orders*

2.079 A *Beddoe* application is a specific type of application which trustees can make to a court 'for directions … as to whether to bring, continue or defend court proceedings in their capacity as trustee'[205] and takes its name from the case of *Re Beddoe.*[206] It likely also applies to arbitration proceedings[207] and as the alternative is potential personal liability by the trustees for all costs incurred,[208] it is an extremely important type of application.

Re Benjamin *orders*

2.080 A *Benjamin* order permits, 'personal representatives to distribute an estate on the footing that missing beneficiaries whom it has been impossible to trace predeceased the deceased.'[209] The effect of such an order is that, 'the trustees are protected, in that they cannot afterwards be accused of a breach of a trust as they have acted under the authority of an order of the court, but it preserves the right of any person actually entitled to follow the trust property if he later appears'.[210] The name of the order comes from the case of *Re Benjamin*,[211] and although not as important as *Beddoe* orders, a *Benjamin* order can be crucial in situations where it has proven impossible to trace certain beneficiaries. This is because trustees are unlikely to distribute the trust funds without the protec-

---

202 S 40 Trustee Act 1925.

203 Hayton et al. (n 182) 1048–1057.

204 Trustee Act 1925 s 61; Tucker and others (n 196) 1922.

205 Kate Davenport and Tiaan Nelson, 'The Court's Role in Assisting Trustees: *Re Beddoe* Orders and Other Directions' (2017) 23:3 Trusts Trustee 343.

206 [1891–94] All ER Rep Ext 1697

207 Sara Collins, *International Trust Disputes* (Oxford University Press 2012) 268.

208 *In re Beddoe* [1891–94] All ER Rep Ext 1697, 1704.

209 Collins (n 207) 241.

210 Tucker and others (n 196) 1119.

211 *In re Benjamin* (1902) 1 Ch 723 (High Court).

tion of such an order due to the risk of later breach of trust proceedings if the missing beneficiary reappears.[212]

Authorising actions which would otherwise constitute a breach of trust

2.081 The court also has the power, under its inherent jurisdiction, to authorise actions which would otherwise constitute a breach of trust,[213] for example allowing a trustee to buy trust property in his personal capacity where no one else was willing to buy the property at a fair price.[214]

Applications under the Matrimonial Causes Act 1973

2.082 This statute regulates divorce in England and Wales, including the procedure for making financial provision orders, and allows the court to vary an 'ante-nuptial or post-nuptial settlement [trust]' as part of an order under s 24. Although this term is broad, it does not refer to all trusts held by either party to the marriage but rather only to 'marriage settlement[s]';[215] unfortunately, the test for determining whether a trust is or is not a marriage settlement is unclear. One opinion is that in order to determine whether a trust is a marriage settlement you have to determine whether the trust is 'upon the husband in the character of a husband or on the wife in the character of a wife or both in the character of husband and wife'.[216] In the past, this test was useful due to the former practice of marriage settlements, but as these have fallen into disuse, the test is no longer helpful. An alternative test is to determine whether the trust has the requisite 'nuptial element' by looking at: (i) 'the existence of a marriage or proposed marriage at the time the settlement is made'; (ii) the terms of the settlement themselves; and (iii) '[t]he nature of the trust property. A settlement holding the family home is almost bound to be a marriage settlement'.[217]

2.083 The English courts can make orders for both domestic and foreign divorce, nullity or judicial separation decrees,[218] and can vary both English and foreign trusts.[219] As always when there is a foreign element, for example when the trustees and/or the property are outwith the jurisdiction, enforcement of orders under the Act becomes considerably more complex.[220] The Act also contains

212 Tucker and others (n 196) para 27-027.

213 Richard C Nolan, '"The Execution of a Trust Shall Be Under the Control of the Court": A Maxim in Modern Times' (2016) 2:2 Canadian Journal of Contemporary and Comparative Law at 473.

214 *Campbell v Walker* (1800) 5 Ves Jun 678, albeit in that case prior approval was not obtained and so the court advised that the transaction would not stand if it was not to the advantage of the beneficiaries.

215 James Kessler, *Drafting Trusts and Will Trusts: A Modern Approach* (Sweet & Maxwell 2017) 60.

216 ibid.

217 ibid 60–61.

218 Hayton, *Law Relating to Trusts and Trustees* (n 134) para 43.105.

219 ibid para 43.106.

220 ibid para 43.109.

anti-avoidance provisions in s 37 so that a court can prevent dispositions or transfers from being made which have 'the intention of defeating the applicant's claim for ancillary relief'.[221] The court can also set aside any transactions which have already been made, which means that it can 'unwind' trusts made to defeat claims under the Act.[222] Dispositions of foreign property come within the scope of the Act,[223] but dispositions made under a will or in a codicil to a will are excluded.[224]

Applications under the Inheritance (Provision for Family and Dependants) Act 1975

2.084 This piece of legislation provides that where a testator has not made reasonable provision for his dependants or where the rules of intestacy do not do so, something that is defined via a *numerus clausus* which is nevertheless broad in effect,[225] the court can make a variety of orders to ensure they are fairly provided for.[226] The courts' powers explicitly extend to the varying of any trusts 'on which the deceased's estate is held (whether arising under the will, or the law relating to intestacy, or both'.[227]

Applications Under the Insolvency Act 1986

2.085 Although, as with the above two acts, this statute is not primarily a 'trust Act', it contains two provisions which are of significant relevance in trust disputes, namely s 339 and s 423. Section 339 applies when a person has been declared bankrupt and enables his trustee in bankruptcy to make an application regarding transactions which were at an 'undervalue' and the court can 'make any order as it thinks fit for restoring the position to what it would have been if that individual had not entered into that transaction'.[228] There is, however, a time limit so that applications under the section must be made within five years of the presentation of a bankruptcy petition, if (a) the settlor was at that time insolvent, or (b) became insolvent as a result of that transaction.[229] However, if the petition is brought within two years, the transaction in question can be set aside without needing to fulfil either of these requirements.[230] The definition of 'undervalue' is a common-sense one as being (i) a transaction made with no consideration, or (ii) a transaction in consideration of marriage or

---

221 Collins (n 207) para 2.61.

222 ibid paras 2.61–2.68.

223 ibid para 2.66.

224 Hayton, *Law Relating to Trusts and Trustees* (n 134) para 18.4.

225 Inheritance (Provision for Family and Dependants) Act 1975 s 1.

226 ibid s 2.

227 ibid s 2(h).

228 Insolvency Act 1986 s 339(2).

229 Nicholas Le Poidevin, 'Going Bust: Insolvency and Trusts' (2010) 16 Trusts & Trustees 299, 300.

230 ibid 299–300.

a civil partnership, or (iii) a transaction for consideration, the value of which is significantly more than the value of the consideration provided by the other person.[231] These definitions are especially problematic in the trust context, as usually trusts are created for no consideration and thus will generally be transactions at an undervalue liable to being set aside or compensated under the Act.[232]

Section 423 of the Act concerns transactions which defraud creditors; as with s 339, there is a requirement for such transactions to be at an 'undervalue', with an identical definition of that term being provided. Despite the name of the section, it is not necessary to prove 'a fraudulent or dishonest intent'.[233] Instead, one must only prove that the transaction was entered into, 'for the purpose – (a) of putting assets beyond the reach of a person who is making, or may at some time make, a claim against him, or (b) of otherwise prejudicing the interests of such a person in relation to the claim which he is making or may make'.[234] The remedies which the court can grant under this section are slightly broader under s 339, however, as the court can make any 'order as it thinks fit for – (a) restoring the position to what it would have been if the transaction had not been entered into, and (b) protecting the interests of persons who are victims of the transaction'.[235] **2.086**

Claims can be brought not just by the relevant insolvency practitioner, as with s 339, but also by a victim of the transaction,[236] and crucially the limitation period for such actions is substantially longer than under s 423. In the case of claims for monetary relief, the limitation period is six years from the date on which the cause of action became complete, while for claims requesting non-monetary relief it is 12 years.[237] However, in the case of claims brought by an insolvency practitioner, an action 'becomes complete only on the date of the commencement of the formal insolvency proceedings in which the insolvency practitioner has been appointed'.[238] In consequence, where there are no formal insolvency proceedings, the clock does not start to run, with the result that there is always the possibility of bringing such proceedings in the future and, **2.087**

231 Insolvency Act s 339(3).

232 Le Poidevin (n 229) 299–300.

233 David Alexander and Stephen Robins, 'Settlor Insolvency and Fraudulent Dispositions: England and Wales' (2011) 17 Trusts & Trustees 132, 133.

234 Insolvency Act s 423(3).

235 ibid 423(2).

236 ibid 424.

237 Alexander and Robins (n 233) 134.

238 ibid 135.

thereby, effectively there is no limitation period to such claims.[239] Equally, s 32(2) of the Limitation Act 1980 means that the prescription period does not start to run until the victim of such a transaction, 'discovers, or could with reasonable diligence discover, that a transaction at an undervalue has been entered into for the purpose of putting an asset beyond the reach of creditors'.[240]

(ii) Exercise by an arbitral tribunal of a court's powers in relation to trusts and trustees

Issues with an arbitral tribunal granting proprietary remedies

2.088 The primary issue with arbitral tribunals attempting to grant proprietary remedies is that they operate *in rem* and are thus clearly beyond an arbitrator's powers. [241] As discussed below in the context of vesting orders, it would appear that the best an arbitral tribunal could do is order a trustee to convey the property to the claimant, and, if they refused to do so, the claimant could seek to enforce such an order via the courts, with the possibility of contempt proceedings being initiated if the trustee refused. However, this is not necessarily the case in all jurisdictions: for example, the relevant legislation in New Zealand provides that an arbitrator can grant all the same remedies and forms of relief as the High Court could if the case was before them in a civil proceeding.[242] In consequence, it would appear that an arbitral tribunal seated in New Zealand would be competent to grant proprietary remedies. As a last point it is worth noting that as one of the main benefits of such claims is that they can be pursued against third parties, they would arguably often fall outside the scope of the arbitration agreement, and indeed also the scope of this work.

Issues with an arbitral tribunal removing a trustee

2.089 Lawrence Cohen and Joanna Poole argue that as the power to remove and appoint new trustees was specifically granted to courts by statute, it cannot be removed by the private agreement of the parties.[243] Unfortunately, they do not analyse the issue in any great deal, but one can assume that they relied on Lawrence Cohen's earlier seminal article with Marcus Staff,[244] where it is argued, with reference to *Czarnikow v Roth, Schmidt*,[245] that powers specifically

---

239 ibid.

240 ibid.

241 See by analogy regarding vesting orders Matthew Conaglen, 'The Enforceability of Arbitration Clauses in Trusts' (2015) 74 The Cambridge Law Journal 450, 457.

242 Arbitration Act 1996 (NZ) s 12(1)(a).

243 Lawrence Cohen and Joanna Poole, 'Trust Arbitration – Is it Desirable and Does It Work?' (2012) 18:4 Trusts and Trustees 324, 329.

244 Lawrence Cohen and Marcus Staff, 'The Arbitration of Trust Disputes' (1999) 7 Journal of International Trust and Corporate Planning 203.

245 *Czarnikow v Roth, Schmidt and Company* (n 48).

granted to the courts by statute cannot be ousted via an arbitration clause.[246] In that case, which concerned an attempt to exclude the stated case provisions of the relevant Arbitration Act, the court held that the provisions were void as contrary to public policy as an attempt to oust '... not the common law jurisdiction of the courts to give a remedy for breaches of contract, but the special statutory jurisdiction of the court to intervene...'.[247] Consequently, as the power to remove and appoint trustees under s 41 of the Trustee Act 1925 and the power to appoint a Judicial Trustee under the Judicial Trustee Act 1896 is granted to the courts, it follows that these provisions cannot be disapplied by an arbitration clause in a trust deed.[248] Cohen and Poole's argument is not that arbitrators cannot remove trustees but rather that the courts have coterminous jurisdiction in such matters.[249]

Although it might seem impractical for a court and arbitral tribunal to have coterminous jurisdiction to remove trustees, this situation is not unprecedented, it is the same as that regarding interim measures. As stated by Born, 'Provisional measures in connection with an international arbitration are, in principle, available from either an arbitral tribunal or a national court'.[250] This represents an exception to the general rule that the existence of a valid and enforceable arbitration agreement 'creates an exclusive forum for the resolution of the disputes covered by its scope'.[251] This exception is justified by the so-called 'principle of complementarity',[252] which, in England and Wales, is enshrined in s 44 of the Arbitration Act 1996, which grants courts several powers exercisable in support of arbitral proceedings. These include measures regarding the taking and preservation of evidence, and a variety of conservatory measures as regards property, the sale of goods, the granting of an interim injunction and the appointment of a receiver.[253] **2.090**

The possibility of conflicting decisions by the court and the arbitral tribunal are eliminated by the conditions for obtaining such relief from the court as, if the situation is not urgent, the court can only grant relief with the permission of the tribunal or agreement of all the parties.[254] Moreover, such relief can only **2.091**

246 Cohen and Staff (n 244) 215–216.

247 *Czarnikow v Roth, Schmidt and Company* (n 48) 491.

248 Cohen and Staff (n 244) 215–216.

249 Cohen and Poole (n 243) 330.

250 Gary Born, *International Commercial Arbitration* (2nd edn, Kluwer Law International 2014) 2428.

251 Giacomo Marchisio, *The Notion of Award in International Commercial Arbitration: A Comparative Analysis of French Law, English Law, and the UNCITRAL Model Law*, vol 44 (Kluwer Law International 2017) 145.

252 ibid.

253 Arbitration Act 1996 s 44(2).

254 ibid 44(3)–(4).

be granted if the arbitral tribunal, institution or other person endowed by the parties with such a power 'has no power or is unable for the time being to act effectively'.[255] Additionally, the court can even provide that its order will cease to have effect when the arbitral tribunal, institution or other person gains power to act as regards the subject-matter of the order.[256]

2.092 However, it is difficult to see how the example of coterminous jurisdiction to grant provisional measures could be applied to the power of removing trustees. The removal of a trustee is not an interim measure but rather will often go to the merits of a dispute. Indeed, the entire dispute might have resulted from irreconcilable views about whether to remove a trustee, or all the trustees, or not. It is therefore obvious that the court and the arbitral tribunal cannot share jurisdiction over the merits of the dispute, and thus it is suggested that Cohen and Poole's conclusion is wrong.

2.093 Cohen and Poole's position suffers from further logical inconsistencies noted by Daniel Clarry, who states that they 'fail to explain how the Court can have an "exclusive jurisdiction" which comprise powers that can also be exercised by an arbitrator'.[257] In his view, the courts' jurisdiction to appoint and remove trustees is non-exclusive and 'can be outsourced to arbitration where it is expedient to do so without ousting the supervisory jurisdiction over trust administration'.[258] This view is certainly more logically consistent than that of Cohen, Poole and Staff's; moreover it avoids the issue of conflicting decisions between the court and arbitral tribunal.

2.094 Daniel Clarry also addresses another argument against the arbitration of trustee removal: the alleged need for public scrutiny regarding trustees. He notes that in reality this argument is a weak one as trustees can resign from office without this being publicised. Moreover, they can be removed by other powerholders in a trust structure, such as protectors, without any publicity, and even if removed by a judge this could be done privately, in the judge's chambers, for example.[259] It is difficult to fault Daniel Clarry's reasoning, and the practical reality is that removal by an impartial arbitral tribunal following a hearing of both sides' cases and after a reasoned decision by the tribunal, is significantly better than potentially unreasoned removal by a protector who may well reflect the settlor's

---

255 ibid 44(5).

256 ibid 44(6).

257 SI Strong and Tony Molloy (eds), *Arbitration of Trust Disputes: Issues in National and International Law* (Oxford University Press 2016), 261.

258 ibid 261.

259 ibid 282.

interests.[260] In consequence, there doesn't seem to be any particular reason not to permit the arbitration of actions as regards trustee removal.

Vesting orders

As noted by Matthew Conaglen, a vesting order 'concerned as it is with property ownership, operates in rem, and is thus beyond the power of an arbitrator',[261] and 'the court often makes a vesting order ... where trustees are removed from office'. [262] Furthermore, the power to make such orders is usually, though not always, narrowly circumscribed so that courts cannot vest property in beneficiaries but only trustees, and one cannot, therefore, speak of a power allowing 'the court ... a general power to put property wherever it ought to be'.[263] This in itself represents a relaxation of the earlier position, by statute, whereby the Courts could only order a defendant to make the desired transfer and imprison them if they refused.[264] The result of all this is that it is difficult to see how arbitral tribunals could make such orders when appointing a trustee following the removal of a prior trustee. A sensible alternative in such cases would be to adopt the course of action outlined by Bathurst CJ in *Rinehart*,[265] namely for the court to order the trustee to resign and convey the property to the new trustee. This course of action would not be too dissimilar to that adopted by courts prior to the passing of vesting statutes, and if this formed part of the relief granted in an arbitral award then a party could, as discussed below, enforce it via the s 66 procedure, with the result that a recalcitrant party would open themselves to the penalty of contempt for non-compliance. If this remedy was not made in an award, it could amount to a peremptory order under s 41 of the Arbitration Act which would be eligible for enforcement via s 44. This section permits courts to exercise their powers to secure compliance with peremptory orders and includes the possibility of contempt for non-compliance.[266] **2.095**

Another alternative, as discussed in *Fulham Football Club*, would be for the arbitral tribunal to give directions authorising a party to go before the court and request a vesting order on the basis of the arbitral award.[267] Again, non-compliance with such an order would be punishable as contempt via the **2.096**

260 Lawrence A Frolik, 'Trust Protectors: Why They Have Become "The Next Big Thing"' (2015) 50 Real Property, Trust and Estate Law Journal 267, 268–270.

261 Conaglen (n 241) 457.

262 ibid.

263 'Unravelling Proprietary Restitution' (2004) 40 The Canadian Business Law Journal 317, 336.

264 ibid 335.

265 *Rinehart v Welker* (n 153).

266 'Report on the English Arbitration Bill' (n 13) para 212.

267 *Fulham Football Club (1987) Ltd v Richards and another* (n 15) para 83.

s 44 procedure. In consequence, even if the arbitral tribunal could not itself make a vesting order, this is unlikely to undermine its ability to decide actions for the removal of a trustee or other disputes which result in the need for a vesting order.

Issues with an arbitral tribunal varying, rectifying or rescinding a trust

2.097 Although the varying of a trust does not, in and of itself, raise public policy or arbitrability issues, the problem arises because the statutory powers to vary a trust are most often used for tax minimisation or efficiency purposes.[268] Equally, applications to rectify or rescind trusts, for example under the rule in *Re Hastings-Bass*,[269] are very often done in order to avoid unforeseen adverse tax consequences or otherwise to mitigate or avoid tax.[270] Note, however, that the courts will not order rectification of a trust if the application is made purely in order to avoid or mitigate tax and the rights of the parties in question would not be affected.[271] Taxation is a matter of public interest, with the UK tax authority having adopted a hard line towards offshore tax evasion[272] as well as the introduction in 2013 of General Anti-Abuse Rule (GAAR)[273] to prevent tax avoidance. Indeed, the UK Supreme Court noted in *Pitt v Holt* that:

> In some cases of artificial tax avoidance the court might think it right to refuse relief, either on the ground that such claimants, acting on supposedly expert advice, must be taken to have accepted the risk that the scheme would prove ineffective, or on the ground that discretionary relief should be refused on grounds of public policy.[274]

2.098 In consequence, it is arguable that requests to vary, rescind or rectify a trust on the basis of a taxation law issue involve extremely sensitive matters of public policy and thus are unlikely to be arbitrable.[275] It is true that it is not necessarily the case that disputes involving tax are non-arbitrable as investment tribunals

---

268 See the comments of Harman LJ *Re Weston's Settlements* [1968] 3 All ER 338, 342; Tucker and others (n 196) 2223.

269 *In re Hastings-Bass, decd* [1975] Ch 25.

270 Tucker (n 135) paras 29–272; *Pitt v Holt* (2013) 2 AC 108 [132].

271 Tucker and others (n 196) para 4-073.

272 'No Safe Havens: Our Offshore Evasion Strategy 2013 and Beyond' (HM Revenue & Customs 2013) <https://assets.publishing.service.gov.uk/government/uploads/system/uploads/attachment_data/file/193112/offshore-strategy_1_.pdf>; 'No Safe Havens: 2019 HMRC's Strategy for Offshore Tax Compliance' (HM Revenue & Customs 2019) <https://assets.publishing.service.gov.uk/government/uploads/system/uploads/attachment_data/file/802253/No_safe_havens_report_2019.pdf>.

273 'General Anti-Abuse Rule (GAAR) Guidance' (HM Revenue & Customs 2018) <https://assets.publishing.service.gov.uk/government/uploads/system/uploads/attachment_data/file/695255/gaar_parts_a_b_c_2018.pdf>.

274 *Pitt v Holt* (n 270) para 135.

275 For examples of cases where the English Courts have held disputes to be non-arbitrable on public policy grounds see David St John Sutton, Judith Gill and Matthew Gearing, *Russell on Arbitration*, vol 24 (Sweet & Maxwell 2015) para 2-084.

have often dealt with matters involving actual or asserted tax liabilities,[276] although the relevant treaties often contain a tax carve out or veto,[277] and business transactions often raise matters of tax,[278] while some international tax disputes can be settled by inter-state arbitration.[279] However, it is submitted that, at least in the context of commercial as opposed to investment arbitration, tax disputes which involve 'substantive tax law issues are too important for the state to be left for settlement by a private jurisdiction'.[280] In consequence, such disputes should not be arbitrable.[281] In consequence, applications for the rectification, variation or rescission of a trust, in order to avoid undesirable or to achieve favourable tax consequences would not be arbitrable as they would clearly involve substantive tax law issues.[282]

It is also important to note that rectification and rescission are retrospective so that 'the settlement will be deemed always to have been in its rectified state, or if rescinded, never to have been made at all'.[283] HMRC has long accepted this retrospectivity[284] with the result that such relief, in turn, might result in *prima facie* eligibility for a tax refund.[285] In that situation, it is not hard to see that HMRC will have considerable incentive to challenge the validity of the arbitrator's decision. In any event, claims for restitution of overpaid tax are problematic enough[286] without the added complication of a trust arbitral award and would almost inevitably result in costly litigation. **2.099**

In conclusion, it is suggested that the granting by an arbitral tribunal of the remedies of rectification, rescission or variation would be fraught with all manner of complications and thus it is more sensible to exclude such matters **2.100**

---

276 See the discussion in Mistelis (n 1) 179–206.

277 See the discussion in 'Resolution of Tax Disputes in International Arbitration' (2017) 4 McGill Journal of Dispute Resolution 86.

278 Mistelis (n 1) 181.

279 ibid 181–182.

280 Lauren Brazier, 'The Arbitrability of Investor-State Taxation Disputes in International Commercial Arbitration' (2015) 32 Journal of International Arbitration 1, 15.

281 ibid.

282 This being why HMRC often seeks to be joined or intervene in Re Hastings-Bass Applications; for the offshore experience see Simon Davies and Jonathon Ellis, 'HMRC Wades in Offshore: Gresh v RBC Trust Company (Guernsey) Ltd & HM Revenue and Customs, Court of Appeal of Guernsey, 16 September 2009' (2010) 16 Trusts & Trustees 331; see also the advice in Tucker and others (n 196) para 4-080; Cf Hayton et al. (n 182) para 15.34.

283 Tucker and others (n 196) para 4-061.

284 See generally Michael Furness and Tiffany Scott, 'In the Post-Pitt World ...' (2014) 20 Trusts & Trustees 871.

285 Tucker and others (n 196) para 4-080.

286 See generally Steven Elliott, Birke Hacker and Charles Mitchell, *Restitution of Overpaid Tax* (Hart Publishing 2013).

from the ambit of an arbitration clause. Although strictly speaking this would only be necessary with regard to tax matters, drafting a clause to exclude only tax matters would likely lead to disputes about the exact interpretation of 'tax matters'. It is therefore probably better to simply exclude the grant of such remedies altogether. It is also worth noting that although, as discussed above, it is possible to select the procedural law of a jurisdiction which grants broader powers to arbitrators than English law and thereby get around the procedural limitations of English law, this would not solve the problem as regards rectification, rescission or variation. This results from the fact that the issue in these cases is not a procedural limitation: rather it is a matter of public policy and thus selecting a foreign procedural law would make no difference to the outcome.

Issues regarding non-contentious relief such as Re Beddoe *and* Re Benjamin *orders*

2.101 As noted above, many of the powers that the courts exercise over trusts are non-contentious, this is the case not only with regard to *Re Beddoe* and *Re Benjamin* orders but also when trustees request authorisation to commit an act which would otherwise be a breach of trust or when they are merely asked, without dispute, to interpret the terms of a trust instrument.[287] This poses a problem for the arbitrability of such disputes, as 'International arbitration conventions and national legislation are generally limited to agreements to arbitrate "disputes", or "differences"'.[288] This is certainly the case for the Arbitration Act 1996 s 6(1), which defines an arbitration agreement as 'an agreement to submit to arbitration present or future disputes (whether they are contractual or not)'. Although it is true that the former requirement for there to be a dispute between the parties in order for a stay to be granted was changed in the 1996 Act,[289] this was done to avoid technical arguments over whether it included situations where one party was clearly in the right because there was no defence, or it was hopeless, or vice versa.[290] In any event, this does not solve the definition of disputes in s 6(1) of the Act which excludes non-contentious issues.

2.102 However, the above problem is not necessarily insoluble due to a peculiarity of the Act: Schedule 1 to the Act lists which provisions are to be considered mandatory, and thereby not subject to party autonomy. It is notable that s 6 is not listed as a mandatory provision and therefore it is arguable that a party

287 See generally Paul Matthews, 'What Is a Trust Jurisdiction Clause?' October 2003 The Jersey Law Review 232, paras 21–22.

288 Gary Born, *International Commercial Arbitration* (2nd edn, Kluwer Law International 2014) 338.

289 'Report on the English Arbitration Bill' (n 13) para 55.

290 See the reference to in the DAC report above *Hayter v Nelson and Others* (1990) 2 Lloyd's Rep 265.

could make provision for an arbitration clause to include both contentious and non-contentious matters. Against this argument, one might note that the section which itself sets out the consequences of provisions being mandatory or not, s 4, is not listed as mandatory in the schedule of the Act, nor is the provision on limitations to arbitration, s 1(b), and these provisions are obviously intended to be mandatory.[291] Furthermore, considering that arbitration is concerned with the resolution of disputes and the issues enforcing consent awards under the New York Convention,[292] discussed below, it seems more likely than not that the courts would not enforce such provisions. Consequently, settlors and other interested parties should be aware that an arbitration clause in a trust deed is unlikely to prevent non-contentious relief from being granted by the courts and, although it is not necessary, they may want to clarify the scope of the clause by explicitly providing this. In that regard, some lessons might be learnt from the 'exclusive jurisdiction' v 'forum for the administration of the trust' clauses saga discussed below.[293]

Issues regarding the Matrimonial Causes Act 1973

The primary issue regarding an arbitral tribunal's exercise, attempted or otherwise, of powers granted under this Act is that it governs a very sensitive matter which is generally thought to be at the heart of private law and at the core of a state court's jurisdiction.[294] This is reinforced by the fact that, in the international context, the provisions under the act constitute mandatory rules of the forum under Art 15 enabling an English court to override a settlor's choice of law for the trust.[295] Equally, in deciding such applications, the English courts will always apply their own law regardless of the domicile of the parties.[296] **2.103**

Notwithstanding all the above issues, since February 2012 there has existed a family law arbitration scheme in England and Wales, which covers a variety of family law issues including applications for financial support under the Matrimonial Causes Act (MCA). [297] The guide to the scheme makes it clear that the scheme is intended to be enforceable under the Arbitration Act 1996 **2.104**

291 'Report on the English Arbitration Bill' (n 13) paras 18–22, 28–30.

292 See generally Yaraslau Kryvoi and Dmitry Davydenko, 'Consent Awards in International Arbitration: From Settlement to Enforcement' (2015) 40 Brooklyn Journal of International Law; cf Born (n 250) 3021–3027.

293 See generally Matthews, 'What Is a Trust Jurisdiction Clause?' (n 287); Gareth Jones, 'Trusts on Tour: Jurisdiction Clauses in Trust Instruments' [2015] The Jersey & Guernsey Law Review 309.

294 Lew and others (n 2) paras 19.33–19.36.

295 *Floros Charalambous v Martha Joannou Charalambous* [2004] EWCA Civ 1030 [26–43].

296 AV Dicey, *Dicey, Morris and Collins on the Conflict of Laws* (Sweet & Maxwell/Thomson Reuters 2012) paras 18–230.

297 'A Guide to the Family Law Arbitration Scheme: An Introductory Guide for Family Arbitrators, Judges and Professional Referrers' (Institute of Family Law Arbitrators) Third Edition para 5.1.

as well as under the NYC.[298] The extent to which awards under the scheme are likely to be internationally enforceable evidently depends on each state's views on the arbitrability of family law disputes[299] and the extent to which it will impose those views on foreign awards, i.e. whether they only form part of a state's national public policy or also its international public policy.[300]

2.105 In England and Wales, the scheme received judicial approval from the then President of the Family Division in the case of *S v S*,[301] where a consent order was lodged with the court in order to give effect to an arbitral award made under the scheme.[302] The court made extensive reference to the approval of pre-nuptial agreements in English law as a result of the Supreme Court decision of *Radmacher (formerly Granatino) v Granatino*[303] and made an analogy between such agreements and arbitration stating:

> There is no conceptual difference between the parties making an agreement and agreeing to give an arbitrator the power to make the decision for them. Indeed, an arbitral award is surely of its nature even stronger than a simple agreement between the parties.[304]

2.106 The court also helpfully outlined the enforcement process for contested and uncontested awards. In the event that a party attempted to 'resile from the award'[305] there would likely be an abbreviated hearing, although in certain cases this may be more elaborate, and the recalcitrant part would have to 'make good one of the limited grounds of challenge or appeal permitted by the Arbitration Act 1996'.[306] As regards uncontested awards, 'The judge will not need to play the detective unless something leaps off the page to indicate that something has gone so seriously wrong as to vitiate the arbitral award'.[307]

2.107 However, the above position changed somewhat following the recent Court of Appeal case of *Haley v Haley*.[308] In that case, the court disagreed with the argu-

298 ibid 2.

299 See generally Wendy Kennett, 'It's Arbitration, But Not As We Know It: Reflections on Family Law Dispute Resolution' (2016) 30 International Journal of Law, Policy and the Family 1.

300 This is dealt with in detail below in the chapter on the New York Convention

301 *S v S (Arbitral Award: Approval) [Family Division]* [2014] EWHC 7 (Fam).

302 ibid 1.

303 *Radmacher (formerly Granatino) v Granatino* [2010] UKSC 42.

304 *S v S (Arbitral Award: Approval) [Family Division]* (n 301) para 19.

305 ibid 25.

306 ibid 26.

307 ibid 21.

308 *Russell Haley v Kelly Haley* [2020] EWCA Civ 1369.

ment that an arbitral award was stronger than an actual agreement between the parties, stating that:

> An agreement as between the parties themselves is … an agreement to the actual terms; the parties, therefore, know precisely the outcome and have agreed to it. That is not the case in arbitration, where the parties have agreed to nominate a third party to determine fair terms intended to be final and binding, but subject to the courts ultimate discretion.[309]

Crucially the court distinguished court orders reflecting the terms of arbitration in commercial and civil cases from such orders made in relation to family law cases, by stating that the former 'derive their authority from the arbitration agreement'[310] whilst the latter 'derive [their] authority from the court and not from the arbitration agreement'.[311] The consequence of this was that appeals regarding such orders in family law cases were not limited to the narrow grounds of the Arbitration Act 1996, but rather those grounds found in the Matrimonial Causes Act 1973. This meant that 'the court will … substitute its own order if the judge decides that the arbitrator's award was wrong; not seriously, or obviously wrong, or so wrong that it leaps off the page, but just wrong'.[312] This is a clear repudiation of the test formulated by the court in *S v S* and means that it will be substantially easier to challenge such awards as compared to commercial or civil arbitration awards. **2.108**

The judgment in *Haley* is not completely negative for family law arbitration however, as the Court of Appeal gave its stamp of approval to the scheme, stating that 'I do not wish it to be thought that I am in any way undermining the arbitration process … parties must go into arbitration with their eyes open with the understanding that, all other things being equal, the award made at the end of the process will thereafter be incorporated into a consent order'.[313] On the other hand, the history of English arbitration legislation makes it clear that a bar for appeals allowing mere error to be grounds for overturning an award is unlikely to deter parties in family law cases, whether merely recalcitrant or genuinely aggrieved, from challenging arbitral awards when they are unhappy with the result. The court's decision is nevertheless not surprising as the MCA is a mandatory rule in English law. It was therefore always somewhat unrealistic to expect that the English courts would allow their efforts to do justice to be frustrated by the technicalities of arbitration law. **2.109**

---

309 ibid 67.

310 ibid 68.

311 ibid.

312 ibid 74.

313 ibid 72.

Issues regarding the Inheritance (Provision for Family and Dependants) Act 1975

2.110 This statute has equivalents in various Commonwealth jurisdictions,[314] and in both Australia as well as in several Canadian provinces it is an issue of public policy,[315] although the situation in England would appear to be more nuanced.[316] In any event, as with issues under the MCA, issues under the Act can be arbitrated via the family law arbitration scheme,[317] and given the judicial approval of that scheme, no arbitrability concerns should arise in England and Wales. That said, the approach of the Court of Appeal in *Haley* might bleed over into decisions under the Inheritance Act 1975: courts may therefore approach arbitrations regarding provision for family and dependents differently than those concerning civil or commercial matters. On the other hand, as discussed above, this act does not seem to have reached the same dizzying heights of mandatory law which its equivalents in other Commonwealth jurisdictions have. In consequence, the risk of the courts adopting a palm tree justice approach to arbitral awards in such cases should not be exaggerated. As regards the issue of enforcing such awards abroad, the situation is the same as with the MCA; namely the possibility of their recognition or enforcement depends on the public policy of the state in which enforcement is sought in each case, as well as an interpretation of the NYC. The latter issue will be dealt with in the chapter on enforcement below.

Issues with regard to claims arising under the Insolvency Act 1986

2.111 As an initial point, it is likely that the vast majority of claims arising under the Insolvency Act 1986 will be made by third parties who have no relation to the trust whatsoever, namely third-party creditors, whether they be banks, loan companies or other persons who are owed money by the settlor. All these cases fall outwith the scope of this work as they are external and not internal trust disputes. However, it is not impossible to conceive of situations where the Insolvency Act 1986 could have relevance in an internal trust dispute situation; for example, it has been suggested that it is at least conceivable that the heirs of the settlor could frame a claim under s 423 on the basis of their forced heirship rights.[318]

314 In the Canadian Context see AH Oosterhoff and others, *Oosterhoff on Wills* (8th edn, Thomson Reuters 2016) 882–883; cf *Re Kent* [1982] DLR (3d) 139. In the Australian context see *Re Gaynor* [1960] VR 640; *Re Chester* (1978) 19 SASR 247; *Shah v Perpetual Trustee Co* (1981) 7 Fam LR 97.

315 John K De Groot and Bruce W Nickel, *Family Provision in Australia* (4th edn, LexisNexis Butterworths 2012) paras 2.45–2.48; *Re Kent* (n 314) 322–323; Oosterhoff and others (n 314) 883–882.

316 See generally *Nathan v Leonard & Ors* (2003) 1 WLR 827.

317 'A Guide to the Family Law Arbitration Scheme: An Introductory Guide for Family Arbitrators, Judges and Professional Referrers' (n 297) para 5.1.

318 Hayton, *The International Trust* (n 134) paras 14.156–14.161.

Another possibility is where trust decanting has taken place. This essentially 'allows a trustee (or other empowered party), without court permission or involvement, to abandon or modify problematic provisions of an existing trust by "decanting" or pouring out some or all of the contents of that trust into a new trust with the desired provisions'.[319] It has been suggested that decanting could be used to dissuade a recalcitrant litigant who is threatening to bring a claim to set aside or change the provisions of a trust by moving all the assets into a trust with a forfeiture clause.[320] It is submitted that such an action would likely, or at least conceivably, fall within the provisions of s 423 as a transaction at an undervalue. Although it is true that the forfeiture clause may not, in any event, be effective in such a situation assuming the claim is brought in good faith, with probable cause or is successful, there may be situations where there is an advantage to bringing a claim under s 423. For example, where the new trust contains other problematic provisions aside from the forfeiture clauses, and the claimant wishes to unwind it completely, or where for some other reason it would be beneficial to have the transaction undone. **2.112**

Although insolvency is clearly a sensitive area, in essence, the issues raised by an arbitral tribunal exercising such powers are the same as those raised by other powers granted by statute, such as a petition for the winding up of a company on the basis of unfair prejudice or for the removal of a trustee. As those issues have already been dealt with above and as, in general, those sorts of claims are arbitrable, the same applies *mutatis mutandis* to applications made under the Insolvency Act, and there is no need to say anything further on the matter. **2.113**

319 Alexander A Bove, 'Another Look at Trust Decanting' (2018) 24 Trusts & Trustees 338, 338.

320 ibid.

3

BINDING PARTIES TO TRUST ARBITRATION CLAUSES

A. INTRODUCTION

3.001 There are three main strands in this chapter: the first will look at the general requirements under English law for a valid arbitration agreement which can bind parties to it, whilst the second will analyse these requirements in the context of trust arbitration. As English and Commonwealth courts have barely addressed the subject of trust arbitration clauses, this part will involve significant analysis and application by analogy of the jurisprudence surrounding trust jurisdiction clauses. The third main part will discuss who the 'parties' to a trust arbitration clause might be, as well as the means of binding them to it.

This section will have a particular focus on how to bind third parties, such as beneficiaries.

B. REQUIREMENTS UNDER ENGLISH AND COMMONWEALTH LAW FOR A VALID AND BINDING ARBITRATION AGREEMENT

The basic requirements for an arbitration agreement to be effective and binding under English law can be found in ss 5–6 of the Arbitration Act, which provide for the arbitration agreement to be in writing and define what an arbitration agreement is. Each of these sections will be examined in turn below. **3.002**

1. The writing requirement

Section 5 of the English Arbitration Act 1996 section provides for an extremely liberal 'writing requirement', setting out that the requirement can be met where the arbitration agreement is made in writing, regardless of whether the parties sign it or not, if it is made by an exchange of written communications or if it is evidenced in writing.[1] Section 2A of the Singapore International Arbitration Act is framed to similar effect, but goes even further in making explicit provision for agreements in electronic form, among other things; Article 7, Schedule 2 of the Australian Arbitration Act 1974 incorporates option 1 of the post-2006 model law which is similarly broad; s 6 of the 2009 Bahamas Act is very similar to the Singapore provision; and s 1 of the 2016 Guernsey Arbitration Law is clearly based on the English provisions. Option II of the 2006 amendment to the model law effectively does away with the writing requirement altogether,[2] and its implementation in the 2020 British Columbia Arbitration Act demonstrates how liberal the provision is. Section 5 of the British Columbia Acts states that: **3.003**

> (1) Two or more persons may make an agreement to resolve, by arbitration, a matter that
> (a) is the subject of a dispute, or
> (b) may be the subject of a dispute in the future …
> (5) For certainty, an arbitration agreement
> (a) need not be writing,

1 Arbitration Act 1996 s 5.

2 'Report of the United Nations Commission on International Trade Law on the Work of its Thirty-Ninth Session' (United Nations 2006) A/61/17 paras 163–167.

(b) need not relate to the interpretation, application or performance of a contract, and
(c) may, but need not, be part of another agreement.[3]

3.004 All of these provisions are very liberal, indeed to paraphrase the DAC report on the Arbitration Act 1996 they 'greatly extend … the definition of "writing"',[4] and it is not therefore surprising that there have been very few cases where a court considers enforcement of a clause at common law due to failure to meet the writing requirement.[5] In consequence, it is hard to see any reason why an arbitration in a trust deed would not meet the writing requirement, and thus no problems should arise for trust arbitration under this section.

2. Definition of an arbitration clause

3.005 Section 6 of the English Act provides a definition of arbitration clause and states that 'an "arbitration agreement" means an agreement to submit to arbitration present or future disputes (whether they are contractual or not)'. As noted above, most other Commonwealth arbitration acts have provisions with broadly similar wording. The fundamental issue which arises for trust arbitration is whether an arbitration clause in a trust deed, as opposed to a contract, can be brought within the scope of this section. If it cannot then, notwithstanding the possibility for discretionary enforcement by the courts under its inherent jurisdiction,[6] much of the progress arbitration has made over the past few decades, such as the mandatory stay and limited court review, is lost. This has the result that arbitration would be significantly less attractive than litigation. The key challenge for trust arbitration is that these sections are usually understood to refer to the need for a contractual agreement,[7] albeit this is clearly not the case for the British Columbia Arbitration Act discussed above, and this would seem to be something that trust arbitration clauses lack.

3.006 It is notable, and perhaps unsurprising, that there is no definition of 'agreement' in the Arbitration Act itself, neither is there any helpful guidance in the departmental advisory committee report on it and thus one is very much left to first principles, namely the use of dictionaries, in order to ascertain what

---

3 Arbitration Act 2020 s 5.

4 'Report on the English Arbitration Bill' (UK Departmental Advisory Committee on Arbitration Law 1996) para 36.

5 For a rare example see *TTMI Sarl v Statoil ASA* [2011] EWHC 1150 (Comm) (High Court).

6 Matthew Conaglen, 'The Enforceability of Arbitration Clauses in Trusts' (2015) 74 The Cambridge Law Journal 450, 472–478.

7 See e.g. David St John Sutton, Judith Gill and Matthew Gearing, *Russell on Arbitration* (24th edn, Sweet & Maxwell 2015) para 2-002.

constitutes an 'agreement' under the Act. A similar situation faced the Texas Supreme Court in the case of *Rachal v Reitz*[8] which also used the word 'agreement' without providing any definition or guidance on the term.[9] The court noted that the Act did not provide only for the enforcement of arbitration provisions in a contract although it had used that term elsewhere in the Act and thus the two terms were not synonymous.[10] In ascertaining the meaning of 'agreement' the court referred to Black's Law Dictionary which provided the definition of 'a manifestation of mutual assent by two or more persons' and noted that several contract treatises stated that the term 'agreement' was broader and less technical than contract.[11] The court adopted the definition provided in Black's Law Dictionary and noted that whilst mutual assent was usually demonstrated through the signing of an agreement, it could also be demonstrated 'when a party has obtained or is seeking substantial benefits under an agreement under the doctrine of direct benefits estoppel'.[12]

The court went on to note that a beneficiary could disclaim their interest in a trust or challenge the validity of the trust itself and in either case, would not be bound by an arbitration clause in the trust deed.[13] On the other hand, **3.007**

> a beneficiary who attempts to enforce rights that would not exist without the trust manifests her assent to the trust's arbitration clause. For example, a beneficiary who brings a claim for breach of fiduciary duty seeks to hold the trustee to her obligations under the instrument and thus has acquiesced to its other provisions, including its arbitration clause.[14]

As this was exactly the situation in the case before the court, it held that the arbitration clause bound the beneficiary notwithstanding the lack of an underlying contract.[15] In effect, the court held that an arbitration clause in a trust deed to which a beneficiary manifested his or her assent, implicitly or otherwise, constituted an agreement for the purposes of the Texas Arbitration Act. **3.008**

Although the decision in *Rachal v Reitz* rested on the doctrine of direct benefit estoppel, which is not known to Commonwealth law,[16] this is not particularly **3.009**

---

8 *Rachal v Reitz* [2012] Supreme Court of Texas No. 11-0708.

9 ibid 845.

10 ibid.

11 ibid.

12 ibid 845–846.

13 ibid 847.

14 ibid.

15 ibid 847–848.

16 Conaglen (n 6) 475–476.

problematic as the importance of this case lies not in legal technicalities but rather its finding that 'agreement' and 'contract' are not synonymous and its common-sense definition of 'agreement'. It is suggested that these findings are both applicable in English law, as leading English contract law textbooks also accept that 'agreement' is broader in meaning than 'contract' and discuss numerous examples of agreements which are not contracts.[17] English law dictionaries also provide a similar definition as Black's Law Dictionary, with Jowitt's defining agreement as '(1) A consensus of two or more minds in anything done or to be done'.[18] Stroud's judicial dictionary provides several judicial definitions of a similar ilk including:

> Aggreamentum is a word compounded of two words -, namely of aggregate and mentium, so that aggreamentum est aggregation mentium in re aliquia facta vel facienda. And so by the contraction of the two words, and by the short pronunciation of them, they are made one word, viz. aggreamentum, which is no other than an union, collection, copulation and conjunction of two or more minds in anything done or to be done.[19]

3.010 It would seem then that in English and Commonwealth law, an arbitration clause in a trust deed would also amount to an agreement under the Arbitration Act. This conclusion can perhaps be fortified by the case of *The Law Debenture Trust Corporation Plc v Elektrim*.[20] The case concerned a not particularly well-drafted dispute resolution clause in a trust deed regarding a bond issue which it was held constituted a unilateral arbitration clause.[21] Although in the circumstances, the court held that the dispute did not fall within the scope of the arbitration agreement, in so doing the court must necessarily have held that the arbitration clause was valid, notwithstanding the fact it was in a trust deed as opposed to a contract.[22] It is difficult to place much reliance on this case, however, given that the court did not address the point and, moreover, the line between contracts and trusts in international financial transactions is somewhat blurred.[23] It is suggested, in any event, that the *Rachal v Reitz* argument discussed above would be sufficiently convincing in order for an English

---

17 Edwin Peel and GH Treitel, *The Law of Contract* (13th edn, Sweet & Maxwell 2011) paras 4-002–4-020; Joseph Chitty, *Chitty on Contracts* (Sweet & Maxwell 2012) paras 2-168–2-192.

18 Daniel Greenberg and William Allen Jowitt, *Jowitt's Dictionary of English Law* (Sweet & Maxwell 2010) 91.

19 Daniel Greenberg, Yisroel Greenberg and Frederick Stroud, *Stroud's Judicial Dictionary of Words and Phrases* (Sweet & Maxwell 2016) 89–90.

20 *The Law Debenture Trust Corporation Plc v Elektrim BV* [2005] EWHC 1412 (Ch) (High Court).

21 ibid 38–47.

22 ibid 38–48.

23 Martin Hughes, 'More Good News than Bad for Bond Trustees' (2004) 8 Journal of International Banking and Finance Law 310, 311.

or Commonwealth Court to hold that an arbitration clause in a trust deed was an 'agreement' for the purposes of the Arbitration Act.

It is also worth noting that the analysis of the court in *Rachal v Reitz* may not go far enough. For example, if the arbitration clause explicitly mentions the trustee, as well as the settlor, and they both manifest their assent to it then, even if the beneficiaries do not manifest an assent, there is still an agreement. The issue in such a case is not whether there is an agreement at all, as there clearly is mutual assent between the settlor and the trustee, but rather whether the beneficiaries are parties to that agreement. That is a different question and would have to be answered within the framework of the Arbitration Act. In consequence, it is possible to say that if the court follows the reasoning discussed above, there should be very few cases where a trust arbitration clause falls outwith the scope of the Arbitration Act. Indeed, any such cases would likely be the result of the shortcomings of the drafters rather than the limitations of English or Commonwealth law. Having established that arbitration clauses in trust deeds meet the threshold requirements for the application of the Arbitration Act, it is now possible to discuss the Commonwealth case law concerning trust arbitration clauses and subsequently trust jurisdiction clauses. **3.011**

C. CASE LAW REGARDING TRUST ARBITRATION CLAUSES

Unsurprisingly there are very few cases which discuss trust arbitration clauses, the very few early cases which did so have been discussed above in the section on ouster clauses and this section will therefore only look at cases which have arisen in the modern period. It also does not analyse the cases of Rinehart *v Welker* and *Fitzpatrick and Ors v Emerald Grain Pty Ltd* (discussed above), as in neither case was the arbitration clause in the trust deed. In *Rinehart* it was in settlement agreements, as regards a trust dispute, which were explicitly consented to by all the parties, and in *Fitzpatrick* it was in a contract which was explicitly consented to by both parties. In consequence, neither decision has much relevance to the usual case where the arbitration clause will be contained in the trust deed and will not have been expressly assented to by the beneficiaries (or indeed possibly other parties such as the trustee, any protector and so on). There are however two reported Commonwealth decisions which deal with arbitration clauses in trust deeds, the Bahamas first instance decision of *Matteo Volpi v Delanson Services Limited & Gabriele Volpi*[24] and the Indian **3.012**

24 *In the Matter of the Winter Trust, the Summer Trust and Spring Trust; Matteo Volpi v Delanson Services Limited & Gabriele Volpi* [2018] Supreme Court of the Bahamas CLE/gen/00474.

Supreme Court decision of *Vimal Kishor Shah & Ors v Jayesh Dinesh Shah & Ors.*[25]

3.013 *Matteo Volpi* concerned a family dispute between Gabriele Volpi, a successful Italian-born businessman who established a business empire in Nigeria, and his son Matteo Volpi. The assets of Gabriele's business empire were held in several trusts for the benefit of his family, including Matteo. However, father and son had a falling out (and indeed Gabriele's marriage also broke up), and subsequently the trustee (Delanson Services Limited) terminated the trusts and distributed all the assets to Gabriele. Matteo therefore brought a claim alleging that this was a breach of trust and requesting an account of assets among other things. The trust deed provided that the trusts were governed by Bahamian law, 'Any dispute relating to the validity of the Trust will be decided by the above Governing law',[26] and also included an arbitration clause. In full, the arbitration clause provides:

> 27. Arbitration Clause
>
> [1] Any other dispute relating to the establishment or effects of the Trust, or between the Settlor and Trustee or between Protectors, or between the parties to the Trust, will have to be submitted to an arbitration board for assessment, with this board consisting of three members, one appointed by each part and the third as President of the Board by the two others. The Board will decide according to a standard procedure within 180 days.
>
> [2] Any dispute concerning rights or ownership in other Countries around the world, will be dealt with on a case-by-case basis, and regulated in consideration of International Agreements, where applicable.
>
> [3] Any proceedings that aim to have Trustees or Protectors appointed by the Court, or directives be given to the Trustee, must be brought exclusively under the law of the Bahamas as long as the registered office of the trust is located there.
>
> [4] For any matters that cannot be brought to arbitration, the Court having exclusive jurisdiction is the court at the registered office of the Trust, currently the Court of Appeal of the Commonwealth of the Bahamas.[27]

3.014 Although the clause is quite extensive, several aspects of the drafting are unclear, and this led to significant issues before the courts. The primary problem is that 'registered office of the trust' is not a term of art in Bahamian law and subsequent clauses had the effect of interpreting this as the registered

25 *Vimal Kishor Shah v Jayesh Dinesh Shah* [2016] A contribution by the ITA Board of Reporters, Kluwer Law International (Supreme Court of India).

26 *In the Matter of the Winter Trust, the Summer Trust and Spring Trust; Matteo Volpi v Delanson Services Limited & Gabriele Volpi* (n 24) para 15.

27 ibid 19.

office of the Trustee which could be changed at the Trustee's discretion. Delanson (the trustee) began life as a Panamanian company but subsequently relocated to the Bahamas and then New Zealand. The result of this was that Gabrielle argued that New Zealand and not Bahamian law applied, as another clause provided for the governing law of the trust to be changed and it was suggested that the trustees' change of location implied the exercise of the change of governing law clause. The court rejected this argument on the basis that there was no evidence to suggest that the trustees had exercised the change of law clause, and there was no need to imply such an exercise.[28]

3.015 The consequence of the court deciding that Bahamian law applied was that it could analyse the dispute in the context of the trust arbitration provisions of the Bahamian Trustee Act, s 91A(2). This provision states that:

> Where a written trust instrument provides that any dispute or administration questions arising between any of the parties in relation to the trust shall be submitted to arbitration (a 'trust arbitration'), that provision shall, for all purposes under the Arbitration Act, have effect as between those parties to an agreement and as if those parties were parties to that agreement.

3.016 As noted by the court, the clear intention of these provisions is that even though the parties are 'not parties to an agreement or even technically privy to the transaction they are nonetheless deemed to be parties to an arbitration agreement'.[29]

3.017 Notwithstanding the above clear provisions Matteo challenged the clause, arguing that as discretionary beneficiary he was not a party to the trust and therefore not caught by the clause. The court rejected this argument, noting that the term 'parties to the trust' was not the same as 'parties to the trust deed' and that a beneficiary (including a discretionary beneficiary) was necessarily a party to the trust.[30] This was because 'Having identified the trustee, the settlor and the protector there are no other classes of persons who could properly fit within the definition of "parties to the Trust".'[31] An additional argument regarding a section which gave the courts power to appoint a replacement trustee, and thereby excluded trustee removal claims from arbitration, was also rejected. This was on the basis both of the drafting of the deed and because s 91B(2) of the Act stated that 'The arbitral tribunal ... may in addition to all

28 ibid 23–26.

29 ibid 34.

30 ibid 37–38.

31 ibid 38.

other powers of the tribunal, at any stage in a trust arbitration, exercise all the powers of the Court ...'[32]

3.018 The court also rejected the argument that Matteo was not suing Gabriele in his capacity as beneficiary or settlor and his claims did not therefore fall within the provisions of the arbitration clause. It stated that 'This is a claim about allegedly improper distributions made by a Trustee to a beneficiary. Gabrielle is being sued in the capacity of a beneficiary and clearly both of these claims arise out of the Trust relationship and the allegations of Gabriele's receipt of an improper distribution.'[33]

3.019 As a whole, the case is useful in showing that even where there are statutory provisions regarding trust arbitration this will not prevent individuals making technical arguments in order to escape their scope. In particular, it is clear that a trust arbitration clause should clearly set out who is intended to be bound under it rather than simply providing 'the parties to the trust'. This is all the more so given that 'parties' is a term more suited to contract law, and one should (perhaps even the English language forces us to do so) be wary of using it in the context of trusts. It would perhaps be better to provide a list setting out all the classes of individuals caught by such a clause, a simple way of doing this might be to state 'any actual or alleged beneficiaries of whatever class'. It is also clear that clauses regarding the governing law of the trust must be drafted clearly, and their overlap with any other governing law or exclusive forum clauses must be clearly outlined. This is particularly important in cases where the intended law has a trust arbitration statute, and it is intended that the trust should benefit from the application of it. It is impossible to draw more from the case in the context of trust arbitration clauses in general as it was decided against the backdrop of a specific statutory scheme and many elements of the decision may not therefore be relevant elsewhere. However, as will be seen below, the case is also important in the trust jurisdiction clause context.

3.020 The earlier Indian Supreme Court Case of *Vimal Kishor Shah & Ors v Jayesh Dinesh Shah & Ors* unfortunately comes to a much less positive result for trust arbitration in holding that trust arbitration is not possible in India. The court's objections to trust arbitration were three-fold. Firstly the court stated that:

> In the case of a Will, the testator executes the Will in favour of legatee(s) whereas in the case of a Trust, the settlor executes the deed in favour of the beneficiaries. In both the

32 ibid 46.

33 ibid 48.

> cases, it is the testator/settlor who signs the document alone. That apart, both the deeds convey the interest in the estate in favour of the legatees or/and beneficiaries. However, since legatee/beneficiaries do not sign the document or we may say are not required to sign such document, they are not regarded as party to such deed despite legatee/beneficiaries/trustees accepting the deed. Such deed, therefore, in our opinion, does not partake the nature of an agreement between such parties.
>
> We are, therefore, of the view that if the Will is held not to constitute an arbitration agreement despite containing an arbitration clause therein – a fortiori, the Trust Deed can also not be held to constitute an agreement much less an arbitration agreement despite containing an arbitration clause therein.[34]

The court's reasoning is not at all convincing given that, as shown above, it is perfectly possible for an arbitration clause in a trust deed to amount to an agreement where a party seeks to take a benefit under it. Moreover, as already noted, in many trust arbitration cases the question will not be whether there is a trust arbitration agreement (as there will be explicit agreement between the settlor and the trustee(s), or even the trustees *inter-se*) but rather whether the beneficiaries and other third-parties are caught within the scope of such a clause. It is also unfortunate that the court relies on an excessively formalistic view of the arbitration acts by highlighting the fact that only the testator or settlor signs the trust deed. It is unclear why this is a relevant consideration given that contracts (as well as individual terms of contracts), including arbitration contracts, can often arise without one party signing a document, for example through implication, trade custom, conduct etc. **3.021**

The court's second objection highlights its formalistic reasoning as it states that **3.022**

> there is always a proposal and then its acceptance in the case of every agreement, which is not required in the case of creation of the Trust because in the case of a Trust, the trustee and beneficiary though accept its creation but by such acceptance, they merely undertake to carry out the terms of the Trust Deed in so far as the same may be in accordance with law.[35]

The problem with this strict view is that it does not accord with the reality of how beneficiaries, or legatees, benefit under a trust or will: they are not obliged to accept a benefit but can disclaim it,[36] in consequence if they take under the trust or will they impliedly agree to abide by its terms. As will be seen below, it **3.023**

34 *Vimal Kishor Shah v Jayesh Dinesh Shah* (n 25) para 33.

35 ibid 41.

36 See a discussion of the authorities in the recent case of *Smith & Anor v Michelmores Trust Corporation Ltd & Ors* [2021] EWHC [64–72].

is for this reason that leading trust jurisdictions have upheld the choice of court clauses and this reasoning is applicable by analogy to trust arbitration clauses.

3.024 The court's third objection is an evolution of the rule against ouster of the court's jurisdiction combined with an excessively formalistic interpretation of the applicable statutes as it states that:

> in our considered view, there exists an implied bar of exclusion of applicability of the Arbitration Act for deciding the disputes relating to Trust, trustees and beneficiaries through private arbitration. In other words, when the Trust Act exhaustively deals with the Trust, Trustees and beneficiaries and provides for adequate and sufficient remedies to all aggrieved persons by giving them a right to approach the Civil Court of principal original jurisdiction for redressal of their disputes arising out of Trust Deed and the Trust Act then, in our opinion, any such dispute pertaining to affairs of the Trust including the dispute inter se Trustee and beneficiary in relation to their right, duties, obligations, removal etc. can not [sic] [be] decided by the arbitrator by taking recourse to the provisions of the Act. Such disputes have to be decided by the Civil Court as specified under the Trust Act.[37]

3.025 As the reasoning in this and subsequent paragraphs would appear to rely on idiosyncrasies of Indian statutory interpretation and constitutional law it isn't necessary, or indeed possible, to critique them in any depth: it suffices to say that the reasoning is profoundly unconvincing. In any event, the Indian Supreme Court's decision in this case means that trusts subject to Indian law cannot include arbitration clauses and individuals considering settling trusts which will have links to India should think carefully before including a trust arbitration clause, due to potential enforceability issues.

D. CASE LAW REGARDING TRUST JURISDICTION CLAUSES

3.026 Although arbitration clauses are different from jurisdiction clauses, there is a certain similarity between them,[38] with the US Supreme Court famously stating, 'An agreement to arbitrate before a specified tribunal is, in effect, a specialized kind of forum-selection clause that posits not only the situs of suit but also the procedure to be used in resolving the dispute'.[39] Although the English Courts have not gone this far, it is clear that they will refer to cases regarding jurisdiction clauses in appropriate cases when interpreting arbitration

37 *Vimal Kishor Shah v Jayesh Dinesh Shah* (n 25) para 58.

38 Gary Born, *International Commercial Arbitration* (2nd edn, Kluwer Law International 2014) 72–73.

39 *Scherk v Alberto-Culver Co* [1974] US Supreme Court No. 73-781, 417 US 506 519.

clauses or ruling on matters related to them.[40] Moreover, the same fundamental issue arises in both trust jurisdiction and arbitration clauses, namely that as trusts are not contracts,[41] it would seem to follow then, that the nature of the obligation which such clauses impose, if merely included in the trust deed, cannot be contractual.[42] Questions, therefore, arise surrounding the nature of the interpretation to be used when analysing such clauses (it cannot be contractual)[43] as well as the legal principles to be applied, for example the fundamental principle of contract law, *pacta sunt servanda*, is not necessarily relevant. [44] In consequence, given the almost complete dearth of case law on trust arbitration clauses from any Commonwealth jurisdiction (with the exception of Australia where there are a handful of cases) it is helpful to analyse the courts' approach to trust jurisdiction clauses and consider their application by analogy.

As a preliminary point, it should be noted that trust jurisdiction clauses are relatively novel, albeit less so than trust arbitration clauses, and thus there is an unfortunate lack of English law authorities. Fortunately, however, the close links which are maintained between English lawyers, judges and academics on the one hand and various offshore legal systems[45] on the other means that the authorities which exist in these systems can legitimately be applied to English law. As there is relatively little case law on trust jurisdiction clauses, even offshore, this section will examine each of the cases individually and attempt to extract some general principles from them. **3.027**

40 See e.g. the landmark case of *Fiona Trust & Holding Corporation & Ors v Yuri Privalov & Ors EWCA Civ 20* [2007] EWCA Civ 20.

41 Paul Matthews, 'What Is a Trust Jurisdiction Clause?' (October 2003) The Jersey Law Review 14, para 10; *Baker v JE Clark & Co (Transport) UK Ltd* [2006] Court of Appeal of England and Wales A3/2005/1939, EWCA Civ 464 para 19; Alastair Hudson, 'The Trust as an Equitable Response', Staff seminar paper (2002) 12–16.

42 But see the discussion in Paul Matthews, 'Remuneration for Professional Trustees' (1995) 9 Trust Law International 50.

43 *EMM Capricorn Trustees Limited v Compass Trustees Limited* [2001] JLR 205 (Royal Court, Jersey); *E Crociani v C Crociani & Ors* [2014] (2) JLR 508 (Judicial Committee of the Privy Council).

44 *EMM Capricorn Trustees Limited v Compass Trustees Limited* (n 43); *E Crociani v C Crociani & Ors* (n 43).

45 For examples of English lawyers appointed as judges to offshore courts see 'Justices of Appeal' (*Cayman Islands Judicial & Legal Website | An official website of the Cayman Islands Government*) <https://www.judicial.ky/judicial-administration/justices-of-appeal> accessed 3 May 2020; 'Governor Rankin Appoints Two New Justices' (*Bernews*, 9 April 2018) <https://bernews.com/2018/04/governor-rankin-appoints-two-new-justices/> accessed 3 August 2020; 'Judiciary' <https://www.jerseylaw.je/courts/Pages/Judiciary.aspx> accessed 3 August 2020; St Peter Port King's Road, 'Judge of the Royal Court' (13 September 2011) <http://www.guernseyroyalcourt.gg/article/3385/Judge-of-the-Royal-Court> accessed 3 August 2020; News Staff, 'Clarke Appointed New Court of Appeal President | The Royal Gazette: Bermuda News' (*The Royal Gazette*) <http://www.royalgazette.com/court/article/20181115/clarke-appointed-new-court-of-appeal-president> accessed 3 August 2020.

1. *EMM Capricorn Trustees Limited v Compass Trustees Limited*[46]

3.028 As far as this author can determine this was the first case which dealt with an exclusive jurisdiction clause in a trust and thus it remains a point of reference for all literature in the field. As with many cases in trust law, the case concerned breach of trust proceedings and the issue before the Jersey Courts was whether they should stay the proceedings on the basis that there was an exclusive jurisdiction clause in favour of the Guernsey courts in the trust deed. The Court noted the novelty of the issue, stating that none of the lawyers before it was able to refer to any authorities which could guide the court in making its decision.[47]

3.029 The Court explored the matter from first principles, namely *pacta sunt servanda*,[48] and rejected the idea that jurisdiction clauses in trusts should be given the same weight as those in a contract.[49] This was on the basis that whilst contractual parties agreed jurisdiction clauses between themselves, and therefore the principle of *pacta sunt servanda* applied, this was not the case for the beneficiaries of a trust. [50] The Court went further, however, and, counterintuitively, rejected the argument that a successor trustee should be held to an exclusive jurisdiction clause because in accepting their office, they accepted the clause. The court justified this on the basis that it would be difficult to adopt a different approach for trustees as opposed to beneficiaries because 'in some cases, it might be a matter of chance as to whether an action for breach of trust against a former trustee was brought by the present trustees or by a beneficiary'.[51]

3.030 Despite the difference between trusts and contracts, the Court stated that because beneficiaries and trustees 'assume their rights and obligations under the terms of the trust deed. One cannot simply ignore an important provision of the trust deed, namely, an exclusive jurisdiction clause'.[52] It then set out a modified version of the famous *Aratra Potato Company*[53] test which '[it]

---

46 *EMM Capricorn Trustees Limited v Compass Trustees Limited* (n 43).

47 ibid 11.

48 For a historical overview of the development and reception of this doctrine see Anthony Jeremy, 'Pacta Sunt Servanda the Influence of Canon Law upon the Development of Contractual Obligations' (2000) 144 Law & Justice – The Christian Law Review 4.

49 *EMM Capricorn Trustees Limited v Compass Trustees Limited* (n 43) para 16.

50 ibid.

51 ibid 17.

52 ibid 18.

53 *Aratra Potato Company Ltd v Egyptian Navigation Company (El Amria)* [1981] EWCA Civ J0515 (Court of Appeal).

modified … so as to reduce the level of the burden on plaintiffs as compared with contractual cases'.[54]

The case illustrates the difficulty courts face when dealing with cases that involve trust jurisdiction clauses. Doctrinally they are at pains to distinguish them from contractual jurisdiction clauses, but in practice they apply virtually the same principles. In other words, courts find it very hard to free themselves from the 'contractual paradigm', which they apply to all agreements that come before them regardless of their legal category. This has been criticised by some writers who argue that the contractual paradigm, as well as the 'benefit and burden' approach, are not appropriate in the context of trust agreements and the emphasis should instead be on respecting the settlor's autonomy.[55] However, this argument does not take the matter very far as the principle of settlor autonomy is itself derived from party autonomy, which is equally foreign to trust law and which some have argued is problematic in the context of trusts.[56] It is clear then that courts are faced with a very difficult balancing exercise when analysing trust jurisdiction clauses and, so far, have not been able to satisfactorily reconcile the various competing doctrines.[57] **3.031**

2. *Koonmen v Bender and Seven Others*[58]

The primary issue, in this case, was whether the designation of Anguilla as the 'forum for the administration [of the trust]' could be interpreted as an exclusive jurisdiction clause or not. As explained by Paul Matthews in his article commenting on the case, the forum of administration had long been used by trust draughtsmen to refer to the jurisdiction which would resolve any non-contentious administrative issues regarding the trust, for example *Benjamin* orders, *Beddoe* orders and so on.[59] Jurisdiction for contentious matters, however, would be determined by the general Conflict of Laws principle of the state before whose courts the matter was brought.[60] **3.032**

---

54 *EMM Capricorn Trustees Limited v Compass Trustees Limited* (n 43) para 20.

55 Gareth Jones, 'Trusts on Tour: Jurisdiction Clauses in Trust Instruments' [2015] The Jersey & Guernsey Law Review 309, para 55.

56 Lionel Smith, 'Give the People What They Want? The Onshoring of the Offshore' (2018) 103 Iowa Law Review 2155, 2164.

57 *EMM Capricorn Trustees Limited v Compass Trustees Limited* (n 43) para 19.

58 *Koonmen v Bender and Seven Others* [2002] JLR 407 (Royal Court Jersey).

59 Matthews, 'What Is a Trust Jurisdiction Clause?' (n 41) paras 20–22.

60 ibid.

3.033 The Jersey Court of Appeal, however, interpreted the clause as conferring exclusive jurisdiction on the Anguillan courts to resolve the dispute and held that although, unlike arbitration, it still retained a discretion not to enforce the clause, it would only do so 'in exceptional circumstances'.[61] Paul Matthews was extremely critical of the decision noting that the court had treated the clause as if it was a contractual jurisdiction clause, referred to authorities who discussed only contractual and not trust jurisdiction clauses and that the members of the bench lacked any real experience in trust law.[62]

3.034 The decision again illustrates the difficulties courts face when interpreting trust jurisdiction clauses and the difficulty of escaping the 'contractual paradigm' as regards jurisdiction clauses. No doubt this was exacerbated by the appellate bench's inexperience in trust law and the fact that one of them was an arbitration specialist used to dealing with contractual dispute resolution clauses.[63]

3. *Helmsman Limited v BNY (Cayman) Limited*[64]

3.035 The facts of this case were very similar to those of *Koonmen*, involving a clause which used the wording 'forum for the administration [of the trust]'. However, the Court did not have to make a binding ruling on the matter as the trustees always had the power to change said forum and had in fact done so. Nevertheless, the Court stated that it suspected Paul Matthews' article on *Koonmen* was correct, and the clause likely did not encompass contentious matters such as the breach of trust action before it.[65]

4. *Representation of AA*[66]

3.036 This case was very similar to *Koonmen* and again involved a 'forum for administration' clause. There was, however, no use of the word 'exclusive' and the court, therefore, distinguished the case from *Koonmen*, holding that in the case before it the clause did not grant exclusive jurisdiction to the Jersey courts.[67] Although distinguishing the case from *Koonmen* may have been done for entirely legitimate reasons, it is notable that the court referred extensively to

61 ibid 14.

62 ibid 16–18.

63 ibid 16.

64 *Helsman Limited & Hotham Trustee Company Limited v Bank of New York Trust Company (Cayman) Limited* [2009] CILR 490 (Grand Court).

65 ibid 13–14.

66 *Representation of AA* [2010] JRC164 (Jersey Royal Court (Samedi Division)).

67 ibid 29.

Paul Matthews' article in its judgment, albeit without concluding on it one way or the other. It is therefore entirely possible that the court engaged in the time-honoured common law tradition of distinguishing otherwise binding cases that would prevent it from reaching the 'correct' decision.

5. *In The Matter of a Trust*[68]

This case, as with all others considered so far, again involved a clause with 'forum for administration' wording. Although the Royal Court cited *Koonmen* approvingly and held that Bermuda was the exclusive forum for administering the trust,[69] it nevertheless accepted that some matters would not be caught by the clause, for example claims against third parties or claims asserted abroad relating to trust administration. [70] The court, however, rejected the argument that claims for breach of trust would not fall within the ambit of the clause and also explicitly rejected Paul Matthews' arguments in this regard.[71] It can be seen that at this point, the divisive legacy of *Koonmen* continued to propagate throughout the offshore world. **3.037**

6. *Crociani v Crociani*[72]

As with many cases that reach the courts, the deed, in this case, was far from a model of clear drafting and as with all the cases that have been analysed so far the clause in question used the phrase 'forum for the administration of the trusts'.[73] In the light of the previous cases, it's unsurprising that the argument was again made that 'forum for the administration of the trusts' constituted an exclusive jurisdiction clause, but the JCPC rejected this argument, instead holding that it meant 'the place where the affairs of the trust are run'.[74] This was notwithstanding the fact that, as in *Koonmen*, the wording 'shall be subject to the exclusive jurisdiction' was used in the clause; the Board thereby implicitly overruled that case. The JCPC held that the circumstances of the case meant that it was feasible to consider that the draughtsmen of the deed were stipulating the place where the trust's affairs 'were to be organised or run'. If the draughtsman had intended it to be an exclusive jurisdiction clause, **3.038**

---

68 *In the Matter of a Trust* [2012] Supreme Court of Bermuda 2009: 361, SC (Bda) 72 Civ.

69 ibid 64.

70 ibid 67.

71 ibid 68.

72 *E Crociani v C Crociani & Ors* (n 43).

73 ibid 7.

74 ibid 14.

they would have referred to the courts of that country rather than the country alone.[75]

3.039 As for the phrase 'shall be subject to the exclusive jurisdiction', the JCPC held that this was not a forum jurisdiction clause but was rather intended to address 'the risk of *dépeçage* i.e. that different aspects of the Grand Trust [would be] subject to different proper law'.[76] Interestingly, the JCPC did not consider any previous decisions regarding jurisdiction clauses in its decision, holding that they are irrelevant as there was no judicial consensus on the issue at the time the clause was drafted.[77] However, this does not change the fact that the JCPC vindicated Paul Matthews' criticism of *Koonmen* and adopted an approach similar to that laid down in *EMM Capricorn*.[78]

3.040 The court noted that less weight should be given to trust jurisdiction clauses than to contractual jurisdiction clauses. Moreover, although 'a beneficiary who wishes to take advantage of a trust can be expected to accept that she is bound by the terms of the trust',[79] this was 'not a commitment of the same order' as it was for parties to a contract. [80] Although the case is the highest-level judicial pronouncement on trust jurisdiction clauses in the offshore and English legal world to date, its value is significantly reduced as a result of the court confining its reasoning to the facts of the case before it.[81] As noted above, the Privy Council's refusal to address previous case law on the matter is one symptom of this, another is the court's statement that a lower test applies for the enforcement of trust jurisdiction clauses than contractual jurisdiction clauses, without, however, providing any guidance on said test.[82]

7. *Matteo Volpi v Delanson Services Limited & Gabriele Volpi*

3.041 As noted above, the trust arbitration clause in this case also included an exclusive jurisdiction clause for claims which could not be the subject of trust arbitration. The court applied the decision of the Privy Council in *Crociani* and held that the wording 'for any court matters that cannot be brought to arbitration, the Court having exclusive jurisdiction is the court at the registered

75 ibid 19–20.

76 ibid 23.

77 *E Crociani v C Crociani & Ors* (n 43).

78 *EMM Capricorn Trustees Limited v Compass Trustees Limited* (n 43).

79 *E Crociani v C Crociani & Ors* (n 43) paras 35–36.

80 ibid.

81 Jones (n 55) paras 9–12.

82 ibid.

office of the Trust'[83] demonstrated that it was an exclusive jurisdiction clause (in favour of the New Zealand courts) and not merely a forum for the administration of the trust clause.

The court further held that the exclusive jurisdiction clause should be applied unless Matteo could make out a case to avoid it, an application of the *Crociani* test, and determined that no case had been made out. This was because the only connection with the Bahamas was the fact that the governing law of the trust was Bahamian law. Neither the assets of the trust nor the trustees were located in the jurisdiction, nor did any of the complained of acts occur in the Bahamas and there were no relevant witnesses in the Bahamas either.[84] On the other hand, the registered office of the trustees was in New Zealand, one of its trustees was in New Zealand, and New Zealand therefore had territorial jurisdiction over the trustees. Finally, 'New Zealand is a developed common law jurisdiction with a history of trust law and its courts are quite capable of applying Bahamian law where necessary'.[85] **3.042**

The last factor mentioned by the court raises intriguing questions, as it appears to show that a court enforcing a trust jurisdiction clause which points to another jurisdiction but where the underlying trust is governed by the court's law will consider the capabilities of the chosen court when deciding whether to enforce the clause. What would happen then if the jurisdiction clause pointed to a civil law jurisdiction which was not familiar with trusts? Or if it pointed to a jurisdiction where there was a different type of trust from the common law trust (e.g. Malta or Liechtenstein)? The possibility of a court refusing to enforce a trust jurisdiction clause on this basis introduces significant uncertainty into the process, although it might be thought to be a relatively infrequent occurrence. Notwithstanding these uncertainties, the case is a useful guide to how courts will apply trust jurisdiction clauses post *Crociani* and illustrates that the test laid down in *Crociani* for the enforcement of trust jurisdiction clauses remains the leading one in Commonwealth law. **3.043**

E. LESSONS TO BE LEARNT FOR TRUST ARBITRATION

The lessons which can be learnt for Trust Arbitration are essentially fourfold: **3.044**

83 *In the Matter of the Winter Trust, the Summer Trust and Spring Trust; Matteo Volpi v Delanson Services Limited & Gabriele Volpi* (n 24) para 56.

84 ibid 59.

85 ibid 60.

3.045 Firstly, much as it is possible to specify one jurisdiction for the administration of a trust and another for dealing with contentious trust issues, it may be possible to draft an arbitration clause which only covers contentious trust issues and leaves the courts of a particular jurisdiction to address administrative issues. This might indeed be desirable as it is inefficient to constitute a three-member arbitral tribunal every time an administrative issue which would otherwise be brought before the courts arises. However, if it is to be done, the drafters must explicitly state their intentions to avoid any uncertainty which might lead to the trustees and others being tied up in unnecessary and expensive litigation.

3.046 Secondly, it is clear that courts will enforce 'agreements' in trust deeds, i.e. jurisdiction clauses, even if the theoretical basis underpinning their enforcement has not yet been fully worked out.[86] This is so even where the beneficiaries have not 'signed' or otherwise consented to them.[87] The justification for this is two-fold; firstly, respect for the settlor's wishes and, secondly, the common-sense equitable view that one should not take a gift given on certain conditions and then refuse to abide by those conditions.[88]

3.047 Thirdly, if courts are happy to enforce jurisdiction clauses in trusts which have not been explicitly consented to by the beneficiaries or others, then they should be equally willing to do so for arbitration clauses. It is, of course, true that one key difference between litigation and arbitration is the need for consent,[89] but it is not difficult to see that in trust arbitration cases the necessary consent could be inferred from acceptance of the gift or a claim based on entitlement under the trust.[90] It is only in cases where the trust, or will, is challenged as a whole that it would be difficult to garner the consent necessary for there to be a valid arbitration agreement. For example, in the California case of *McArthur v McArthur*,[91] a trust was amended, *inter alia*, to include an arbitration clause. The plaintiff challenged the amendments, and the court held that she could not be held bound to the clause as she had never accepted any benefits under the amended trust, rather she had challenged it *in toto*.[92]

---

86 Jones (n 55) para 55.

87 *EMM Capricorn Trustees Limited v Compass Trustees Limited* (n 43) para 18; *E Crociani v C Crociani & Ors* (n 43) para 36.

88 *EMM Capricorn Trustees Limited v Compass Trustees Limited* (n 43) para 18; *Crociani v Crociani* (n 43) para 36.

89 'Report on the English Arbitration Bill' (n 4) para 19; Blackaby N and others, *Redfern and Hunter on International Arbitration* (5th edn, Oxford University Press 2009) para 2.01.

90 For an approach based on the US doctrine of direct benefits estoppel see *Rachal v Reitz* (n 8).

91 *McArthur v McArthur* Court of Appeal of the State of California A137133.

92 ibid 656–660.

In cases like that discussed above, the principle of separability embodied in s 7 of the Act does not assist as it merely provides that an arbitration agreement does not become invalid, non-existent or ineffective because the agreement in which it was contained has become or is alleged to have been invalid, non-existent or ineffective.[93] However, in a trust arbitration case, the only means through which consent can be obtained (unless obtained explicitly) is through some form of affirmation by the beneficiary which leads to the necessary implication of their consenting to the arbitration clause. As they are necessarily third parties to the trust deed, there is no question of them having entered into both the trust deed agreement and the arbitration agreement, with the latter being inside and surviving the former.[94] It is perhaps for this reason that the 2018 DIFC Trust law, whilst explicitly making provision for trust arbitration,[95] states that the doctrine of separability is not to apply to such arbitrations.[96] It is true that the doctrine of Kompetenz-Kompetenz embodied in s 30 of the Act allows the tribunal to rule on its jurisdiction, but the tribunal would equally have to rule that it had no jurisdiction in such a case, and in any event a party can still object to this under s 67 of the Act, providing it has not lost the right to object,[97] so this adds little to the discussion. **3.048**

In consequence, one can state that trust arbitration clauses should be upheld except where the beneficiary or third party has not in any way impliedly consented, and it is likely that most cases challenging the trust or testament *in toto* will fall into this category. It is important not to overstate this limitation as it means that breach of trust actions, actions regarding the interpretation of the trust deed and actions to vary, rectify or rescind the trust to name but a few, will all usually fall within the scope of a trust arbitration clause. The limitation assumes even less importance in the case of *inter vivos* trusts, as in such cases there is no temptation to challenge the trust *in toto* so that one can acquire the assets via intestacy. Nevertheless, it does mean that settlors would be well advised not to rely merely on the analogy with trust jurisdiction clauses in order to ensure the enforcement of any arbitration clause in their trust. **3.049**

Fourthly, although the courts will generally uphold trust jurisdiction clauses, they reserve the right to interfere in their operation to a greater extent than **3.050**

---

93 Arbitration Act 1996 s 7.

94 This being how the doctrine of separability is explained in English law, Sutton, Gill and Gearing (n 7) para 2-007.

95 DIFC Trust Law ss 31–32.

96 ibid Schedule 2(5).

97 Arbitration Act 1996 s 73.

they would under contractual jurisdiction clauses. However, it is questionable whether this reasoning would apply to trust arbitration clauses as these fall within a statutory scheme which leaves very little room for discretion.[98] In this regard, the Court of Appeal stated in a recent case that:

> Either the arbitration agreement is valid … or the court is satisfied that it is 'null and void' or 'inoperative' or 'incapable of being performed' … There is no halfway house in which the court can decide whether, on the facts, it would be an 'abuse of right' or 'inequitable' to rely on an otherwise valid arbitration agreement.[99]

3.051 In consequence, aside from clearly established doctrines such as, perhaps, unconscionability[100] or fraud on a power,[101] for example, if a trustee used a power of amendment to stifle an otherwise legitimate claim by requiring procedurally unfair arbitration,[102] it would seem that there is very little scope indeed for the court to refuse to enforce a valid arbitration clause. The courts would, of course, retain a power of review over the arbitral process, and that should lessen the unease or regret which they might feel in upholding such clauses. In view of this lack of discretion, trust arbitration clauses have another theoretical advantage over trust jurisdiction clauses: they should be more likely to be upheld by the English courts than trust jurisdiction clauses.

F. MEANS OF BINDING PARTIES TO TRUST ARBITRATION CLAUSES

3.052 This second half of the chapter will discuss the various means by which parties in a trust relationship, whether the trustees (as well as protectors, enforcers and so on), the settlor or the beneficiaries, can be bound to a trust arbitration clause. The first means, that of explicit agreement, will usually (but not always) be reserved for trustees, protectors, enforcers and the settlor, while the rest of the suggested means will usually (but, again, not always) be reserved for beneficiaries. This section also discusses the use of a particular statutory provision in arbitration acts throughout the Commonwealth, which, it has been argued, could bind beneficiaries, trustees and others to arbitrate; but (as will be discussed below) this is a complete misreading of the statute.

---

98 *Joint Stock Company 'Aeroflot-Russian Airlines' v Berezovsky & Ors* [2013] EWCA Civ 784.

99 ibid.

100 See the Ontario Court of Appeal judgment based on similar statutory provisions in *Heller v Uber Technologies* [2019] ONCA 1 (Ontario Court of Appeal); upheld by the Canadian Supreme Court *Uber Technologies Inc v Heller* 2020 SCC 16.

101 Tucker L and others, *Lewin on Trusts* (19th edn, Sweet & Maxwell/Thomson Reuters 2015) paras 29-289–29-293.

102 See by analogy *Heller v Uber Technologies* (n 100).

1. Explicit agreement

This is by far the most certain means of ensuring arbitration among all the interested parties to a trust deed, and it is easy to see how the settlor and the trustees could enter into a written agreement to arbitrate all disputes arising between them.[103] Although it would be rarer to enter into an agreement with beneficiaries, as the beneficiaries may not be ascertained in many trusts, it would still be possible in some cases, for example where the agreement is entered into after the dispute arises.[104] The most problematic issue with a contract between all the various interested parties is that it will only be binding *inter partes* and thus future trustees, beneficiaries and so on will not be bound by it. **3.053**

However, it is possible for the contract to be transferred to new parties via novation, which is where 'the two contracting parties agree that a third, who also agrees, shall stand in the relation of either of them to the other. There is a new contract and it is therefore essential that the consent of all parties shall be obtained'.[105] The situation of an arbitration agreement as regards a trust dispute is more complicated as there will be more than two parties, but the principle holds good. How practical it would be to obtain the consent of all the parties is another matter. However, where there is no dispute and one is merely replacing one trustee for another, novating the contract need not be contentious or problematic. Although, in one sense it would be easier to assign the contract, as this does not require consent,[106] this is not possible as one cannot assign liabilities.[107] In consequence there would be no release of the assigning party from their obligations, with the result that an assignee could, unless they agreed otherwise, only ever be a claimant and not a respondent.[108] **3.054**

2. Forfeiture clauses

A forfeiture or 'no contest' clause is a clause 'which provides that a beneficiary who contests a will or trust forfeits their interest',[109] and although they are **3.055**

103 Lawrence Cohen and Joanna Poole, 'Trust Arbitration – Is It Desirable and Does It Work?' (2012) 18:4 Trusts and Trustees 324, 327; *Rinehart v Welker* [2012] NSWCA 95 (Court of Appeal, New South Wales); *Hancock Prospecting Pty Ltd v Rinehart* [2017] FCAFC 170 (Federal Court of Australia).

104 'Arbitration of Trust Disputes' (Trust Law Committee 2011) 3; *Rinehart v Welker* (see n 103).

105 Chitty (n 17) para 19-086.

106 ibid.

107 ibid para 19-077.

108 Audley Sheppard and Michael Jervis Chaston, 'Third-Party Rights under the English Arbitration Act 1996' (2004) 6 Asian Dispute Review 43, para 10.26.

109 James Kessler, *Drafting Trusts and Will Trusts: A Modern Approach* (Sweet & Maxwell 2017) para 29.7.

not much used in England, they are common offshore.[110] Such clauses can vary significantly in scope, from those which cover any attempt whatsoever to challenge the will or trust to those which only include unreasonable challenges to decisions by a trustee or protector.[111] It is also important to note that they are a form of condition subsequent, that is to say, a condition 'where the event is to destroy or divest an existing right; [e.g.] if I give an annuity of £100 to C so long as she shall remain my widow, this creates a condition subsequent, because the performance of it is subsequent to the vesting of the right'.[112]

3.056 As will be seen below, the law surrounding forfeiture clauses is complex and obscure, with only a handful of reported cases addressing them and even fewer of those relating to trusts as opposed to wills in general, as they have only recently started finding their way into *inter vivos* trust deeds.[113] The clauses are of interest because it has been suggested that they could be used to force disgruntled beneficiaries into arbitration. Instead of providing for forfeiture in the case of any dispute with regard to the trust, they would provide for forfeiture if the beneficiaries refused to be bound by the arbitration clause in the trust deed.[114] Consequently, this section will firstly analyse the law surrounding such clauses in general and then consider their application in the case of trust arbitration.

3.057 It would seem that the first reported case which considered such a clause is the case of *Comes Sterling contra Levingson*,[115] where there was a forfeiture clause in the will but an issue subsequently arose regarding the interpretation of the will and which parts the heirs general were entitled to. Consequently, they brought an action in court in order to determine their entitlements and the court held that, 'It was most fit that a Trial at Law be had touching the Plaintiff's Right and Title, and that such Action to be brought shall not be taken or construed as Breach of the [Forfeiture clause]'.[116]

---

110 ibid.

111 ibid.

112 Greenberg and Jowitt (n 18) 500.

113 *AN v Barclays Private Bank and Trust (Cayman) Limited and others* (2006) 9 ITELR 630 (Cayman Islands Grand Court) 421–422.

114 For an early albeit unsuccessful example see *Rhodes v The Muswell Hill Land Company* (1861) 54 ER 745; cf Gerardo J Bosques-Hernández, 'Arbitration Clauses in Trusts' [2008] InDret 7–8; J Blattmachr, 'Reducing Estate and Trust Litigation Through Disclosure, In Terrorem Clauses, Mediation and Arbitration' (2008) 9 Cardozo Journal of Conflict Resolution 237, 258–263.

115 *Comes Sterling contra Levingston* (1672) 21 ER 620.

116 ibid 620.

The next case, *Powell v Morgan*,[117] concerned a situation where a 'Legacy [was] given on condition the legatee shall not dispute the will'[118] and the legatee subsequently commenced a suit contesting the validity of the will. The court ruled that there was no forfeiture as there was 'probabilis causa litigandi',[119] that is, some level of probable cause.[120] **3.058**

The next case is that of *Cleaver v Spurling*,[121] in which 'the testator gave a legacy to his wife, on condition she should not trouble his executor, or sue or molest him for her widow's share'.[122] In the event she did so there was a 'devise' or 'gift over' so that the legacy went to someone else.[123] In consequence, the court held that the clause was valid and not merely *in terrorem*.[124] The latter term can mean 'in fear' or 'as a warning' and refers to the legal fiction that 'the condition in question is judged to be a threat, and in the absence of a gift over, an empty threat at that'.[125] The phrase has caused considerable difficulties in the interpretation of forfeiture clauses in wills generally,[126] and is in no small part responsible for the thicket of confusing case law which practitioners must wade through when drafting them. However, it is not clear from the report whether it was only counsel that used this term or the court itself. **3.059**

The next case is that of *Morris v Burroughs*,[127] which held that a forfeiture clause was not binding on the beneficiary, as it was 'in terrorem only, and … no such forfeiture could be incurred by contesting any disputable matter in a court of justice'.[128] The court referred to the earlier case of *Cleaver*, noting that such clauses would not be held merely *in terrorem* where there was a devise or gift over.[129] As noted in the literature, the justification for this rule is 'that the testator had not really intended to impose the condition, and that therefore the condition would only be given effect if the testator demonstrated, by the inclusion of a gift over, that he was indeed in earnest'.[130] As with many legal **3.060**

---

117 *Powell v Morgan* 23 (1688) Eng Rep R 668.

118 ibid 668.

119 ibid.

120 S Collins, *International Trust Disputes* (Oxford University Press 2012) para 9.19.

121 *Cleaver v Spurling* 25 (1729) ER 336.

122 ibid 337.

123 ibid.

124 ibid.

125 PG Lawson, 'The Rule Against "In Terrorem" Conditions: What Is It? Where Did It Come from? Do We Really Need It?' (2005) 25 Estates, Trusts & Pensions Journal 71, 73.

126 See generally Lawson (n 125).

127 *Morris v Burroughs* 1 (1737) Atkyns 399.

128 ibid 404.

129 ibid.

130 Lawson (n 125) 74–75.

fictions, the rule does not, in practice, accord with reality, as it is quite clear in most cases that the testator did intend to disinherit the beneficiary if he contravened the clause.

3.061 A new tactic to get around such clauses was used in *Cooke v Turner*,[131] where it was argued that the clauses were contrary to public policy. The court, however, held that they were valid and not contrary to public policy because:

> … the state has no interest whatever apart from the interest of the parties themselves … It matters not to the state whether the land is enjoyed by the heir or the devisee; and we conceive therefore, that the law leaves the parties to make just what contracts and what agreements they may think expedient … the sole result of which is to give the enjoyment of property to one claimant rather than another.[132]

3.062 *Cooke v Turner* led to further litigation that resulted in the case of *Cooke v Cholmondeley*,[133] which reveals that the clause in question was quite extensive. It required the parties not just to not dispute the will but also to actively resist any attempt by anyone else to impugn it.[134] As the testator had been declared a 'lunatic' the court held that the circumstances surrounding the creation of the will had to be tried before a jury, in order to determine whether the testator was of sane mind when making the will or not. The court noted that it was very unusual for a solicitor on the commission of lunacy to be involved in making a will with a person who was still declared insane by that very commission. This was particularly the case when he had not consulted the court under whose protection lunatics were put.[135]

3.063 The court went on to state that 'I think that it is most important to the due administration of the affairs of mankind that such a transaction should be thoroughly sifted'.[136] This was so even though neither the heiress nor her husband wanted the action to proceed to trial,[137] as the court noted that 'the question in this case really is … there has not been a fraud practised on the Great Seal'.[138] The court further provided directions that protected the heiress and her husband from the effects of the forfeiture clause.[139] The case is important for showing that the court has power to grant relief from the effect of

131 *Cooke v Turner* 15 (1846) M & W 727.
132 ibid 1047.
133 *Cooke v Cholmondeley* 60 (1849) ER 757.
134 ibid 757.
135 ibid 761–762.
136 ibid 762.
137 ibid.
138 ibid.
139 ibid 763.

forfeiture clauses, at least in appropriate cases, and whilst not allowing them to completely shut out access to a court, will not necessarily take the simpler, and blunter, option of declaring them invalid.

In the 1874 Canadian Privy Council case of *Evanturel v Evanturel*,[140] the court praised[141] the decision in *Cooke v Turner*, whilst, in the context of Quebec law, stating that 'Upon principle, it is to be observed that the prohibition cannot be absolute, and can be invoked only where the validity of a will has been unsuccessfully contested'.[142] This would seem to be in line with the more equitable interpretation in *Cooke v Cholmondeley* protecting the heiress from forfeiture, although it clearly goes even further. **3.064**

The case of *Adams v Adams*[143] continued the more restrictive approach of the courts, holding that where a *bona fide* action was brought disputing a will, this would not fall within the scope of a forfeiture clause. However, as the case in question was clearly '*frivolous and vexatious*' the clause operated to forfeit the appellant's legacy.[144] It would appear that from this point forward there have been no more English cases for over a century and thus we will turn to the jurisprudence of the Canadian courts, which have, unlike their American brethren, adopted the English approach to forfeiture clauses.[145] **3.065**

One of the earliest reported cases is the Ontario case of *Harrison v Harrison*,[146] which concerned a clause stating that: **3.066**

> if any beneficiary refuses to accept the portion or provision allotted to him and shall take any proceedings to set aside, cancel, or modify in any manner any part of the will, or to obtain any benefit other than that plainly and distinctly given to him, then any benefit given to him shall absolutely cease, and his share shall be divided equally among the other beneficiaries.[147]

The court held that this clause did not apply to an action 'to obtain a construction of the will and a declaration of plaintiff's rights as to present payment'.[148] It would seem that this conclusion is entirely logical in so far as the action is **3.067**

---

140 *Evanturel v Evanturel* (1874) 6 PC LR 1.

141 ibid 29–30.

142 ibid 26.

143 *Adams v Adams* (1892) 1 Ch 369.

144 ibid 375.

145 Lawson (n 125) 84.

146 *Harrison v Harrison* (1904) 3 OWR 247.

147 ibid 247.

148 ibid.

not a hostile one, and thus can be assumed not to be the type of action such clauses are intended to prohibit.

3.068 The case of *Williams v Williams*[149] concerned a will with a forfeiture clause that provided that if any action was taken in the High Court in the names of the beneficiaries their shares would be forfeited to the trustees, in the first place to pay for all the legal proceedings, and that trust would have priority over any other declared in favour of such plaintiffs.[150] Allegations of wilful default were nevertheless brought against the trustees as they had delayed realising the estate for several years, not accounted for the moneys they had received, and not paid moneys due to the plaintiffs.[151] The court held that the clause did not apply as there was *probabilism causa litigandi* given that 'capital moneys have been withheld for years and the trustees have been guilty of wilful default and the cestuis que trust have been driven to take proceedings to enforce their rights'.[152] Moreover, if the clause had applied, it would have been void for repugnancy as a result of giving the beneficiaries a gift but denying them any means of enforcing their rights to it.[153]

(a) Fork in the road: matrimonial and familial provision statutes

3.069 At this stage, as will become apparent below, there is a divergence, or fork in the road, between the approach of the Australian and Canadian courts, on the one hand, and English courts on the other, as regards the validity of forfeiture clauses in the context of matrimonial or familial provision statutes. These statutes were first introduced in New Zealand in 1900 with the passing of the Testator's Family Maintenance Act and subsequently spread to all the states of Australia, throughout Canada and to England itself.[154] In England the first familial provision statute was the 1938 Inheritance (Family Provision) Act, which in turn was used as the basis for similar statutes in Singapore[155] and Hong Kong.[156] The New Zealand Act, and arguably all Commonwealth familial provision statues, was based on two fundamental principles '(i) the testator should do justice to her or her dependents; (2) those persons should

149 *Williams v Williams* (1912) 1 Ch 399.

150 ibid 399–400.

151 ibid 400.

152 ibid 403.

153 ibid 404.

154 Oliver Stone, 'Recent Developments in Family Law in British Common Law Jurisdictions' (1967) 67 Columbia Law Review 1241, 1241–1242.

155 *AOS v Estate of AOT, deceased* [2012] SGCA 30 [36].

156 'Law of Wills, Intestate Succession and Provision for Deceased Persons' Families and Dependants' (The Law Reform Commission of Hong Kong 1990) 15 para 13.3.

not, through the testator leaving his property away from them, be left perhaps a burden on the state'.[157] Another key principle in familial provision statutes is that of there being a 'moral obligation to provide for surviving dependants'[158] on the part of the testator.

3.070 The unique characteristic of familial provision statutes is that they set out 'neither a fixed limitation on the testator's bounty nor a minimum disposable portion';[159] instead the matter is left to the discretion of the court.[160] However, it is important that this discretion is circumscribed in many jurisdictions[161] by mandatory factors which a court must take into account when exercising its discretion under the relevant act.

3.071 The issue posed by familial provision statutes for forfeiture clauses is that they can be considered an issue of public policy which allows the court to void, or at least disregard, forfeiture clauses in a will where an individual has challenged a will on the basis of a familial provision statute, thereby potentially triggering forfeiture. The key case in this regard is *Re Gaynor*,[162] which concerned a challenge to a will made by the daughter of the testator on the basis of the familial provision statute in the Australian state of Victoria. The court first considered whether an application for provision under the statute was an act which challenged the will, thereby triggering the forfeiture clause, and held that it was, overruling the first instance court on this point.[163] The court then held that the condition was void not only because it did not provide for gift over,[164] but also because it was contrary to public policy. This resulted from the fact that:

> the Act … is designed to serve a public purpose as well as to benefit individuals, and that the authority conferred upon the public was so conferred not merely in the interests of the widow, widower or child … but of the public, because it is a matter of public concern

157 Joseph Dainow, 'Restricted Testation in New Zealand, Australia and Canada' (1938) 36 Michigan Law Review 1107, 1109.

158 John G Ross Martyn, *Williams, Mortimer and Sunnucks on Executors, Administrators and Probate* (Sweet & Maxwell/Thomson Reuters 2013) para 58-08; Cf Dainow (n 157) 1111; 1127; *AOS v Estate of AOT, deceased* (n 155) paras 37–39.

159 Dainow (n 157) 1107.

160 ibid.

161 (England) Inheritance (Provision for Family and Dependants) Act 1975 s 3; (Alberta) Wills and Succession Act 2010 s 93; (Hong Kong) Inheritance (Provision for Family and Dependants) Ordinance 1995 s 5; (Australian Capital Territory) Family Provision Act 1969 s 8(3); (New South Wales) Succession Act 2006 s 60.

162 *Re Gaynor* [1960] VR 640

163 ibid 641.

164 ibid 642.

that they should not be left without adequate provision for their proper maintenance and support.[165]

3.072 The court also rejected the argument that the forfeiture clause was designed to put legatees on their election so that they had to choose between their rights under the will and their rights under the Act. This was because 'a condition subsequent never can effectively prohibit a beneficiary from doing what he chooses to do. If he chooses to break the condition, he will work a forfeiture of the gift to which the condition is attached'.[166] In consequence, 'the condition is opposed to public policy because the object and effect of it is to deter the beneficiary from having recourse to the courts in a matter in which it is in the public interest that he should be free to have recourse'.[167]

3.073 The primary issue with the court's analysis, in this case, is that it adopted a literal interpretation of the clause; unlike in earlier case law, it did not hold the clause as only operating to prevent non *bona fide* actions, or actions which were not brought in *probabilism causa litigandi*, or which were unsuccessful. If it had adopted any of these tests the result would have been the same without, however, attacking the important principle of freedom of testation.

3.074 Another issue is that it is not clear whether the application under the familial provision statute was or would have been successful, as the court stated, 'The vice in this sort of condition is that a testator may leave a beneficiary a legacy or other provision by will which may or may not be adequate for his proper maintenance and support'.[168] In other words, according to the court, all such conditions are *ex ante* void as violating public policy, regardless of whether the amount left was or was not adequate for the applicant's proper maintenance and support and, going further, they are presumably void even without an application under the familial provision statute. It would, therefore, seem to be the case that when such wills came before the court, whether by probate or otherwise, it would have to void such conditions *ex proprio motu*. This is an extraordinary inroad to make on the principle of freedom of testation and would also seem imprudent.

3.075 On the other hand, notwithstanding the above practical and doctrinal criticisms of the decision in *Re Gaynor*, it would seem that it is supported by two cases of high authority (both of which are cited in the decision), the first is

165 ibid 642–643.

166 ibid 643.

167 ibid.

168 ibid.

the Privy Council case of *Dillon v Public Trustee*[169] and the second is the High Court of Australia case of *Lieberman v Morris.*[170] Both cases involved attempts to contract out of familial provision legislation via agreements between the testator and their wife, now widow, that in consideration for X property the widow would not make an application under the familial provision legislation after the testator's death. In both cases, the contracts were held to be ineffective, but not void, due to the public policy embodied in the act with the court in *Dillon* stating:

> The manifest purpose of the Family Protection Act … is to secure, on grounds of public policy, that a man who dies, leaving an estate which he distributes by will, shall not be permitted to leave widow and children inadequately provided for, if the court in its discretion thinks that the distribution of the estate should be altered in their favour.[171]

Importantly, however, the court held that the act did not oblige the husband to actually make adequate provision for his dependants nor limit his will-making power: instead, it allowed the court 'to interpose in order to carve out of his estate what amounts to adequate provision for these relations if they are not sufficiently provided for'.[172] In other words, contrary to the decision in *Re Gaynor*, such provisions are not void *ex ante* but merely ineffective following an application from a dependant. In consequence, a court in such a situation would not have to declare them void *ex proprio motu.* In the same way, in *Lieberman*[173] the court did not declare the contract void,[174] agreeing that 'it does not impose any duty upon testators',[175] and further stated that 'If no application is made under the Act the will is not affected by the Act'.[176] **3.076**

It can be seen therefore that the court in *Re Gaynor* wrongly applied both *Dillon* and *Lieberman*, which, moreover, are, in any event, arguably distinguishable as they concern contracts, albeit in relation to a will, and not provisions in a will itself. Although it might be said that the distinction is a technical one, it is nevertheless important, as there is a long tradition of interpreting such conditions benevolently rather than holding them void. In consequence, the court in *Re Gaynor* not only misinterpreted these decisions, it also misapplied **3.077**

---

169 *Dillon v Public Trustee* [1941] Judicial Committee of the Privy Council 2, Privy Council Appeal No. 1 of 1940.

170 *Lieberman v Morris* (1944) 69 CLR 69 (High Court of Australia).

171 *Dillon v Public Trustee* (n 169) 4.

172 ibid 3.

173 *Lieberman v Morris* (n 170).

174 ibid 80–81.

175 ibid 81.

176 ibid.

them and ignored a long line of case law regarding benevolent or restrictive interpretation of forfeiture clauses in wills.

3.078 Notwithstanding these issues, the decision in *Re Gaynor* was unfortunately applied with little comment in the later South Australian case of *Re Chester*[177] and the New South Wales case of *Shah v Perpetual Trustee Co*,[178] and going further afield, a first instance court also applied it in British Columbia in the case of *Re Kent*.[179] In that case, the court held that the clause was void as being against public policy as it purported to deprive the petitioners of their right to apply for relief, under the Wills Variation Act, for inadequate provision under a will.[180] The court noted that 'It is important to the public as a whole that widows, widowers and children be at liberty to apply for adequate maintenance and support in the event that sufficient provision for them is not made in the will of their spouse or parent'.[181]

3.079 The decisions in all those cases can be criticised for the same reasons as the decision in *Re Gaynor*, there were other means to reach the same result which were supported by earlier case law and would not have damaged the principle of freedom of testation in the same way. Moreover one should always be wary of turning to the 'very unruly horse'[182] of public policy, which should always be a means of last resort as 'once you get astride it you never know where it will carry you'.[183] Notwithstanding these issues, it would appear that the line of case law proceeding from *Re Gaynor* is now firmly entrenched in Australian law.[184] The position is somewhat more nuanced in Canada, for example in New Brunswick one may contract out of the legislation[185] and thus presumably a forfeiture clause in a will would not be invalid. Notwithstanding this, *Re Kent* remains good law and is referred to authoritatively in one of the leading Canadian textbooks on wills.[186]

---

177 *Re Chester* (1978) 19 SASR 247, 262.

178 *Shah v Perpetual Trustee Co* (1981) 7 Fam LR 97, 101.

179 *Re Kent* [1982] DLR (3d) 139.

180 ibid 322–323.

181 ibid 323.

182 *Richardson v Mellish* (1824) 2 Bingham 229, 252.

183 ibid.

184 See the commentary on contracting out and forfeiture clauses in De Groot JK and Nickel BW, *Family Provision in Australia* (4th edn, LexisNexis Butterworths 2012) paras 2.45–2.48.

185 Oosterhoff AH and others, *Oosterhoff on Wills* (8th edn, Thomson Reuters 2016) 883.

186 ibid 727–732.

3.080 The situation in England and Wales would appear to be very different as the approach set out in the above line of case law was rejected in the English case of *Nathan v Leonard and others*.[187] In that case, the court considered whether a no-contest clause would be void as a result of the Inheritance (Provision for Family and Dependants) Act 1975. The court noted that the key argument in *Re Kent* and *Re Gaynor* was the fact that the clause might deter individuals who were entitled to adequate provision under the will from making applications for further provision and was thus contrary to public policy.[188] However, in contrast to the cases of *Re Gaynor* and *Re Kent*, the court stated that 'it is the policy of the law to uphold testamentary freedom … that policy is reflected in the fact that English law has no concept of forced heirship',[189] with the closest it had come to this being the 1975 Act.[190] In consequence, the court rejected the approach taken by *Re Gaynor* and *Re Kent*, stating that:

> … the condition does not prevent an applicant making his claim; and if he does so, and forfeits his interest under the will, that can be taken into account by the court. The court will determine whether reasonable provision has been made; and in doing so one of the circumstances it will take into account is that, because of the condition, the applicant has received nothing at all from the estate … I can see no reason why policy considerations which can be attained in that way should require the condition itself to be invalidated.[191]

3.081 The court also went on to make several relevant *obiter* remarks, holding that 'Nothing in the authorities … supports any suggestion that there is a rule of law that forfeiture conditions only apply to unsuccessful conditions'.[192] The previous authorities which stated this were explained away on the basis that the reason for 'a successful challenge escap[ing] the condition, accordingly, seems to be that the challenge has the effect of setting aside both will and condition'.[193] As this was not always the case, however, it followed that sometimes even successful challenges would result in the clause operating to effect forfeiture of a litigant's interests,[194] and the key task for the court was to correctly construe the clause's scope.[195]

---

187 *Nathan v Leonard & Ors* (2003) 1 WLR 827.

188 ibid 832.

189 ibid 831.

190 ibid.

191 ibid 832–833.

192 ibid 837.

193 ibid 836.

194 ibid 836–837.

195 ibid.

3.082 Although the court's conclusion is certainly interesting, it is surprising that the court did not discuss the disapplication of such clauses where there was *probabilis causa litigandi* or a *bona fide* case, and if the cases approving this outcome were correctly decided it might be thought that the court's decision is largely academic. This is likely because in most cases where there was a successful challenge to the will there was *probabilis causa litigandi* or a *bona fide* case and thus in most, if not all, successful cases the clause would not operate. Even if the case could be held as disagreeing with this line of authority, that in itself is problematic as one of those cases, *Adams v Adams*,[196] is a Court of Appeal case and thus binding on it. It is at least arguable therefore that this part of the court's reasoning is either purely *obiter* or also *per incuriam* as a result of ignoring a binding precedent.

3.083 One last important point which can be taken from the case is that the court likely can grant relief from forfeiture clauses, even if they provide for gift over and are thus valid.[197] However, the court will be unlikely to grant such relief if it would do 'real damage' to the testator's intentions.[198] It should also be noted in passing that the court ultimately declined to uphold the clause as it was void for uncertainty because it was not clear what events would trigger it.[199]

3.084 The artificiality of the approach put forward in *Re Gaynor* and *Re Kent*, as opposed to the approach set out in *Nathan v Leonard*, is further demonstrated by the recent Alberta Court of Appeal case of *Mawhinney v Scobie*.[200] In that case, the no-contest clause was carefully drafted so that it did not oust the court's jurisdiction as regards 'necessary judicial interpretation or for the assistance of the court in the course of administration of [the] estate' and 'permit[ed] litigation that [sought] "to enforce or obtain any rights or benefits conferred by the laws of the Province of Alberta"'.[201] This was clearly a response to the line of case law regarding familial provision statutes discussed above and the court held that the clause permitted not only 'dependants' relief type applications [but also] other types of substantive rights or benefits created by statute which should not be extinguished by a no contest clause'.[202] The consequence of this is that what a testator is unable to do via benevolent judicial

196 *Adams v Adams* (n 143).

197 *Nathan v Leonard & Ors* (n 187) 837.

198 ibid.

199 ibid 835.

200 *Mawhinney v Scobie* Court of Appeal 1701-0243-AC, 2019 ABCA 76.

201 ibid 29.

202 ibid 41.

interpretation, as in earlier case law, he is able to do via cautious drafting. This highlights the formalism of the approach set out in *Re Gaynor* and *Re Kent* and further undermines its attractiveness.

The case also provides useful guidance regarding the purpose and effect of forfeiture clauses as well as what types of actions trigger them. Notwithstanding the drafting of the clause, the court rejected the argument that an action challenging a will on the statutory basis of 'suspicious circumstances' stating that: **3.085**

> the no contest clause does not prohibit an outright challenge to the validity of the will or litigation in connection with any provision of the will. If the challenge is unsuccessful then Ms. Mawhinney will forfeit the bequest. However, if she were to be successful in challenging the validity of the will, then it would no longer be valid and neither would the no contest clause. Therefore, the effect of the no contest clause is to test the fortitude of a potential challenger to the validity of the will and how strongly they believe they can successfully challenge the will. The clause is designed to discourage litigation not prohibit it.[203]

The approach of the Alberta Court of Appeal is clearly in line with earlier case law regarding such clauses not encompassing successful challenges nor being able to prevent all litigation, and therefore has much to recommend it. It also makes intuitive sense; such clauses cannot prohibit all litigation as this would violate the rule against ouster. Rather they are designed to make those who challenge wills 'put their money where their mouth is' and by increasing the cost-benefit ratio of such challenges discourage frivolous or purely emotional litigation. Moreover the court also repeatedly demonstrated deference to the intentions of the testator, stating that it 'must also be concerned about its obligation to give effect to the intentions of the JC who put the no contest clause in the will: Wills and Succession Act, s 26 (wills must be interpreted in a manner that gives effect to the intent of the testator)'.[204] In consequence, the court's decision is more in line with the public policy in favour of testamentary freedom by minimising state interference with the testator's wishes. **3.086**

Unfortunately, there is also no further guidance in England and Wales on the issue of familial provision statutes and forfeiture clauses, or merely on forfeiture clauses, and the few Australian and Canadian cases on the issue do not advance the matter, so it is now time to consider how offshore courts have addressed forfeiture clauses. **3.087**

203 ibid 49.
204 ibid 50.

(b) Forfeiture clauses: the offshore perspective

3.088 The first reported offshore case and the first case addressing forfeiture clauses in the context of *inter-vivos* trusts[205] is *AN v Barclays Private Bank and Trust (Cayman) Limited and others.*[206] The case concerned a clause which provided that:

> Whosoever contests the validity of this deed and the trust created under it, of the provisions of any conveyance of property by any person or persons to the trustees to form and be held as part of the trust fund and of the decisions of the trustee and/or of the protection committee shall cease to be a beneficiary of any of these trusts and shall be excluded from any benefits ...[207]

3.089 The court reviewed almost all the authorities discussed above and held that it would 'adhere to the relevant principles of construction which have been developed by the cases dealing with testamentary dispositions',[208] which meant that such clauses were to be strictly construed.[209] The court began by noting that in order to be upheld, such clauses had to be sufficiently certain so as to allow the relevant person or court to 'know with certainty the exact event the happening of which will result in the defeasance or forfeiture of the beneficial interest'.[210] The court held that the first two 'limbs' of the clause were sufficiently certain, but the provisions relating to decisions of the trustee or protection committee were not as it was not clear what 'decisions' were caught by the clause.[211]

3.090 The next issue which the court considered was whether the clause was void as repugnant to the trust or as an attempt to oust the courts' jurisdiction. The argument being made was that 'as it is fundamental to the existence of the trust that there are beneficiaries who can enforce it ... it is therefore repugnant to the very nature of the trust to prevent a beneficiary from doing so'.[212] The court conflated these submissions with a general public policy argument against such clauses and rejected them. It held that 'in the case of a challenge to the essential validity of the trust itself ... there is no general public policy reason why a no-contest provision should not be valid' but even in such challenges, 'a no-contest clause cannot be validly construed so as entirely to shut out chal-

---

205 *AN v Barclays Private Bank and Trust (Cayman) Limited and others* (n 113) 641–642.

206 ibid.

207 ibid 633.

208 ibid 642.

209 ibid 644.

210 ibid.

211 ibid 649–651.

212 ibid 651.

lenges which are based on probable cause or good faith or which are not taken merely frivolously and vexatiously or without good reason'.[213]

However, no-contest clauses could not act as a total prohibition on litigation, for example by entirely preventing litigation against a defaulting trustee, as 'this would be repugnant to the trusts themselves, to the beneficial interests of the beneficiaries and to their right to seek vindication of their positions before the court in an appropriate case where such vindication may be necessary'.[214] In consequence, challenges based on probable cause, in good faith and which were not vexatious would not and could not be caught by such a provision. This was so regardless of the settlor's intentions,[215] as the principle 'is one derived from the corpus of the common law as it has developed'. [216] As a result of this, and because the trust deed included a clause that it should be construed in accordance with Caymanian law, the court held that the clause should be read as follows 'Whosoever unjustifiably contests the validity of this deed and the trust created under it, of the provisions of any conveyance of property by any person or persons to the trustee …'[217] **3.091**

As in the case of *Nathan v Leonard*, the court then considered whether it had the power to grant relief from the operation of forfeiture clauses. The court held that: **3.092**

> jurisdiction must exist to grant relief in respect of the … beneficial interests, however described, as cl 23 might operate to defeat or divest. The jurisdiction, which is equitable in nature, derives from the principle that equity acts on the conscience of the parties, and is not to be excluded simply by virtue of the formal context in which the parties may act. By their very nature the settlements are not merely contractual but equitable also.[218]

However, this did not apply where the condition was a condition precedent with the result that there was a gift over, as 'this would involve a fundamental "re-writing" of the settlement'.[219] **3.093**

The next relevant case, *AB Jnr v MB*, is also from the Cayman Islands and involves the same judge as *AN*. This was a complex case concerning a claim for equitable compensation brought by the beneficiaries against the trustees **3.094**

---

213 ibid 666.

214 ibid.

215 ibid 666–667.

216 ibid 667.

217 ibid 668.

218 ibid 669.

219 ibid 675.

in, as is so often the case, a situation where there was significant animosity between them and allegations that relevant information was not disclosed to them whilst negotiating their exit from the trust. Relevantly for our purposes, there was a no-contest clause in the trust, and the court had to consider the interaction between this and the doctrines of estoppel and laches. Although not required to do so, the court discussed the validity of the no-contest clause stating that:

> I am persuaded that the no-contest clause is valid. In particular, it meets the test of 'certainty' and can, and should, be construed as complying with the public policy requirement of not seeking to preclude a challenge before the court on justifiable grounds. The no-contest clause is a valid expression of the intention of the settlor that those who would wish to enjoy his bounty should do so on the conditions expressed in his trust and should forfeit the right to do so if they should seek to impede or challenge the purposes of the trust.[220]

3.095 This analysis is merely a restatement or a summary of the judge's earlier statements in *AN*, although it helps confirm his consistent view on this matter. More interesting, however, is the court's discussion of the specific circumstances that caused the no-contest clause to come into effect, where it stated:

> Mme. B's conduct triggered the operation of the no-contest clause and (but for the estoppel per rem judicatam), operated a forfeiture of her interests under the trust. This is for all the reasons … involving the sealing of the art collection; the unauthorized and wilful sale of some of it; the invocation of diplomatic immunity … the challenge in the European courts to the proprietary entitlements of the trust; and the breaches of the confidentiality of the affairs of the trust compelled at her behest by judicial mandate and warrant …[221]

3.096 All of this confirms that *mala fides* actions will certainly cause a no-contest clause to come into effect and the court also confirmed that in these circumstances the plaintiff would not have been able to claim relief from forfeiture.[222] Most interesting of all, however, is the court's discussion on the interaction of the doctrine of estoppel and the no-contest clause. The issue arose because after contested proceedings came about, which would have caused the no-contest clause to have come into effect, the parties entered into a settlement agreement which was confirmed by the court. The court stated:

> Mme. B's primary response to the counterclaim for declaration of forfeiture is that the trustees and the beneficiaries of the trust (through KB) are estopped from so asserting

---

220 *AB Jnr and Madama B v MB and Four Others* (2013) 1 CILR 1 [275].

221 ibid 276.

222 ibid 279.

> … I am compelled to agree that an estoppel operates to block KB's counterclaim. My primary reasons for this conclusion … is that this issue was compromised and determined by the 1999 agreement as approved by the 1999 order by this court on June 30th, 1999 …[223]

The consequence of this was 'that an estoppel per rem judicatam arose and still exists'[224] with the effect of such an estoppel being: **3.097**

> to prevent a party to an action from asserting or denying, as against the other party, the existence of a particular cause of action, the non-existence or existence of which has been determined by a court of competent jurisdiction in previous litigation between the same parties.[225]

One important point to take from this judgment is that the dead hand of the settlor can be frustrated by the actions of the beneficiaries and trustees. Even if he provides for a forfeiture clause, this can be overridden by a settlement agreement and compromise amongst the relevant parties which is approved by the court. Equally, it is important for parties who consider entering into such an agreement to realise that, if a recalcitrant party later starts other litigation, the effect of a no-contest clause may well be lost. In the context of using a no-contest clause to enforce an arbitration clause, this might have particularly severe consequences, in that the party may no longer be required to arbitrate the proceedings. **3.098**

The Bermudan case of *Estate of PQR*[226] is unique in that it concerned a homemade will which contained a forfeiture clause that provided, 'If my daughter or her affiliates initiate any litigation of any type relating to this will or to my wife's ownership of the [AB] property, or to my wife in general, then she shall forfeit [her] cash legacy and investment legacy, and shall receive no benefit from this will'.[227] It is worth noting at the outset that the clause was held invalid for failure to provide for a gift over in the event of the clause being contravened.[228] The fact that the clause failed to provide this is no doubt a result of the fact it was homemade. **3.099**

However, prior to this, the court nevertheless outlined how it would interpret the clause and followed the approach adopted in *AN v Barclays Private Bank*, **3.100**

223 ibid 239–242.

224 ibid 257.

225 ibid 261.

226 *In the Matter of the Estate of PQR, Deceased* [2014] SC (Bda) 95 Civ.

227 ibid 6.

228 ibid 52.

stating that it would interpret the clause as 'only prohibiting unjustified claims brought by D against W be they related or unrelated to the will. A claim would be "unjustified" if it was either not advanced in good faith or if there was no good reason for it being pursued ...'[229]

3.101 The court also considered the rule regarding ouster of the jurisdiction of the court and held that 'One seeks to construe a clause which, literally read, would oust the jurisdiction of the courts (and accordingly be void), in a way which: (a) does not offend the relevant public policy rule; and (b) subject to (a), gives effect so far as is possible to the intentions of the maker of the instrument in question'.[230] The Bermudan courts, therefore, appear to be quite generous to such clauses and reluctant to strike them down, as with the English courts, and unlike the Canadian or Australian courts. Indeed, the court went on to explicitly reject those cases.[231] However, the persuasive value of this decision is somewhat blunted by the court's explicit reference to the importance of wealth management to the Bermudan economy where trusts are generally based on English precedents with English legal input. In particular, the court stated that 'this Court should generally lean towards rules of construction which are consistent with the corresponding English law approach'.[232]

3.102 Notwithstanding the court's reference to economic realities, the decision in *PQR*, like that in *AN v Barclays Bank*, is well reasoned, with a full discussion of the relevant authorities and is in line with the many cases discussed above. Although the case will certainly not be the last word on the matter, it can safely be regarded as the last word for now and neatly sums up the current state of the law. However, there is one last issue which must be addressed before discussing the application of forfeiture clauses in the context of trust arbitration, namely, can forfeiture clauses bind minor, incapable or unascertained beneficiaries?

(c) Forfeiture clauses and minor, incapable or unascertained beneficiaries

3.103 The issue simply has not been addressed by any of the cases discussed above, and it does not seem to have been considered by the relevant textbooks either. Approaching the matter from first principles, namely freedom of testation,[233] it would seem that as the courts generally strive to uphold a settlor or testator's

---

229 ibid 34.

230 ibid 40–41.

231 ibid 48.

232 ibid 51.

233 For the historical development of this doctrine see Frederick Pollock and Frederic William Maitland, *The History of English Law before the Time of Edward I, by Sir Frederick Pollock and Frederic William Maitland* (Cambridge University Press 1898) 348–356 <http://archive.org/details/historyofenglish00polluoft> accessed

will, there is no reason why they would refuse to do so merely because a trust included minor, incapable or unascertained beneficiaries. It could be said that it would be unfair to allow someone else, for example, a parent or guardian *ad litem* to dispute on their behalf with the result that they would lose the benefit of the trust through no fault of their own. However, it can be seen from *Nathan v Leonard* that the mere fact that an individual can lose benefit under a trust through no fault of their own is not a reason to hold the clause invalid.

Moreover, as the beneficiaries obtain their rights and obligations under the trust deed, it can be said that it would not generally be just to allow them to ignore their obligations while assuming their rights.[234] It is important to note in that regard that *Crociani v Crociani* itself concerned minor beneficiaries, as can be seen from reference to the Jersey Court of Appeal judgment,[235] and no suggestion was made that the jurisdiction clause did not apply to them as they were minors. It is true that in that case the minors were represented by guardians *ad litem*, what in England would now be called litigation friends, but this merely indicates that any problems relating to such clauses are likely to be merely due process rather than validity issues. In consequence, they will not be dealt with in this chapter but rather in the chapter on due process and human rights below. **3.104**

(d) Forfeiture clauses in the context of trust arbitration

As noted above, there is at least one reported case where a testator sought to use a forfeiture clause to force those claiming under the will to arbitrate any disputes as opposed to litigating them, the case of *Rhodes v The Muswell Hill Land Company*. [236] Unfortunately, in that case, the court held that the clause was 'absurd, inconsistent and repugnant'[237] because its result was that: **3.105**

> no devisee could take any proceedings to compel the payment to him of the rent, or bring an action of ejectment to establish his right to the property as against a stranger … if a servant was to embezzle the effects bequeathed he could not indict the man for the offence, or take proceedings of a civil character for compensation or damages, without the property going over …[238]

---

4 April 2020; cf Richard Schaul-Yoder, 'British Inheritance Legislation: Discretionary Distribution at Death' (1985) 8 Boston College International and Comparative Law Review 205.

234 See the discussion in *EMM Capricorn Trustees Limited v Compass Trustees Limited* (n 43); *E Crociani v C Crociani & Ors* (n 43).

235 *Crociani v Crociani* [2014] JCA 89.

236 *Rhodes v The Muswell Hill Land Company* (n 114).

237 ibid 446.

238 ibid 746.

3.106 The decision is best seen as an outlier reflecting the excessive breadth of the clause which, if read literally, would include any legal dispute whatsoever about the estate or anything to do with it, as well as a lack of benevolence on the part of the judge. It is clear from the other cases discussed above that such clauses will be read in such a way as to preserve their validity, even if this goes against their literal wording, and thus the judge's literalistic approach is not to be recommended. The overly strict approach of the court perhaps stems from the fact that at this time the courts were not as supportive of arbitration as they presently are, something that can be seen from the similarly dated decisions discussed above in the section on arbitrability. It is submitted then that the only lessons which can be taken away from this case are: (i) that the use of a forfeiture clause to force disputes by beneficiaries into arbitration is not entirely novel; and (ii) that such clauses should be worded so as to make clear that they do not apply to external trust disputes.

3.107 The main issue that falls to be considered is whether the limitations imposed on no-contest clauses by the courts also apply to no-contest except through arbitration clauses, and it is suggested that the answer is no. This is because whereas the former clauses purport to prevent the parties from disputing the trust or will altogether, the latter only purport to prevent them from litigating such matters: they can still dispute them through the quasi-judicial procedure of arbitration. The arbitral proceedings will be under the supervision of the court, as discussed above in the section on arbitrability, and the final award can be challenged, albeit on narrow grounds, in the courts.

3.108 In consequence, it is arguable that there is no need for such clauses to be read down and even in those cases which do not involve hostile litigation, for example where a party is merely asking for the court to interpret the will, the clause should still apply as there is no reason an arbitral tribunal cannot decide such matters.

3.109 Another issue worth considering is whether the clause should provide that challenges to the arbitral award will trigger it. The decision on whether to draft the clause in such a way depends on whether the clause is merely being used to force the parties into arbitration, or rather to restrict disputes more generally. Additionally, it is unclear whether the courts would uphold such a clause as the sections of the Arbitration Act 1996 which provide for court review of arbitral awards,[239] aside from errors of law,[240] are mandatory and cannot be contracted

239 Arbitration Act 1996 ss 67–68.

240 ibid 69.

out of by the parties.[241] Arguably, the forfeiture clause might nevertheless work as it is not strictly speaking excluding review, it is rather only laying down certain consequences for insisting on court review, i.e. forfeiture of all benefits otherwise available under the trust. The better view, however, is that as arbitration is only available under the Act under certain conditions, such a clause would be struck out by the court. Moreover, it would possibly open up the whole arbitration clause to attack for violating the principle of the irreducible core and excessively ousting the courts' jurisdiction. It is therefore safer not to provide for such a clause.

It is also worth noting that if the settlor is interested in simply reducing any disputes under the trust to a minimum, as opposed to forcing parties into arbitration, the effect of a no-contest except through arbitration clause may be weaker, as parties could bring unjustifiable or vexatious claims through arbitration without triggering the clause. In order to avoid this, it may be possible to provide for a two-step no-contest clause to prevent this: **3.110**

- The first step would provide that any unjustifiable or vexatious legal proceedings resulting out of a dispute about the trust would lead to a forfeiture of the beneficiaries' interest under the trust;
- The second step would provide that any justifiable or *bona fides* dispute about the trust is to be settled by arbitration, and any resort to the courts, not in relation to an arbitration, would lead to a forfeiture of the beneficiaries' interest under the trust.

Having exhausted what there is to say about no-contest clauses, it is now possible to move on to the possibility of using a condition precedent to enforce an arbitration clause in a trust deed. **3.111**

3. Conditions precedent

A condition precedent is defined by Stroud's as 'the sine qua non to getting the thing'[242] and by Jowitt's as 'one which delays the vesting of the right until the event happens; thus, if I give £100 to A if he shall act as my executor, A's right to the legacy is dependent on a condition precedent, because the performance of it must precede his receipt of the £100'.[243] These general definitions are applicable in the case of trusts, as can be seen from *Underhill and Hayton*,[244] **3.112**

241 ibid Schedule 1; 'Report on the English Arbitration Bill' (n 4) paras 275–283.

242 Greenberg, Greenberg and Stroud (n 19) 464.

243 Greenberg and Jowitt (n 18) 500.

244 DJ Hayton and others (n 244) para 8.95.

and there are numerous examples of such conditions in trusts, for example conditions regarding retaining a particular religion, not marrying people of a particular religion, residing in a particular place and so on.[245] Crucially, the courts treat conditions precedent more liberally in terms of enforcement than conditions subsequent, i.e. forfeiture clauses, so that there is a looser test for certainty.[246] It is questionable whether there is any jurisdiction for the courts to grant relief from failure to meet conditions precedent.[247] Therefore, it seems that if a requirement to arbitrate disputes arising under a trust can be framed as a condition precedent as opposed to a condition subsequent, these would be far harder to circumvent: it is for that reason that they are explored in this chapter.

3.113 There are essentially two proposed ways in which to frame a requirement to arbitrate any disputes under a trust as a condition precedent:

- The first is to provide 'that a beneficiary's interest only arises upon his or her actual acceptance of the terms of an arbitration clause'.[248] This could be done by preventing 'the trustee from … exercising their powers in favour of a beneficial object who has not agreed to the terms of the arbitration clause or … restricting the beneficial class itself to those beneficiaries who have … submitted to future arbitration'.[249]
- The second, and significantly more controversial option, is to provide that 'a beneficiary who wishes to bring proceedings to enforce any of his or her rights as beneficiary must first obtain an arbitral award'.[250] This would effectively be a form of *Scott v Avery* clause but operating in a trust deed as opposed to a contract. Each of the above suggestions will be examined in turn below.

(a) Requirement for actual acceptance of arbitration clause as a condition precedent

3.114 This is the more straightforward of the two approaches. One means of obtaining acceptance could be the need to send the executor or trustee 'an acknowledged instrument in writing agreeing, in consideration of the bequest hereby offered to him, that any challenge he wishes to make or issue he wishes to raise

245 Ibid paras 8-100–8-110.

246 ibid paras 8.95–8.97; Tucker and others (n 101) para 4-039.

247 *AN v Barclays Private Bank and Trust (Cayman) Limited and others* (n 113) paras 108–115; *Lucius Henry Cary Lord Viscount Falkland, Son and Heir of Edw. Cary, an Infant, by his Guardian v James Bertie and Elizabeth his Wife, Sir William Whitlock, John Grout, and others* (1696) 23 ER 814 333.

248 A Holden, 'The Arbitration of Trust Disputes: Theoretical Problems and Practical Possibilities' (2015) 21 Trusts & Trustees 546, 550; see also Blattmachr (n 114) 263–265.

249 Holden (n 248) 550.

250 ibid.

relating to the validity, construction or effect of all or any portion of this document ... or any complaint he may have ... shall be resolved ... by mediation and arbitration as provided ...'.[251] An issue arises, however, as is so often the case, in the case of minor, unborn, unascertained and incapable beneficiaries, as none of these would be able to manifest the requisite consent to benefit from the trust.[252]

In the case of mentally incapable beneficiaries, the best solution to this problem would be the deputy or other representative (e.g., the parents) consenting to the arbitration clause on behalf of the beneficiary. Although this will require an application to the court or other tribunal for someone to be appointed in order to exercise this power, this would have to be done in any event, whether or not there was a trust arbitration clause, as the beneficiary will require someone to make decisions on their behalf to administer their property as well as any number of other decisions involving their well-being and their life as a whole. In other words a trust arbitration provision would not complicate the already complex situation of leaving property for the benefit of a mentally incapable person, although it would be wise to specifically bring the arbitration clause (and the need for someone to consent to it) to the attention of the relevant court or tribunal. **3.115**

It is also worth noting that where a deputy or other representative has the authority to act on behalf of the mentally incapable beneficiary, they should, in principle, be able to bind the beneficiary via implied consent, i.e. by taking a benefit under the trust subject to the arbitration clause. The consequence of this is that, counterintuitively, binding a mentally incapable beneficiary to a trust is not actually that different from binding a normal beneficiary: always assuming, however, that there is someone who can legitimately act on their behalf. **3.116**

The situation is somewhat more complex in the case of minor and unborn beneficiaries, this is because, at common law, 'there is no adult who is competent to make contracts on behalf of an infant, nor does the concurrence in or sanction for a contract by a parent or other guardian in any way enhance its validity'.[253] The situation has changed in some jurisdictions, for example in Alberta the court can confirm minors' contracts and they then have the same **3.117**

251 Blattmachr (n 114) 264.

252 Holden (n 248) 550.

253 HJ Hartwig, 'Infants' Contracts in English Law: With Commonwealth and European Comparisons' (1966) 15 The International and Comparative Law Quarterly 780, 786–787.

effect as if the minor had made them as an adult,[254] but as a general rule the above principle holds good. In consequence, it would seem that the parents cannot consent to the arbitration clause on a minor beneficiary's behalf: moreover, even if the trust required as a condition precedent that the beneficiary reach the age of majority and then consent to the arbitration clause to benefit, this wouldn't capture claims made against the trustees before they reached the age of majority. The minor beneficiaries would be empowered to bring claims at this stage even if their interest had not yet crystallised.

3.118 The issue is unique to attempts to use conditions precedent to enforce arbitration clauses, because whilst allowing a beneficiary bringing a claim in court before they reached an age set as a condition precedent (or another condition) would not undermine the entire point of the condition, allowing a beneficiary to litigate such claims instead of arbitrating them would clearly undermine the entire point of the condition precedent. One solution would be using a forfeiture clause to encourage beneficiaries not to litigate, but again this would not solve the problem of consent as minors cannot consent nor can their parents consent for them. Does this mean that arbitration clauses cannot be used in trusts with minor beneficiaries?

3.119 The answer to this is complex but can be discovered by making an analogy with trust litigation. In trust litigation it is the parents or guardian who will act on behalf of the minor beneficiary; they will decide whether to bring a claim, where to bring a claim, against whom to bring a claim, and what claim to bring. All of this will bind the beneficiary and may result in the beneficiary losing procedural rights, for example submitting to the jurisdiction of a particular court to the exclusion of others and so on.[255] Arguably there is little difference between such actions and consenting to an arbitration clause, the minor beneficiary does not lose any substantive legal rights and should be able to enforce their legal rights just as effectively in arbitration as they would do so via court actions. Indeed, as noted above, there are several advantages including international enforceability, the prevention of parallel proceedings, confidentiality, and so on.

3.120 The above argument can be set out syllogistically as follows:

I. The parents, guardians, or litigation friend (as the case may be) are competent to choose a forum in which to sue on behalf of the infant and can bind the infant to that choice,

---

254 Minors' Property Act 2004 ss 3–4.

255 For a general discussion concerning submission to the jurisdiction of a foreign court see *New Cap Reinsurance Corporation Ltd (in Liquidation) v Grant; Rubin v Eurofinance SA* [2012] UKSC 46.

II. Arbitration is merely a special type of forum,
III. Therefore the parents, guardians, or litigation friend can bind an infant to an arbitration clause.

In consequence, it is suggested that in order to bind minor beneficiaries to an arbitration clause a condition precedent should be included in the trust deed which will provide that they will only benefit under the trust when they reach the age of majority and consent to the arbitration clause. Additionally, the parents, guardians or litigation friend to be appointed under the representation clause in the trust deed can be required to waive any rights to bring any claims in relation to the trust, on behalf of the child, except according to the arbitration provisions in the deed. Such a person should also be required to explicitly consent to the arbitration clause themselves in order to avoid any other complications. **3.121**

The issue is effectively academic as regards unascertained beneficiaries since as 'such potential beneficiaries ... have no present right to protection of their potential interest and hence no locus standi ... it is striking that such potential beneficiaries cannot sue for breach of trust in any circumstances [and] have no right to seek disclosure'.[256] In consequence, such beneficiaries are unlikely to cause any problems, and they can, for all practical purposes, effectively be ignored. **3.122**

Other solutions to the problem of minor or unborn beneficiaries include the creation of a 'black hole trust' where the trustees have extremely broad discretion to add in further beneficiaries, with the default beneficiaries never being intended to benefit,[257] and minor beneficiaries can be added in on their majority, after consenting to the condition. A final option for all beneficiaries would be for the matter to be brought before the courts and they could then consent on behalf of the beneficiary, perhaps as part of their supervisory jurisdiction,[258] or via specific statutes granting the courts power to deal with minors' property or to contract on their behalf. **3.123**

(b) Creating a Scott v Avery *clause in a trust deed*

The case of *Scott v Avery*[259] has already been discussed above, and so current **3.124**

256 Tucker and others (n 101) para 23-080.

257 Nichola Jackson, 'Certainty of Beneficiaries in Jersey and the First Principles of Trust Law' [2015] The Jersey & Guernsey Law Review 236, 238–240.

258 This jurisdiction is very extensive and the courts have been willing to apply it in novel circumstances, as shown in RC Nolan, '"The Execution of a Trust Shall Be under the Control of the Court": A Maxim in Modern Times' (2016) 2 CJCCL 2, 469.

259 *Scott v Avery* V (1856) HLC 809.

discussion will be limited to whether that sort of clause could be adopted in a trust instrument. The issue with applying a *Scott v Avery* clause to a trust deed is that in contractual *Scott v Avery* cases the courts 'have no jurisdiction whatsoever, and no cause of action accrues until the arbitrators have determined'.[260] However, in trust cases, the court has its supervisory jurisdiction, regardless of any provision in the trust deed, and, as has been discussed above, this cannot wholly be ousted even by a valid arbitration clause. Moreover, given the numerous problems caused by *Scott v Avery* clauses,[261] the courts are unlikely to be particularly enthusiastic about their application in a trust deed where the beneficiaries will not, unlike in a contract, have consented to them. This is particularly problematic given that freedom of contract was one of the main justifications for upholding the clause in *Scott v Avery*.[262] It is therefore unlikely that such clauses would be upheld by the courts.

4. Section 82(2) Arbitration Act 1996 and equivalent provisions

3.125 Section 82(2) of the Arbitration Act 1996 provides that 'References in this Part to a party to an arbitration agreement include any person claiming under or through a party to the agreement'. Section 9 in the same part of the Act provides for a mandatory stay of court proceedings, on the request of a party to an arbitration agreement, unless 'the arbitration agreement is null and void, inoperative, or incapable of being performed'. As a result, several scholars have argued that s 82(2) could be used to enforce a trust arbitration agreement against non-signatories such as beneficiaries.[263] This would be on the basis that beneficiaries derive their rights from the settlor and/or the trustee and therefore claim 'under or through' them.[264]

3.126 The contrary view is held by a roughly equal number of scholars. They argue that the subsection likely refers only to assignees and not third-party beneficiaries.[265] This section will therefore engage in a two-fold analysis of the argument. Firstly, it will analyse the relevant jurisprudence concerning the section and equivalents to it to see how it has been interpreted. Secondly, it will

260 ibid 1138–1139.

261 'Report on Commercial Arbitration' (Law Reform Commission of New South Wales 1967) para 4.2.3; Andrew Tweeddale and Keren Tweeddale, 'Scott v Avery Clauses: O'er Judges' Fingers, Who Straight Dream on Fees' (2011) 77 Arbitration International 423, 424–427.

262 *Scott v Avery* (n 259) 852–853.

263 Cohen and Poole (n 103) 327–328; Le Poidevin, 'Arbitration and Trusts: Can It Be Done?' (2012) 309.

264 Cohen and Poole (n 103) 328; Le Poidevin, 'Arbitration and Trusts: Can It Be Done?' (2012).

265 Toby Graham, 'The Problems with Compulsory Arbitration of Trust Disputes' (2014) 20 Trusts & Trustees 20, 23; Tony Molloy QC and Toby Graham, 'Arbitration of Trust Disputes' (2012) 18:4 Trusts and Trustees 279, 282–286.

consider whether as a matter of doctrine, it is possible to include beneficiaries within the scope of s 82(2).

(a) Relevant statutes and case law

The origin for the concept of 'party' including anyone claiming 'through or under' them lies, as with much of modern English arbitration law,[266] in the 1854 Common Law Procedure Act, specifically section 11. The wording of that section, as was the style in that age, is incredibly verbose and thus it will not be quoted here in full but, paraphrased, it provides that: **3.127**

> Whenever the Parties to any Deed or Instrument in Writing to be hereafter made or executed, or any of them, shall agree that any existing or future Differences between them … shall be referred to Arbitration, and any One or more of the Parties so agreeing, or any Person or Persons claiming through or under him or them … it shall be lawful for the court in which [an] Action or Suit is brought … to make a Rule or Order staying all Proceedings in such Action or Suit …[267]

This provision was re-enacted, although in a less verbose formula, in s 4 of the Arbitration Act 1889 and that formula was then re-enacted in s 4 of the Arbitration Act 1950, s 1 of the Arbitration Act 1975 and finally, read together, ss 9 and 88 of the Arbitration Act 1996. In consequence, cases and academic commentary under all of these acts are potentially relevant in understanding the scope of the phrase 'through or under a party'. **3.128**

It is likely that the first reported case addressing the meaning of the words 'through or under a party' is the 1856 case of *Pennell & Ors v Walker*[268] which held that assignees of a bankrupt did not claim through or under a bankrupt.[269] The next relevant case, *Piercy v Young*,[270] also concerned bankruptcy, specifically the trustee in bankruptcy of a partner in a partnership which provided that disputes between the partners should be settled by arbitration. A court action was brought against the trustee in bankruptcy, who, having adopted the partnership agreement, asked the court to stay the action. Although the court refused to do so it stated, 'We also do not desire to hear counsel on the question whether the Defendant is a party who can make this application within the meaning of the Common law Procedure Act'.[271] It would seem then that **3.129**

266 See generally Stavros Brekoulakis, 'The Historical Treatment of Arbitration under English Law and the Development of the Policy Favouring Arbitration' (2019) 39 Oxford Journal of Legal Studies 124.

267 Common Law Procedure Act 1854 s 11.

268 *Pennell & Ors v Walker* (1856) 18 CB 650.

269 ibid 657–658.

270 *Piercy v Young* (1879) 14 ChD 200.

271 ibid 203.

the court held that a trustee in bankruptcy who adopted a contract with an arbitration clause was a person who claimed 'through or under' the bankrupt, and this is the conclusion of *Mustill & Boyd*, who cite the case to support this point. [272] As will be seen below, the matter is put on more solid footing by the Arbitration Act 1934.

3.130 The next case is an 1883 Privy Council case on appeal from Mauritius, *Martin, Deceased v Boulanger*[273] and although the case concerned Art 474 of the Mauritian Code of Civil Procedure, the code used wording similar to that in the 1854 Act and thus the court explicitly referred to the 'through or under a party' wording.[274] The case concerned the settling of the accounts between a firm and one of its debtors by arbitration. Subsequently, the judgment creditors of the firm challenged the award,[275] and the court of first instance held that they were not bound by it as they were not parties to the arbitration.[276] The Privy Council disagreed with this and stated, 'It certainly seems to their Lordships that this is not quite accurate. What was found on the reference is binding, not only on the parties to the reference, but also on every one who would, in English law, by claiming through or under them, be privy to it.'[277] The court goes on to explain the policy reasons for this, stating that:

> It is not merely that a judgment shall be binding on the parties who are the actual parties to the suit, but it must be binding upon all who claim under or through the party to it in respect to the property in dispute. Otherwise there would be interminable litigation, and every judgment would be opened again and again, and the maxim 'interest reipublicae ut sit finis litium' to say nothing of justice and convenience between parties, would be completely lost sight of.[278]

3.131 The court goes on to note that once they obtained the judgment against the firm, they were claiming under that firm and thus were bound by the arbitral award.[279] Two important things can be taken from the decision. Firstly, judgment creditors will in certain circumstances be bound by arbitral awards which bind their judgment debtors, and, secondly, the aim of the 'through or under' wording is to further the public interest of preventing endless litigation as well as to ensure justice and convenience between parties.

---

272 Michael J Mustill, *The Law and Practice of Commercial Arbitration in England* (Butterworths 1989) 137.

273 *Martin, Deceased v Boulanger* (1883) 8 App Cas 296.

274 ibid 302, 304.

275 ibid 300–301.

276 ibid 302.

277 ibid.

278 ibid.

279 ibid 302–304.

It would appear that the next case addressing this matter is the 1910 case of *Bonnin v Neame*,[280] where a partnership agreement between three partners provided for arbitration between them as well as their executors or administrators. The complication was that one of the partners had mortgaged his share and the mortgagees brought an action against all of the partners for an account of that partner's share as from the date of the partnership's dissolution. The partners applied for a stay of the action on the basis of the arbitration deed, but the court refused, as the mortgagee's right to account arose 'under s.31 of the Partnership Act'[281] and not from the partnership deed. **3.132**

Additional reasons for refusing to stay included the fact that the articles did not explicitly include persons claiming under the parties,[282] matters of law arose[283] and the arbitrators were not free from partiality or bias.[284] It is not entirely certain what can be drawn from this case, but it would seem that, at a minimum, in order for a person to be claiming 'through or under a party' they cannot be claiming a right which is 'independent of the deed'.[285] In other words, if a person's right arises independently from the deed, for example from statute, they cannot be held to be claiming through or under a party. **3.133**

The next relevant case is the 1929 case of *Aspell v Seymour*,[286] which was a construction dispute where the contract in question included an arbitration clause and the contractors assigned the contract to the plaintiff who subsequently brought an action against the defendants, who were the employers under the construction contract. The defendants argued that the case should be stayed by reason of the arbitration clause in the contract and the fact that the plaintiff was claiming through the contractors who were a party to that contract. The court held that the plaintiff was bound as 'Sect. 4 provided that the right to a stay under an arbitration claim should arise not only as between the parties to the submission but also as between assignees as persons claiming through the original parties'.[287] The exception to this, in line with an earlier case dealing with assignment in general, *Cottage Club Estates Ltd v Woodside Estates Co*,[288] was where the persons in question had 'assigned all money to become due under **3.134**

280 *Bonnin v Neame* (1910) 1 Ch 732.
281 ibid 738.
282 ibid.
283 ibid 739.
284 ibid 740.
285 Russell (2021) 86.
286 *Aspell v Seymour* [1929] WN 152.
287 ibid 152.
288 *Cottage Club Estates Ltd v Woodside Estates Company (Amersham) Ltd* (1928) 2 KB 463.

the contract … as they had divested themselves of any interest'.[289] The case, therefore, establishes one of the classical means of binding non-signatories or third parties to an arbitration clause, namely, assignment.

3.135 The next evolution in the understanding of 'through or under' came not from a case but rather from the Arbitration Act 1934. Section 1 of that Act provides that an arbitration agreement can be enforced by or against the personal representative of a deceased person and s 2 provides that an arbitration agreement can be enforced by or against the trustee in bankruptcy of a bankrupt if the trustee adopts the contract. Although neither the wording 'through or under' nor the relevant section of the 1889 Arbitration act is mentioned in the 1934 Act, subsequent editions of the leading Arbitration textbook at the time, *Russell on Arbitration*, hold that the Act had the effect of broadening the scope of those words to include personal representatives and trustees in bankruptcy.[290] The Act established two of the other classical exceptions to privity of contract in English arbitration: arbitration agreements bind personal representatives of deceased persons and trustees in bankruptcy who have adopted the contract containing the arbitration clause.

3.136 The next relevant case, *Smith v Pearl Assurance Company Ltd*,[291] addressed the provisions of the *Third Parties (Rights against Insurers) Act 1930*, section 1 of which vested an insured person's rights against the insurer in their debtor when they went bankrupt. This allowed persons whom they had injured and were unable to pay, hence their bankruptcy, to recover from the insurer through subrogation. In the case at hand, the insurance policy included an arbitration clause, and the issue was whether the plaintiff was bound by it; the court held that they were as they were claiming through the insured person.[292] The case, therefore, established one of the other classical exceptions to privity of contract in English arbitration theory, subrogation.

3.137 The next case which addresses the wording 'through or under', *Shayler v Woolf*,[293] builds upon *Aspell* and holds that the fact 'that an arbitration clause is assignable in its nature seems to me to be quite clearly contemplated by s.4 of the Arbitration Act, 1889, and it has been recognized in … Aspell v. Seymour'.[294] The combined effect of these two cases is that, in general, arbitra-

---

289 *Aspell v Seymour* (n 286) 152.

290 Russell (2021) 86; Anthony Walton, *Russell on the Law of Arbitration* (18th edn, Stevens and Sons 1970) 143–144.

291 *Smith v Pearl Assurance Company Ltd* (1939) 63 LIL Rep 1.

292 ibid 2.

293 *Shayler v Woolf* [1946] Ch 320.

294 *Aspell v Seymour* (n 286) 323.

tion clauses are assignable and assignees will be individuals who claim through or under their assignor and are thus bound by the arbitration clause.

It was quite some time before the next relevant reported case, the 1978 case of *Roussel-Uclaf v GD Searle & Co. Ltd*,[295] which concerned a patent licensing dispute where the plaintiff had brought an action before the court and the defendant argued that the action should be stayed on the basis of an arbitration clause in the licensing agreement.[296] The plaintiff argued, however, that the defendant was not a party to the arbitration agreement as it was signed only by the US 'mother' company and not the defendant.[297] The court disagreed, stating that 'I see no reason why these words ... should be construed so narrowly as to exclude a wholly-owned subsidiary company claiming ... a right to sell patented articles which it has obtained from and been ordered to sell by its parent'.[298] It went on to say that 'The two parties and their actions are ... so closely related on the facts in this case that it would be right to hold that the subsidiary can establish that it is within the purview of the arbitration clause ... on the basis that it is claiming "through or under" the parent ...'.[299] **3.138**

At first sight, the interpretation given to 'through or under' in *Roussel* is significant in that it would appear to be close to adopting the 'group of companies' doctrine in English law, although subsequent commentary has suggested that perhaps it was justified on the basis of agency.[300] The judge in *Grupo Torras S.A. v Al-Sabah*[301] appeared to doubt whether this was so and stated that 'I do not find it easy to extract any principle from the reasoning',[302] before going on to discuss the possibility of a broadening of the basis on which agreements can bind third parties or non-signatories.[303] In any event, the case is of merely academic interest as it was overruled by the Court of Appeal in *City of London v Sancheti*,[304] which held that *Roussel* was wrongly decided as 'a mere legal or commercial connection is not sufficient'[305] to trigger the stay of proceedings before a court. Despite this, *Roussel* remains of interest as its subsequent treat- **3.139**

295 *Roussel-Uclaf v GD Searle & Co Ltd and GD Searle & Co* 1 Ch D 225 (1978).

296 ibid 225–228.

297 ibid 230.

298 ibid 231.

299 ibid.

300 Mustill (n 272) 137 fn 2.

301 *Grupo Torras SA and Torras Hostencg London Ltd v Sheikh Fahad Mohammed Al-Sabah* (1995) 1 Lloyd's Rep 374.

302 ibid 451.

303 ibid.

304 *City of London v Sancheti* [2009] Lloyd's Rep 117.

305 ibid 122.

ment by the English Courts, including its overruling, demonstrate the inherent conservatism of the English courts when it comes to binding third parties or non-signatories.

3.140 The next relevant case is that of *Rumput (Panama) SA v Islamic Republic of Iran Shipping Lines ('The Leage')*,[306] which expanded the types of assignees that could claim 'through or under' the assignor, by holding that 'an assignee of a debt does claim against the debtor "through or under" the assignor'.[307] The court went on to justify its view, stating that:

> The entitlement of the assignor is an essential ingredient of the assignee's claim, to be properly pleaded and proved. The derivative nature of the assignee's claim is underlined by the rule that an assignee takes subject to equities and by the practice of joining the assignor as either plaintiff or defendant in bringing suits on an equitable assignment of a legal chose in action.[308]

3.141 This case effectively overturned the rule drawn out of the case *Cottage Club Estates*[309] that, 'The benefit of [an arbitration] clause will however not pass to the assignee of a debt arising out of the contract containing it'. [310]

3.142 The next relevant case is the English case of *Through Transport Mutual Insurance Association v New India Assurance Co (No 2)*.[311] There were many complications in this case, but the relevant one for our purposes is that New India was not an assignee as such but rather, had 'the right under the Finnish Insurance Contracts Act to enforce the obligations of the [defendant] under the contract of insurance'. [312] In consequence, it was not clear whether New India was, 'a statutory transferee or simply … the beneficiary of a statutory provision',[313] but the court held that regardless of how exactly New India's right was to be characterised, it was 'subject to certain inherent limitations, including the obligation to enforce it by arbitration in London'.[314] Moreover, it was also a party claiming 'through or under a party to the agreement'.[315] This was so even where New India did not wish to pursue a claim in arbitration or

306 *Rumput (Panama) SA and Belzetta Shipping Co SA v Islamic Republic of Iran Shipping Lines (The 'Leage')* (1984) 2 Lloyd's Rep 259.

307 ibid 262.

308 ibid 276.

309 *Cottage Club Estates Ltd v Woodside Estates Company (Amersham) Ltd* (n 288).

310 Ernest Wetton, *Russell on Arbitration* (14th edn, Stevens and Sons 1949) 73.

311 *Through Transport Mutual Insurance Association (Eurasia) Ltd v New India Assurance Co Ltd (No 2)* [2005] EWHC 455.

312 ibid 24.

313 ibid.

314 ibid 25.

315 ibid.

even to pursue a claim at all because, 'as soon as a third party in the position of New India makes a demand on the insurer there is the potential for a dispute to arise, as indeed happened …, and once a dispute has arisen … it is one which must be determined by arbitration in accordance with the contract'.[316]

3.143 It is difficult to reconcile the judge's laissez-faire approach to determining whether New India was a statutory transferee or a mere statutory beneficiary, with the holding in *Bonnin* that where a third party's right arose from statute, and consequently independently of the deed, the party would not be claiming 'through or under' a party to the arbitration clause.[317] If New India had an independent statutory right to bring a claim and was not a quasi-assignee, then it was not claiming 'through or under' a party to the arbitration clause and should not have been held bound to it. The matter was subsequently clarified when the judge, now on the Court of Appeal, clarified in the case of *London Steamship Owners' Mutual Insurance Association Ltd v Spain*[318] that, *Through Transport* was 'an example [where] the terms of the legislation make it reasonably clear that the claimant is intended to be given a right to enforce the contract in place of the insured'.[319] In other words, this was an example of simple subrogation, as in *Smith v Pearl Assurance Company*.[320]

3.144 The next case also involves subrogation as well as shipping and builds on *Through Transport*, *West Tankers Inc v RAS Riunione Adriatica Sicurta SpA*.[321] The case again concerned proceedings in several jurisdictions as well as anti-suit jurisdiction and the issue of whether a third party who had a right to arbitrate a dispute but had instead gone to a foreign court was bound by the clause. Moreover, the case again involved statutory subrogation, this time under Italian law.[322] The court stated that:

> On the face of it the words 'any person claiming [under or through a party to the agreement] might be given a narrower or a wider meaning: a narrower interpretation limiting the term to persons who have invoked the arbitration machinery to make a claim [sic] (which the insurers have not done), or a wider interpretation including any person who (as the insurers do in the proceedings in Sicily) asserts a right which, if disputed, would have to be enforced through the procedure stipulated in the arbitration agreement. Mr

316 ibid 28.

317 *Bonnin v Neame* (n 280) 738.

318 *London Steamship Owners' Mutual Insurance Association Ltd v Spain* (2015) 1 CLC 596.

319 ibid 608.

320 *Smith v Pearl Assurance Company Ltd* (n 291).

321 *West Tankers Inc v RAS Riunione Adriatica Sicurta SpA, Generali Assicurazioni Generali SpA* [2007] EWHC 2184 (Comm).

322 ibid [8].

> Bailey submits that the term is to be given the wider interpretation … I … accept the first stage of Mr. Bailey's reasoning.[323]

3.145 The case confirms that statutory subrogation can bring a party under s 82(2) of the Arbitration Act 1996 and also puts forward 'a broad interpretation of when a 'party is claiming' … so that it includes a party asserting a right which, if disputed, must be referred to arbitration'.[324] Neither *West Tankers* nor *Through Transport* is therefore particularly revolutionary, and the fact that the English courts are still discussing subrogation close to seventy years after it was first recognised as a means of binding third parties or non-signatories, demonstrates their inherent conservatism.

(b) Application of the above to trust arbitration

3.146 It can be seen from the above cases and statutes that at no point in the 165-year-long history of the 'through or under' wording has a beneficiary been held to be claiming 'through or under' a trustee or settlor in English law. It could be argued this is merely because arbitration of trust disputes is a relatively recent phenomenon. However even if one looks at the matter from first principles, namely the classical definition of a trust as 'an equitable fiduciary obligation, binding a person (called a trustee) to deal with property … owned and controlled by him as a separate fund … for the benefit of persons (called beneficiaries)',[325] it is hard to see how beneficiaries could be argued to obtain their rights through or under the settlor. This is because, as noted above, traditionally in a trust, the settlor has no rights or obligations as regards the trust.[326] He has quite simply stepped out of the picture and has 'no rights under the trust that [he] can assign onto the beneficiaries'.[327]

3.147 Moreover, unlike in the legal situations discussed above, such as assignment or subrogation, a trust is not a case where a person or persons are being transplanted, either fully or partially, into an existing legal relationship, nor is it a case where a new legal relationship is being created to replace an existing one, as in novation. Instead, a trust involves the creation of a new legal relationship with new rights, obligations and parties. Indeed, strictly speaking, even the proprietary rights under a trust are new, as a settlor never had a proprietary beneficial interest in his property given that it is impossible for a proprietary

323 ibid para 10.

324 Sutton, Gill and Gearing (n 7) 112, fn 82.

325 Hayton and others (n 244) para 1.1(1).

326 ibid 1.1.

327 Graham (n 265) 23.

beneficial interest to exist unless split from the legal title.[328] As an illustration, an owner of land does not hold both an equitable and a legal interest in the land but is rather 'the absolute owner of an estate in fee simple in the land'.[329] Thus, where a person who holds one of the two interests has the other transferred to him, they would merge to form 'a single absolute interest in the land'.[330]

In consequence, it is submitted that, despite the intuitive attraction of the idea, it is clear that beneficiaries do not claim through or under a settlor: thus s 82(2) could not be used to hold them bound to an arbitration clause to which the settlor is a party. **3.148**

Counterintuitively, the matter is a little more complex with regard to the trustee, as many scholars state that, in one sense, the beneficiaries' rights are derivative from the trustees' rights[331] and it is clear that a determinative aspect for a holding that an individual is claiming through or under another is that their right is in some way derivative from another person's.[332] However, it is important to analyse the sense in which beneficiaries' rights are said to be derivative from the trustees. It is clear from the literature that beneficiaries' rights are derivative legal rights in the sense that equitable rights are derivative legal rights. Thus, in the case of a trust, if the trustees never had the right to something the beneficiaries cannot claim it as part of the trust fund.[333] **3.149**

To put it another way 'It's of no use for Equity to say that A is a trustee of Blackacre for B, unless there be some court that can say A is the owner of Blackacre. Equity without common law would have been a castle in the air, an impossibility'.[334] The beneficiaries' rights are derivative in another sense too; in general, it is the trustee who sues or is sued by third parties, with the beneficiaries only able to do so if the trustee wrongfully refuses to do so, and even in these cases the beneficiaries sue in the name of the trustee.[335] Does this **3.150**

328 Hayton and others (n 244) para 1.1(11); *Duggan v Governor of Full Sutton Prison and another* (2004) 1 WLR 1010 [26–28]; *Westdeutsche Landesbank Girozentrale v Islington London Borough Council* [1996] AC 669 HL (E), 706.

329 *Re DKLR Holding Co (No 2) Pty Limited v Commissioner of Stamp Duties* (1982) 149 CLR 431, 463.

330 ibid.

331 See the discussion in JE Penner, 'The (True) Nature of a Beneficiary's Equitable Proprietary Interest under a Trust' (2014) 27 Canadian Journal of Law & Jurisprudence 473, 475–476.

332 See for example *Rumput (Panama) SA and Belzetta Shipping Co SA v Islamic Republic of Iran Shipping Lines (The 'Leage')* (n 306) 276.

333 Penner (n 331) 475–476.

334 FW Maitland, *Equity, Also the Forms of Action at Common Law: Two Courses of Lectures* (Cambridge University Press 1910) 19.

335 Hayton and others (n 244) para 1.1(3).

mean that the beneficiaries' rights are derivative in the sense that is required by s 82(2) and the jurisprudence on it?

3.151 It is submitted that this is not the case, as the same basic differences which distinguish the relationship between settlor and beneficiary and assignees, subrogates and parties to a novated contract also exist with regard to the relationship between trustee and beneficiary, namely the relationship in both cases is a wholly new and distinct one. Moreover, the beneficiaries have rights, such as the right to benefit from the trust fund,[336] and obligations, in the sense of complying with any conditions for benefit under the trust deed that the settlor has imposed, which the trustees do not have, never had and never will have.

3.152 In summary, it is now possible to conclude that there is no legal or doctrinal support for the view that beneficiaries claim 'through or under' the settlor or trustee, and thus any argument in favour of trust arbitration clauses binding beneficiaries based on s 82(2) is fundamentally misconceived.

G. CONCLUSION

3.153 It is now possible to briefly summarise the outcome of this chapter. Firstly, arbitration agreements in trust deeds meet the threshold requirements of ss 5–6 of the Arbitration Act 1996 and thus come within the statutory scheme. Secondly, forfeiture clauses in trust deeds are usually effective and should also be effective to enforce arbitration by the beneficiaries. Thirdly, the use of a condition precedent should also be effective to enforce arbitration by the beneficiaries, although their use in the case of minor, incapable and unascertained beneficiaries is fraught with difficulty. Fourthly, s 82(2) does not apply to beneficiaries under a trust, and thus it would not be an effective means of enforcing an arbitration clause in a trust deed.

336 See generally Tucker and others (n 101) ch 20.

4

TRUST ARBITRATION AND DUE PROCESS: THE ECHR AND COMMON LAW PRINCIPLES OF NATURAL JUSTICE

A. INTRODUCTION

4.001 This chapter and the following chapter deal with two interrelated, but nevertheless highly distinct, legal 'ecosystems' which protect individuals' due process rights. This chapter examines the European Convention on Human Rights, specifically the Art 6(1) right to a fair trial, and the following chapter deals with the common law rules of natural justice as well as their statutory equivalents in the context of arbitration.

4.002 Although the particular importance of the ECHR and the principles of natural justice, as well as their statutory arbitration equivalents, to trust arbitration has been discussed above it is worth briefly re-emphasising this before beginning the chapter proper. There are four main reasons why the ECHR and the principles of natural justice pose a particular challenge to trust arbitration.

4.003 Firstly, as already explained above, beneficiaries under a trust are unlikely to be parties to any arbitration agreement under the trust instrument and may not even know of its existence. In consequence, serious issues arise regarding their natural justice right to be heard and their ECHR right of access to a court, as well as their ECHR right to a fair trial more generally.

4.004 Secondly, trusts will often involve minors and legally incapable parties who cannot explicitly, or perhaps at all, consent to arbitrate their disputes under the trust and thus, again, issues arise regarding their natural justice right to be heard, as well as their ECHR right of access to a court and ECHR right to a fair trial more generally.

4.005 Thirdly, there is an inherent imbalance, or inequality,[1] in the relationship between the beneficiaries on the one hand, and the trustees and any other powerholders in the trust on the other. Although the beneficiaries are, excluding reasonable reimbursement of expenses and agreed for fees, the only ones entitled to benefit under the trust, they do not actually manage it. It is the trustees, and to a lesser extent any powerholders, who manage the trust fund, the beneficiaries are wholly dependent on the former to ensure that they receive what they are due. This applies *a fortiori* in the case of discretionary trusts, particularly those with widely drawn classes, where the beneficiaries may find it very hard to hold trustees and other powerholders to account for purportedly erroneous or unlawful decisions.[2]

---

1 Andrew S Gold and Paul B Miller (eds), *Philosophical Foundations of Fiduciary Law* (Oxford University Press 2014) 73 <http://www.oxfordscholarship.com/view/10.1093/acprof:oso/9780198701729.001.0001/acprof-9780198701729> accessed 3 June 2020; Leonard I Rotman, 'The Vulnerable Position of Fiduciary Doctrine in the Supreme Court of Canada' (1996) 24 Manitoba Law Journal 60.

2 See generally David Hayton, 'The Strength of Beneficiaries' Rights under English Law and the Laws of Caribbean States' (Transcontinental Trust Conference, Geneva, 19 June 2013).

The above imbalance also exists between the settlor, the trustee and the beneficiaries as, even if the settlor has usually stepped out of the picture, it is only he and the trustees who have drawn up the trust deed. There is therefore every possibility for him to tilt the scales in favour of the trustees with widely drawn exemption clauses and restrictions on litigation, and the situation is exacerbated where he has reserved powers in his favour or otherwise restricted the rights of beneficiaries. In consequence, there is a risk that arbitration clauses could be unfairly drafted, leading to breaches of either the natural right to be heard or the *nemo judex in causa sua* principle, or the ECHR right to a fair trial. **4.006**

Fourthly, with the exception of high value trusts, there is a much greater risk of procedural unfairness due to the number of unsophisticated legal parties involved, while the difficulty, or even impossibility, involved in obtaining legal aid for trust disputes (and even more so for trust arbitration) means that there is a much greater risk of breaching the natural justice right to be heard, the *nemo judex in causa sua* principle or the ECHR right to a fair trial than in other forms of arbitration. In particular, as will be seen below, there is a significant risk that adopting the same approach as arbitrators do with regard to sophisticated parties, or a lack of legal aid, will cause a breach of the natural justice right to be heard or the ECHR right to a fair trial. **4.007**

B. THE EUROPEAN CONVENTION ON HUMAN RIGHTS AND THE EUROPEAN COURT OF HUMAN RIGHTS – AN OVERVIEW

The European Convention on Human Rights was finalised in 1950 and entered into force in 1953.[3] However, the European Court of Human Rights (ECtHR) only came into existence nine years later in 1959 and is the oldest, and arguably most important, regional human rights court, possessing jurisdiction over the 800 million residents of the 47 member states of the Council of Europe.[4] The evolution of the European Convention on Human Rights, as well as the European Court of Human Rights, is a complex one, with entire books written on the subject.[5] However, it is not necessary to enter into those matters as what is important for our purposes is that the ECHR as a human rights instrument protects a whole host of rights. These include the right to life (Art 2), the right to liberty (Art 5), the right to a fair trial (Art 6), the right to **4.008**

3 Ed Bates, *The Convention of 1950 and Key Features of its Subsequent Evolution* (Oxford University Press 2010) 134 <https://www.oxfordscholarship.com/view/10.1093/acprof:oso/9780199207992.001.0001/acprof-9780199207992-chapter-5> accessed 2 November 2019.

4 *The Conscience of Europe: 50 Years of the European Court of Human Rights* (Third Millennium Publishing Limited 2010) 16.

5 See e.g. Bates (n 3).

respect for private and family life (Art 8) and the right of freedom of thought, conscience and religion (Art 9), to name only a few. Crucially individuals can petition the court directly regarding alleged violations of their right (Art 34), and the court can, in certain circumstances, award them 'just satisfaction' for such violations (Art 41).

4.009 It is important to note that there is a significant limitation on applications to the court regarding alleged violations of convention rights, namely the Art 35(1) requirement to exhaust domestic remedies. The reasoning behind this requirement 'reflects the fact that the primary responsibility for observing the provisions of the Convention rests with the states who are parties to it'.[6] Moreover, 'The Convention also affords member states an opportunity, in accordance with general principles of international law, to redress any violation … within the domestic arena'.[7] It is therefore not usually possible for an applicant to simply ignore domestic courts and apply directly to the ECtHR, although the requirement is applied flexibly as, *inter alia*, there is no need to apply for purely theoretical remedies or to seek remedies which would likely be futile.[8] There may also be circumstances in which even when domestic remedies would resolve a breach of an applicant's right, they may nevertheless be exempted from the requirement to exhaust them.[9]

4.010 Equally, enforcement of the ECHR varies throughout the Council of Europe, with the matter being significantly more complex than the usual contrasting approaches of monist and dualist legal systems.[10] For example, although Belgium is formally dualist, its courts adopted a monist approach to the ECHR, while the Austrian courts, despite a constitutional amendment incorporating the ECHR, remained reluctant to give it direct effect for several decades.[11]

4.011 The position in the UK is a complicated one. Prior to the Human Rights Act 1998 (HRA), the ECHR had no formal status in domestic law, with the result that ECHR rights effectively only existed on the international law plane.[12] The HRA 1998 radically changed this position, however, incorporating the ECHR into domestic law and requiring 'courts and other public authorities to

6 Mr Justice Bratza and Alison Padfield, 'Exhaustion of Domestic Remedies under the European Convention on Human Rights' (1998) 3 Judicial Review 220, 221.

7 ibid.

8 ibid 221–223.

9 ibid 223–224.

10 Bates (n 3) 158–159.

11 ibid 158–160.

12 ibid 163.

apply the ECHR directly within the British legal system [and empowering] individuals to plead the ECHR against public authorities in the courts'.[13] In particular, under s 6 of the HRA public authorities, including courts, 'must apply convention rights directly when reaching their decisions, [consequently] convention rights are today used regularly to interpret both legislation and the common law'.[14] However, it should be noted that the common law is of continued relevance in the human rights context,[15] and as stated by the UKSC 'the natural starting point in any dispute is to start with domestic law, and it is certainly not to focus exclusively on the Convention rights, without surveying the wider common law scene'.[16]

One of the most important features of the HRA 1998 is its requirement for legislation to 'So far as … possible … be read and given effect in a way which is compatible with the Convention rights',[17] although this 'does not affect the validity, continuing operation or enforcement of any incompatible primary legislation'[18] nor subordinate legislation if primary legislation prevents the removal of any incompatibility.[19] However, it should be noted that although this provision allows the courts to go beyond the traditional approach of ascertaining 'the true meaning of the statute, or establishing the intention of … Parliament',[20] they cannot adopt an interpretation which is 'inconsistent with a fundamental feature of [the] legislation'.[21] **4.012**

An example of a reading which would be held to be inconsistent in such a way can be found in the family court case of *In the Matter of Z (A Child)*.[22] The case concerned a child who was conceived with the plaintiff's sperm and a donor's egg, which was implanted into an American surrogate mother.[23] The issue was that under the relevant legislation in order for the child to be treated as the child of the plaintiff, a parental order from the court was required and this **4.013**

---

13 Pablo Santolaya Machetti and Javier García Roca, *Europe of Rights: A Compendium on the European Convention of Human Rights* (Martinus Nijhoff Publishers 2012) 43 <http://catdir.loc.gov/catdir/toc/fy13pdf01/2011050529.html> accessed 2 November 2019.

14 ibid 52.

15 See generally Mark Elliott, 'Beyond the European Convention: Human Rights and the Common Law' (2015) 68 Current Legal Problems 85.

16 *Kennedy v The Charity Commission* [2014] UKSC 20 [46].

17 Human Rights Act 1998 s 3(1).

18 ibid 3(1)(b).

19 ibid 3(1)(c).

20 Santolaya Machetti and García Roca (n 13) 52.

21 *Ghaidan v Godin-Mendoza* [2004] UKHL 30 [33].

22 *In the Matter of Z (A Child)* [2015] EWFC 73.

23 ibid 2.

had to be made by a couple and not a single parent.[24] As the plaintiff and the American surrogate mother were not a couple or in a relationship, the father asked the court to read down the relevant statutory provision as allowing an application to be made by only one person as opposed to a couple.[25]

4.014 The court refused to read down the legislation in this way, holding that the consistent statutory limitation of parental orders only being granted to couples, and not single parents, 'always has been, and remains … a "fundamental feature", a "cardinal" or "essential" principle of the legislation'. The court went on to note that the suggested interpretation 'would … ignore what is, as it has always been, a key feature of the scheme and scope of the legislation'.[26] In such a case the court can make a declaration of incompatibility under s 4 of the Act, although this remedy does little more than place political pressure on parliament to remedy the situation,[27] and that is in fact what the court did.[28]

4.015 Although the above brief introduction to the ECHR, the ECtHR and the HRA is by necessity an extremely compressed one, it suffices to lay the foundations for the remainder of this chapter, and it is not necessary or desirable to examine the matter as a whole any further. Instead, the next section will analyse ECtHR jurisprudence regarding the right that has been frequently considered with regard to arbitration, the Art 6(1) right to a fair trial.

C. ART 6(1) ECHR AND ARBITRATION

4.016 Art 6(1) ECHR provides that:

> In the determination of his civil rights and obligations or of any criminal charge against him, everyone is entitled to a fair and public hearing within a reasonable time by an independent and impartial tribunal established by law. Judgment shall be pronounced publicly but the press and public may be excluded from all or part of the trial in the interests of morals, public order or national security in a democratic society, where the interests of juveniles or the protection of the private life of the parties so require, or to the extent strictly necessary in the opinion of the court in special circumstances where publicity would prejudice the interests of justice.

24 ibid 1–6.

25 ibid.

26 ibid 37.

27 Santolaya Machetti and García Roca (n 13) 53.

28 *In the Matter of Z (A Child) (No 2)* [2016] EWHC 1191 (Fam).

The most important rights in the arbitration context,[29] which are encompassed within Art 6(1)[30] are: **4.017**

I. The right of access to a court;
II. The right to an independent and impartial tribunal established by law;
III. The right to a fair hearing, which includes the right to effectively participate in the trial, to have equality of arms and the right to a reasoned judgement;
IV. The right to trial within a reasonable time;
V. The right to a public trial.

It should be noted that although there are other ECHR rights which are potentially applicable to arbitration, for example, the Art 1 Protocol 1 right to peaceful enjoyment of possessions,[31] in general, the literature has focused on, and in many cases exclusively addressed, Art 6(1),[32] and this section will also only address that article. This is primarily because the procedural rights of Art 6(1) are the most important and applicable ECHR rights in the practice of, at least commercial, arbitration[33] and secondarily due to space constraints. **4.018**

It is also important to outline the structure of this section at this stage, as, unsurprisingly given the complexities of the ECHR, this is the most complicated section of this work so far. Firstly, this section will analyse the fundamental difference in ECHR law between voluntary and compulsory arbitration, including discussion about how third parties or non-signatories fit into this distinction. Secondly, it will analyse ECtHR jurisprudence regarding voluntary jurisprudence which mostly revolves around the waiver of ECHR rights, including discussion about whether there are any rights which cannot be waived or derogated from. Thirdly, it will look at ECtHR jurisprudence regarding compulsory arbitration and the ECHR rights which might be violated by such arbitrations. Fourthly and lastly, it will look at the possibility of remediating the violation of Art 6(1) rights through later court proceedings. **4.019**

---

29 Sebastian Besson, 'Arbitration and Human Rights' (2006) 24 ASA Bulletin 394, 396–397.

30 DJ Harris and others, *Law of the European Convention on Human Rights* (4th edn, Oxford University Press 2018) 399–459; cf Besson (n 29) 396–397.

31 *Case of OAO Neftyanaya Kompaniya Yukos v Russia* [2011] Application no 14902/04 (European Court of Human Rights); Besson (n 29) 397.

32 Besson (n 29); Marius Emberland, 'The Usefulness of Applying Human Rights Arguments in International Commercial Arbitration' (2003) 20 J. Int'l Arb. 355; Adam Samuel, 'Arbitration, Alternative Dispute Resolution Generally and the European Convention on Human Rights' (2004) 21 Journal of International Arbitration 413; William Robinson, 'The Effects of the Human Rights Act 1998 on Arbitration' (2002) 2002 Amicus Curiae 24; L Clover Alcolea, 'Trust Arbitration and the European Convention on Human Rights' (2018) 24 Trusts & Trustees 976.

33 Besson (n 29) 398.

1. Compulsory or voluntary arbitration?

4.020 The case of *X v The Federal Republic of Germany*,[34] which was a complicated employment case regarding a German teacher in a German school based in Spain where the employment contract contained an arbitration clause, laid the foundations of the fundamental difference in ECtHR jurisprudence between compulsory and voluntary arbitration. The court stated that:

> the inclusion of an arbitration clause in an agreement between individuals amounts legally to a partial renunciation of the exercise of those rights defined by Article 6 (I); nothing in the text of that Article nor of any other Article of the Convention explicitly prohibits such renunciation; whereas the commission is not entitled to assume that the Contracting states, in accepting the obligations arising under Article 6 (I), intended to prevent persons coming under their jurisdiction from entrusting the settlement of certain matters to arbitrators; whereas the disputed arbitration clause might have been regarded as contrary to the Convention if X. had signed it under constraint, which was not the case, whereas even though … the clause was a perfectly normal and indispensable insertion made at the request of the Minister for Foreign Affairs this fact did not invalidate the Applicant's consent, and he remained free to refuse his services …[35]

4.021 The seeds of the fundamental distinction between compulsory and voluntary arbitration can be seen in the courts holding that consent to an arbitration agreement amounts to a partial renunciation of Art 6(1) rights, but this would not have been so if X's consent was invalidated by 'constraint'. *A fortiori* a situation where consent was simply irrelevant, i.e. compulsory arbitration, would potentially violate Art 6(1).

4.022 The case of *Bramelid and Malmstrom v Sweden*,[36] which concerned a system of compulsory arbitration for the valuation of minority shares under Swedish law, built upon the above holding and firmly established the distinction between compulsory and voluntary arbitration in ECHR law. The Court stated that:

> a distinction must be drawn between voluntary arbitration and compulsory arbitration. Normally Article 6 poses no problem where arbitration is entered into voluntarily (cf Application No 1197/61, Yearbook 5, pages 88, 94 and 96). If, on the other hand, arbitration is compulsory in the sense of being required by law, as in this case, the parties have no option but to refer their dispute to an arbitration Board, and the Board must offer the guarantees set forth in Article 6 (1).[37]

---

34 *X v The Federal Republic of Germany* (1961) 5 Yearbook of the European Convention on Human Rights 88.

35 ibid 96.

36 *Bramelid & Malstrom v Sweden* [1983] Application nos 8588/79 & 8589/79 (European Court of Human Rights).

37 ibid 30.

The fundamental difference between voluntary and compulsory arbitration is that in the former a party has waived, either in whole or in part, their Art 6(1) rights, while in the latter they have not. As a result, the arbitral tribunal is required under the ECHR to act in accordance with Art 6(1). It is important to note that another key difference between voluntary and compulsory arbitration is the extent of state liability for breaches of Art 6(1). **4.023**

The case of *R v Switzerland*[38] held that states remain liable for voluntary arbitration, although only if 'and only insofar as, the national courts were required to intervene'.[39] This was confirmed by the later case of *Jakob Boss Sohne KG v Germany*,[40] which stated that the fact an arbitration is voluntary: **4.024**

> does not mean … that the respondent State's responsibility is completely excluded … as the arbitration award had to be recognised by the German Courts and be given executory effect by them. The courts thereby exercised a certain control and guarantee as to the fairness and correctness of the arbitration proceedings which they considered to have been carried out in conformity with fundamental rights and in particular with the right of the applicant company to be heard.[41]

The case of *Nordström v Netherlands* further developed this point in dealing with a voluntary arbitration agreement, stating that: **4.025**

> the Commission considers that account must be taken not only of the arbitration agreement between the parties and the nature of the private arbitration proceedings, but also of the legislative framework providing for such proceedings in order to determine whether the domestic courts retained some measure of control of the arbitration proceedings and whether this control has been properly exercised in the concrete case. The Commission notes in particular that Dutch law contains rules which permit the courts to quash arbitral awards …[42]

The court then went on to consider the specific grounds of review under Dutch law as well as judgments of the Dutch Supreme Court, stating that: **4.026**

> Under Dutch law an arbitral award may be quashed on, inter alia, grounds of public order interests … In view of this interpretation of the Supreme Court of what could be considered to be contrary to public order interests, the Commission observes that the applicant's argument … has no basis in Dutch law. It considers that Art 6-1 … does not require the Dutch Courts to apply a different criterion in determining whether or not to quash an arbitral award. It finds it reasonable that in this respect Dutch law requires

38 *R v Switzerland* [1987] Application no 10881/84 (ECtHR).

39 ibid 102.

40 *Jakob Boss Sohne KG v Germany* [1991] Application no 18479/91 (European Court of Human Rights).

41 ibid.

42 *Nordström v Netherlands* [1996] Application no 28101/95 (European Court of Human Rights).

> strong reasons for quashing an already rendered award, since the quashing will often mean that a long and costly arbitral procedure will become useless.[43]

4.027 The most recent ECtHR case on the matter, *Mutu and Pechstein v Switzerland*,[44] concerning a sports law arbitration in Switzerland, held that even though the Court of Arbitration for Sport (CAS) was 'neither a domestic court nor any other institution of Swiss public law',[45] Switzerland's liability under the ECHR could still be engaged,[46] because:

> Swiss law confers jurisdiction on the Federal Court to examine the validity of CAS awards … In addition, that supreme court dismissed the appeals of both applicants in the present case, thereby giving the relevant awards force of law in the Swiss legal order.[47]

4.028 The above leads to two conclusions; firstly, it would seem that states can only be liable to the extent that their legal framework allows the courts to intervene in an arbitration, whether by supervising the tribunal or enforcing its awards. Furthermore, if the courts have such supervisory powers, the ECtHR will not interfere even if these powers are limited or narrow in scope, for example reasonable limitations on annulment, or set aside. Secondly, if a state's legal framework does not allow its courts to intervene in voluntary arbitrations, as arguably happens in the case of ICSID arbitrations, it may be that a state is simply not liable for any alleged breaches of Art 6(1). This would seem to follow from the fact that all of the above cases mention that the courts had a supervisory power over arbitration and from the explicit wording in *R v Switzerland* discussed above.[48] Furthermore, the case of *Tabbane v Switzerland*[49] held that Art 6(1) did not prevent parties from waiving their right to court review of an arbitral award[50] and in such circumstances, the scope for court intervention, and thus state liability, will be extremely limited.

4.029 The cases also give us one definition of compulsory arbitration, an arbitration which is 'required by law', and by implication also voluntary arbitration, an arbitration based on an arbitration agreement which the parties have entered into without constraint, freely and voluntarily. However, although the definition of a compulsory arbitration provided by *Bramelid* remained good law until

43 ibid.

44 *Mutu and Pechstein v Switzerland* [2018] Applications nos 40575/10 and 67474/10.

45 ibid 65.

46 ibid 67.

47 ibid 25.

48 See also ibid 65–66.

49 *Tabbane v Switzerland* [2016] Application no 41069/12 (ECtHr).

50 ibid 30–36.

2016,[51] it requires updating in the light of *Mutu and Pechstein v Switzerland*,[52] where the court held that:

> the only choice in the second applicant's case was between accepting the arbitration clause and thus earning her living by practising her sport professionally, or not accepting it and being obliged to refrain completely from earning a living from her sport at that level ... Having regard to the restriction that non-acceptance of the arbitration clause would have entailed for her professional life, it cannot be asserted that she had accepted that clause freely and unequivocally. The Court thus concludes that, even though it had not been imposed by law but by the ISU regulations, the acceptance of CAS jurisdiction ... must be regarded as 'compulsory' arbitration within the meaning of its case-law ... The arbitration proceedings therefore had to afford the safeguards secured by Article 6(1) of the convention.[53]

It is possible to draw two conclusions from the above paragraphs. Firstly, compulsory arbitration includes arbitrations procured by what can loosely be called 'economic duress' and, *a fortiori*, arbitrations procured by actual duress or compulsion such as threats of violence. Secondly, it would seem from the courts wording that all arbitrations where the clause was not freely and unequivocally accepted[54] are classified as compulsory. This would be a radical departure from existing ECtHR jurisprudence,[55] for example, *Suda v Czech Republic*.[56] That case concerned minority shareholders in a public limited company, which was being taken over, and who wanted to have the courts re-evaluate the value of their shareholdings. However, this was not possible as the company in which they held shares and the purchasing company had signed a contract in which shares were to be valued by an arbitral tribunal and all the minority shareholders attempts to challenge this in the Czech courts failed. The court nevertheless stated: **4.030**

> In the present case, it should be noted that the applicant himself did not waive the possibility of submitting the dispute to an ordinary court or the exercise of the guarantees provided for in Article 6(1) of the Convention. The parties nevertheless agree that it was not a compulsory arbitration, that is to say imposed by law, but an arbitration contracted by third parties ...[57]

---

51 ibid 26.

52 *Mutu and Pechstein v Switzerland* (n 44).

53 ibid 113–115.

54 *Mutu and Pechstein v Switzerland* (n 44) para 114.

55 'Sports Arbitration Revisited Pt II: Mutu and Pechstein v Switzerland' (*Keep Calm Talk Law*) <http://www.keepcalmtalklaw.co.uk/sports-arbitration-revisited-pt-ii-mutu-and-pechstein-v-switzerland/> accessed 7 November 2019.

56 *Suda v Czech Republic* [2010] Application no 1643/06 (ECtHR).

57 ibid 50.

4.031 It is uncertain whether the court was merely acquiescing in the parties' joint categorisation of the arbitration agreement, or whether it really did not consider it a compulsory arbitration. In any event, after *Mutu* cases involving facts such as those that arose in *Suda* would be categorised as compulsory arbitration, and this seems more logical than inventing another term for arbitration which is neither voluntary nor compulsory. However, as will be shown below, this does not mean that all or even most cases where a third party or non-signatory is held bound to an arbitration clause constitute cases of forced arbitration.

(a) The problems of classifying arbitrations involving third parties or non-signatories

4.032 In general, when a court finds that a third party or non-signatory is bound by an arbitration clause it does so based on 'a common intent of the parties',[58] and such rulings are therefore based 'on consent'.[59] In consequence, 'The basic issue therefore remains: who is a party to the clause, or has adhered to it, or eventually is estopped from contending that it has not adhered to it'.[60] It is true that the consent we are discussing here is merely 'assumed consent',[61] but ultimately 'the methodological basis for being bound by an arbitration agreement is, in principle, the same for signatories as for non-signatory third parties'.[62]

4.033 The result of this is that one cannot say third-party or non-signatory arbitrations go against the consent of those parties and thus necessarily violate their Art 6(1) rights. Instead, the issue is whether the doctrines used to infer or assume such consent are compatible with Art 6(1) ECHR, and this, in turn, entails determining whether a doctrine is compatible with the requirements for waiver under the ECHR. Such an investigation would be outside the scope of this work, particularly as many of the techniques used to bind third parties or non-signatories to arbitration, such as agency, group of companies,[63] assignment or subrogation,[64] are not applicable to trust arbitration. In consequence, this book will analyse the compatibility of the various solutions proposed to bind third parties, i.e. the beneficiaries, to a trust arbitration clause alongside the requirements for a valid waiver of Art 6(1) ECHR rights.

---

58 Albert Jan Van den Berg, *International Arbitration 2006: Back to Basics?*, ICCA Congress series no 13 (ICCA & Kluwer Law International 2007) 343.

59 ibid.

60 ibid.

61 Nathalie Voser, 'Multi-Party Disputes and Joinder of Third Parties', in *50 Years of the New York Convention*, ICCA Congress series no 14 (2009) 343, 371.

62 ibid.

63 ibid 372–377.

64 Audley Sheppard, 'Chapter 10: Third Party Non-Signatories in English Arbitration Law' (2016) 37 The Evolution and Future of International Arbitration, International Arbitration Law Library 183, 188–189.

However, before doing so, it is possible to say as a general point that where a third party or non-signatory is bound without any imputed or assumed consent, as would appear to have been the case in *Suda*, this will almost certainly be a violation of Art 6(1). Indeed, given the holding of *Mutu*, it would seem that such arbitrations would be considered compulsory arbitrations and thus subject to the requirements of Art 6(1) in their entirety. **4.034**

2. Requirements for a valid waiver of ECHR rights

As will be seen below, the ECtHR has established four requirements in its jurisprudence in order for a waiver to be effective, it must be: **4.035**

I. Free;
II. Unequivocal;
III. Permissible;
IV. Attended by minimum safeguards commensurate to its importance.

(a) The need for free and informed consent

The leading case on the need for free consent in order to waive one's Art 6(1) rights is *Deweer v Belgium*.[65] The case concerned proceedings brought against a Belgian butcher for exceeding the allowed price for pork.[66] The prosecutor ordered that his shop be closed within 48 hours and until the trial, unless he chose to close the case by paying a set sum of 10,000 BF, which was considerably less than the cost of the potential closure of his shop and the maximum 30,000,000 BF fine if the matter went to court.[67] The court held that the applicant had not waived his Art 6(1) right of access to the courts as his consent was subject to constraint, because of 'the closure order of 30 September 1974',[68] which would have resulted in Mr Deweer suffering 'considerable loss'.[69] Moreover, there was a 'flagrant disproportion between the two alternatives facing the applicant. The relative moderation of the sum demanded in fact tells against the Government's argument since it added to the pressure brought to bear by the closure order. The moderation rendered the pressure so compelling that it is not surprising that Mr. Deweer yielded.'[70] **4.036**

The court, therefore, adopts a liberal interpretation of what duress or coercion may amount to, with one writer stating that 'the Court seems to be attached **4.037**

65 *Deweer v Belgium* [1980] Application no 6903/75 (European Court of Human Rights).
66 ibid 7–8.
67 ibid 9–13.
68 ibid 23.
69 ibid.
70 ibid.

to a realistic understanding of what coercion or duress may mean, especially in a bargaining process'.[71] This approach continues to be applied by the ECtHR, as can be seen in the case of *Mutu and Pechstein v Switzerland* where the court held that an arbitration clause was not accepted freely[72] where:

> the [applicant's] only choice … was between accepting the arbitration clause and thus earning her living by practising her sport professionally, or not accepting it and being obliged to refrain completing from earning a living from her sport at that level.[73]

4.038 On the other hand, the ECtHR has set a high bar for what can broadly be called 'economic duress', stating that there was no issue with the validity of the waiver in the three most recent arbitration cases which had come before the court[74] as:

> in those three cases, the applicants – a businessman and commercial companies – had been free to establish commercial relations with the partners of their choosing without affecting their freedom and capacity to engage, with other partners, in projects within their respective fields of activity.[75]

4.039 Furthermore, in *Mutu* itself the court rejected the argument of the first applicant, a footballer, that the disparity in contractual negotiating power between him and Chelsea meant that his consent was not free, stating that:

> The court is able to accept that a major football club with considerable financial resources may have a greater negotiating strength than an individual player, even a famous one. That being said, not only has the first applicant failed to adduce evidence that all Chelsea players were obliged to give their consent to the arbitration clause, he has also failed to show that other professional football clubs, which perhaps have more modest financial means, would have refused to hire him on the basis of a contract providing for dispute settlement in the ordinary courts.[76]

4.040 The difference in treatment as regards the two applicants would seem to mean that 'The Court appears to make a distinction between the freedom to earn a living from sports and the freedom to earn the highest possible salary in the

71 Olivier De Schutter, 'Waiver of Rights and State Paternalism under the European Convention on Human Rights' (2000) 51 Northern Ireland Legal Quarterly 481, 489.

72 *Mutu and Pechstein v Switzerland* (n 44) para 114.

73 ibid 113.

74 *Tabbane v Switzerland* (n 49); *Eiffage SA v Switzerland* [2009] Application no 1742/05 (European Court of Human Rights); *Transado-Transportes Fluviais do Sado, SA v Portugal* [2003] Application no 35943/02 (European Court of Human Rights).

75 *Mutu and Pechstein v Switzerland* (n 44) para 107.

76 ibid 120.

discipline'.[77] It would seem then that 'economic duress' in the sense which invalidates a waiver of Art 6(1) ECHR means not just a loss of financial opportunities but, effectively, an inability to make a living from one's discipline if one does not agree to an Art 6(1) waiver. In the case of a company, it would mean an inability to exist as a company in that field of activity.[78]

The importance of the court's strict approach to invalidating a waiver of Art 6(1) on economic grounds for our purposes lies in the fact that one could argue that a forfeiture clause or condition precedent in a trust deed requiring one to accept arbitration in order to benefit from that instrument amounts to a form of duress or coercion. It is clear, however, from the ECtHR's case law, that a mere lack of receiving, even a very significant, financial gain on pain of submitting to arbitration would not amount to duress or coercion sufficient to invalidate an Art 6(1) ECHR waiver. It may be that the court would be more sympathetic to the plight of a person who is completely dependent on receiving a benefit under the trust in order to live, but it is submitted that such a situation would be rare. **4.041**

It is not, however, sufficient for waivers to be free in the sense that duress or coercion is absent from the bargaining process, they must also be 'informed'[79] or 'made in full knowledge of the surrounding circumstances'.[80] The leading case in this regard is *Pfeifer and Plankl v Austria*,[81] which concerned criminal proceedings where the applicants had argued bias by the judges in their domestic case but were found by the domestic courts to have waived their right to challenge the composition of the court.[82] The court held that: **4.042**

> In the instant case it is sufficient to note that Judge Kaiser on his own initiative approached Mr Pfeifer in the absence of his lawyer, the latter not having been summoned ... He put to him a question which was essentially one of law, whose implications Mr Pfeifer as a layman was not in a position to appreciate completely. A waiver of rights expressed there and then in such circumstances appears questionable, to say the least. The fact that the applicant stated that he did not think it necessary for his lawyer

77 Guest Blogger, 'Mutu and Pechstein v. Switzerland: Strasbourg's Assessment of the Right to a Fair Hearing in Sports Arbitration' (*Strasbourg Observers*, 30 November 2018) <https://strasbourgobservers.com/2018/11/30/mutu-and-pechstein-v-switzerland-strasbourgs-assessment-of-the-right-to-a-fair-hearing-in-sports-arbitration/> accessed 8 November 2019.

78 *Mutu and Pechstein v Switzerland* (n 44) para 107.

79 De Schutter (n 71) 491.

80 *Looking to the Future: Essays on International Law in Honor of W. Michael Reisman* (Brill Nijhoff 2011) 23 <https://brill.com/view/title/15834> accessed 8 November 2019.

81 *Pfeifer and Plankl v Austria* [1992] Application no 10802/84 (European Court of Human Rights).

82 ibid 35–37.

> to be present makes no difference. Thus … the circumstances surrounding the applicant's decision deprived it of any validity from the point of view of the Convention.[83]

4.043 Another example is the case of *DH v The Czech Republic*,[84] which concerned the placement of special needs Roma children in special schools under a regime where the consent of the parents was crucial. The court held:

> the Court is not satisfied that the parents of the Roma children, who were members of a disadvantaged community and often poorly educated, were capable of weighing up all the aspects of the situation and the consequences of giving their consent. The Government themselves admitted that consent in this instance had been given by means of a signature on a pre-completed form that contained no information on the available alternatives or the differences between the special-school curriculum and the curriculum followed in other schools. Nor do the domestic authorities appear to have taken any additional measures to ensure that the Roma parents received all the information they needed to make an informed decision or were aware of the consequences that giving their consent would have for their children's future.[85]

4.044 It would appear from these cases that the circumstances in which the court has found a lack of informed consent are usually extreme, and far removed from the situation in a trust arbitration case, where one would expect the trustees, or possibly the executor in the case of a will trust, to explain the situation to the beneficiaries. Moreover, if the trust is a high value one, then it is likely independent legal advice would be taken by the beneficiaries. In such circumstances, it is hard to see how an argument could be made that consent to a trust arbitration clause was not 'informed' or 'made in full knowledge of the surrounding circumstances', unless, of course, the person had special characteristics such as a lack of education, or a disability or was a minor. Equally, if the trustees and/or the executor did not explain the situation to the beneficiaries, and the latter didn't take legal advice then perhaps an argument could be made that the waiver was invalid. The special issues regarding minors or otherwise mentally incapable individuals will be addressed below, but it can be seen that in general trust arbitration clauses should not raise issues regarding free and informed consent.

(b) The need for an unequivocal waiver

4.045 It is, unfortunately, more difficult to define what is meant by an unequivocal waiver in ECtHR case law, as the court has not provided a standalone definition of the term but rather has merely ruled on situations which do or do not

83 ibid 38–39.

84 *DH v The Czech Republic* [2007] Application no 57325/00 (European Court of Human Rights).

85 ibid 203.

amount to an unequivocal waiver. The fact that the ECtHR has repeatedly upheld the compatibility of voluntary arbitration clauses[86] would seem to imply that arbitration clauses generally constitute an unequivocal waiver of Art 6(1). Indeed, in *R v Switzerland* the court stated, 'In the present case arbitration was not required by law. In signing an arbitration agreement, the applicant waived his right to bring the dispute before an ordinary court ... It follows that an arbitration agreement entails a renunciation of the exercise of the rights secured by Article 6 para 1, provided that the agreement was not signed under duress.'[87]

Sadly, this position is somewhat complicated by the cases of *Suovaniemi v Finland*[88] and *Mutu and Pechstein v Switzerland.*[89] In *Suovaniemi*, the court stated: **4.046**

> Not only was the submission to arbitration voluntary but, in addition, during the proceedings before the arbitrators the applicants clearly abstained from pursuing their challenge against [that] arbitrator ... [Although] the impartiality of one of the arbitrators was open to doubt under domestic law ... the applicants unequivocally accepted this state of affairs in the course of the arbitration proceedings.[90]

The wording of the court would seem to raise the possibility that if a party maintains their challenge to an arbitrator their waiver of Art 6(1) rights, or at least of the right to an impartial tribunal, might not be waived. This was, in fact, explicitly confirmed in the case of *Mutu,* where the court stated: **4.047**

> In the present case, the court notes that ... the applicant brought a challenge against the arbitrator appointed by Chelsea ... whose independence and impartiality he was disputing ... Consequently, unlike the decision reached in Suoveniemi and others ... it cannot be considered that, by accepting the arbitration clause in his contract and by choosing to take his case to the CAS – and not to a national court, as authorised by Article 42 of the 201 Rules –, the applicant had 'unequivocally' waived his right to challenge the independence and impartiality of the CAS in any dispute that might arise between him and Chelsea.[91]

---

86 *X v The Federal Republic of Germany* (n 34); *R v Switzerland* (n 38); *Jakob Boss Sohne KG v Germany* (n 40); *Osmo SUOVANIEMI and others v Finland* [1999] Application no 31737/96 (ECtHR); *Eiffage SA v Switzerland* (n 74); *Tabbane v Switzerland* (n 49); *Transado-Transportes Fluviais Do Sado, SA v Portugal* [2003] Application no 35943/02 (European Court of Human Rights).

87 *R v Switzerland* (n 38) 100–101.

88 *Osmo SUOVANIEMI and others v Finland* (n 86).

89 *Mutu and Pechstein v Switzerland* (n 44).

90 *Osmo SUOVANIEMI and others v Finland* (n 86) 5–6.

91 *Mutu and Pechstein v Switzerland* (n 44) para 122.

4.048 As noted by commentators, 'This part of the judgment has potentially extremely wide implications beyond sports arbitration, as the Court seems to indicate that any challenge to the independence or impartiality of an arbitrator could harm the validity of an arbitration clause freely consented to.'[92] If this interpretation is correct, it would be deeply troubling as even unsuccessful or unmeritorious challenges to arbitrators could be sufficient to impugn the validity of a waiver of Art 6(1) rights and render the arbitral process a violation of the ECHR. It would also seem to be a wholly illogical approach to the issue of consent, as the mere fact that a person challenges an arbitrator does not mean that they do not consent to arbitration, rather it means that they are disputing that the arbitration should be conducted by person X or Y.

4.049 Moreover, it seems absurd that if a person is making a wholly unmeritorious complaint about an arbitrator's impartiality in order to delay or complicate the arbitration, a clear case of engaging in unethical guerrilla tactics,[93] this should be interpreted as a revocation of a valid waiver of Art 6(1) rights or at least as rendering their waiver equivocal. It is unclear how the court will approach the issue in future cases, but it is to be hoped that it will clarify the matter in a rational manner, particularly due to the advantages it accepts arbitration has over state court litigation,[94] and its earlier more reasonable jurisprudence in *Deweer*.[95] In any event, as will be shown later, given that ECHR compliant court proceedings can remediate earlier non-compliant proceedings, as well as the requirement for exhaustion of domestic remedies, it is unlikely that this will have as much practical effect. This is because in most cases parties would be able and required to challenge the proceedings in state courts before raising a claim before the ECtHR and as long as these proceedings are Art 6(1) compliant this should remedy any violations in the arbitral procedure.

4.050 Another key issue to note is that it is accepted that a waiver need not be explicit,[96] or in writing,[97] but can be merely tacit, something that the ECtHR has

---

92 'Asser International Sports Law Blog | The "Victory" of the Court of Arbitration for Sport at the European Court of Human Rights: The End of the Beginning for the CAS' <https://www.asser.nl/SportsLaw/Blog/post/the-victory-of-the-court-of-arbitration-for-sport-at-the-european-court-of-human-rights-the-end-of-the-beginning-for-the-cas> accessed 9 November 2019.

93 Günther J Horvath and Stephen Wilske (eds), *Guerrilla Tactics in International Arbitration* (Kluwer Law International 2013) 10–11.

94 *Deweer v Belgium* (n 65) para 49; *Tabbane v Switzerland* (n 49) para 36; *Mutu and Pechstein v Switzerland* (n 44) paras 97–98.

95 *Deweer v Belgium* (n 65) 100–101.

96 De Schutter (n 71) 493; *Looking to the Future: Essays on International Law in Honor of W. Michael Reisman* (n 80) 23.

97 *Looking to the Future: Essays on International Law in Honor of W. Michael Reisman* (n 80) 23.

confirmed on multiple occasions.[98] One case of this would be where a person has a right to ask for a public hearing but does not ask for one.[99] Another example would be where it would be unusual to have a public hearing, and so an applicant would be expected to ask for one if they wanted one.[100] Some authors have therefore concluded that in certain circumstances, mere passivity on the part of an applicant can lead to a tacit waiver of an ECHR right,[101] although the circumstances in which the ECtHR will accept this as valid are complicated, at least in criminal cases.[102] In any event, it would seem clear that the taking of a benefit under a trust by a beneficiary would amount to a valid waiver, as the beneficiary would be taking in circumstances where it was clear that they would have to arbitrate any disputes about their benefit or that their right was otherwise conditional on, or limited by, the requirement to arbitrate disputes under the trust.

(c) Permissible

In the interest of succinctness, this section will include several elements of permissibility: **4.051**

I. First, a waiver must 'not relate to underogable rights';[103]
II. Second, a waiver must be permitted by domestic law;[104]
III. Third, waivers must not be contrary to an important public interest.[105]

Each of these aspects will be considered in turn below.

(i) Underogable rights

One clear example of an underogable right can be seen in *DH v The Czech Republic*,[106] where the court stated, 'In view of the fundamental importance of the prohibition of racial discrimination ... the Grand Chamber considers that, even assuming the conditions referred to ... above were satisfied, no waiver **4.052**

98 *Hakansson and Struesson v Sweden* [1990] Application no 11855/85 (European Court of Human Rights); *Axelsson v Sweden* [1989] European Court of Human Rights 12213/86; *Schuler-Zgraggen v Switzerland* [1993] Application no 14518/89 (European Court of Human Rights); *Strag Datajanster AB v Sweden* [2005] Application no (European Court of Human Rights).

99 *Hakansson and Struesson v Sweden* (n 98); *Axelsson & Ors v Sweden* [1990] Application no 11960/86 (European Court of Human Rights); *Strag Datajanster AB v Sweden* (n 98).

100 *Schuler-Zgraggen v Switzerland* (n 98).

101 Jorgen Aall, 'Waiver of Human Rights' (2010) 28 Nordic Journal of Human Rights 300, 324–329.

102 ibid.

103 *Looking to the Future: Essays on International Law in Honor of W. Michael Reisman* (n 80) 427.

104 ibid 428.

105 ibid; Aall, 'Waiver of Human Rights' (n 101) 319–321.

106 *DH v The Czech Republic* (n 84).

of the right not to be subjected to racial discrimination can be accepted, as it would be counter to an important public interest'.[107] In the context of Art 6(1) it has been stated that its 'basic requirements … are mandatory',[108] with such requirements including the right to an independent and impartial tribunal, which in arbitration would mean the right to independent and impartial arbitrators.[109] However, this is directly contrary to the judgment of the ECtHR in *Suovaniemi v Finland*[110] where the court stated:

> Without having to decide whether a similar waiver would be valid in the context of purely judicial proceedings the Court comes to the conclusion that in the circumstances of the present case concerning arbitral proceedings the applicants' waiver of their right to an impartial judge should be regarded as effective for Convention purposes.[111]

4.053 This judgment, moreover, emphasises the flexibility and leniency of the ECtHR when dealing with cases concerning voluntary arbitration, which was restated in the most recent case of *Mutu*:

> in matters of commercial and sports arbitration to which consent has been given freely, lawfully and unequivocally, the notions of independence and impartially may be construed flexibly, in so far as the very essence of the arbitration system is based on the appointment of the decision-making bodies, or at least part of them, by the parties to the dispute.[112]

4.054 In any event, the right to an impartial and independent tribunal under the ECHR is unlikely to have much practical effect in arbitral disputes, as almost all jurisdictions recognise lack of impartiality or independence as a ground for challenging an arbitrator or arbitral award,[113] as do all major institutional rules,[114] and it is also a possible ground for challenge under the NYC in certain circumstances.[115]

---

107 ibid 204.

108 Jorgen Aall, 'Waiver of Human Rights' (2011) 29 Nordic Journal of Human Rights 206, 210–211.

109 ibid.

110 *Osmo SUOVANIEMI and others v Finland* (n 86).

111 ibid 6.

112 *Mutu and Pechstein v Switzerland* (n 44) para 146.

113 UNCITRAL Model Law on International Commercial Arbitration s 12(2); Federal Arbitration Act s 10(a)(2).

114 See e.g. International Chamber of Commerce Rules of Arbitration 2017 s 14; London Court of International Arbitration Rules 2014 s 10; Stockholm Chamber of Commerce Arbitration Rules 2017; ibid 19; Vienna International Arbitral Centre Rules 2018 s 20; Hong Kong International Arbitration Centre Rules 2018 s 11; UNCITRAL Arbitration Rules 1976 s 10; Singapore International Arbitration Centre Rules 2016 s 14.

115 Stavroula Angoura, 'Arbitrator's Impartiality Under Article V(1)(D) of the New York Convention' (2019) 15 Asian International Arbitration Journal 29.

(ii) Permissible by domestic law

This requirement has been alluded to in several cases,[116] and as it is self-explanatory, it is not necessary to examine it in any detail. In any event, it is clear that a state in legislating for arbitration must be taken as permitting the relevant Art 6(1) waiver necessary for that legislative scheme to function, and it appears unlikely that any European state would explicitly legislate to forbid ECHR waivers given all the complications that would cause. **4.055**

(iii) Not contrary to an important public interest

This requirement was formulated in the case of *Hakansson and Strusesson v Sweden*[117] where the court stated, 'a waiver must be made in an unequivocal manner and must not run counter to any important public interest'.[118] Unfortunately, as noted by the literature,[119] the ECtHR has not elaborated or explained this condition in any great depth. However, one possible interpretation is that, 'it coincides, at least partly, with the condition that an individual cannot renounce rights the abandonment of which would or could adversely affect the rights of others or the functioning of the European mechanism for the protection of human rights'.[120] **4.056**

One example that is reflected in the literature is an alleged waiver of the 'right not to be subjected to racial discrimination',[121] and it had been stated that cases where there would be 'important public interests' such that a waiver of the right to the ordinary courts in favour of arbitration would not be suitable, include 'disputes concerning family law in a wide sense: conditions for marriage and its dissolution, paternity, custody …'.[122] In general, it does not seem that trust arbitration clauses would reach the seemingly high bar necessary to be contrary to an important public interest. **4.057**

---

116 *Colozza v Italy* [1985] Application no 9024/80 (European Court of Human Rights) [28–29]; *Andandonskiy v Russia* [2006] Application no 24015/02 (European Court of Human Rights) [54]; *Vozhigov v Russia* [2007] Application no 5953/02 (European Court of Human Rights) [57].

117 *Hakansson and Struesson v Sweden* (n 98).

118 ibid 66.

119 *Looking to the Future: Essays on International Law in Honor of W. Michael Reisman* (n 80) 428.

120 ibid.

121 *DH v The Czech Republic* (n 84) para 204.

122 Aall, 'Waiver of Human Rights' (n 108) 208.

(d) The need for a waiver of a right to be attended by minimum guarantees commensurate to its importance

4.058 This requirement was established in the case of *Pfeifer and Plankl v Austria*,[123] where the court stated, 'the Court agrees with the Commission that in the case of procedural rights a waiver, in order to be effective for Convention purposes, requires minimum guarantees commensurate to its importance'.[124] The case of *Suovaniemi v Finland* sheds some light on what those 'minimum guarantees' might consist of, stating that 'considering that throughout the arbitration the applicants were represented by counsel, the waiver was accompanied by sufficient guarantees commensurate to its importance'.[125]

4.059 It is obvious that in most trust dispute cases parties will be represented by legal counsel and at the point of accepting or disclaiming a benefit under the trust will also have access to legal advice, particularly if the trust is of a high value, or at the very least the matter will be explained to them by the trustees or executor who may also be legally qualified. In consequence, it is unlikely that trust arbitration clauses would be found not to be attended with minimum guarantees commensurate to the importance of waiving one's Art 6(1) rights.

4.060 The above covers all the requirements necessary for a valid waiver to one's Art 6(1) rights and demonstrates that in most cases there should be no issue with a trust arbitration clause amounting to a waiver of Art 6(1) rights. Nevertheless, this work will next discuss, *in abundantia cautio*, the rulings of the ECtHR as regards compulsory arbitration, and consider the possible issues that might arise in the context of trust arbitration.

3. The ECHR and compulsory arbitration

4.061 This chapter will analyse the various ECtHR cases which have considered situations of compulsory arbitration and look at the most problematic rights under the ECHR for such arbitrations. It is not possible to discuss all of the possibly relevant rights under Art 6(1), particularly as some, such as the right to an impartial and independent tribunal, have already been discussed above, and thus this section will only address the following three rights:

I. The right of access to a court including the possibility of receiving legal aid to exercise that right;

123 *Pfeifer and Plankl v Austria* (n 81).

124 ibid 37.

125 *Osmo SUOVANIEMI and others v Finland* (n 86) 6.

II. The right to a public hearing;
III. The right to present your case.

Each of these rights will be discussed in turn below.

(a) The right of access to a court

The wording of Art 6(1) requires that a case be heard 'by an independent and impartial tribunal established by law'. Each of these two requirements will be dealt with below, in reverse order, as the latter condition is harder to satisfy than the former; thus if an arbitral tribunal is not established by law under the ECHR then there is no need to consider issues of independence and impartiality. **4.062**

(i) Established by law

The most recent case addressing this requirement in the context of arbitration is *Mutu and Pechstein v Switzerland*,[126] where the court stated: **4.063**

> This access to a court is not necessarily to be understood as access to a court of the classic kind, integrated within the standard judicial machinery of the country; thus, the 'tribunal' may be a body set up to determine a limited number of specific issues, provided always that it offers the appropriate guarantees ... Article 6 therefore does not preclude the establishment of arbitral tribunals in order to settle certain pecuniary disputes between individuals [here the court makes reference to *Suda v Czech Republic*].[127]

The court further noted that:

> A court or tribunal is characterised in that substantive sense by its judicial function, that is to say determining matters within its competence on the basis of legal rules, with full jurisdiction and after proceedings conducted in a prescribed manner ... In addition, only an institution that has full jurisdiction and satisfies a number of requirements, such as independence from the executive and also from the parties, merits the designation 'tribunal'.[128]

Surprisingly the court went on to hold that the CAS met these requirements, even though it was 'the emanation of a private-law foundation',[129] as a result of 'the combined effect of the PILA and the Federal Court's case-law'.[130] In particular, the court observed that the CAS: **4.064**

126 *Mutu and Pechstein v Switzerland* (n 44).
127 ibid 94.
128 ibid 140.
129 ibid 149; ibid 150–159.
130 *Mutu and Pechstein v Switzerland* (n 44) para 149.

> was endowed with full jurisdiction to entertain, on the basis of legal rules and after proceedings conducted in a prescribed manner, any question of fact or law submitted to it in the context of the disputes before it … Its awards resolved such disputes in a judicial manner and they could be appealed to the Federal Court … Moreover, the Federal Court, in its settled case-law, has regarded the CAS awards as 'proper judgements comparable with those of a national court'.[131]

(ii) The need for an independent and impartial tribunal

4.065 The seminal case regarding compulsory arbitration and issues of independence and impartiality is *Bramelid and Malmstrom v Sweden*,[132] where it was stated that:

> in the arbitration system designed for dealing with the compulsory purchase of shares, it is inevitable that the Arbitration Board's independence of one of the parties cannot always be guaranteed. In regard to their relationship with the arbitrators they have themselves appointed, the parties may not always be on an equal footing. In this case, the minority shareholders, who included the applicants, had no practical means of reaching an agreement over the choice of their arbitrator, since the law states that their choice must be unanimous. They were therefore obliged to have their arbitrator appointed by an authority …
>
> On the other hand, the opposing party, Ahlens, was able to choose its arbitrator for itself; it chose Mr Lofgren, chartered accountant. It is no secret that Ahlens is one of a number of high-powered commercial enterprises that are constantly having to entrust chartered accountants with important assignments … in which the agent is required to take the company's side and defend its interests.
>
> Considering the position of the arbitrators in relation to the parties appointing them, the Commission notes a degree of imbalance in this case which the appointment of the third arbitrator did nothing to correct … it considers that there must be a rigorous guarantee of equality between the parties in regard to the influence they exercise on the composition of the court.[133]

4.066 In some respects, the issue of bias and party appointed arbitrators is a perennial one, and the current leading case regarding arbitration and the ECHR, *Mutu and Pechstein v Switzerland*[134] likewise had to consider the issue in the context of the CAS system for selecting arbitrators. The court held that:

> In the present case, the arbitral panel which ruled on the dispute … was made up of three arbitrators, all chosen from the list drawn up by the ICAS … Even the applicant's ability to appoint the arbitrator of her choosing was limited by the obligation to

131 ibid.

132 *Bramelid & Malstrom v Sweden* (n 36).

133 ibid 38–39.

134 *Mutu and Pechstein v Switzerland* (n 44).

> use this list … such that the applicant did not have full freedom of choice – whereas such freedom is the rule, for example, in commercial arbitration … While the Court is prepared to acknowledge that the organisations which were likely to be involved in disputes with athletes before the CAS had real influence over the mechanism for appointing arbitrators, as applicable at the relevant time, it cannot be concluded that, solely on account of this influence, the list of arbitrators, or even a majority thereof, was composed of arbitrators who could not be regarded as independent and impartial, on an individual basis, whether objectively or subjectively, vis-à-vis those organisations.[135]

The above might be seen to reflect a softening of approach by the ECtHR, but it is important to note the fundamental differences between *Bramelid* and *Mutu*. In the former, only one party was able to pick an arbitrator and selected one who had a potential financial interest in being sympathetic to it; in the latter, however, both parties were able to pick an arbitrator of their choice, albeit from a list that was vetted by the CAS. Even if many of the arbitrators on this list may have had interests in common with the sports organisations which appointed them, a set number of independent arbitrators was required.[136] This list consisted of over 300 persons, and the applicant did not submit any evidence to impugn their impartiality.[137] In short, it appears that the court is willing to adopt a realistic and flexible approach in arbitration cases, so that even 'imperfect' systems of arbitrator appointment will not necessarily lead to a ruling of a lack of impartiality or independence on the part of the arbitral tribunal. **4.067**

In the context of trust arbitration, the issue of party appointment is also a problematic one as different beneficiaries, or classes of beneficiaries, may have different interests, as might different trustees and power holders such as enforcers, protectors and so on. For example, imagine a situation where a beneficiary sues a trustee for breach of trust for incorrectly paying out trust funds to a purported beneficiary, and also sues that beneficiary for wrongful receipt. The trustee then defends himself on the basis that he was acting on the instructions of an enforcer who, under the trust deed, had the power to instruct him about whom to pay out trust funds to. In this situation, the beneficiary, trustee, purported beneficiary and the enforcer all potentially have separate interests. Equally, where a beneficiary sues a trustee for breach of trust and the trustee claims that responsibility for the breach of trust actually lies with another trustee or where one class of beneficiaries sues for breach of **4.068**

135 ibid 157.

136 ibid 153–154.

137 ibid 157.

trust claiming that the trustee is favouring another class of beneficiaries, all the parties involved would again have separate interests.

4.069 The general approach of arbitral institutions to this problem has been to allow the parties to agree to joint nomination; for example, all the claimants and respondents agree to nominate one arbitrator each or all parties might agree to nominate a sole arbitrator, and if they fail to do so, then the institution will appoint all the arbitrators itself.[138] This approach is not perfect as it removes one of the main benefits of arbitration, the ability to choose one's judge, and essentially means that although no one party is advantaged over another, they are all, arguably, equally disadvantaged. On the other hand, it may be that there is much to be gained and little lost from allowing an experienced arbitral institution to appoint arbitrators as they are arguably likely to be well placed to pick the best arbitrators for the dispute.[139] It does not appear that this approach would lead to any ECHR concerns as the appointment process would not be imbalanced, although the institution would have to be careful in its choice to ensure that there were no issues of potential financial dependence as in *Bramelid*. However, *Mutu* shows that there is a high bar for parties to impugn the process of arbitrator selection and thus it is unlikely the ECtHR would find it ECHR violative.

4.070 An alternative approach is to specifically address the matter in the parties' agreement. For example, it could be provided that where the respondents cannot jointly agree on an arbitrator, their claims should be separated,[140] or each party could be allowed to appoint an arbitrator even if this leads to a panel greater than three.[141] In these cases, it would be possible to agree on an even number of arbitrators, in order to avoid absurdly large arbitral panels with all the added expense and administrative headache; but in such cases provision should be made for a tie-breaking mechanism to avoid deadlock or an invalid award.[142] Equally, if there is a desire to keep the costs of such disputes down, or more likely for speed and efficiency perhaps to prevent excessive acrimony building up, the clause might provide that a sole arbitrator is to be appointed, who, where the parties cannot agree, would be appointed by the institution,

---

138 See generally Ricardo Ugarte and Thomas Bevilacqua, 'Ensuring Party Equality in the Process of Designating Arbitrators in Multiparty Arbitration: An Update on the Governing Provisions' (2010) 27 Journal of International Arbitration 9.

139 ibid 48.

140 Jeffrey Maurice Waincymer, *Procedure and Evidence in International Arbitration* (Kluwer Law International 2012) 511.

141 ibid 510–511.

142 Voser (n 61) 362.

and this should not raise any particular issues.[143] Again, it does not appear that any of these solutions would lead to an imbalance between the parties or any independence or impartiality issues, provided, of course, that there are no special circumstances in a case and that the arbitral institution exercises any power of default appointment in a prudent manner.

The issue of arbitrator appointment is, therefore, one which drafters of trust arbitration clauses should have at the forefront of their minds and they should provide a mechanism for selecting arbitrators in the arbitration clause and ensure they select rules that will respect this choice. The selection of institutional rules in such cases is potentially crucial, as some institutions might consider the method of arbitrator selection provided in their rules as mandatory and therefore refuse to administer the arbitration.[144] In this regard it should be noted that although an arbitral institution's refusal to administer an arbitration certainly complicates matters, it will not necessarily invalidate the arbitration agreement, and courts may still enforce it notwithstanding the practical problems this causes.[145] On the other hand, if the settlor does not wish to address the matter of arbitrator appointment, he should at least ensure that he selects rules that address the matter in a way that he considers appropriate.[146] **4.071**

(b) The 'right' to legal aid

Art 6(3)(c) ECHR provides the right to legal aid in criminal proceedings in a variety of circumstances, but there is no equivalent explicit provision in the ECHR for civil legal aid, and thus, although the ECtHR has held there might be a right to civil legal aid in certain specific circumstances, this right is a limited one. The leading case is *Airey v Ireland*,[147] which concerned a lady who had separated from her abusive husband but alleged that she needed legal aid to obtain a judicial separation. The court held that: **4.072**

> In certain eventualities, the possibility of appearing before a court in person, even without a lawyer's assistance, will meet the requirements of Article 6 para. 1 ...; there may be occasions when such a possibility secures adequate access to the High Court … much must depend on the particular circumstances … however ... Article 6 para.1 … may sometimes compel the State to provide for the assistance of a lawyer when

143 ibid 363.

144 *Samsung Electronics Co Ltd v Mr Michael Jaffe, administrator/liquidator of Qimonda AG* [2010] Tribunal de Grande Instance of Paris 10-50604, ITA Board of Reporters; cf Andrea Carlevaris, 'The Bounds of Party Autonomy in Institutional Arbitration' [2015] International Arbitration Under Review: Essays in Honour of John Beechey.

145 For several examples see Carlevaris (n 144).

146 For a discussion of the different possibilities see Ugarte and Bevilacqua (n 138).

147 *Airey v Ireland* [1979] Application no 6289/73 (European Court of Human Rights).

> such assistance proves indispensable for an effective access to court either because legal representation is rendered compulsory, as is done by the domestic law of certain Contracting States for various types of litigation, or by reason of the complexity of the procedure or of the case ...[148]

4.073 The result of the ECtHR's judgment is that the decision as to whether legal aid is or is not required in a civil case is determined on a case-by-case basis. For example, in *McVicar v the United Kingdom*,[149] the court stated:

> So far as the law of defamation is concerned, the Court does not consider that this was sufficiently complex to require a person in the applicant's position to have legal assistance ... The outcome of the libel action turned on the simple question of whether or not the applicant was able to show on the balance of probabilities that the allegations at issue were substantially true.[150]

4.074 The case-by-case nature of the right to legal aid is further emphasised by the judgment in *Steel and Morris v United Kingdom*,[151] where the court held that the complexity of a trial regarding alleged defamation by anti-McDonald's protestors meant that the lack of legal aid had violated their Art 6(1) rights.[152] The court distinguished the case from its earlier judgment in *McVicar* by holding that, whereas in that earlier case the applicant had been 'required to prove the truth of a single, principal allegation ... in the course of a trial which lasted just over two weeks',[153] the trial in the current case had 'lasted 313 court days ... [and] the factual case the applicants had to prove was highly complex, involving 40,000 pages of documentary evidence and 130 oral witnesses, including a number of experts...'.[154] The result of this was that 'the denial of legal aid to the applicants deprived them of the opportunity to present their case effectively ... and contributed to an unacceptable inequality of arms with McDonald's'.[155]

4.075 It can be seen then that the complexity of a case is crucial in determining whether there has been a violation of the right to legal aid and, moreover, the case-by-case nature of the matter makes it impossible to say with any certainty whether a lack of legal aid in a particular matter will or will not lead to a violation of Art 6(1). The picture is further complicated by the fact that the court

---

148 ibid 26.

149 *McVicar v The United Kingdom* [2002] Application no 46311/99 (European Court of Human Rights).

150 ibid 55.

151 *Steel and Morris v United Kingdom* [2005] Application no 68416/01 (European Court of Human Rights).

152 *McVicar v The United Kingdom* (n 149) paras 64–72.

153 ibid 64.

154 *Steel and Morris v United Kingdom* (n 151) para 65.

155 ibid 72.

will also analyse legal aid schemes, in general, to determine if they violate the ECHR or not. For example, in *Aerts v Belgium* the court held 'By refusing the application on the ground that the appeal did not at that time appear to be well-founded, the Legal Aid Board impaired the very essence of Mr Aert's right to a tribunal'.[156]

4.076 Although it is impossible to distil all the principles from the many cases where the ECtHR has dealt with the issue into a short summary,[157] it seems that the overriding concern of the court is whether the denial or lack of legal aid 'deprive[s] them of the opportunity to present their case effectively'.[158] In the English context, it is worth noting that civil legal aid is governed by the Legal Aid, Sentencing and Punishment of Offenders Act 2012, which lists the circumstances in which civil legal aid can be granted in Part 1 Schedule 1 and which, unsurprisingly, does not include trust disputes. Consequently, unless they can make out an exceptional case as provided for in s 10 of the Act, it does not seem that parties to a trust dispute would be able to claim legal aid.

4.077 In general, beneficiaries will not be able to charge their costs in trust disputes against the trust fund[159] and thus they will either have to pay out of their own funds, secure a no win, no fee arrangement,[160] or possibly seek third-party funding.[161] It need not be said that third-party funding is likely only available for high-value trust disputes, whilst a no win, no fee arrangement, although offered by law firms in contentious probate situations,[162] will likely not be offered where the risk of losing is too high or the payoff is not sufficient.

---

156 *Aerts v Belgium* [1998] European Court of Human Rights Application no. 61/1991/845/1051 [60].

157 For an overview see 'Guide on Article 6 of the European Convention on Human Rights – Right to a Fair Trial (Civil Limb)' (European Court of Human Rights 2019) 32–33.

158 *Steel and Morris v United Kingdom* (n 151) para 72.

159 Tucker L and others, *Lewin on Trusts* (19th edn, Sweet & Maxwell/Thomson Reuters 2015) paras 27-165–21-188; cf the recent British Columbia case of *Xie v Lai*, 2021 BCSC 1768, at para 24 where the court held that 'the plaintiffs having obtained the certificate of pending litigation on the footing of an arguable, triable, proprietary claim to the Fund … must satisfy the threshold requirement of showing that they cannot reasonably afford to pay their legal expenses without recourse to the Fund. If they meet this threshold, I must go on to balance the potential injustice to both parties.'

160 See generally Terry McGuinness, 'No Win, No Fee Funding Arrangements' <https://researchbriefings.parliament.uk/ResearchBriefing/Summary/CBP-7607> accessed 11 November 2019.

161 James M Sheedy and Stephen M Baker, *Litigating Trust Disputes in Jersey: Law, Procedure & Remedies* (Hart Publishing 2017) paras 1-149–1-154; note however that the offence of maintenance and champerty no longer exists in England and Wales, see s 13(1)(a) of the Criminal Law Act 1967.

162 See e.g. 'Contesting Probate | Contentious Probate' (*Myerson Solicitors*) <https://www.myerson.co.uk/personal/contested-probate> accessed 11 November 2019; 'Dispute Resolution – Clarkson Wright & Jakes Solicitors (Orpington, Kent)' (*Clarkson Wright and Jakes Ltd*) <https://www.cwj.co.uk/site/individualservices/civildisputes/> accessed 11 November 2019; 'Will Disputes Solicitors | George Green | Wolverhampton' (*George Green Solicitors*) <https://www.georgegreen.co.uk/site/our-services/litigation-solicitors-birmingham/will-disputes-inheritance-claims/> accessed 11 November 2019.

Consequently, there may be situations where impecunious individuals who wish to bring a claim as regards a trust may be unable to do so without legal aid, although given the availability of alternative funding discussed above, this should only happen in low value or high-risk cases.

4.078 In the context of trust arbitration, it should be noted that there is pre-HRA authority that mere impecuniosity will not be sufficient to invalidate an arbitration agreement,[163] or prevent a stay in favour of arbitration due to the lack of legal aid.[164] One exception to this, in so far as the stay is concerned, may be where, 'the plaintiff has established, to the required standard of proof, that his alleged inability to obtain redress by arbitration may have been due to breaches of contract by the defendants'.[165] The post HRA and Arbitration Act 1996 case of *El Nasharty v J Sainsbury PLC*,[166] which also dealt with a situation where an arbitration agreement was impugned on the grounds of impecuniosity, did not refer to this earlier case but rejected Art 6(1) ECHR arguments, stating that:

> In my view it is irrelevant to the question whether the Claimant has waived his Article 6 rights that, if it be proved, he cannot afford to pursue an arbitration … However if it is relevant and necessary to examine the question, I would go further and hold that the costs rules of the ICC pursue the legitimate aim of ensuring that arbitrators are properly remunerated and that the administrative expenses of the ICC are paid. The Rules are proportionate to this aim.[167]

4.079 Although the court's treatment of the ECHR is not thorough, it suffices to state that the English Courts are not any more sympathetic to impecuniosity claims with regard to arbitration post the HRA than they were before. It does not seem therefore that the use of trust arbitration clauses would cause any particular issues with regard to the potential right to legal aid in civil cases, or at least it is unlikely to cause any more problems than existing trust deeds already do in the context of trust litigation.

(c) The right to a public hearing

4.080 This right is 'a fundamental principle enshrined in paragraph 1 of Article 6'[168] and 'protects litigants against the administration of justice in secret with no public scrutiny; it is also one of the means whereby confidence in the courts can

---

163 *Paczy v Haendler & Natermann G.m.bH* [1980] 11–19.

164 *Goodman v Winchester & Alton Railway Plc* (1985) 1 The Weekly Law Reports 141; *Trustee of the Property of Andrews v Brock Builders (Kessingland) Ltd* [1996] QB 674.

165 *Trustee of the Property of Andrews v Brock Builders (Kessingland) Ltd* (n 164) 682–683.

166 *El Nasharty v J Sainsbury Plc* [2003] EWHC 2195 (Comm).

167 ibid 34.

168 *Malhous v the Czech Republic* [2001] Application no 33071/96 [55].

be maintained'.[169] It is closely related to the right to a public pronouncement of judgment, which, unlike the right to a public hearing, does not have exceptions in the text of Article 6(1).[170] It is also one of the most problematic rights in terms of compulsory arbitration as even in *Mutu* where the court adopted a very flexible approach to sports arbitration and rejected all other violations of Art 6(1), it found a violation of the right to a public hearing.[171]

The requirement to hold a public hearing is not however absolute; even in criminal cases where it is most strictly applied there may be exceptions to it,[172] for example in cases where 'there are no issues of credibility or contested facts'[173] or highly technical cases which do not raise issues of public importance such as social security disputes.[174] The court takes a particularly strict approach to disciplinary hearings,[175] and hearings where 'the sanction imposed on the applicant carried a degree of stigma and was likely to adversely affect her professional honour and reputation'.[176] In the context of trust arbitration, it is important to note that cases involving breach of trust or professional negligence are clearly cases which would affect a trustee's 'professional honour and reputation' and thus the court is likely to apply a particularly strict approach to them. **4.081**

One particular countervailing interest in the context of trust arbitration which has been discussed by scholars, is the consideration that the interests of minors might be sufficient to dispense with the obligation to hold a public hearing.[177] It is true that the ECtHR has held that the rights of children can take priority over the right to a public trial in certain cases, for example in *B and P v The United Kingdom* it stated: **4.082**

> The proceedings which the present applicants wished to take place in public concerned the residence of each man's son following the parents' divorce or separation. The Court considers that such proceedings are prime examples of cases where the exclusion of the

169 ibid.

170 Aall, 'Waiver of Human Rights' (n 108) 238.

171 *Mutu and Pechstein v Switzerland* (n 44) paras 181–184.

172 *Grande Stevens v Italy* [2014] Application no 18640/10 (European Court of Human Rights) [119–120].

173 *Suhadolc v Slovenia* [2011] Application no 57655/08 (European Court of Human Rights) 13.

174 *Schuler-Zgraggen v Switzerland* (n 98) para 58; *Dory v Sweden* [2002] Application No 28394/95 [41].

175 *Ramos Nunes De Carvalho E Sa v Portugal* [2018] Application nos 55391/13, 57728/13 and 74041/13 (European Court of Human Rights) [208–211].

176 *Mutu and Pechstein v Switzerland* (n 44) para 182.

177 'Arbitration of Trust Disputes' (Trust Law Committee 2011), para 44.

press and public may be justified in order to protect the privacy of the child and parties and to avoid prejudicing the interests of justice.[178]

4.083 However, it is clear from the court's wording that the rights of the children took priority over the right to a public hearing not just because they were children but also because of the specific circumstances of the case at hand. In other words, it does not follow that in all cases involving children, a court would be justified in dispensing with a public trial. Indeed, in the case of *Khrabrova v Russia*,[179] which concerned a complaint from a teacher who had been sacked because of alleged excessive disciplining of a student, the court held that *in camera* hearings were not justified as:

> it is worth noting that the District Court held in camera not only the last hearing of 7 February 2003 … but all other hearings as well. Secondly, the holding of the hearings in camera was not linked to the intention of any specific minor… Thirdly, it does not appear from the Government's submissions that during the hearings the court sought to protect from the glare of publicity any private or otherwise sensitive information which was not mentioned later in the text of the judgment or the appeal decision, the latter being held in public…[180]

4.084 In consequence, it is not certain that the mere fact that an arbitration concerns minors will be sufficient to justify holding proceedings in private and therefore it would appear that, in most circumstances, compulsory arbitration will violate the Art 6(1) right to a public hearing and likewise the right to a public judgment. As will be seen later, however, this may not be the end of the story as subsequent public court hearings may remedy the earlier violation in the arbitral procedure.

(d) The right to present your case

4.085 As explained by the ECtHR, this entails 'the right of the parties to the trial to submit any observations that they consider relevant to their case … this right can only be seen as effective if the observations are actually "heard", that is duly considered by the trial court'.[181] This, in turn, imposes a right of 'due diligence', so that if a court did not properly examine the case, for example where a judge did not properly examine the file,[182] there would be a violation of Art 6(1).

---

178 *B and P v The United Kingdom* [2001] Applications nos 36337/97 and 35974/97 (European Court of Human Rights) [38].

179 *Khrabrova v Russia* [2012] Application no 18498/04 (European Court of Human Rights).

180 ibid 51.

181 *Perez v France* [2004] Application no 47287/99 (European Court of Human Rights) [80].

182 See the discussion in *Kraska v Switzerland* [1993] Application no 13942/88 (European Court of Human Rights) [28–34].

As will be discussed further below in the context of incapable parties, the right to present your case does not prevent states from imposing limitations on access to a court. For example, in *Lithgow v The United Kingdom*,[183] disputes regarding the valuation of shares which arose in the context of nationalisation had to be brought before an arbitral tribunal, not the courts, and there was no right of individual access.[184] Instead, shareholders would be represented as a class by an appointed representative.[185] Despite this, the court held there was no violation of Art 6(1), as shareholders could give instructions as a class to the appointed representative or apply for his removal and could also bring individual claims alleging that he was failing to properly represent their interests whether under statute or the common law.[186] It is true that this case concerned very unique circumstances and the court made mention of the fact that the procedure aimed to avoid 'a multiplicity of claims and proceedings brought by individual shareholders' in its judgment.[187] However, as will be seen below, similar circumstances can arise in trust law cases, and thus the case is of general interest. **4.086**

4. Remediation of Article 6(1) violations through later proceedings

The ECtHR has held on multiple occasions that violations of the ECHR can be remedied through later ECHR compliant proceedings. For example, in the case of *Schuler-Zgraggen v Switzerland*,[188] the court stated that: **4.087**

> The Court finds that the proceedings before the Appeals Board did not enable Mrs Schuler-Zgraggen to have a complete, detailed picture of the particulars supplied to the Board. It considers, however, that the Federal Insurance Court remedied this shortcoming by requesting the Board to make all the documents available to the applicant ...[189]

The key issue is that the later proceedings must be before 'a judicial body that has full jurisdiction and ... provide[s] the guarantees of Article 6 para. 1 ...'[190] and thus proceedings before a court of cassation which 'does not take cogni- **4.088**

183 *Lithgow and Others v The United Kingdom* [1986] Application nos 9006/80; 9262/81; 9263/81; 9265/81; 9266/81; 9313/81; 9405/8 (ECtHR).

184 ibid 10–36.

185 ibid.

186 ibid 196.

187 ibid 197.

188 *Schuler-Zgraggen v Switzerland* (n 98).

189 ibid 52.

190 *Albert and Le Compte v Belgium* [1983] Applications nos 7299/75 & 7496/76 (European Court of Human Rights) [29].

sance of the merits of the case'[191] would not remedy earlier Art 6(1) noncompliant proceedings.[192] The same may well be true if court review of an arbitral award is excessively limited, as in *Bramelid and Malmstrom v Sweden*,[193] where the court stated, 'the remedy before the District Court ... was of so limited a character as to be of negligible relevance to its present investigations. It did not provide a means for the applicants to challenge the arbitrators' decision on the purchase of the shares or on the price payable for them'.[194]

4.089 In the context of ss 67–69 of the English Arbitration Act 1996, although it is a trite point that the English Courts rarely set aside or annul an award, they can nevertheless address any number of serious irregularities, including violations of due process under s 68, which can include issues of fact,[195] as well as errors of law under s 69, unless the parties have excluded this, and such issues include issues of mixed fact and law.[196] A challenge to the jurisdiction of the tribunal under s 67 is *de novo* and 'not merely a review of the way in which the tribunal determined its substantive jurisdiction'.[197] These grounds are substantially broader in scope than those available in many other arbitration-friendly jurisdictions, and it has been said that 'The English Arbitration Act can be considered to take a maximalist approach to court review'.[198]

4.090 It would seem then that review is more substantial than that available in *Bramelid*, and possibly also than the court of cassation in *Le Compte*, but as the ECtHR has not addressed the matter in its jurisprudence, it is an open question whether court review under ss 67–69 would remediate earlier ECHR non-compliant proceedings. In conclusion, although it is not certain that subsequent review by the English courts would suffice to remediate earlier Art 6(1) violations by the arbitral tribunal, it is arguably more likely than not that this is the case.

---

191 ibid 36.

192 ibid 36–37.

193 *Bramelid & Malstrom v Sweden* (n 36).

194 ibid 30.

195 Julian DM Lew and others (eds), *Arbitration in England: With Chapters on Scotland and Ireland* (Kluwer Law International 2013) 534–536.

196 ibid 548–549.

197 ibid 533–534.

198 'What to Expect from the Review of Arbitral Awards by Courts at the Seat' (2015) 33 ASA Bulletin 293, 301.

5. The application of Art 6(1) ECHR to arbitration in English law

There are essentially three possibilities regarding the applicability of Art 6(1) ECHR in English arbitration:[199] **4.091**

I. The first is that arbitral tribunals are considered public tribunals and thus are required by s 6 of the HRA to apply the ECHR;
II. The second is that arbitral tribunals, in cases where English law governs the trust deed, are required to apply English law, and this includes the HRA which incorporates the ECHR;
III. The third is that English-seated tribunals are subject to review by the English Courts, and as these are required to act in conformity with the ECHR via Art 6 of the HRA they could refuse to enforce or set aside an award which is not in conformity with the ECHR.

It can be seen that there is a fundamental difference between options 1 and 2, and option 3, in the former the HRA and thus the ECHR is directly applicable by the arbitral tribunal, whereas in the latter it is only indirectly applicable via court supervision. Each of these possibilities will be considered in turn below. **4.092**

(a) Arbitral tribunals as public authorities required to directly apply Art 6(1) ECHR

It has been stated in the literature that as far as compulsory arbitration is concerned such tribunals would be required to directly apply Art 6(1) ECHR as they would be public authorities under s 6 of the HRA.[200] However, this was in the context of the more conservative definition of 'compulsory arbitration' adopted by the ECtHR at the time, namely arbitration required by law, and does not capture situations such as that which occurred in *Suda* where third parties were bound by the outcome of an arbitration but were not themselves positively required to arbitrate. Equally, post *Mutu*, it is clear that the ECHR must, at least in the context of professional athletes who have little choice but to agree to an arbitration clause, be applied to proceedings before bodies such as the Court of Arbitration for Sport. This is the case even though such bodies would likely not amount to public authorities under English law; for example, it has been held that the FA was not susceptible to judicial review as it was not a public authority.[201] In consequence, the issue of whether arbitral tribunals are **4.093**

199 See generally Robinson (n 32); William Robinson and Boris Kasolowsky, 'Will the United Kingdom's Human Rights Act Further Protect Parties to Arbitration Proceedings?' (2002) 18 Arbitration International 453.

200 Robinson (n 32) 25.

201 *R v Football Association Ltd, Ex parte Football League Ltd* [1991] Times Law Reports.

required to directly apply the provisions of the ECHR remains a live issue with regard to which there are two diametrically opposed views.

4.094 The majority view in the literature would seem to be that arbitral tribunals are not public authorities bound to apply the HRA, as:

I. Tribunals do not exercise functions of a public nature, and this was considered by the Lord Advocate to be crucial for a body to be a public authority;[202]
II. Judicial review is not available in respect of voluntary arbitration;[203]
III. The CJEU has not recognised voluntary arbitration as an organ of the state, and thus an arbitral tribunal cannot make a reference for a preliminary ruling;[204]
IV. Arbitral proceedings are not legal proceedings nor is a voluntary arbitral tribunal a tribunal in which such proceedings may be brought in terms of the Act[205]

An alternative view, however, has been put forward by Clare Ambrose, who argued that arbitral tribunals are public authorities bound to apply the HRA, as:

I. The HRA should be interpreted in a liberal and purposive fashion and doubts regarding whether arbitral proceedings are legal proceedings or whether an arbitral tribunal is a tribunal in which such proceedings may be brought, are based on an overly formalistic interpretation of it;[206]
II. The availability or lack thereof, of judicial review, does not determine whether a body is a public authority under the HRA and the fact that arbitrators have always been subject to a system of statutory review implies that they do in fact exercise a public function;[207]
III. The approach of the CJEU to arbitral tribunals should be distinguished as it results from the unique character of EU law and the need to ensure its uniformity[208]

---

202 Robinson and Kasolowsky (n 199) 456.

203 ibid.

204 ibid 457; see the most recent CJEU case, *Slovak Republic v Achmea BV* [2018] Court of Justice of the European Union Case C-284/16 [43–49].

205 Robinson and Kasolowsky (n 199) 457.

206 Clare Ambrose, 'Arbitration and the Human Rights Act' [2000] Lloyd's Maritime and Commercial Law Quarterly 468, 473–478.

207 ibid 478–479.

208 ibid 485–487.

The English Courts have generally held that voluntary submission to arbitration entails a waiver of one's ECHR rights and thus have not considered the issue of applicability in any great depth.[209] As regards the Strasbourg jurisprudence, it cannot really shed much light on domestic constitutional matters such as these and international literature is equally divided concerning whether the ECHR applies directly to voluntary arbitration.[210] In consequence, broadening our scope to include the approach of other jurisdictions does not assist in clarifying the matter. The issue, therefore, has to be considered from first principles, namely that: (i) determination of whether a body is a public authority is to be done on a case-by-case basis;[211] (ii) when interpreting the ECHR UK courts must take into account ECtHR jurisprudence,[212] such jurisprudence is often broader than the public authority concept as understood in UK judicial review law;[213] and (iii) a determination of whether a body is a public authority or not depends on whether they exercise a public function.[214] It would appear that as regards all these points, the fundamental question to be answered is: what role do arbitrators play in the English arbitral system? **4.095**

The answer to the above question dovetails with a long-standing theoretical debate in international arbitration – namely, should arbitrators be assimilated to state judges or should they be considered as private individuals drawing their powers solely from the parties' will?[215] Although it is isn't possible to address the subject in great detail, it is suggested that, at least for the purposes of the ECHR, arbitrators should be assimilated to state court judges. The primary reason for this is the fact that arbitrators act as substitute judges and they therefore necessarily 'exercise a jurisdictional mission even if their intervention is conditional upon an agreement between the parties'.[216] In consequence they can no longer be considered ordinary subjects or citizens but have certain *ex officio* 'rights and duties, which are normally exercised by the courts'.[217] This is arguably recognised in the statutory scheme in support of arbitration, which, **4.096**

---

209 See generally *Stretford v FA* [2006] EWHC 479 (Ch) (High Court of England & Wales).

210 See generally Aleksandar Jaksic, *Arbitration and Human Rights* (P Lang 2002) 183–219; cf Besson (n 29).

211 Nicholas Bamforth, 'The Application of the Human Rights Act 1998 to Public Authorities and Private Bodies' (1999) 58 The Cambridge Law Journal 159, 160.

212 Human Rights Act s 2; see generally Brenda Hale, 'Argentoratum Locutum: Is Strasbourg or the Supreme Court Supreme?' (2012) 12 Human Rights Law Review 65.

213 Bamforth (n 211) 162–163.

214 ibid 161; Ambrose (n 215) 479.

215 See generally Emmanuel Gaillard, *Legal Theory of International Arbitration* (Martinus Nijhoff Publishers 2010).

216 Besson (n 29) 402.

217 ibid.

by going 'further than simply enforcing contractual rights',[218] should be seen as establishing and regulating 'the public nature of an arbitrator's judicial role in determining legal rights'.[219]

4.097 The fact that the English statutory framework goes further than simply enforcing contractual rights cannot be seriously disputed as it, *inter alia*, permits the coercive powers of the courts to be engaged in favour of arbitration,[220] gives arbitrators an immunity similar to that given to judges in respect of their acts as arbitrators,[221] with a similar immunity applying to arbitral institutions,[222] and otherwise permits court intervention.[223] An additional reason for considering that arbitral tribunals could be considered public authorities includes the fact that other seemingly 'private' authorities have been held to be public authorities, for example 'the governors of a private school or a privatized utility could be public authorities within the meaning of the Act'.[224] Moreover, given the strong parallels between Art 6 ECHR and the rules of natural justice, it is worth noting that, as discussed above, the rules of natural justice apply to all decision makers, including arbitrators.

4.098 It is not possible to decide the matter with certainty in the absence of English authority, but it is nevertheless suggested that, at present, it seems more likely than not that arbitral tribunals are public authorities required to apply the HRA directly. In the alternative, they are bound to do so as a result of their duty to apply English law as the law of the trust deed, as will be discussed below.

(b) Arbitral tribunals required to apply English law as the law of the trust deed

4.099 This argument essentially flows from the fact that under the principle of party autonomy, given statutory form in s 46(1) of the 1996 Act, the tribunal must decide the dispute in accordance with the law chosen by the parties. As the Human Rights Act 1998 is clearly part of English law, it would seem to follow that the arbitral tribunal is under a duty to apply the HRA when adjudicating a dispute. There are, however, two further complications caused by this thesis, each of which will be dealt with below.

---

218 Ambrose (n 215) 479.

219 ibid.

220 See e.g. Arbitration Act 1996 ss 42, 66, 101(2)–(3).

221 ibid s 29.

222 ibid s 74.

223 See e.g. ibid ss 17–19, 24, 44, 67–71.

224 Ambrose (n 215) 479.

(i) *Does the HRA incorporate the ECHR into English law?*

It would seem obvious that the HRA incorporates the ECHR into English law, but the contrary view is held by Clare Ambrose, who notes that: 4.100

> There is no provision to 'give force of law' to the Convention, as is used in other statutes incorporating international treaties. The Government made very clear in the passage of the Bill through Parliament that it did not make Convention rights part of English law. Instead it gives 'further effect' to Convention Rights by requiring legislation to be construed compatibly with Convention rights so far as possible, secondly by requiring public authorities to act compatibly with Convention rights.[225]

This is a very formalistic approach which although likely correct from a formal perspective does not tell the whole story as 'Even if the Convention were not incorporated into English law in the manner traditional for public international law instruments, both the purpose of the Act and the wording of section 1(2) make plain that the identified Convention rights are to "have effect" in English law'.[226] Moreover, consider the not uncommon situation where an arbitral tribunal is called upon to interpret an English statute, can it really be the case that it can do so in a manner completely different to a state court merely because it considers itself not bound by the ECHR? This would seem to be problematic, particularly where the tribunal would be bound to apply English case law interpreting that statute even if this was based on an otherwise unlikely interpretation which was nevertheless mandated by the HRA. 4.101

In conclusion, it can be said that the HRA does, in some sense, incorporate the ECHR into English law, at least as far as an arbitral tribunal is concerned, albeit the manner of that incorporation is unique and indirect,[227] so as to 'preserve the separation of powers and Parliamentary sovereignty'.[228] 4.102

(ii) *Is Art 6(1) part of English substantive law, English procedural law or merely part of public policy?*

Even if the ECHR was in some sense incorporated into English law, it might be said that as the rights in Art 6(1) ECHR are essentially procedural rights, they are not part of English substantive law but merely part of English procedural law. In consequence, an arbitral tribunal would only be obliged to apply them in so far as the parties had also chosen English procedural law or where 4.103

225 ibid 472.

226 Robinson and Kasolowsky (n 199) 457.

227 Harris and others (n 30) 30.

228 Ambrose (n 215) 473.

the proceedings were seated in the UK.[229] As an initial point it is worth noting that although the HRA does not make any distinction between procedural and substantive rights in its wording, the literature on the ECHR generally does make such a distinction[230] and so does the ECtHR.[231] In consequence, this argument does not appear to be unfounded, even if in reality it can be expected that where an arbitration clause is contained in a trust deed and that deed is governed by English law the clause will in most cases likewise be governed by English law, so that the tribunal would be bound to apply both English substantive and procedural law.

4.104 A more complicated possibility is that the ECHR forms part of English public policy and thus arbitral tribunals would have to consider it, either because 'an arbitration derives its legitimacy from, and its award is enforced through, national laws',[232] or because of a duty to render an enforceable award which may apply under the relevant institutional rules or legislation.[233] The issue is debatable because it might be argued that arbitrators should only apply transnational or truly international public policy,[234] but this view is underlain with an arbitration philosophy,[235] the transnational approach,[236] which has traditionally been rejected in English law,[237] and thus a more conservative approach is likely to be applied by the English courts. Although there does not appear to be any explicit judicial or statutory statement that the ECHR via the HRA forms part of English public policy, this would seem to follow from its nature as a human rights instrument,[238] which must necessarily embody 'fundamental conceptions of morality and justice'.[239] Moreover, at the European level, it has been argued that the ECHR 'represent[s] a 'constitutional instrument of

229 Robinson and Kasolowsky (n 199) 458.

230 See generally Jorgen Aall, 'Waiver of Human Rights' (2011) 29 Nordic Journal of Human Rights 56.

231 See e.g. *Pfeifer and Plankl v Austria* (n 81) para 37.

232 Lew and others (n 195) paras 12–53.

233 ibid.

234 See generally Pierre LaLive, 'Transnational (or Truly International) Public Policy and International Arbitration' (1987) 3 Comparative Arbitration Practice and Public Policy in Arbitration 258; see also in the context of non-enforcement of foreign arbitral awards under the NYC, Pierre Mayer and Audley Sheppard, 'Final ILA Report on Public Policy as a Bar to Enforcement of International Arbitral Awards' (2003) 19 Arbitration International 249.

235 See in particular LaLive (n 234) paras 40–49.

236 See in particular Gaillard (n 215) 35–66, 126–135.

237 F Mann, '"Lex Facit Arbitrum", in *International Arbitration. Liber Amicorum for Martin Domke*. Edited by Pieter Sanders (The Hague, Nijhoff, 1967) [Reprinted under the title 'The UNCITRAL Model Law – Lex Facit Arbitrum' in (1986) 2(3) Arbitration International 241]; R Goode, 'The Role of the Lex Loci Arbitri in International Commercial Arbitration' (2001) 17 Arbitration International 19.

238 See Jan Oster, 'Public Policy and Human Rights' (2015) 11 Journal of Private International Law 542.

239 DStJ Sutton, J Gill and M Gearing, *Russell on Arbitration* (24th edn, Sweet & Maxwell 2015) para 8-050.

European Public order ("ordre public")'.[240] This would also apply at the UK level, and, in consequence, it seems more likely than not that the ECHR, as implemented in the HRA, forms part of English public policy.

In conclusion, arbitrators adjudicating cases governed by English law, which are seated in England and Wales or where enforcement is likely to be sought in England, should take the ECHR into account when rendering their decisions either because it forms part of substantive or, in the case of Art 6(1), procedural law or because it forms part of English public policy. It is worth noting, however, that the English courts have yet to refuse enforcement of or set aside an award because of incompatibility with the ECHR and thus arguably the risk of this happening in practice is very low. Arguably this is not due to a lack of appreciation of the ECHR by the English courts but rather the fact that many of the provisions of the ECHR, the violation of which would justify the setting aside or refusal of enforcement of an award, are already embodied in the rules of natural justice. As has already been noted and will be discussed further below, the English courts have refused enforcement of or set aside awards on multiple occasions for breaching the rules of natural justice. **4.105**

(c) Art 6(1) ECHR as indirectly applicable via the supervisory jurisdiction of the English courts

This is the least controversial of the methods discussed in this section and follows from the plain wording of s 6 of the HRA 1998 which states that '(1) It is unlawful for a public authority to act in a way which is incompatible with a Convention right … (3) In this section "public authority" includes – (a) a court or tribunal'. It is, of course, true that this obligation is not absolute, as subsection 2 provides an escape clause where the public authority in question is required to act in this way because of primary legislation. Moreover, as discussed above, s 3 of the Act also places an obligation on the courts to interpret legislation in a way which is compatible with Convention rights in so far as possible, and this would also apply to the Arbitration Act 1996 and associated legislative provisions. **4.106**

Although, as noted above, the English courts have not yet set aside or refused to enforce an award due to incompatibility with the ECHR, they have discussed its provisions and the HRA in several arbitration cases,[241] including **4.107**

240 Helmut Ortner and Franz Schwarz, 'Chapter III: The Arbitration Procedure – Procedural Ordre Public and the Internationalization of Public Policy in Arbitration' in Gerold Zeiler and Irene Welser (eds), *Austrian Arbitration Yearbook*, vol 2008 (Manz'sche Verlags- und Universitätsbuchhandlung 2008) 164.

241 See the cases discussed in Robinson and Kasolowsky (n 199) 460–461.

most famously the cases of *Stretford v Football Association Ltd*[242] and *Sumukan Ltd v Commonwealth Secretariat (No 2)*.[243] In the former case, the court stated:

> It is common ground that, as a public authority, the court is bound to give effect to Mr Stretford's rights under article 6. The question is therefore whether Mr Stretford will be deprived of any of those rights if the proceedings are stayed under section 9(4) of the 1996 Act. It is not in dispute that the arbitrators will be determining his civil rights and obligations. It follows that, on the face of article 6 ... the mandatory provisions [of the 1996 Act] ensure that the High Court has power to put right any want of impartiality or procedural fairness ... In our judgment the cases support the general proposition that, where parties have voluntarily or (as some of the cases put it) freely entered into an arbitration agreement they are to be treated as waiving their rights under article 6.[244]

4.108 In *Sumukan* the court also entered into an in-depth discussion regarding the application of the ECHR to arbitration, specifically concerning whether Art 6 prevented parties from excluding their right to appeal to the high court on a matter of law under s 69, and stated:

> ... parties who, by entering into an arbitration agreement, contract into the restricted supervisory regime of Section 69 of the 1996 Act, are not by agreeing to such restrictions acting inconsistently with the human rights of the opposite party ... Although they are to have a very restricted right of appeal, that is not impermissible under the Convention. Equally, if they mutually agree to go down the route of entirely excluding a right of appeal, they are also acting entirely consistently with Article 6 ...[245]

4.109 It can be seen that in both cases the English courts entered into a detailed analysis of the relevant statutory provisions and the ECHR, so it is clear that this is something that the English courts are comfortable with doing. In consequence, it can be stated with certainty that the ECHR does apply indirectly to arbitration via the supervisory jurisdiction of the courts, even if this has yet to lead them to set aside or refuse enforcement to an award.

4.110 As regards the practical means by which the courts could enforce Art 6 ECHR, this could occur in any of the following ways:

I. The court could refuse leave to enforce a domestic award under s 66 of the Act, even in unchallenged cases;[246]

---

242 *Stretford v FA* (n 209).

243 *Sumukan Ltd v Commonwealth Secretariat (No 2)* [2006] EWHC 304 (Comm).

244 *Stretford v FA* (n 209) paras 33–34, 38, 45.

245 *Sumukan Ltd v Commonwealth Secretariat (No. 2)* (n 243) para 26.

246 As happened in *Sterling v Rand & Anor* [2019] EWHC 2560 (Ch).

II. The court could set aside the award on the request of a party due to serious irregularity under s 68, most likely under subsection (a) due to the tribunal's failure to comply with its mandatory duties in s 33;
III. The court could uphold an appeal on a point of law under s 69, if this section had not been excluded;
IV. The court could refuse recognition or enforcement to a New York Convention award on the basis of s 103, most likely on the ground provided in subsection 3 that 'it would be contrary to public policy to recognise or enforce the award'.

To summarise this entire subsection, it is possible to say that Art 6 ECHR applies directly to arbitration either because tribunals are public authorities in the sense required by the HRA, although this is far from certain, or because tribunals acting under English law are required to apply it as part of English procedural law or English public policy. In any event it is applicable indirectly due to the supervisory jurisdiction of the English courts. **4.111**

D. THE COMMON LAW RULES OF NATURAL JUSTICE

In the law of England and Wales, the principles of the ECHR sit alongside the substantially older and 'homegrown' principles of natural justice.[247] These principles are, in some respects, of more importance than the ECHR as their application to arbitration is uncontroversial, being free of either practical or theoretical difficulties. Moreover, as will be discussed below, while the English courts have repeatedly refused to enforce or set aside awards due to a breach of the rules of natural justice, they have yet to do so for breach of Art 6(1) ECHR. It is therefore clear that whilst the rules of natural justice and the ECHR broadly overlap, the former have not been supplanted by the latter and merit independent analysis. This section aims to carry out that independent analysis by, first, briefly outlining the content of the rules of natural justice and, secondly, analysing their application to arbitration. **4.112**

The two cardinal rules of natural justice are as follows:[248] **4.113**

I. *Nemo judex in causa sua* – no man can be a judge in his own cause;

---

247 William Wade and CF Forsyth, *Administrative Law* (10th edn, Oxford University Press 2009) 371–379 <http://catdir.loc.gov/catdir/enhancements/fy1214/2009016251-t.html> accessed 12 November 2019.

248 'Natural Justice – Oxford Reference' <https://www.oxfordreference.com/view/10.1093/oi/authority.20110803100225319> accessed 13 November 2019; see generally Rom KL Chung, 'The Rules of Natural Justice in Arbitration' (2011) 77 Arbitration 167.

II. *Audi alteram partem* – hear the other side.

4.114 As with the elements of Art 6(1) ECHR discussed above, it is possible for the principles of natural justice to be waived by a party[249] or even excluded altogether by statute.[250] The standards applied to such waivers are very similar to those applied to waivers under the ECHR, for example in the case of *R v Institute of Chartered Accountants in England and Wales*[251] the Court of Appeal stated that 'If agreement is to prevent what would otherwise be a breach of the rules of natural justice it cannot be anything less than a voluntary, informed and unequivocal agreement'.[252]

4.115 An awkward example of where a waiver would not meet the above requirements can be found in the case of *Smith v Kvaerner Cementation Foundations Ltd & Anor.*[253] In that case a party found out shortly before the hearing that the judge who was to hear his case was apparently biased and was not given any information about 'how quickly his case could be tried if he insisted that it should be transferred to another judge'.[254] Additionally, his counsel (whose head of chambers was acting as the judge) gave strong advice to the party to have the proceedings heard before the apparently biased judge.[255] The court stated that 'it is not appropriate for counsel to expound on his knowledge of the personal integrity of the individual judge'[256] and went on to note that:

> in a case such as this, we do not think that it is part of counsel's duty or appropriate for counsel to seek to influence the decision to be taken by the lay client. The choice is the client's and, while it is proper for counsel to inform the client of the implications of the choice, it is not appropriate for counsel to urge the client to waive his right to object to the tribunal.[257]

4.116 Although the circumstances in the case were unique the decision nevertheless shows that the technicalities regarding waiver of natural justice rights are no less complex than those involved with the waiver of Art 6(1) ECHR rights.

---

249 Matthew Groves, 'Waiver of Natural Justice' (2019) 40 Adelaide Law Review 641; James Goudkamp, 'The Rule against Bias and the Doctrine of Waiver' [2007] Civil Justice Quarterly 310.

250 Matthew Groves, 'Exclusion of the Rules of Natural Justice' (2013) 39 Monash University Law Review 285.

251 *R v Institute of Chartered Accountants in England and Wales* (2014) 1 WLR 86.

252 ibid 31.

253 *Smith v Kvaerner Cementation Foundations Ltd & Anor* [2006] EWCA Civ 242.

254 ibid 31.

255 ibid 32.

256 ibid 33.

257 ibid 37.

1. *Nemo judex in causa sua*

The classical statement of the *nemo judex in causa sua* rule in Commonwealth legal systems can be found in the House of Lords case of *Dimes v Grand Junction Canal*.[258] In that case the Lord Chancellor heard the case although he held shares, both on his own behalf and for others by virtue of being a trustee, in the Grand Junction Canal company.[259] The House of Lords held that his decree was therefore voidable,[260] and Lord Campbell provided the following classical statement on the *nemo judex* rule: **4.117**

> No one can suppose that Lord Cottenham could be, in the remotest degree, influenced by the interest that he had in this concern; but, my Lords, it is of the last importance that the maxim that no man is to be a judge in his own cause should be held sacred. And that is not to be confined to a cause in which he is a party, but applies to a cause in which he has an interest.[261]

The most celebrated example of the *nemo judex* rule in recent times is undoubtedly the case of *R v Bow Street Metropolitan Stipendiary Magistrate and Others, Ex Parte Pinochet Ugarte (No 2)*.[262] The case revolved around a request by Spain for the extradition of the former Chilean leader Pinochet Ugarte on the basis of alleged crimes against humanity, and the links between one of the judges (Lord Hoffman) in a House of Lords appeal on the matter and Amnesty International. The appeal before the House of Lords held that Pinochet could be extradited,[263] but subsequent to this decision it was discovered that Lord Hoffman was a director of the Amnesty international Charitable Trust.[264] The issue was that Amnesty International had not only repeatedly called for the prosecution of those involved in Chilean human rights violations during the dictatorship of Pinochet, but had also intervened in the appeal regarding Pinochet's extradition to Spain.[265] The organisational structure of Amnesty International was complex with numerous interrelated companies and charities[266] so that whilst Lord Hoffman was a director of Amnesty International Charitable Limited that was not the same body of Amnesty International **4.118**

---

258 *Dimes v the Proprietors of the Grand Junction Canal* (1852) III HLC 759.

259 ibid 764.

260 ibid 792.

261 ibid 793.

262 *R v Bow Street Metropolitan Stipendiary Magistrate, Ex Parte Pinochet Ugarte (No 2)* (2000) 1 AC 119.

263 *R v Bow Street Metropolitan Stipendiary Magistrate, Ex Parte Pinochet Ugarte (No 1)* (2000) 1 AC 61.

264 *R v Bow Street Metropolitan Stipendiary Magistrate, Ex Parte Pinochet Ugarte (No 2)* (n 263) 128–129.

265 ibid 131, 134.

266 ibid 131, 133–135.

which had become a party of the appeal.[267] The House of Lords did not give much importance to these technicalities however and held that:

> The substance of the matter is that A.I., A.I.L. and A.I.C.L. are all various parts of an entity or movement working in different fields towards the same goals. If the absolute impartiality of the judiciary is to be maintained, there must be a rule which automatically disqualifies a judge who is involved, whether personally or as a director of a company, in promoting the same causes in the same organisation as is a party to the suit. There is no room for fine distinctions …[268]

4.119 This led the House of Lords to order a further appeal hearing,[269] which came to very different legal conclusions from the original case, albeit it allowed Pinochet's extradition on a substantially narrower list of charges (although he was in fact never extradited[270]). It is clear from all this that the *nemo judex in causa sua* rule is strictly applied by the English courts and that they will not hesitate to quash rulings of judges who have contravened it no matter their eminence.

4.120 It is important to note at this stage that the *nemo judex in causa sua* rule, now often called 'the rule against bias',[271] contains a number of sub-rules and has given rise to a very complex thicket of jurisprudence with slightly different emphasises in each Commonwealth jurisdiction.[272] In particular, the cases discussed above represent an example of the 'automatic disqualification rule', which provides that 'a decision-maker who is a party to the matter to be decided, or who has a financial interest in the decision to be made (or, exceptionally, a non-financial interest) is "automatically disqualified" as a decision-maker … and if a decision has been made, it will be invalid'.[273]

4.121 The automatic disqualification rule is unfortunately an example of the differences found in different Commonwealth jurisdictions given that it is not accepted in Australia, with the High Court of Australia stating in the case of *Ebner v Official Trustee in Bankruptcy*[274] that 'a rule of automatic disqualification would be anomalous. It is in some respects too wide, and in other

---

267 ibid 128–129, 134.

268 ibid 135.

269 *R v Bow Street Metropolitan Stipendiary Magistrate, Ex Parte Pinochet Ugarte (No 3)* (2000) 1 AC 147.

270 News Unlimited staff and agencies, 'Pinochet Leaves Britain' (*The Guardian*, 2 March 2000) <http://www.theguardian.com/world/2000/mar/02/pinochet.chile2> accessed 2 May 2021.

271 Peter Cane, *Administrative Law* (Oxford University Press 2011) 69.

272 See generally Matthew Groves, 'The Rule Against Bias' [2009] Monash University Law Research Series 485.

273 Cane (n 271) 71.

274 *Ebner v Official Trustee in Bankruptcy* [2000] HCA 63.

respects too narrow. There is no reason in principle why it should be limited to interests that are pecuniary, or why, if it were so limited, it should be limited to pecuniary interests that are direct'.[275] Instead the court held that 'Where, in the absence of any suggestion of actual bias, a question arises as to the independence or impartiality of a judge ... the governing principle is that ... a judge is disqualified if a fair-minded lay observer might reasonably apprehend that the judge might not bring an impartial mind to the resolution of the question the judge is required to decide'.[276]

The case brings us to the next strand of the *nemo judex* principle, the rule against apparent bias. This 'is also known as perceived and ostensible bias [and] occurs when the hypothetical fair-minded and informed observer believes that the judge may be biased'.[277] The classical locus for this strand is the Divisional Court case of *R v Sussex Justices, ex parte McCarthy*,[278] which was a case where the deputy clerk to the lay justices who heard the case, and had retired with them when they were deciding the case, was a partner in the same law firm as the claimant and the brother of one of that law firm's founding partners.[279] The court held that even if, as was alleged, the clerk in question had not been consulted about the case and had abstained from referring to it in anyway the rule against bias was still violated. This was because 'it is of fundamental importance that justice should not only be done, but should manifestly and undoubtedly be seen to be done'.[280] The court went on to note that 'Nothing is to be done which creates even a suspicion that there has been an improper interference with the course of justice'.[281] **4.122**

One of the most famous, and blatant, examples where a judge evinced apparent bias is discussed in the Court of Appeal case of *Howell & Ors v Lees Millais & Ors*.[282] In that case the first instance judge, Mr Justice Peter Smith, wanted to join Addleshaw Goddard but that law firm decided that the idea was not financially viable.[283] Mr Justice Peter Smith did not take this well and in a subsequent case involving Addleshaw Goddard to be heard by the same **4.123**

---

275 ibid 54.

276 ibid 6.

277 James Goudkamp, 'Facing up to Actual Bias' (2008) 27 Civil Justice Quarterly 32, 32.

278 *R v Sussex Justices, ex parte McCarthy* [1923] All ER Rep 233 (High Court of England and Wales).

279 ibid 256–257.

280 ibid 259.

281 ibid.

282 *Howell & Ors v Lees Millais & Ors* [2007] EWCA Civ 270.

283 ibid 9–10.

judge one month later a request was made for the judge to recuse himself.[284] In the hearing on that application the judge acted in an intemperate fashion and cross-examined the Addleshaw Goddard partner who was called as a witness in the application, which led to the Court of Appeal stating that:

> the cross-examination of Mr Twigden and the approach adopted by the judge in the course of Mr Crampin's submissions provides strong support for Mr Flint's submissions that the fair-minded and informed observer having considered the facts would conclude that there was a real possibility that the judge was biased against AG and its partners, one of whom is the first claimant in the application.[285]

The Court of Appeal went on to note that:

> When this evidence is put together with the content and tone of the emails sent by the judge that I quoted earlier, I am quite satisfied that this is a case in which the judge should have recused himself. This is not to my mind a case which is close to the borderline but a case in which there is no doubt that the test laid down in the authorities is satisfied.[286]

4.124 Unfortunately, not all cases are as clear cut and the modern law concerning bias involves a quagmire of complex rules in both England[287] and other Commonwealth jurisdictions.[288] Helpfully, the recent English case of *Trump International Ltd v DTTM Operations LLC*[289] provides a useful recapitulation of the modern English authorities, and states with regard to apparent bias that:

> The test applicable to apparent bias, regardless of whether a justice, member of an inferior tribunal or arbitrator is concerned, is whether, having regard to the relevant circumstances, there is a real possibility of bias on the part of the individual in question, in the sense that he/she might unfairly regard with favour, or disfavour, the case of a party to the issue under consideration by him/her … It is an objective test: i.e. the question is addressed by a fair-minded and informed observer.[290]

4.125 It would appear that this real possibility of bias test is also the same in several other Commonwealth legal systems,[291] and thus we are not faced with the rift between different jurisdictions that has happened with regards to the automatic disqualification rule. In any event we can stop our exploration of

---

284 ibid 1–3.

285 ibid 25.

286 ibid.

287 James Maurici, 'The Modern Approach to Bias' (2007) 12 Judicial Review 251.

288 Simon Young, 'The Evolution of Bias: Spectrums, Species and the Weary Lay Observer' (2017) 41 Melbourne University Law Review 928.

289 *Trump International Ltd v DTTM Operations LLC* [2019] EWHC 769 (Ch).

290 ibid 38.

291 Maurici (n 287) 251.

this overly complex area of law here, as the above more than suffices to set out a foundation for a discussion below on the application of the *nemo judex* rule in arbitration, and trust arbitration in particular.

2. *Audi alteram partem*

The second cardinal rule of natural justice essentially concerns procedural fairness (and indeed in certain jurisdictions the two terms are synonymous), what in the US would be called 'due process',[292] and has now, possibly due to the influence of the ECtHR, been changed into the more amorphous concept of 'the right to a fair hearing'.[293] **4.126**

It would seem the earliest reported case is the 1572 decision in *James Bagg's Case*[294] regarding the disenfranchisement of a burgess, where the court held, among other things, that 'it appears by the return, that they have proceeded against him without (a) hearing him answer to what was objected, or that he was not reasonably warned, such removal is void, and shall not bind the party, (b)… and such removal is against justice and right'.[295] **4.127**

The later case of *The King v The Chancellor, Masters and Scholars of the University of Cambridge*[296] provides us with one of the most memorable restatements of the rule, holding that: **4.128**

> the objection for want of notice can never be got over. The laws of God and man give the party an opportunity to make his defence, if he has any. I remember to have heard it observed by a very learned man upon such an occasion, that even God himself did not pass sentence upon Adam, before he was called upon to make his defence. Adam (says God) where art thou? Hast thou not eaten of the tree, whereof I commanded thee that thou shouldst not eat? And the same question was put to Eve also.[297]

The principle was extended to property rights by the case of *Cooper v Board of Works for the Wandsworth District*,[298] which was a case concerning the statutory right of a district board to alter or demolish a house where the builder had not given adequate notice of his intention to build. The district board demolished the house without giving any notice to the builder, who subsequently brought **4.129**

292 See generally Frederick F Shauer, 'English Natural Justice and American Due Process: An Analytical Comparison' (1976) 18 William & Mary Law Review 47.

293 Wade and Forsyth (n 247) 402.

294 *James Bagg's Case* 11 CO REP 93.

295 ibid 99a.

296 *The King v The Chancellor, Masters and Scholars of the University of Cambridge* (1790) 1 Strange 698.

297 ibid 567.

298 *Cooper v Board of Works for the Wandsworth District* (1863) 143 ER 414.

the matter before the courts, which held that, 'a tribunal which is by law invested with power to affect the property of one of Her Majesty's subjects, is bound to give such subject an opportunity of being heard before it proceeds: and that rule is of universal application, and founded upon the plainest principles of justice'.[299]

4.130 The subsequent case of *Board of Education v Rice*,[300] which concerned a dispute between a local education authority and a school around salaries, confirmed the universality of the obligation and provided more guidance as to the content of the right, stating that:

> I need not add that in doing either they must act in good faith and fairly listen to both sides for that is a duty lying upon every one who decides anything. But I do not think they are bound to treat such a question as though it were a trial. They have no power to administer an oath and need not examine witnesses. They can obtain information in any way they think best, always giving a fair opportunity to those who are parties in the controversy for correcting or contradicting any relevant statement prejudicial to their view.[301]

4.131 Unfortunately, the development of the right hit somewhat of a roadblock in the early 20th century with aspersions being cast on it and a requirement of a person 'acting judicially' being imposed in order for the right to be heard to apply.[302] The House of Lords reversed this trend in the 1963 case of *Ridge v Baldwin*,[303] holding that the idea that 'natural justice is so vague as to be practically meaningless [is] tainted by the perennial fallacy that because something cannot be cut and dried or nicely weighed or measured therefore it does not exist'.[304] It went on to note that if the limitation imposed on natural justice by earlier 20th century cases 'meant that it is never enough that a body simply has a duty to determine what the rights of an individual should be, but that there must always be something more to impose on it a duty to act judicially before it can be found to observe the principles of natural justice, then that appears to me impossible to reconcile with the earlier authorities'.[305] The House of Lords therefore freed the doctrine of natural justice from the shackles imposed on it

299 ibid 418.

300 *Board of Education v Rice* [1911] AC 179.

301 ibid 182.

302 Chief Justice Robert S French, 'Procedural Fairness – Indispensable to Justice?' (The University of Melbourne Law School 2010) 19.

303 *Ridge v Baldwin* [1964] AC 40.

304 ibid 64–65.

305 ibid 75.

in the early 20th century, and the right to be heard, as part of that doctrine, has evolved ever since.[306]

At this stage it is important to emphasise that the rule goes beyond merely hearing the other side and includes: **4.132**

I. 'Prior notice that a decision that may affect a person's interest will be made';[307]
II. 'Disclosure of the "critical issues" to be addressed, and of information that is credible, relevant and significant to the issues';[308] and
III. 'A substantive hearing – oral or written – with a reasonable opportunity to present a case'.[309]

A recent judgment of the High Court of Australia concerning a self-represented litigant in a probate matter, *Homayoun Nobarani v Teresa Anne Mariconte* illustrates these points.[310] The case is complex, but in essence the appellant challenged a grant of probate made without notice to him by filing caveats; he was aware that a trial would occur with regard to his caveats but then three days before the trial it was decided that the trial would be of the claim to probate itself.[311] This meant that he only had 'three clear business days to prepare for a trial of proceedings to which [he] had not yet been joined and in which [he] had not been the subject of pre-trial orders for preparing and filing a defence, preparing and filing evidence, issuing subpoenas, and locating and confirming availability of witnesses'.[312] As a result of the rushed timetable the appellant also could not cross-examine the respondent, could not call certain witnesses and could not properly examine certain evidence during the trial.[313] The court noted that even though the respondent's case was strong, 'a grant of probate in solemn form was not inevitable. The denial of procedural fairness to the appellant amounted to a "substantial wrong or miscarriage" in the sense that the appellant was denied the possibility of a successful outcome'.[314] **4.133**

306 French (n 302) 20–23.
307 'Traditional Rights and Freedoms – Encroachments by Commonwealth Laws Final Report' (Australian Law Reform Commission 2015) 129, para 14.22.
308 ibid.
309 ibid.
310 *Homayoun Nobarani v Teresa Anne Mariconte* [2018] HCA 36.
311 ibid 1–4.
312 ibid 47.
313 ibid 44.
314 ibid 46.

4.134 Another more recent decision of the UKSC illustrates the possibility for bad judicial behaviour to render a trial unfair. The case of *Serafin v Malkiewicz and others*[315] involved a defamation claim brought by a self-represented litigant, albeit one who seemed to benefit from some legal support outside the courtroom,[316] where the judge had (to use the famous phrase) descended into the arena. The UKSC took the unusual step of providing a schedule to their judgment listing all the infelicities committed by the judge during the proceedings, this included stifling explanations by the claimant,[317] consistently showing irritation towards him,[318] indicating to the claimant that he would lose the case,[319] introducing a demand for the production of six years' tax returns,[320] threatening the claimant with HMRC investigation, and threats of imprisonment.[321] It is not therefore surprising that the Court stated that:

> when one considers the barrage of hostility towards the claimant's case, and towards the claimant himself acting in person, fired by the judge in immoderate, ill-tempered and at times offensive language at many different points during the long hearing, one is driven, with profound regret, to uphold the Court of Appeal's conclusion that he did not allow the claim to be properly presented; that therefore he could not fairly appraise it; and, that, in short, the trial was unfair. Instead of making allowance for the claimant's appearance in person, the judge harassed and intimidated him in ways which surely would never have occurred if the claimant had been represented. It was ridiculous for the defendants to submit to us that, when placed in context, the judge's interventions were 'wholly justifiable'.[322]

4.135 Although natural justice is not explicitly mentioned in the judgment it does refer to bias in passing, and it is clear that the decision relates to the right to a fair trial, otherwise known as the right to be heard. It is also interesting to note that the court while highly critical of the judge's conduct stated that the judgment itself was 'on any view a remarkable document … it is intricately constructed and beautifully written … the judge in no way accepted all the defendant's arguments … [and] following a reading of this judgment, but of nothing else, many might ask "how could that trial have been unfair?"'.[323] It is

---

315 *Serafin v Malkiewicz and others* [2020] UKSC 23.
316 ibid 1–4.
317 ibid A1.
318 ibid 2–3.
319 ibid A4.
320 ibid A11.
321 ibid A12.
322 ibid 48.
323 ibid 44.

therefore clear that even a well-written and fair judgment will not save a decision from being quashed if the process which led to it was not fair.

The right to be heard can also be violated not just by anomalous actions by a judge or court but also due to longstanding practice. For example, in the case of *Porto Seguro Companhia De Seguros Gerais v Belcan SA* the Canadian Supreme Court held that the longstanding rule of disallowing expert evidence where the court was already assisted by assessors 'violate[d] the principle of natural justice of the right to be heard, audi alteram partem. This principle confers the right on every party to litigation to bring forth evidence on all material points'.[324] The court went on to note that 'Trial judges possess a discretion to limit evidence or exclude evidence where its relevance is outweighed by the prejudice it may cause to the trial process. But the principle that every litigant has a right to be heard goes against the exclusion of an entire category of evidence'.[325] No doubt many practitioners yearn for the days when there was too little rather than too much expert evidence, and the SCC may well regret its decision, but in any event the case demonstrates the flexibility and importance of the right to be heard. **4.136**

At this stage, as with the *nemo judex* rule, it is necessary to stop an exploration of this area of the law in the abstract and instead explore how it might apply to arbitration: in particular trust arbitration. **4.137**

3. The application of the rules of natural justice to arbitration

As has already been noted above, the application of the rules of natural justice to arbitration is considerably more straightforward than the application of the ECHR: there is no dispute about their applicability to arbitration,[326] nor that they constitute part of English public policy, for example.[327] The situation is even simpler in jurisdictions where the principles of natural justice are explicitly incorporated in the applicable arbitration act, as is the case in Australia,[328] Singapore,[329] and New Zealand[330] for example. **4.138**

---

324 *Porto Seguro Companhia De Seguros Gerais v Belcan SA* (1997) 3 SCR 1293.

325 ibid.

326 Indeed it has even been said that they are applicable not just to judges or arbitrators but to all those acting in a judicial capacity, see *Amec Civil Engineering Ltd v Secretary of State for Transport* [2005] EWCA Civ 291 [46].

327 See Sutton, Gill and Gearing (n 239) paras 5-036–5-056, 8-040–8-041; *Cukurova Holding AS v Sonera Holding BV* [2014] UKPC 15 [30–33].

328 International Arbitration Act s 8(7A), 19(b).

329 ibid s 24(b).

330 Arbitration Act 1996 (NZ) s 34(6)(b), 36(3)(b).

4.139 In consequence, this section will be shorter than the prior one not because the rules of natural justice are less important than the ECHR, they certainly are not, but because their application in arbitration is considerably less complex.

4.140 As an initial point, it is important to note that, as with Art 6(1) ECHR, it may be possible to 'contract out' of at least some principles of natural justice. For example, one can agree that the arbitrator will only be appointed by one party or the incorporation of a custom or trade practice which would be unreasonable and contrary to natural justice.[331] The exception to this in England is that those principles of natural justice which are embodied in s 33, i.e. the requirement to act impartially, to give the parties an opportunity to be heard and so on, cannot be contracted out of as the section is mandatory and thus not subject to party autonomy.[332]

4.141 However, it would appear that common law jurisdictions do not have a uniform practice on waiver of statutory provisions protecting the rules of natural justice. For example, the New Zealand Court of Appeal in the case of *Bidois v Leef*[333] conducted a thorough analysis of the jurisprudence, as well as the relevant statutory provisions, and held that:

> We consider it is wrong in principle that a party, with full knowledge of the facts ... can fail to take a timely object later. If that were possible then it would indeed be in a no-lose situation from the outset. Either its case is accepted, or the award is invalidated. We reject that interpretation of the Act and conclude that a valid waiver of matters that could be raised under art 12 [of schedule 1 to the Act] is effective and binding.[334]

4.142 The approach is appealing in that it ensures that the same approach is applied in both litigation and arbitration: it also prevents the obvious unfairness of a party being in a 'win-win' situation regarding challenge of an arbitrator. On the other hand, it could be argued that comparing arbitrators and judge is comparing 'apples and oranges': the latter can be subjected to extensive and substantive appellate review whilst the former cannot. In that sense, it is reasonable for a jurisdiction to make a policy choice (as England appears to have done) and prohibiting waiver of the rule against bias or the right to be heard by making the applicable statutory provisions mandatory.

---

331 Sutton, Gill and Gearing (n 239) para 5-037.

332 ibid.

333 *Bidois v Leef & Ors* [2015] NZCA 176.

334 ibid 80.

The rule against bias has also been extended in unforeseen ways in the context of arbitration by certain jurisdictions. For example, the Indian Supreme Court outlawed unilateral arbitrator appointment by one party in the case of *Perkins Eastman Architects DPC & Anr. v HSCC (India) Ltd* and held that: **4.143**

> in a case where only one party has a right to appoint a sole arbitrator, its choice will always have an element of exclusivity in determining or charting the course for dispute resolution. Naturally, the person who has an interest in the outcome or decision of the dispute must not have the power to appoint a sole arbitrator.[335]

This decision, while perhaps not pleasing to those who emphasise party autonomy above all else, is not unreasonable, as unilateral appointment of an arbitrator by one party would be contrary to the principle of equality in certain jurisdictions, i.e. France as per the *Dutco* judgment. It would also likely violate the ECHR for the same reason. **4.144**

Before further analysing the jurisprudence regarding breaches of natural justice, it is important to make a small terminological point. In England and Wales, as well as other jurisdictions who have substantially copied the English Act, the tendency is now to talk about serious irregularity under s 68 of the Arbitration Act 1996 rather than a breach of natural justice. In consequence, it is now relatively rare to find references to a breach of natural justice in English, and certain other overseas jurisdictions', case law except where the cases quote classic decisions which preceded the Arbitration Act 1996. On the other hand, it goes without saying that in jurisdictions where natural justice is explicitly (as opposed to implicitly) incorporated into the Act one continues to find references to breaches of natural justice in the case law. Notwithstanding this difference in terminology the same principles (and case law) are, to a large extent, applied in most Commonwealth jurisdictions although, as will be seen below, it may be that statutes which require 'serious irregularity' or the like impose a higher standard for breach than those which simply mention breach of the rules of natural justice. **4.145**

The most recent case of high authority concerning a breach of the rules of natural justice (or serious irregularity under the statute) can be found in the Judicial Committee of the Privy Council case of *RAV Bahamas Ltd and another v Therapy Beach Club Incorporated*.[336] The appeal revolved around two main issues, firstly it was alleged that the arbitrator had not addressed a point that **4.146**

335 *Perkins Eastman Architects DPC & Anr v HSCC (India) Ltd* [2019] Arbitration Application No. 32 of 2019 [16].

336 *RAV Bahamas Ltd and another v Therapy Beach Club Incorporated* [2021] UKPC 8.

was put to him, and secondly it was alleged that the arbitrator had discounted the alleged losses in a way which neither party had requested or addressed in their submissions. The JCPC held that the arbitrator's failure to address a claim which had been pleaded to him constituted a serious irregularity as 'It was central to the proper determination of Therapy's entitlement to damages for lost profits and would potentially at least halve the quantum of an award'.[337] As regards the issue of the discounting of losses, the JCPC quoted an earlier case referring to the principles of natural justice and stated that 'An arbitrator will not have acted fairly if a party is learning for the first time in the award about findings and matters in the decision of the arbitrator which that party has not had the opportunity to address'.[338] Subsequently, it also found that the arbitrator's discounting of losses amounted to a serious irregularity as 'It goes without saying and is self-evident that an arbitrary deduction of damages by a third (when it might be a much higher deduction) is seriously prejudicial to RAV'.[339]

4.147 Notwithstanding this high-profile successful challenge, it is important to emphasise that challenges based on breaches of natural justice are almost always dismissed. For example, in 2019 in England no challenge on the basis of serious irregularity was successful, and in 2020 only 1/16 were successful.[340] One of the reasons for this low success rate is that the English Act requires that there was not just an irregularity of a kind listed in the Act but also that said irregularity must 'cause substantial injustice to the applicant'.[341] Similar restrictions have been read into the statute by courts in other jurisdictions. For example, in Australia the Full Court of the Federal Court held in the case of *TCL Air Conditioner (Zhongshan) Co Ltd v Castel Electronics Pty Ltd*[342] that 'An international commercial arbitration award will not be set aside or denied recognition or enforcement … unless there is demonstrated real unfairness or real practical injustice in how the international litigation or dispute resolution was conducted or resolved, by reference to established principles of natural justice or procedural fairness'.[343]

4.148 In Singapore the Court of Appeal has stated that 'an applicant will have to persuade the court that there has been some actual or real prejudice caused

337 ibid 68.

338 ibid 46.

339 ibid 84.

340 'November Meeting Minutes' (Commercial Court User Group 2020) para 10.

341 Arbitration Act 1996 s 68(2).

342 *TCL Air Conditioner (Zhongshan) Co Ltd v Castel Electronics Pty Ltd* [2014] Federal Court of Australia – Full Court 83.

343 ibid 55.

by the alleged breach. While this is obviously a lower hurdle than substantial prejudice, it certainly does not embrace technical or procedural irregularities that have caused no harm in the final analysis. There must be more than technical unfairness'.[344] In particular, in Singapore a party must show 'the breach of the rules of natural justice [has]… actually altered the final outcome of the arbitral proceedings in some meaningful way'.[345] Despite the court, at least to an extent, drawing a clear distinction with the English approach which requires 'substantial injustice', it cannot be seriously argued that Singapore is a less arbitration-friendly jurisdiction than England and it is unclear that challenges on the basis of natural justice are more likely to be successful in the latter than the former. It is therefore unclear whether there really is a difference in practice between the English and Singaporean approaches to natural justice in the context of arbitration.

It should also be noted that none of the above prevents challenges which might appear technical from succeeding where the court holds that the required high bar for challenge was met. For example in *P v D*[346] where the English High court allowed a s 68 application as the arbitrators had decided the case on, *inter alia*, a ground which a key witness had not been cross-examined about and where that witness's credibility was in question. The court stated that: **4.149**

> fairness to a witness requires that, if his evidence is to be disbelieved, he must be given a fair opportunity to deal with the allegation. There is then … the further point that there was also not put … any case as to conditionality or contingency, as to which he was given no opportunity to explain his case, or meet what it seems the Arbitrators subsequently concluded, without such cross-examination, was … the 'proper analysis of his evidence'.[347]

In the more extreme case of *CBS v CBP*[348] the Singapore Court of Appeal held that a tribunal's refusal to hear witnesses, where neither the arbitral rules nor the parties' agreement provided them with such a power, amounted to a breach of natural justice. The court stated that: **4.150**

> The arbitrator had no power in this case to impose a condition that a party could be required to show that its evidence had 'substantive value' before he decided whether to allow it being adduced into the evidence through an oral hearing or to disallow it … It is

344 *Soh Beng Tee & Co Pte Ltd v Fairmount Development Pte Ltd* [2007] 30 SGCA 28, para 91.

345 ibid.

346 *P v D* [2019] EWHC 1277.

347 ibid 34.

348 *CBS v CBP* [2021] SGCA 4.

> clear to us that the arbitrator's directions in excluding the entirety of the Buyer's witness evidence is a material breach of the rules of natural justice.[349]

4.151 In the context of trust arbitration the main problems which are likely to arise are: (i) the self-evident complications posed by self-represented litigants, whether their lack of legal counsel is due to impecuniosity or otherwise; and (ii) failure to give proper notice to all parties or allow them to participate. A good example of the first type of situation can be found in the New Zealand High Court case of *Coromandel Land Trust Limited v MilkT Investments Limited*.[350] The facts of the case are complex but revolve around the fact that Coromandel Land Trust Limited ('Coromandel') was allegedly rendered impecunious by a district court order sought by MilkT Investments Limited ('MilkT') which required the former to pay a sum into its solicitor's trust account. Coromandel subsequently requested an adjournment of the arbitration to allow it to raise funds for the arbitration which the arbitrator denied and held the proceedings with Coromandel self-represented, allegedly due to lack of funds, before rendering its award.[351] The court therefore held that:

> In this case Coromandel's former counsel had raised legal issues earlier in the course of the arbitration, the Arbitrator was advised that there were complex legal and farming issues to be considered, Coromandel had previously been represented by counsel and wished to be represented at the hearing, and MilkT had been, and continued to be, represented by counsel. In those circumstances Coromandel was required to be given a reasonable opportunity to obtain legal representation. I am satisfied that the brief adjournment [of 28 days] did not afford Coromandel that opportunity, and that the Arbitrator's refusal to allow a longer adjournment was a breach of natural justice.[352]

4.152 Although the court elsewhere stated that 'I am not satisfied that Coromandel's funding difficulties were grounds on which the Arbitrator should have adjourned the arbitration hearing',[353] it seems fairly clear that the issues with counsel were due to funding difficulties and thus the impecuniosity of Coromandel was of crucial importance in the case. It is also important to note that there were other issues, such as Coromandel being unable to present expert witnesses to the tribunal due to the arbitrator's refusal to grant adjournments and unilaterally setting a date for the arbitration: the case therefore included multiple breaches of natural justice.[354]

---

349 ibid 71.

350 *Coromandel Land Trust Limited v MilkT Investments Limited* [High Court of New Zealand] CIV 2009.

351 ibid 8–26.

352 ibid 59.

353 ibid 68.

354 ibid 60.

The decision illustrates the need for arbitrators to be flexible when dealing with self-represented parties, particularly if they want legal representation but are having issues securing it and facing funding problems. It can be supposed that this sort of situation will not be uncommon in trust arbitrations if provision for funding legitimate trust disputes is not made in the trust deed, and it is therefore important for parties and arbitrators not to railroad proceedings in circumstances where this may lead to difficulties in enforcing the award, or even to its being set aside. The same goes for a party's desire to lead expert witnesses, these may well be relevant in complex trust arbitrations, and it is important to schedule proceedings accordingly instead of blindly barrelling along on a pre-set timetable. **4.153**

The reader is reminded that the decisions of *Homayoun Nobarani* and *Serafin* discussed above, albeit arising in the context of litigation, also involved self-represented parties, and in both cases an apex court found a breach of natural justice which led to the decision being set aside. It is therefore important for parties to be alive to the complications that dealing with self-represented litigants may pose and not treat them unfairly, even if their ignorance of legal matters (or their behaviour) complicates lawyers' or decision-makers' lives or irritates them. As the UKSC noted in *Serafin*, 'a judgment which results from an unfair hearing is written in water',[355] in consequence it is in everyone's interest to treat self-represented litigants fairly no matter how much this might go against the grain in certain circumstances. **4.154**

The Hong Kong case of *Sun Tian Gang v Hong Kong & China Gas (Jilin) Limited*[356] is an extreme example of the second type of situation discussed above. In that case the defendant was arrested and remained in detention in China, with little or no communication with the outside world during the entirety of the arbitral proceedings and for several years thereafter.[357] The issue was complicated by the fact that service was allegedly proven via a forged document.[358] The court began by noting that: **4.155**

> the fundamental principle of the law and of natural justice – that a person against whom any claim is made or any relief or remedy is sought in any proceedings must be given due and fair notice of those proceedings, so as to enable him to answer and defend these claims – applies to arbitration as much as it applies to legal proceedings in court.[359]

---

355 *Serafin v Malkiewicz and others* (n 315) para 49.

356 *Sun Tian Gang v Hong Kong & China Gas (Jilin) Limited* [2016] Construction and Arbitration proceedings No 46 of 2015 (High Court of the Hong Kong Special Administrative Region).

357 ibid 11–14, 48.

358 ibid 26–29.

359 ibid 4.

4.156 The court held that Sun clearly had not been able to attend or participate in the arbitration, even via an authorised agent, with the result that the award could be set aside for lack of notice.[360] The court went on to note that:

> fundamental principles of natural justice require a fair opportunity to be given to a person against whom claims are made, to answer and properly present his case against such claims. Our notions of open justice dictate that a party is entitled to know the case asserted against it, to see the evidence put against it, and to be given the opportunity to meet the case advanced against it. To deprive a party against whom claims are made of any fair or real opportunity, as in this case, to know the case against him, the evidence given against him, and to correct or contradict the statements made which affect him, when he is unable to do so or prevented by circumstances beyond his control from doing so, would in my view be shocking to the court's conscience and our fundamental conceptions of justice.[361]

4.157 Although the case is an extreme one it illustrates the point that parties must be given notice, and an opportunity to be heard, even in difficult circumstances. There are obvious challenges in doing this in trust arbitration where there are widely drawn classes of beneficiaries or children or otherwise legally incapable parties: but, as discussed below in Chapter 5, section B, there are tried and tested means of overcoming these challenges in court proceedings which can be applied (with some modifications) in arbitration.

4.158 The means by which the courts could sanction breaches of the rules of natural justice are essentially the same as those discussed above in the context of the ECHR with one addition, in England a court could also, on the application of a party, remove an arbitrator or the entire arbitral panel under s 24 for failure to comply with their mandatory duties in s 33(1).[362] As the latter section embodies several of the rules of natural justice, it follows that failure to comply with the rules it embodies would permit the court to grant an application for removal under section 24 of the Act. However, the section is not found in arbitration laws based on the UNCITRAL Model Law and thus is not found, for example, in the Singapore International Arbitration Act, the Australian Arbitration Act 1974, the New Zealand Arbitration Act 1996 or the Hong Kong Arbitration Ordinance. On the other hand, s 16 of the (domestic) Singapore Arbitration Act provides for the court to remove the arbitrator in similar terms to s 24, as does s 18 of the Arbitration (Guernsey) Law 2016 and s 35 of Bahamas Arbitration Act 2009.

---

360 ibid 57.

361 ibid 59.

362 *Benaim (UK) Ltd v Davies Middleton & Davies Ltd* [2005] EWHC 1370 (TCC) [22–26].

5

REPRESENTATION OF BENEFICIARIES IN ARBITRAL PROCEEDINGS

A. THE PROBLEM OF BINDING UNBORN, MINOR, INCAPABLE OR UNASCERTAINED BENEFICIARIES

A perennial problem that has arisen for trust arbitration is how to ensure that unborn, minor, incapable or unascertained beneficiaries are represented in an acceptable manner, in order that they can be bound by the arbitration clause in the trust. This is not a novel issue, and the English Courts have been dealing with the problem for centuries in the context of litigation. In consequence, this chapter will firstly look at how the English Courts have addressed the problem, including a discussion of relevant ECHR case law, and then consider how the problem might be addressed in the context of trust arbitration. **5.001**

B. SOLUTIONS TO THE PROBLEM OF REPRESENTING UNBORN, UNASCERTAINED, MINOR AND INCAPABLE BENEFICIARIES IN LITIGATION

5.002 There are essentially two solutions to this problem in litigation. The first can apply to all the above categories of beneficiaries and is to appoint a litigation friend, what used to be called a guardian *ad litem*, who will represent them. The second, which only applies to unborn or unascertained beneficiaries, is to make a representation order. Each of these will be discussed in turn below.

1. Appointing a litigation friend

5.003 As an initial point it should be noted that this section will, for the sake of conciseness, only explicitly address the English provisions: however, much of what is said will also apply to other Commonwealth jurisdictions as their provisions are broadly the same.[1]

5.004 The requirement and procedure for appointing a litigation friend is set out in Part 21 of the Civil Procedure Rules, which stipulates that a party who is a child or lacks capacity to conduct proceedings 'must have a litigation friend to conduct proceedings on his behalf'.[2] However, the court can make provision for a child to conduct proceedings without a litigation friend.[3] Further protections for children and protected parties include the fact that if they do not have a litigation friend a person cannot, without the court's permission, make an application against them before proceedings have started,[4] or take any step in the proceedings except issuing and serving the claim form or applying for appointment of a litigation friend.[5] Crucially, 'any step taken before a child or protected party has a litigation friend has no effect unless the court orders otherwise'.[6]

5.005 A person can become a litigation friend, either by court order[7] or without a court order.[8] The former situation can occur where the person is a deputy

1 'Seen and Heard: Priority for Children in the Legal Process' (Australian Law Reform Commission 1997) 84, para 13.6; Order 76 Singapore Rules of Court; Rules 4.29–4.48 New Zealand High Court Rules 2016.
2 Civil Procedure Rules, r 21.2(1).
3 ibid r 21.2(3)–(5).
4 ibid r 21.3(2)(a).
5 ibid r 21.3(2).
6 ibid r 21.3(4).
7 ibid r 21.4.
8 ibid r 21.5.

appointed by the court of protection with power to conduct proceedings on the person's behalf,[9] or where the court has not yet appointed anyone. The rules require that such a person, not being a deputy with the power to conduct such proceedings from the Court of Protection, must:

I. Be able to 'fairly and competently conduct proceedings' on behalf of the person;[10]
II. Have 'no interest adverse to that of' the person;[11]
III. Undertake to pay the costs which the person may be ordered to pay by the court, although they may have a right of indemnity[12]

In order to become a litigation friend, a deputy appointed by the Court of Protection (CoP) with the power to conduct proceedings on the party's behalf must file an official copy of the CoP's order, either at the time the claim is made or, in the case of a defendant, when he takes a first step in the proceedings.[13] Any other person, not appointed by court order, must instead 'file a certificate of suitability stating that he satisfies the conditions specified in rule 21.4(3)'.[14] **5.006**

The procedure for the appointment of a litigation friend by court order is set out in rule 21.6, which provides that an application can be made by someone who wishes to be the litigation friend or a party,[15] and a person claiming against a child or incapable person must apply for one to be appointed where: **5.007**

I. A person 'not entitled to be a litigation friend files a defence'[16]; or
II. The claimant wants 'to take some step in the proceedings'.[17]

Unsurprisingly such an application must be supported by evidence, but the rules do not provide many further details, neither do the practice directions, although if one seeks to appoint the Official Solicitor 'provision must be made for payment of his charges'.[18] In the event of a litigation friend being appointed **5.008**

---

9 ibid r 21.4(2).
10 ibid r 21.4(3)(a).
11 ibid r 21.4(3)(b).
12 ibid r 21.4(3)(c).
13 ibid r 21.5(2).
14 ibid r 21.5(3).
15 ibid r 21.6(2).
16 ibid r 21.6(3)(d)(i).
17 ibid r 21.6(3)(d)(ii).
18 'PRACTICE DIRECTION 21 – CHILDREN AND PROTECTED PARTIES – Civil Procedure Rules' s 3.4 <https://www.justice.gov.uk/courts/procedure-rules/civil/rules/part21/pd_part21> accessed 15 November 2019.

for a child their appointment ceases when they turn 18,[19] and where it is an incapable person, their appointment ceases only on the issuance of a court order, even if the person regains or acquires capacity.[20]

5.009 Although it is clear from the above that the court exercises a paternalistic jurisdiction over children and incapable parties, the extreme extent of this jurisdiction is demonstrated by Rule 21.10, which provides that if the party is a claimant no settlement, compromise, payment or acceptance of money paid into court is valid without the court's approval. Equally any money so recovered or paid into court will be dealt with under directions given by the court under Rule 21.11. The court is likewise protective regarding the expenses incurred by a litigation friend, which must only have been 'reasonably incurred'[21] and 'reasonable in amount',[22] and restrictions are placed on the total amount of such costs depending on the value of the claim.[23] In the case of protected parties who are incapable, the situation is even more complex because of the involvement of the CoP as will be discussed below.

2. The Court of Protection and incapable parties

5.010 The Court of Protection is a statutory court which was set up in 2007 by the Mental Capacity Act 2005, although it exercises powers of the Crown that have existed since the Middle Ages and has existed in some form or another since the creation of Commissioners of Lunacy in 1842.[24] The Court's purpose is to 'deal with all personal welfare, including health care, and financial decisions on behalf of adults lacking capacity',[25] and to this end, the court has extensive powers under ss 15–21 of the Act, including the power to:

I. 'make declarations, decisions, and orders on financial and welfare matters affecting people who lack, or are alleged to lack, capacity (the lack of capacity must relate to the particular issue being presented to the court)';
II. '[a]ppoint deputies to make decisions for people who lack capacity to make those decisions'; and

19 'PART 21 – CHILDREN AND PROTECTED PARTIES – Civil Procedure Rules' r 21.9(1) <https://www.justice.gov.uk/courts/procedure-rules/civil/rules/part21> accessed 9 September 2018.

20 ibid r 21.9(2).

21 ibid r 21.12(1)(a).

22 ibid r 21.12(1)(b).

23 ibid r 21.12(6)–(7).

24 Martin Terrell, *A Practitioner's Guide to the Court of Protection* (3rd edn, Tottel Publishing 2009) para 2.2.

25 Richard Dew, Olya Marine and Georgia Bedworth, *Trust and Estate Practitioners' Guide to Mental Capacity* (LexisNexis/Butterworths 2007) para 6.1.

III. '[r]emove deputies or attorneys who act inappropriately'.[26]

In the context of litigation, the primary issue is that the court can appoint a deputy and that deputy can be granted the authority, by the CoP, to act as a litigation friend for the person lacking capacity.[27] The procedure is more complicated than the appointment of a litigation friend under the Civil Procedure Rules (CPR), as the deputy must not only show that the appointment of a litigation friend is in the incapable person's best interests and that the deputy has no adverse interests, but must also discuss the person's liability for costs and their chances of success.[28] Moreover, this may well require the production of an opinion from counsel to be attached to the application.[29] **5.011**

It should be noted that there are no exact equivalents to the Court of Protection in other Commonwealth jurisdictions, and there is a divergence of approach between those jurisdictions which entrust matters concerning legally incapable person to tribunals separate from the ordinary courts,[30] and those which have left it to the ordinary courts to resolve the matter.[31] It is also important to note that in many jurisdictions the powers of the Court of Protection are split between different bodies, for example in Queensland the Office of the Public Guardian is responsible for many of the supervisory functions of the Court of Protection while disputes are raised before the Queensland Civil and Administration Tribunal. **5.012**

3. The Official Solicitor

As described by its website, the Official Solicitor acts, 'as a last resort litigation friend and in some cases solicitor for children (other than those who are the subject of child welfare proceedings) and for adults who lack mental capacity'.[32] The fact that the Official Solicitor is only a 'last resort' litigation friend means that he 'operates what is referred to as a last resort acceptance policy. This means that he will need to be satisfied that there is no other suitable and **5.013**

26 ibid 7.17.

27 Terrell (n 24) para 10.5.

28 ibid.

29 ibid.

30 Victorian Guardianship and Administration Act 2019; Queensland Guardianship and Administration Act 2000; New Zealand Protection of Personal and Property Rights Act 1988 s 2; Singapore Mental Capacity Act s 2.

31 Substitute Decisions Act 1992 s 1; British Columbia Patients Property Act s 1.

32 'About Us' (*GOV.UK*) <https://www.gov.uk/government/organisations/official-solicitor-and-public-trustee/about> accessed 16 November 2019.

willing person who can be appointed to represent a person.'[33] However, in practice the Official Solicitor is almost always appointed in CoP proceedings[34] for the reasons outlined in *RP v Nottingham City Council*,[35] where the court stated:

> The first and overriding duty of a litigation friend is to conduct the proceedings 'fairly and competently'. Making every allowance for the feelings of RP's parents and brother (the only persons put forward as being suitable) I do not think that any one of these three would have been able to act in this way. A litigation friend is a great deal more than the protected person's advocate … But it is of the essence of … an appointment that the litigation friend has no conflict of interest with the protected party … In the instant case, there were clear conflicts … A moment's thought makes it clear that no family member could advance RP's case whilst putting themselves forward as carers for KP in opposition to RP's wishes.[36]

5.014 It is clear that in most cases before the Court of Protection, a conflict of interest would arise and thus unsurprisingly the Official Solicitor would usually be appointed.[37] However, the situation is more nuanced in trust disputes, with the result that 'In most cases a parent will be the natural choice of litigation friend'.[38] Moreover, modern practice even allows one defendant to act as a litigation friend for another defendant.[39] Nevertheless, if there are conflicts of interest, it is to be supposed that the Official Solicitor should be appointed as a litigation friend unless some independent third party can be found. In the case of incapable parties assuming a deputy has been appointed, they are likely to be the obvious choice of litigation friend, and in all other cases, The Official Solicitor or an independent third party should be appointed.

5.015 As with the Court of Protection, there are no exact equivalents in other Commonwealth jurisdictions, but the Office of the Public Guardian in several jurisdictions deals with the matters discussed above, and thus much of what is said above can be applied to them.

---

33 Marc Marin, *The Family Lawyer and the Court of Protection* (Family Law 2010) para 6.4.

34 ibid 6.17.

35 *RP v Nottingham City Council* [2008] EWCA Civ 462.

36 ibid 129–130.

37 Marin (n 33) para 6.17.

38 S Collins, *International Trust Disputes* (Oxford University Press 2012) para 16.54.

39 ibid 16.54.

4. Representation orders

Another means of dealing with representation is available in the case of parties who: **5.016**

I. are unborn; or
II. cannot be located; or
III. are unascertained or cannot be easily ascertained; or
IV. have the same interests in a claim as a person in the first three categories or appointing a representative would further the overriding objection under the CPR.[40]

In such cases, the court can make a representation order so that 'the interests of such persons are represented by persons who are parties to the proceedings'[41] under the provisions in Rules 19.6–19.7A of the Civil Procedure Rules. The power is not a new one and has been exercised by the English Courts since at least the early 19th century 'not as a rigid matter of principle but "a flexible tool of convenience for the administration of justice"'.[42] It is true that the power has mostly been exercised in pensions cases,[43] likely due to the extreme complexity of pension trusts litigation, but the CPR does not restrict it to such cases, and the courts have held that 'it would be wrong in principle for there to be one law for pensions cases and another for other types of trust cases'.[44] Moreover, there is no bar to parties being represented despite objecting or refusing consent to this even if there is no reported case where the court has done this,[45] and that suggests a great reluctance on their part to do so. **5.017**

A party cannot appeal directly against a representation order, essentially for reasons of practicality, as explained by the Court of Appeal in the case of *Watson v Cave (No 1)*[46] 'If Mr. Lovering could appeal, every other bondholder would have a like right; and if we decided against Mr. Lovering on the appeal, somebody else might appear to say that Mr. Lovering did not represent him, or did not do it well, and therefore he had a right to do it'.[47] However, where 'a person professing to represent the parties is not really representing them'[48] **5.018**

40 ibid 16.39.
41 ibid 16.38.
42 *PNPF Trust Company Ltd v Taylor & Others* [2009] EWHC 1693 (Ch) [37–38].
43 Collins (n 38) para 16.38.
44 *PNPF Trust Company Ltd v Taylor & Others* (n 42) para 44.
45 ibid 26–69.
46 *Watson v Cave (No 1)* 17 (1881) ChD 19.
47 ibid 21.
48 ibid.

then the supposedly represented party can apply to 'be added as a defendant, and then he could apply as a Defendant to get rid of the order, or to take the conduct of the suit out of the hands of the Plaintiff'.[49] A party can also prospectively object to the making of a representative order and seek to be joined to the proceedings as a party, as happened in *PNPF Trust Company Ltd v Taylor*.[50]

5.019 Although in general, a representative party should have similar interests to the party they are purportedly representing, this is not strictly necessary, and in circumstances where the litigation is extremely complex and where it would be inappropriate to appoint yet further parties, the Court has shown itself to be flexible regarding this requirement. [51] It is even possible for a party to represent another party where there is a conflict of interest between them, at least where the parties have so agreed.[52]

5.020 It should be noted that as in the case of litigation friends, 'The court's approval is required to settle a claim in which a party is acting as a representative under this rule'[53] and 'the court may approve a settlement where it is satisfied that the settlement is for the benefit of all the represented persons'.[54] The court's paternal jurisdiction is therefore engaged just as much in such cases as in cases involving incapable parties or children, albeit minus the complication of the Court of Protection and the Official Solicitor.

5.021 The scheme of representative proceedings is not unique to England but is also found, in very similar terms, in other Commonwealth jurisdictions,[55] and therefore what has been said above can, subject to jurisdictional idiosyncrasies, be applied generally in many other Commonwealth jurisdictions.

---

49 ibid.

50 *PNPF Trust Company Ltd v Taylor & Others* (n 42).

51 See e.g. *NBPF Pensions Trustees Ltd v Warnock-Smith and another* [2008] EWHC 455 (Ch); *Bestrustees v Stuart* [2001] Pens LR 283.

52 *NBPF Pensions Trustees Ltd v Warnock-Smith and another* (n 51) paras 14–17; *Bestrustees v Stuart* (n 51) para 26.

53 'PART 19 – PARTIES AND GROUP LITIGATION – Civil Procedure Rules' r 19.7(5) <https://www.justice.gov.uk/courts/procedure-rules/civil/rules/part19> accessed 15 November 2019.

54 ibid r 19.7(6).

55 'Representative Proceedings' (Law Reform Commission of Western Australia) Final Report 103; Rule 10 Ontario Rules of Civil Procedure; Order 15 Rules 13, 15 Singapore Rules of Court; in different terms but to a similar effect see Rule 7.6 New Zealand High Court Rules 2016; cf New South Wales Uniform Civil Procedure Rules 2005.

C. LITIGATION FRIENDS, THE OFFICIAL SOLICITOR AND REPRESENTATION ORDERS: ART 6(1) ECHR

The appointment of litigation friends by the court, the representation of parties by the Official Solicitor, and the use of representation orders all raise obvious Art 6(1) ECHR issues which will be addressed in this section. **5.022**

The key ECtHR case in this regard is *Ashingdane v The United Kingdom*,[56] which concerned an individual involuntarily detained at a mental institution due to psychiatric problems, a restriction on proceedings brought by detained persons regarding their detention, and a limited immunity to persons involved in their detention under the Mental Health Act 1959. In considering whether this violated the applicant's Art 6(1) right of access to the courts, the court held that: **5.023**

> the right of access to the courts is not absolute but may be subject to limitations, these are permitted by implication since the right of access 'by its very nature calls for regulations by the State ... which may vary in time and in place according to the needs and resources of the community and of individuals' ... Nonetheless, the limitations applied must not restrict or reduce the access left to the individual in such a way or to such an extent that the very essence of the right is impaired ... Furthermore, a limitation will not be compatible with Article 6 para.1 ... if it does not pursue a legitimate aim and if there is not a reasonable relationship of proportionality between the means employed and the aim sought ...[57]

The court held that, in the circumstances, a bar on proceeding against the responsible authorities unless the act was done negligently or in bad faith 'did not impair the very essence of Mr. Ashingdane's "right to a court" or transgress the principle of proportionality'.[58] **5.024**

The next case, that of *Lithgow v The United Kingdom*,[59] built on *Ashingdane*, although it involved very different circumstances, namely the nationalisation of shipyards by the British Government and disputes about the compensation received by shareholders for their shareholdings. As an arbitral tribunal carried out the valuation of shares, Art 6(1) issues also arose, and in this regard, the court stated: **5.025**

56 *Ashingdane v The United Kingdom* [1985] Application no 8225/78 (European Court of Human Rights).

57 ibid 57.

58 ibid 59.

59 *Lithgow and Others v The United Kingdom* [1986] Application nos 9006/80; 9262/81; 9263/81; 9265/81; 9266/81; 9313/81; 9405/8 (ECtHR).

Notwithstanding this bar on individual access, the Court does not consider that … the very essence of [his] right to a court was impaired.

The 1977 Act established a collective system for the settlement of disputes concerning compensation, in that the parties to proceedings before the Arbitration Tribunal would be the Secretary of State for Industry, on the one hand, and the Stockholders' Representative on the other. The latter was appointed by and represented the interests of all [shareholders] … and thus the interests of each individual shareholder were safeguarded, albeit indirectly. … [T]he Act made provision for meetings of shareholders at which they could give instructions or express their views to the Representative … [I]n addition to the power of removal … remedies were available to an individual who alleged that the Representative had failed or was failing to comply with his duties under the Act or with his common-law obligations as agent …[60]

5.026 It can be seen then that, in certain circumstances, the court is willing to be very flexible, perhaps even more flexible than might be expected, so that even a lack of any right to bring an individual claim in court or even to the arbitral tribunal set up in the court's place, will not necessarily violate Art 6(1). It is apparent from the court's reasoning, however, that the applicant in this case still had individual rights to go to court and allege that his group representative did not properly represent his interests. Equally he could, albeit only as a member of the large group, have him removed or give him instructions. In any event, the parallel between this procedure and representative actions is striking, as both are often used in cases of extreme complexity, such as bondholder or pension fund disputes, and both affect the right to bring an individual dispute to court. It is likely then, that the system of representative actions under English law is also compatible with Art 6(1) ECHR, at least where it is used in cases that are complex and where there would otherwise be a multiplicity of proceedings.

5.027 The ECtHR's flexibility is not, however, unlimited, as can be seen from the case of *Philis v Greece*,[61] which concerned a unique piece of Greek legislation whereby engineers were not paid directly but instead paid by the Technical Chamber of Greece (T.E.E). Moreover, the T.E.E. was subrogated to them, so that only it, and not the engineers, could sue for recovery of their fees.[62] The system was designed to prevent the engineers from being pressured to excessively reduce their fees, to ensure contributions to an insurance fund, and to free them from the awkwardness of suing their own clients.[63] The applicant got into a fee dispute as regards a particular project and accused the T.E.E. of,

---

60 ibid 196.

61 *Philis v Greece* [1991] Application nos 12750/87; 13780/88; 14003/88 (European Court of Human Rights).

62 ibid 45, 60–62.

63 ibid 46, 58.

inter alia, negligence in failing to prosecute his claim in time as well of miscalculating his fees and of failing to enforce the court's judgment.

Although the court held that there were advantages to the Greek system, for example the T.E.E would bear the legal costs of proceedings and provide experienced counsel, the system violated Art 6(1) as: **5.028**

> the applicant was not able to institute proceedings, directly and independently, to seek the payment from his clients – even to the T.E.E. in the first instance – of fees which were owed to him, the very essence of his 'right to a court' was impaired, and this could not be redressed by any remedy available under Greek law.[64]

It would appear that the key distinction between this case and *Lithgow* was the applicant's lack of remedies as against the T.E.E: he could sue the T.E.E for damages if they failed to pursue his claim and it became time barred, but his claim would only arise from the moment it became barred.[65] Moreover, although he could intervene in or object to proceedings brought by the T.E.E., this relied on them actually commencing the action, and the independent claim for damages he could bring 'makes it possible for the engineer to claim compensation, but not his fees as such'.[66] In *Lithgow*, on the other hand, a party could try to have their representative removed, whether as a group or via individual court action alleging that they were failing in their duties as an agent and could also instruct them as a group. **5.029**

Another interesting case is that of *T v The United Kingdom*,[67] where the court had to consider whether a child delinquent's ECHR rights, including his Art 6(1) rights, were violated by the criminal court proceedings against him. The court stated that: **5.030**

> the applicant's trial took place over three weeks in public in the Crown Court. Special measures were taken in view of the applicant's young age and to promote his understanding of the proceedings ... Nonetheless, the formality and ritual of the Crown Court must at times have seemed incomprehensible and intimidating for a child of eleven ... Dr Vizard found ... that the post-traumatic stress disorder suffered by the applicant, combined with the lack of any therapeutic work since the offence, had limited his ability to instruct his lawyers and testify adequately in his defence ... In such circumstances, the Court does not consider that it was sufficient for the purposes of Art 6(1) that the applicant was represented by skilled and experienced lawyers.[68]

---

64 ibid 65.

65 ibid 50.

66 ibid 64.

67 *T v The United Kingdom* Application no 24724/94 (European Court of Human Rights).

68 ibid 86–88.

5.031 The case demonstrates that in certain extreme circumstances even the provision of a lawyer and seemingly uninhibited access to a court will not suffice to meet the requirements of Art 6(1). Moreover, as will be shown in the next case, these sorts of circumstances are not necessarily limited to criminal cases but may also apply in civil ones.

5.032 The case of *RP and Others v The United Kingdom*[69] is a follow-on from the *RP v Nottingham City Council* case discussed above, and is the only ECtHR case to date where the court has considered the compatibility of the litigation friend and official solicitor system with Art 6(1) ECHR. The court held that:

> It is clear that in the present case the proceedings were of the utmost importance to R.P. ... Moreover, while the issue at stake was relatively straightforward ... the evidence that would have to be considered before the issue was addressed was not ...
>
> In light of the above ... the Court considers that it was not only appropriate but also necessary for the United Kingdom to take measures to ensure that R.P.'s best interests were represented in the childcare proceedings. Indeed ... the Court considers that a failure to take measures to protect R.P.'s interests might in itself have amounted to a violation of Article 6(1) ... (see ... *T v the United Kingdom* ...).[70]

5.033 It is clear then that, in the abstract, the system of litigation friends and the Official Solicitor in cases involving children and incapable persons may not only be justified under Art 6(1) ECHR but actually required by it in both criminal and civil proceedings, at least where those proceedings are of importance to the party and where the issues or evidence in dispute are complex. The court went on to discuss the appointment of the Official Solicitor in the case at hand and noted that:

> he was only invited to act following the commissioning of an expert report by a consultant clinical psychologist. ... The Court is satisfied that the decision to appoint the Official Solicitor was not taken lightly. ...
>
> The Court considers that in order to safeguard R.P's rights under Article 6(1) of the Convention, it was imperative that a means existed whereby it was possible for her to challenge the Official Solicitor's appointment or the continuing need for his services. ... R.P. could have applied to the court at any time to have him discharged...[71]

5.034 The Court held that in the circumstances these safeguards were provided and there was, therefore, no violation of Art 6(1).[72] The case demonstrates the

---

69 *RP and Others v The United Kingdom* [2013] Application no 38245/08 (European Court of Human Rights).

70 ibid 66–67.

71 ibid 69–70, 72.

72 ibid 74–78.

extent to which the court is concerned to protect the right of access to a court, even in cases where it is obvious that the person in question requires that someone be appointed to exercise this right for them. For example, the court requires that the decision be explained to them in a way that they understand, and they must be able to challenge it. Moreover, the decision to restrict someone's Art 6(1) right by appointing someone to represent them, even against their will, must only be taken after a thorough analysis of their capacity and circumstances.

However, in general, following this decision it can be assumed that the system of litigation friends and the Official Solicitor does not violate Art 6(1) ECHR and a system of that kind may even be mandatory in order to ensure compliance with it. Equally, it may be that one could combine the system of representative actions and the involvement of the Official Solicitor, for example where there was a complex group claim brought by multiple incapable parties. In that sort of situation, much the same would apply to the representative action system as to the litigation friend via the Official Solicitor system. **5.035**

In conclusion, both the system of representative actions and the, potentially mandatory, involvement of litigation friends or the Official Solicitor in English litigation, are compatible with the ECHR as long as they are only granted in appropriate circumstances and with an individual right of court challenge. **5.036**

D. SUGGESTED APPROACHES TO THE PROBLEM OF REPRESENTING UNBORN, UNASCERTAINED, MINOR AND INCAPABLE BENEFICIARIES IN TRUST ARBITRATION

Two approaches to the problem of representing unborn, unascertained, minor and incapable beneficiaries have been suggested in trust arbitration literature. The first is to provide for some means of representation in the trust deed itself. The second involves the use of a system of virtual representation, a US doctrine which appears to be at least functionally similar to the English representative action. Each of these suggested solutions will be discussed in turn below. **5.037**

1. Representation provisions in the trust deed

This would appear to be the simplest solution and is explicitly provided for in the Bahamas Trustee Act, s 91B(4) of which provides that 'The terms of a trust may provide for the appointment of one or more persons to represent the interests of any person (including a person unborn or unascertained) or class in **5.038** a trust arbitration'. The issue that arises, however, is who should appoint the representatives for such parties? It may be that in certain circumstances the trustees can do so,[73] but that will clearly not be possible where it is a breach of trust case brought against the trustees and a conflict of interest might arise.[74] An alternative would be to provide for a third party, such as a protector or an enforcer or possibly 'the head of a relevant organisation',[75] to represent such parties, assuming again that they were not involved in the proceedings.

5.039 In any event, it is likely that in order to ensure that, if attacked, the provisions are upheld by the courts and are compatible with the ECHR, they should be as similar as possible to those provided in the CPR for proceedings in the courts. Although it might be possible to simply incorporate the CPR *mutatis mutandis*, this might not be sensible if parties want to avoid the inflexibility and formalism of litigation. Consequently, it would seem more sensible to only mirror the provisions of the CPR as regards representative actions or litigation friends in the trust deed, with the necessary changes to reflect that the matter was being arbitrated not litigated.

5.040 Another alternative might be to provide for parties to go to the court to get a litigation friend appointed for children or incapable parties, although whether the courts would entertain that application is an open question. Equally where a minor's parents or guardians, or, in the case of an incapable party, their deputy, could not be appointed and where no other neutral third party was available, it would seem prudent for the tribunal and/or the parties to at least consult with the Official Solicitor about the proceedings. It may be that they would want to intervene in the proceedings on behalf of children or incapable parties, and if that is so issues of public policy might arise if they were not allowed to do so. In consequence, it would seem sensible to provide for the Official Solicitor to represent such parties if they insist on doing so, although given the 'last resort' criteria and the fact that these would not be family law proceedings it might seem unlikely that they would so insist.

5.041 It is also important to note that if an incapable person had a deputy appointed by the CoP, they would have to be informed about it and be involved in the proceedings. It is suggested that if they requested the right to represent the party before the arbitral tribunal, their request should usually be granted.

73 Le Poidevin 'Arbitration and Trusts: Can It Be Done?' (2012) 313.

74 David Hayton, 'Problems in Attaining Binding Determinations of Trust Issues by Alternative Dispute Resolution' (Kluwer Law International 2001).

75 ibid.

Equally, such a party may apply to the CoP for the power to represent the incapable party, and in the event that the CoP granted them such a power, it is hard to see how the arbitral tribunal could refuse to allow them to represent the incapable party without risking contempt of court.

In any event, in order to safeguard compliance with the ECHR, and indeed natural justice, there has to be a body which can decide on objections on legal representation, review a person's capacity if it is contested, judge whether an arbitration friend is sufficiently representing their interests and so on. Assuming that there is no court order on the matter, it would seem logical for the arbitral tribunal to do this subject to court review under the Arbitration Act. For example, a party could apply to remove one or several arbitrators under s 24 for breach of the s 33 duty to act fairly and impartially between the parties. Equally, they could apply for the award to be set aside under s 68 for substantial irregularity on the basis of a violation of due process. It is submitted that these statutory provisions would be sufficient to ensure compliance under the ECHR as they provide a means for an aggrieved party to indirectly challenge the relevant decisions before the court. In the event that an individual had a court order to represent a party, it does not seem that the tribunal would have any other choice but to accede to the individual's request. **5.042**

2. Virtual representation and representative actions

The doctrine was explained by a New York court as follows: **5.043**

> Virtual representation is a doctrine which permits one who is a party (the 'representor') to represent the interests of the person or classes of persons (the 'representees') who otherwise would be necessary parties, without serving them with process or making them actual parties. The whole theory underlying the doctrine is similarity of economic interests. It is presumed that the representor in pursuing his own economic self-interest will necessarily protect the rights of the representees having the same interest.[76]

The court noted that the main issue with that doctrine was 'the possibility inherent in such representation of resulting conflict of interest – a consequence never present where representation is by a guardian ad litem'.[77] Thus, **5.044**

> there is never any absolute assurance that the decree will not be vulnerable. If … it results in an advantage to the representor vis-à-vis the representee, this is prima facie proof of

76 *In the Matter of the Estate of Herbert Silver, Deceased* (1973) 72 Misc 2d 963, 966.

77 ibid.

> either inadequacy of representation or conflict of interest. … [V]irtual representation never assures the same finality as does representation by a guardian ad litem.[78]

5.045 Although the doctrine of virtual representation has obvious parallels with the English system of representative actions, it is in some senses broader and in others narrower than the latter. On the one hand, it does not seem to be limited to those cases where the person is unascertained or unborn or to complex litigation, but on the other, it seems limited to those cases of similar economic interests and is much more vulnerable to attack on the basis of an alleged conflict of interest. It would seem, however, that both are predicated on the desire to simplify litigation and to address situations where it is undesirable or impossible to notify parties of an action, but it is still necessary to bind them.

5.046 David Hayton suggests the use of virtual representation clauses in trust arbitration deeds as a means of improving the enforceability of trust arbitration clauses as against beneficiaries, and even provides a sample clause in his article.[79] He notes, however, that such clauses would have to be extremely lengthy and might not always be able to take into account situations where although the interests of different classes are in harmony, they actually conflict. For example, he states:

> 21 and 19 year old grandsons may want to settle the dispute quickly to obtain cash to meet debts or purchase fast cars, while infant and unborn grandsons would want to settle the dispute for a large sum of money even if this takes longer, or such two grandsons may want the family company owned by the trust to be sold off, although 16 and 14 year old grandsons may be very interested in going into the family business, so that the company should not be sold.[80]

5.047 The use of representative actions would not seem to be as strictly circumscribed as virtual representation, however, and it may be that even when there is a conflict of interest, a representative action could be used. In consequence, clauses based on a representative action rather than virtual representation might not need to be as long as suggested by Hayton, although in the interests of maximising the likelihood of their enforceability they should be based, *mutatis mutandis*, on the representative action provisions in the CPR. Equally it would seem sensible that such clauses be based on a recognised doctrine, namely representative actions, rather than an unrecognised American equivalent, that of virtual representation.

---

78 ibid.

79 Hayton, 'Problems in Attaining Binding Determinations of Trust Issues by Alternative Dispute Resolution' (n 74).

80 DJ Hayton (ed), *The International Trust* (Jordans 2011).

Representative actions are not, however, only relevant in the event that provision is made for the doctrine in the trust deed; it might also be possible for the arbitral tribunal to decide *ex proprio motu* to apply it on the basis of its general power to regulate the proceedings, which is provided for in s 34 of the Arbitration Act as well as under the applicable institutional rules, if any. In such a case it would be up to the tribunal to decide whether to apply the English doctrine of representative actions or the American doctrine of virtual representation, but again it would seem more prudent to apply the English law doctrine if the arbitration is seated in England or English procedural law applies. It would, of course, be open to the settlor to provide for the procedural law of a US state which allows for virtual representation to apply to the arbitration, but issues might arise around, *inter alia*, discovery requirements, which are generally unwelcome in arbitration. In any event, if the tribunal were to decide on such a measure, it would be necessary to provide a means for challenging the rights of a particular party to act as a representative of another in order to ensure compliance with the ECHR. **5.048**

6

CONFLICTS OF LAWS ISSUES AND THE HAGUE TRUST CONVENTION

A. INTRODUCTION

6.001 One of the biggest issues facing trust arbitration is that the trust, as a legal institution, is not known in a vast number of legal systems, although many civil law systems now have some form of trust[1] or quasi-trust law.[2] Equally, some types of trust may not be recognised in all common law legal systems. For example, the Cayman Islands STAR trust does not exist in England and may not be recognised by its courts.[3] This is an unusual problem for the various players in

1 Maltese Trusts and Trustees Act 1989; Johanna Niegel, 'Liechtenstein Trusts: An Overview of the Law and Practice' (2004) 10 Trusts & Trustees 19.

2 See with regard to France and China, Lionel Smith (ed), *Re-Imagining the Trust* (Cambridge University Press 2012) 183–257 <https://www.cambridge.org/core/product/identifier/9780511894879%23c01132-116/type/book_part> accessed 20 November 2019.

3 Paul Matthews, 'Shooting STAR: The New Special Trusts Regime from the Cayman Islands' (1997) 11 Trust Law International 67.

the system of international arbitration, including arbitrators, practitioners and state courts, as usually arbitral awards are about virtually universally recognised legal doctrines such as contract, tort, agency and so on. In consequence, this chapter aims to provide a brief overview of the way in which the trust has been interpreted by civil law legal systems which do not recognise it, as well as the conflict of laws rules which may be applied to it in general, with a particular focus on the 1985 Hague Convention on the Law Applicable to Trusts and on their Recognition. The issue of the appropriate conflict of laws rules to apply to trusts is also intertwined with the question of public policy and the recognition of trusts by legal systems which do not possess either the institution of the trust or the type of trust in question. In the context of trust arbitration, as will be seen below in Chapter 8, the fundamental issue is whether certain jurisdictions might refuse to recognise or enforce trust arbitration awards on the grounds that their legal system does not possess the institution of the trust or that the trust in question violates public policy or mandatory rules. In order to answer such questions under the NYC, it is necessary to first analyse the conflict of laws rules regarding trusts internationally as well as possible public policy issues that might arise in this context and that is the purpose of this chapter.

B. THE CIVILIAN APPROACH TO SITUATIONS INVOLVING A TRUST

As a preliminary point, it is important to note that 'civil law forums do not ordinarily hold a common law trust void per se'.[4] Instead, 'a civil law court will … consider the extent to which code institutions might accomplish the purposes of the trust, in order to determine whether public policy prevents its recognition … and establish a basis of analysis and analogy'.[5] A concrete example of this process in the Italian context resulted in 'an English testamentary trust for sale, conferring a life interest on the testator's children with remainder over to their issue' being 'translated', with the beneficiaries being the testator's heirs and the trustee being an 'administrator sui generis'.[6] Although this situation is better than an outright refusal to recognise the trust, there are obvious issues in terms of predictability, transparency regarding the law[7] and conflict of laws outcomes which would not have been foreseen by the settlor and would not **6.002**

4 'Common Law Trusts in Civil Law Courts' (1954) 67 Harvard Law Review 1030, 1030.

5 ibid.

6 Smith (n 2) 41.

7 ibid 41–42.

have occurred in a common law jurisdiction.[8] It is important to note however that the above process will differ depending on whether the civil law system in question possesses its own 'trusts', as is the case in Malta[9] and Liechtenstein[10] for example, or not, as is the case in most civilian legal systems. However, between these two extremes there is a range of possibilities as some civilian legal systems have trust-like institutions such as the *Treuhand* or *fideicommissum* in Germany and the *Bewind* in the Netherlands.[11] It need not be said that those civilian systems which possess the trust, or a trust-like institution, are more likely to recognise trusts than those which do not.

6.003 Unsurprisingly, the different types of trust tend to be treated differently by civilian legal systems, so that testamentary trusts of immovables are more likely to be upheld in a beneficial fashion, as opposed to being mistranslated, particularly if the legal system allows the law of the testator's domicile to govern, as do France and Belgium.[12] On the other hand, testamentary trusts face unique problems. For example, if the provisions of the trust violate forced heirship rules of the forum, they are likely to be struck down.[13] However, even if the provisions of such a trust are struck down, the courts would appear still to indirectly uphold some provisions of the trust, by holding that the assets not subject to forced heirship do not revert to the testator's estate but are instead subject to a condition subsequent.[14]

6.004 Inter vivos trusts over immovables are less likely to be upheld by a civilian court as 'a civil law court's desire to avoid controversy over title or administration of a trust arrangement is not counterbalanced by the policy favoring a uniform treatment of the donor's dispositions … as the donor is able to make individual gifts … each conforming to the local law'.[15] Testamentary trusts over movables are also less likely to be upheld as the property can be removed from the jurisdiction at any point.[16] On the other hand, inter vivos trusts of movables

---

8 Michele Graziadei and others, *Commercial Trusts in European Private Law* (Cambridge University Press 2005) 61–62 <http://ebookcentral.proquest.com/lib/mcgill/detail.action?docID=244046> accessed 20 November 2019.

9 Maltese Trusts and Trustees Act.

10 Niegel (n 1).

11 See the discussion in Bureau Permanent de la Conference, *Actes et Documents de La Quinzieme Session 8 Au 20 Octobre 1984 Proceedings of the Fifteenth Session Tome II Trust – Loi Applicable et Reconnaissance Trusts – Applicable Law and Recognition* (Imprimerie Nationale 1985) 36–39.

12 'Common Law Trusts in Civil Law Courts' (n 4) 1036–1039.

13 ibid 1038; see generally DJ Hayton (ed), *The International Trust* (Jordans 2011) 711–783.

14 'Common Law Trusts in Civil Law Courts' (n 4) 1038.

15 ibid 1039.

16 ibid.

are likely to be upheld as regards a gift of movables in a common law jurisdiction or where the movables are no longer within the jurisdiction. However, in accordance with general rules of law, civil law will apply when they are within the jurisdiction.[17] An argument could be made that the beneficiaries' rights or lack thereof are a matter of personal status and thus 'should be governed by his personal law', but this argument has had a mixed reception in practice.[18]

In general, and as already noted above, it can be stated that civil law courts will not generally void trusts which would seem to mean that 'a division of legal and beneficial interests does not necessarily violate the situs's public policy if the trustee's obligations and the beneficiary's rights are not unlike rights and obligations that may be created under the Codes'.[19] In consequence, it behoves lawyers dealing with trusts in civilian legal systems to attempt to translate the trust into the most appropriate legal institutions permitted under civil law. This would appear to be much easier today than at the time the article cited above was written – 1950 – given that many civilian legal systems now have some form of quasi-trust institution, and it should be possible to combine it with other institutions permitted in the relevant jurisdiction to achieve a significant measure of recognition for the trust and its terms. Moreover, it would appear that the only public policy issues likely to be raised by the recognition of a trust are, as already discussed, rules regarding forced heirship, tax and the usual complications that arise in divorce or separation proceedings. **6.005**

As an addendum to the above, it should be noted that it is questionable whether the extremely complex types of trust structures seen offshore which involve the use of enforcers and protectors and where the settlor has reserved extensive powers to himself, etc., would be recognised by a civilian court. It would seem to be very hard to 'translate' such complex structures into 'rights and obligations that may be created under the Codes',[20] and any retention of control may create problems as regards forced heirship provisions in the *lex successionis*.[21] **6.006**

As a final point before concluding this short overview of how civil law courts are likely to approach the trust, it is important to note that although the general approach outlined above is valid for civilian courts in general, this approach is **6.007**

17 ibid 1041.

18 ibid 1041–1042.

19 ibid 1041.

20 ibid.

21 David Hayton, 'Trusts and Forced Heirship Problems' (1993) 4 King's College Law Journal 12, 15–16.

affected by the Hague Trust Convention (HTC) in states that are party to it. Indeed as will be seen below, the HTC has even influenced jurisdictions which have not signed or ratified it.

C. A BRIEF INTRODUCTION TO THE HAGUE TRUST CONVENTION

6.008 The Hague Trust Convention, or to give it its full title, the Convention of 1 July 1985 on the Law Applicable to Trusts and on their Recognition, aims not to introduce 'the trust into … civil law countries, but simply … [furnish] to their judges the instruments which are appropriate to grasp this legal device'.[22] The issue is that since the trust 'is not provided for in their substantive laws, they, of course, also do not have rules of private international law to govern it, and they are therefore reduced to seeking laboriously to introduce the elements of the trust into their own concepts'.[23] The Convention rectifies this situation by putting 'at their disposal conflict-of-laws rules for trusts; then it indicates what the recognition of a trust should consist of, but also the limits of this recognition'.[24] Despite this modest description of the Convention's aims in practice, as will be seen below, the Convention has had a far more wide-reaching effect, to the extent that some legal systems have introduced the trust into their domestic law via its provisions, and despite the Convention providing safeguards in order to prevent this outcome.

6.009 Preparatory work on the Convention began in 1980,[25] although, notoriously, only five weeks were available to produce its first draft, which may have led to the Convention's occasionally ambiguous and inelegant wording.[26] It was open for signature from the 1st of July 1985, and it entered into force on the 1st of January 1992.[27] To date, the Convention is applied in only 27 jurisdictions, over half of which consist of the various constituent jurisdictions of the UK as well as its overseas territories, and the majority of the remainder are small civilian jurisdictions, for example, Monaco, Luxembourg, Liechtenstein, San

22 Alfred von Overbeck, 'Explanatory Report by Alfred von Overbeck' (Hague Conference on Private International Law 1985), para 14.

23 ibid.

24 ibid.

25 ibid 1.

26 David Hayton, 'Reflections on The Hague Trusts Convention after 30 Years' (2016) 12 Journal of Private International Law 1, 2.

27 'HCCH | #30 – Status Table' <https://www.hcch.net/en/instruments/conventions/status-table/?cid=59> accessed 21 November 2019.

Marino, Malta and Cyprus. It might, therefore, be said that the Convention is of minor importance, with over half the states being common law jurisdictions which already recognise the trust and the remainder being minor civilian jurisdictions. In consequence, one might argue that both the practical effect and territorial extent of the Convention is so limited as to render it irrelevant. However, this assessment would be an unfair one for several reasons.

Firstly, the size or population of a country does not necessarily correlate with the amount of assets domiciled in the jurisdiction. It is clear that Liechtenstein, Luxembourg and Monaco all have large wealth management industries. Other important wealth management jurisdictions which have ratified the Convention include Switzerland and Panama, as well as, to a lesser extent, Cyprus. Secondly, even if common law jurisdictions already recognise the trust, they do not all recognise the same types of trusts. For example, the British Virgin Islands (BVI) Vista Trust is unique to it, and the Cayman Islands STAR trust is similarly unique. In both cases, issues of recognition by other common law jurisdictions have been raised,[28] and the Convention significantly increases the likelihood of their being recognised by such jurisdictions. **6.010**

Thirdly, there has also been an acceleration of expansion in recent years with Cyprus ratifying it in 2017, Panama acceding to it in 2018 and its application being extended to the province of Ontario in 2018. In general, the trend in recent years has been for the Convention's increasing relevance notwithstanding the limited scope of its direct application. Fourthly, and lastly, the HTC can have an influence even where a country has not ratified it, as in the case of Belgium, which has replicated some of the rules of the HTC in its Private International Law Code as regards trusts.[29] **6.011**

As a result of all of the above, it is therefore clear that the HTC is an important international instrument which merits serious consideration and its most relevant sections will be briefly considered in turn below. **6.012**

1. Function and purpose of the Convention (Article 1)

This article outlines the function and purpose of the Convention, namely to provide choice of law rules for trusts and to govern their recognition. The idea of 'recognition' is an unhappy one as it is typically used with regard to foreign **6.013**

---

28 Raymond Davern, 'Does the Virgin Islands Special Trusts Act Achieve Anything Special?' (2010) 16 Trusts & Trustees 750; Matthews, 'Shooting STAR: The New Special Trusts Regime from the Cayman Islands' (n 3).

29 Hayton, 'Reflections on The Hague Trusts Convention after 30 Years' (n 26) 2.

judgments and awards, but it is clear that that is not what is meant here.[30] Instead, the recognition rules under the HTC 'simply furnish guidance as to what effects a Convention trust should be given in contracting states'.[31]

2. Characteristics of a Convention trust (Article 2)

6.014 The aim of this provision is not so much to provide a definition for what a trust is but rather to 'indicate the characteristics which an institution must show … in order to fall under the Convention's coverage'.[32] The definition covers not just the 'paradigm English express trust'[33] but also civilian legal institutions,[34] although such institutions would have to be structurally analogous to the common law trust as opposed to merely functionally analogous.[35] It is virtually certain then that civil law trusts which are based on the common law trust, such as that of Malta[36] or Liechtenstein,[37] would fall within the definition, as well as possibly the *Treuhand* and *fideicommissum* in Germany and the *Bewind* in the Netherlands.[38]

3. Types of trust governed by the Convention (Article 3)

6.015 This article provides a two-fold limitation on 'the circle of the trusts covered by the Convention'.[39] They must be (i) created voluntarily, and (ii) evidenced in writing. This excludes trusts created *ex lege* or by judicial decision so that 'constructive trusts imposed by the courts and … trusts the courts create by virtue of an express provision of law' are excluded from the Convention.[40] Notwithstanding this provision, some authors have argued either that certain constructive trusts fall within the Convention; for example, where a trust fails due to non-compliance with statutory formalities and the court imposes a constructive trust with the court's decree itself being written evidence for

---

30 Harris JM, *The Hague Trusts Convention: Scope, Application and Preliminary Issues* (Hart 2002), 101.

31 ibid 102.

32 von Overbeck (n 22) para 36.

33 Harris (n 30) 104.

34 ibid 104–105; Emmanuel Gaillard and Donald T Trautman, 'Trusts in Non-Trust Countries: Conflict of Laws and the Hague Convention on Trusts' (1987) 35 The American Journal of Comparative Law 307, 318.

35 Gaillard and Trautman (n 34) 318.

36 Maltese Trusts and Trustees Act.

37 Niegel (n 1).

38 See the discussion in Bureau Permanent de la Conference, *Actes et documents de la Quinzieme session 8 au 20 octobre 1984 Proceedings of the Fifteenth Session Tome II Trust – loi applicable et reconnaissance Trusts – applicable law and recognition* (La Haye: Imprimerie Nationale 1985) at 36–39.

39 von Overbeck (n 22) para 48.

40 ibid 49.

the purposes of the Convention.[41] It is difficult to square this interpretation with the plain wording of the provision,[42] but other less extreme examples of Convention-compliant constructive trusts include those which result from mutual wills and specifically enforceable contracts.[43]

The status of resulting trusts is less contentious as the explanatory report to the Convention itself accepts they may fall within the Convention's scope,[44] but this likely only means 'automatic' resulting trusts as opposed to those which arise from a presumed intention[45] (e.g. when property is purchased in the name of another).[46] Lastly, trusts which arise orally or by delivery of the property to the trustee also come within the scope of the convention as long as they are evidenced in writing.[47] **6.016**

4. Launcher and rocket (Article 4)

This article, which deals with the Convention's scope of application regarding preliminary matters such as the validity of the trust deed, the capacity of the settlor, etc.,[48] has been memorably imagined as drawing a distinction between the 'launcher', the aforesaid preliminary matters, and the 'rocket', that is to say, the trust.[49] The point is that the 'launcher' does not fall within the scope of the Convention, for example, although a transfer of assets is a *sine qua non* for a trust to exist, the acts by which that property is transferred will not be governed by the law designated as applicable by the Convention but rather by whatever law the forum's conflicts rules determine.[50] Equally, although not explicitly mentioned in the Convention, the issue of the capacity of a person, except their capacity to become a trustee, is also excluded from the Convention's scope.[51] **6.017**

41 David Hayton, 'The Hague Convention on the Law Applicable to Trusts and on Their Recognition' (1987) 36 International & Comparative Law Quarterly 260, 264–265.

42 Harris (n 30) 129.

43 ibid 128.

44 von Overbeck (n 22) para 51.

45 Harris (n 30) 126.

46 L Tucker, *Lewin on Trusts* (Sweet & Maxwell 2012) para 9-021 et seq.

47 von Overbeck (n 22) para 52.

48 Harris (n 30) 151.

49 von Overbeck (n 22) para 53.

50 ibid 54.

51 ibid 59.

5. Non-Applicability if non-trust law jurisdiction specified (Article 5)

6.018 The result of this article is fairly straightforward: it ensures that 'the Convention is not applicable if its conflicts rules designate the law of a State which does not have trusts' or does not have the category of trust in question.[52] It is unlikely that the article will be applied often in practice, particularly as it seems inherently improbable that the settlor would choose such a law, and even if he did 'the trust will still fall under the Convention's coverage if the objectively applicable law provides for such a trust'.[53]

6. Express or implied choice of law (Article 6)

6.019 This article has been described as 'the triumph of settlor autonomy'.[54] The 'freedom of a settlor to choose the applicable law under the Convention is quite broad [as] [t]he chosen law need have no objective connection with the trust in question'.[55] There are, however, some standard limitations. For example, the law chosen must be an individual legal system, for example one cannot select 'Canadian law' to govern a trust, one must instead choose a specific province. In the same vein, it has been stated that the law chosen must be of a recognised legal system, references to general principles of law or *lex mercatoria* would not be valid.[56] Equally, it is unlikely that one could choose the law of a national legal system minus its mandatory rules or public policy.[57] On the other hand, the von Overbeck report states that 'The circle of laws which can be chosen is unlimited'[58] and in this respect, the rules regarding trusts in the Draft Common Frame of Reference[59] represent a possible choice, even though they are not the law of a recognised legal system.

6.020 In recent years the Hague Conference seems to have moved towards a greater acceptance of non-national legal systems in its instruments. For example, Art 3 of the Hague Principles on Choice of Law in International Commercial Contracts make explicit provision for such a choice. It states that, 'The law

---

52 ibid 61.

53 ibid.

54 Harris (n 30) 166–169.

55 Gaillard and Trautman (n 34) 323.

56 Harris (n 30) 185–186.

57 ibid 190–191.

58 von Overbeck (n 22) para 64.

59 Christian von Bar and others (eds), *Principles, Definitions and Model Rules of European Private Law: Draft Common Frame of Reference (DCFR)* (Full ed, Sellier European Law Publishers 2009) Bk X.

chosen by the parties may be rules of law that are generally accepted on an international, supranational or regional level as a neutral and balanced set of rules, unless the law of the forum provides otherwise.' The commentary to the principles says that such rules of law include the UN Convention on the International Sale of Goods, the UNIDROIT Principles of International Commercial Contracts and the Principles of European Contract Law.[60] However, it would seem that neither general principles of law nor *lex mercatoria* would be a valid choice of law under the principles.[61]

It goes without saying that the Hague Principles are not directly applicable to trusts and are a non-binding instrument, although implementing legislation has been passed in Paraguay[62] and has been suggested in Australia.[63] Nevertheless, the Principles might be helpful in indicating the general direction of travel in this area in Private International Law and lending credence to the view that a choice of non-national law should be valid in the case of trusts. However, it must be noted that the choice of non-national law to govern a contract, let alone a trust, remains controversial, and compromises had to be made to permit provision for it in the Principles.[64] Indeed, some states made it clear that whilst they would not prevent provision for non-national laws in the Hague Principles, they did not intend to take their national law in such a direction.[65] In any event, it seems highly unlikely that a settlor, lawyer or trustee would choose a non-national law to govern the trust given the complete lack of authority or reported precedent for such a choice, and even in the case of the Draft Common Frame of Reference (DCFR), there is no judicial or statutory authority for the application of its provisions to a trust. **6.021**

As regards implied choice of law, the Convention still attempts to protect the settlor's wishes as 'the implied choice must derive from the terms of the instrument creating, or the writing evidencing, the trust, interpreted if necessary in the light of the circumstances of the case',[66] so that the issue is one of 'implication of intent [which] cannot disregard the purposes of the trust and the **6.022**

60 Principles on Choice of Law in International Commercial Contracts, paras 3.5–3.7.

61 Genevieve Saumier, 'The Hague Principles and the Choice of Non-State "Rules of Law" to Govern an International Commercial Contract' (2014) 40 Brooklyn Journal of International Law 1, 17.

62 'HCCH | #40 - Publications' <https://www.hcch.net/en/instruments/conventions/publications1/?dtid=41&cid=135> accessed 26 December 2019.

63 Michael Douglas and Nicholas Loadsman, 'The Impact of the Hague Principles on Choice of Law in International Commercial Contracts' (2018) 19 Melbourne Journal of International Law 1.

64 Saumier (n 61) 12–18.

65 ibid 28.

66 von Overbeck (n 22) para 64.

context in which the problem arises'.[67] Presumably, the same restrictions apply to an implied choice of law as to an express choice of law. In consequence, it would appear that a choice should not be implied if it would lead to results deemed inconsistent with the settlor's intent.

7. Applicable law in the absence of choice (Article 7)

6.023 This article provides the applicable law where no choice of law has been made as regards the trust, whether express or implied, and where the chosen law does not 'provide for trusts or the category of trusts involved'.[68] The key principle is that the trust will be governed by the law with which it is most closely connected, with four factors given special importance, namely:

I. The place of administration of the trust designated by the settlor;
II. The situs of the trust assets;
III. The place of residence or business of the trustee;
IV. The objects of the trust and the places where they are to be fulfilled.

6.024 It is self-evident that the law applicable under this section cannot be the law of a jurisdiction which does not provide for trusts or for the category of trust in question.[69]

8. Scope of the applicable law (Article 8)

6.025 This article provides a non-exhaustive list of the issues which are subject to the law governing the trust as determined by Arts 6 or 7. Importantly, von Overbeck states that the scope of the applicable law does not include issues of form, these already having been addressed in Art 3.[70] However, Harris argues that some law must govern issues of formal validity regarding the trust as these are more extensive than just the writing requirement in Art 3 and may not always be 'launcher' issues excluded from the Convention.[71] In this regard, he gives the example of an oral trust over land, which fails to meet the requirements of the s 53(1)(b) Law of Property Act 1925 under English law.[72] He argues that notwithstanding the Convention's lack of reference to formal validity, it must be held as providing for the applicable law to govern issues of formal validity in a trust law sense as the alternative is potentially absurd. For

67 Gaillard and Trautman (n 34) 324.
68 von Overbeck (n 22) para 72.
69 ibid 73.
70 ibid 82.
71 Harris (n 30) 272–276.
72 ibid 273–274.

example, would an English court be required to hold that a trust was valid even if it would not be under the law applicable to it nor would it be enforced by the courts of that state?[73]

9. *Dépeçage* (Article 9)

This article provides that *dépeçage*, 'the practice of subjecting certain elements of the trust to different laws',[74] is valid under the Convention. One particular example of this, discussed earlier, is where the validity of the trust is governed by X law, whereas the administration of the trust is governed by Y law.[75] **6.026**

10. Consequences of recognition (Article 11)

This article is the lynchpin of the Convention as it 'requires the recognition of essential elements for all trusts [and] enumerates the supplementary aspects of recognition which may flow from the law applicable to the trust'.[76] Crucially, it provides that the assets of the trust are separate from the personal assets of the trustee, something that 'is an essential element of a trust, without which its recognition would have no meaning'.[77] This is also the most problematic aspect of the trust for civilian legal systems and has had an unintended revolutionary effect on some civil law signatories. For example Italy, which does not under its domestic law have the concept of a trust, has witnessed the growth of the so-called *trust interno*, this is a trust 'involving Italian assets and in favour of Italian beneficiaries but governed by foreign law'.[78] Although there are numerous means for the Italian courts to reject such a possibility under both the Convention and their domestic law, they have refused to do so in the majority of cases brought before them.[79] **6.027**

It should be noted, however, that the Italian example is a unique one and does not appear to have been replicated in the vast majority of Convention states. The importance of the Convention then is not that it introduces trusts into the civil law by the back door but rather that it marks 'the death of translation'.[80] In other words, it requires that 'the trust ... be recognised qua trust and not **6.028**

73 ibid 275–276.

74 von Overbeck (n 22) para 91.

75 Harris (n 30) 281.

76 von Overbeck (n 22) para 104.

77 ibid 108.

78 Hayton, *The International Trust* (n 13) para 15.7.

79 ibid paras 15.6–15.21.

80 Harris (n 30) 335.

by reinvention in the guise of the nearest civil law analogue'.[81] In practice, however, the trust will likely be recognised in some hybrid form of existing civil law substitutes, but this is a price worth paying in order to introduce the trust into the Conflict of Laws rules of states that don't have the trust and ratify the HTC.[82]

11. Non-recognition of trusts more closely connected with non-trust states (Article 13)

6.029 This article is one of several escape hatches in the Convention. Where a trust is more closely connected to a jurisdiction which does not recognise trusts or the type of trust in question, for example because of the habitual residence or nationalities of the relevant parties or the location of the trust assets, a judge can refuse to recognise the trust.[83] Importantly, in the English law context this article was not included in the implementing statute, the Recognition of Trusts Act 1987, with the result that, in theory, an English settlor could create a trust with English beneficiaries, trustees and assets but subject to the law of, for example, the Cayman Islands or the BVI.[84] However, as will be seen below, it might still be possible for courts to refuse recognition on the grounds of public policy.

12. Preservation of mandatory rules of the applicable law (Article 15)

6.030 This article provides that the mandatory rules of the applicable law, not the law of the forum, in certain areas of law are to be preserved and can continue to prevent the recognition of a trust. The areas of law in question are as follows:

I. Laws regarding the protection of minors and incapable parties;
II. Laws regulating the personal and proprietary effects of marriage;
III. Succession rights, and in particular laws regarding forced heirship;
IV. Laws regarding the transfer of title to property and security interests;
V. Insolvency law as regards laws protecting creditors;
VI. Laws protecting third parties acting in good faith.

6.031 It should be noted that the article is permissive and not mandatory, so a judge is not obliged to apply the mandatory rules of the applicable law under the

---

81 ibid.

82 ibid 336.

83 von Overbeck (n 22) paras 122–123.

84 Harris (n 30).

Convention,[85] and indeed the Convention itself states that, 'If recognition of a trust is prevented by application of the preceding paragraph, the court shall try to give effect to the objects of the trust by other means'. However, 'this is an appeal to goodwill rather than a rule of strict law',[86] so it is unlikely to 'have a real substantive impact'.[87]

13. Application of the international mandatory rules of the forum and other closely connected states (Article 16)

The aim of this section is not to safeguard the application of all the mandatory rules of the forum or a closely connected state but rather only those 'which must be applied even in international situations'. Examples of such rules include exchange control regulations,[88] import and export controls,[89] laws protecting weaker or vulnerable parties,[90] laws protecting public health,[91] and possibly, in the English context, certain provisions of the Administration of Estates Act 1925.[92] As regards the provision for the exceptional application of the mandatory rules of a closely connected state, this would be a state which is neither the forum nor the state of the applicable law and depends on the judge's discretion.[93] **6.032**

14. Public policy derogation (Article 18)

This article merely restates the 'public policy clause which is customary in the Hague Conventions',[94] and although potentially capable of undermining the entire Convention, it is likely to be interpreted restrictively.[95] Examples of such situations would be where a law 'brings about a serious infringement of human rights' or where exchange control legislation was used as a system of oppression and discrimination.[96] Other possible examples in the English context would include the non-application of a foreign law which breached the rule against **6.033**

85 ibid 361–362.
86 von Overbeck (n 22) para 147.
87 Harris (n 30) 379.
88 Gaillard and Trautman (n 34) 326; von Overbeck (n 22) para 149.
89 Gaillard and Trautman (n 34) 326; von Overbeck (n 22) para 149.
90 von Overbeck (n 22) para 149.
91 ibid.
92 Harris (n 30) 384.
93 von Overbeck (n 22) para 151.
94 ibid para 164.
95 Harris (n 30) 390–391.
96 Tucker (n 46) para 11-243.

perpetuities or recognised non-charitable purpose trusts.[97] In this context, even if an English court could not avoid the application of BVI or Cayman Islands law under Art 13, it could declare such a trust contrary to public policy under Art 18.

6.034 In bringing this section to a close, it is possible to say that, in general, although trusts cause particular conflict of laws problems due to their unique nature, they should be upheld in some fashion, in most jurisdictions either by analogy with existing legal institutions or via the provisions of the HTC. However, there is still considerable scope for courts in civil law countries, or common law countries which do not recognise the category of trust in question, to refuse to recognise a trust where it would be contrary to public policy. The more complex, or 'wacky', the trust structure is the more unlikely it is to be recognised, although there are particular issues with regard to forced heirship and, in the English context, non-charitable purpose trusts. Crucially, however, trusts are not, in and of themselves, contrary to public policy and thus, as will be seen in the next chapter, it is not possible to argue against the recognition of trust arbitration awards abroad merely because they involve a trust and the legal system in question does not provide for trusts.

97 Hayton, *The International Trust* (n 13) para 3.54.

7

EXISTING STATUTORY FRAMEWORKS FOR TRUST ARBITRATION

It is not surprising given the complexity of the issues involved that some jurisdictions have opted to put trust arbitration on a firmer footing by giving it a statutory basis. The aim of this chapter is to briefly outline and analyse such statutes, as well as to separate the wheat from the chaff in the terms of well and not so well drafted provisions. In terms of structure, Commonwealth jurisdictions will be analysed first, in no particular order, followed by the many US jurisdictions which have implemented such statutes. **7.001**

A. THE BAHAMAS

The relevant provisions are to be found in the Trustee Act 1998 as amended by the Trustee Amendment Act 2011. They are laid out in full below: **7.002**

91A. Arbitration of trust disputes.

(1) The object of this section is to enable any dispute or administration question in relation to a trust to be determined by arbitration in accordance with the provisions of the trust instrument.

(2) Where a written trust instrument provides that any dispute or administration question arising between any of the parties in relation to the trust shall be submitted to arbitration ('a trust arbitration'), that provision shall, for all purposes under the Arbitration Act, have effect as between those parties as if it were an arbitration agreement and as if those parties were parties to that agreement.

(3) The Arbitration Act shall apply to a trust arbitration in accordance with the provisions of the Second Schedule to this Act.

(4) The Minister may by order amend the *Second Schedule*.

91B. Powers of the arbitral tribunal.

(1) This section shall apply except to the extent otherwise provided in the trust instrument.

(2) The arbitral tribunal (hereinafter referred to as 'the tribunal') may, in addition to all other powers of the tribunal, at any stage in a trust arbitration, exercise all the powers of the Court (whether arising by statute (including this Act), under the inherent jurisdiction of the Court or otherwise) in relation to the administration, execution or variation of a trust or the exercise of any power arising under a trust.

(3) Without prejudice to subsection (2), and to any provisions made pursuant to subsection (4), the tribunal has the same powers to appoint one or more persons to represent the interests of any person (including a person unborn or unascertained) or class in a trust arbitration as the court has under Order 15 rule 14 of the Rules of the Supreme Court in relation to proceedings before the court.

(4) The terms of a trust may provide for the appointment of one or more persons to represent the interests of any person (including a person unborn or unascertained) or class in a trust arbitration.

(5) Where an appointment is made under subsection (3) or (4) —

(a) the approval of the tribunal is required in relation to a settlement affecting the person or class represented;

(b) the tribunal may approve a settlement where it is satisfied that the settlement is for the benefit of the person or class represented;

(c) any award given in the trust arbitration shall be binding on the person or class represented by the person or persons appointed.

(6) A person under a disability may not —

(a) bring or make a claim in a trust arbitration except by his next friend;

(b) defend, make a counterclaim or intervene in a trust arbitration except by his guardian *ad litem*; or

(c) take any step in a trust arbitration except by his next friend or guardian *ad litem*, unless otherwise ordered by the tribunal.

(7) The terms of a trust may provide for the appointment of a next friend or guardian *ad litem*, for the cessation of an appointment, and for the service of documents upon a person under a disability.

(8) Subject to subsection (7), the tribunal may appoint a suitable person to be a next friend or guardian *ad litem*, may terminate an appointment, and may give directions for the service of documents upon a person under a disability.

(9) Where a next friend or guardian *ad litem* has been appointed under subsection (7) or subsection (8), no settlement affecting the person under a disability shall be valid, without the approval of the tribunal.

(10) Notwithstanding subsection (1), subsections (5), (6) and (9) shall apply irrespective of any provision in the trust instrument.

(11) The Minister may make regulations to extend or clarify the powers of the tribunal in relation to trust arbitrations.

91C. Interpretation for sections 91A, 918 and the Second Schedule.

For the purposes of sections 91A, 91B and the Second Schedule —

'administration question' means any relief or question in respect of which an action, application or other reference to the court could, subject to section 91 A and the Arbitration Act, be brought or made under Order 74 of the Rules of the Supreme Court under this Act or under the Purpose Trusts Act;

'beneficiary' includes an object of a power, whether or not ascertained or in existence and a charity;

'dispute' includes a difference;

'power holder' means any person holding a power in relation to a trust (including any power of appointment, consent, direction, revocation or variation, and any power to appoint or remove trustees or power holders) and includes a person in the position of a protector;

'the parties in relation to the trust' means any trustee, beneficiary or power holder of or under the trust, in their capacity as such. ...

SECOND SCHEDULE
(section 91A)
APPLICATION OF THE ARBITRATION ACT

The Arbitration Act shall apply and be construed with respect to a trust arbitration, as stated hereunder —

1. The Arbitration Act shall apply and be construed with respect to a trust arbitration, as stated hereunder.
2. In the Arbitration Act, 'dispute' includes an administration question.
3. Section 3(b) of the Arbitration Act shall apply as if it read —
   '(b) the settlor should be free to determine (by provision in the trust instrument) how, in relation to a trust, disputes are resolved, subject only to such safeguards as are necessary in the public interest;'.
4. Other than in sections 42, 43, 73 and Part XII, where in the Arbitration Act reference is made to a matter agreed between the parties to an arbitration agreement (including a matter which may be authorised, chosen, conferred, designated, nominated or vested by the parties) that matter shall (except where no effective provision is made) be determined as provided in the trust instrument.
5. Neither section 7 of the Arbitration Act nor any rule of law or construction treating an arbitration agreement separate to any agreement of which it is a part shall apply in relation to a trust arbitration.
6. The term 'legal proceedings' in sections 9 and 10 of the Arbitration Act includes an application or other reference to the court concerning an administration question which the trust instrument requires to be submitted to arbitration and a stay of that application or other reference may be sought by any of the parties in relation to the trust, whether or not a party to that application or other reference.

7. In any application or other reference to the Court referred to in paragraph 6, the court may stay the proceedings on its own volition unless all parties in relation to the trust affected by the application are before it or are represented by persons before it.
8. The reference to 'contemplation of the parties' in section 12(3)(a) of the Arbitration Act 14 shall apply as if it were a reference to the 'contemplation of the settlor'.
9. Section 83 of the Arbitration Act shall apply as if it included the following subsection —
   '(3) Where a person is or has been a party to a trust arbitration in the capacity of trustee he shall, unless the tribunal otherwise orders, be entitled to the costs of the arbitration, in so far as they are not recovered from or paid by any other person, out of the fund held by the trustee; and the tribunal may otherwise order only on the ground that the trustee has in substance acted for his own benefit rather than for the benefit of the fund.'.
10. Section 85(5) of the Arbitration Act 16 shall apply as if it included the following paragraph —
   '(c) Where a person is or has been a party to a trust arbitration in the capacity of trustee and is entitled to be paid his costs out of the fund held by the trustee any doubt as to whether costs were reasonably incurred shall be resolved in favour of the trustee. Costs shall be presumed to have been unreasonably incurred if they were incurred contrary to the duty of the trustee.'.
11. For the purposes of enforcing an arbitral award under section 88 of the Arbitration Act —
   (a) section 91A shall have effect for the purposes of section[s] 5 and 6 of the Arbitration (Foreign Arbitral Awards) Act, 2009 as it does for the purposes of the Arbitration Act 19;
   (b) section 6(2)(a) of the Arbitration (Foreign Arbitral Awards) Act, 2009 which provides for the refusal of enforcement of an arbitral award against an incapacitated person) shall apply subject to the provisions of section 91B;
   (c) section 6(2)(d) of the Arbitration (Foreign Arbitral Awards) Act, 2009 which provides for the refusal of enforcement of an arbitral award that deals with a difference not contemplated by or not falling within the terms of the submission to arbitration), the term 'difference' includes an administration question.

7.003 It can be seen by comparison with the statutory provisions of other jurisdictions discussed below that the Bahamas trust arbitration provisions are some of the most complete currently in existence. Crucially, the provisions amend the Arbitration Act to ensure that there can be no issue regarding the beneficiaries being bound by the clause, they also outline the powers of an arbitral tribunal in a trust dispute, make provision for representatives of classes of beneficiaries to be appointed by the arbitral tribunal and ensure that vulnerable beneficiaries are protected through the appointment of a representative in trust arbitration proceedings. However, the statute is not perfect, and two issues in particular caught this author's eye: (i) the provision that the doctrine of separability does not apply to trust arbitrations; and (ii) the provision that even administrative questions can be submitted to arbitration.

Although the choice to exclude the application of the doctrine of separability is not unprecedented (as will be seen below the DIFC trust statute does the same), it is not entirely clear why it was done. The legal fiction that the parties entered into a separate contract regarding dispute resolution as well as main contract is no less fictional in contractual than trust cases. Moreover, the agreement between all the parties to arbitrate a trust dispute is no less fictional in cases where the parties challenge the existence or validity of the trust deed than those where they do not. The caveat would make sense if the way in which beneficiaries were bound was by assenting to or seeking some benefit under the trust, but that is not how the statute works – it simply uses the dark arts of legislative fiat to create consent to arbitration where there is none. This raises another general problem, international enforceability. **7.004**

The New York Convention requires that in order to enforce an arbitral award there must actually be an arbitral agreement, which in turns requires consent to arbitrate, and as a result the effect of the Bahamas legislative fiat which invents consent to arbitration among non-consenting parties only extends to the limits of its territory. In consequence, a party wishing to enforce a trust arbitration award or agreement on the basis of the Bahamas Act would still need to prove that the 'parties' to the arbitration agreement actually consented to it. This would likely involve one of the various means of binding 'parties' to the trust discussed above. In other words, as regards international enforceability, the Bahamas Act does not improve on the situation which exists at common law. This may not be an issue where the trust assets and relevant parties are in the Bahamas, which may well often be the case, but in cases where the trust assets or relevant parties are more widely scattered it is likely to be problematic. **7.005**

As regards the provision for administrative questions to be considered disputes, this again raises questions of international enforceability, as, if a trustee is merely seeking guidance or comfort, this is clearly not a dispute and therefore would not fall within the scope of the New York Convention. Additionally, parties need to consider whether to have a different arbitral procedure for administrative questions than the arbitral procedure for actual disputes. This is because it is unlikely to be cost or time effective to convoke a tribunal of three arbitrators to decide on administrative questions. It is of course true that in cases where the parties have elected to have matters decided by a sole arbitrator **7.006** this issue does not arise, but that will not always (or perhaps even often) be the case.

7.007 Another interesting provision is s 91B(2), which imbues the tribunal with all the powers of a court in relation to the administration or execution of trusts, including the power to vary the trust or exercise any power arising under the trust. This is certainly an improvement (although not necessarily from a policy standpoint) on the common law. As onshore jurisdictions are likely to be concerned about the tax effects of such variation, such power is, as discussed above, unlikely to be exercisable by tribunals in onshore jurisdictions. However, tax issues are clearly not a matter of public policy in offshore jurisdictions which benefit greatly from their light touch approach to taxation matters and the provision is therefore a logical one in the context of the Bahamas. It should be noted that, as with the other issues discussed above, the international enforceability of any such decisions, assuming that the taxation effects of such variations affect jurisdictions outside the Bahamas, is open to debate.

7.008 Notwithstanding the above potential issues, many of which are simply caused by the inability of statute to cure every ill, the statute contains one of the most detailed and well-thought-out trust arbitration provisions currently in existence.

B. GUERNSEY

7.009 The relevant provisions in Guernsey can be found in s 63 of the Trusts (Guernsey) Law 2007, which provides that:

> (1) Where —
> (a) the terms of a trust direct or authorise, or the Court so orders, that any claim against a trustee founded on breach of trust may be referred to alternative dispute resolution (**'ADR'**),
> (b) such a claim arises and, in accordance with the terms of the trust or the Court's order, is referred to ADR, and
> (c) the ADR results in a settlement of the claim which is recorded in a document signed by or on behalf of all parties,
>
> the settlement is binding on all beneficiaries of the trust, whether or not yet ascertained or in existence, and whether or not minors or persons under legal disability.
>
> (2) Subsection (1) applies in respect of a beneficiary only if —
> (a) he was represented in the ADR proceedings (whether personally, or by his guardian, or as the member of a class, or otherwise), or

(b) if not so represented, he had notice of the ADR proceedings and a reasonable opportunity of being heard,

and only if, in the case of a beneficiary who is not yet ascertained or in existence, or who is a minor or person under legal disability, the person conducting the ADR proceedings certifies that he was independently represented by a person appointed for the purpose by a court of law.

'Notice' in paragraph (b) means 14 days' notice or such other period as the person conducting the ADR proceedings may direct.

(3) A person who represents a beneficiary in the ADR proceedings for the purposes of subsection (2)(a) is under a duty of care to the beneficiary.
(4) For the avoidance of doubt, the ADR proceedings need not be conducted in Guernsey or in accordance with the procedural law of Guernsey.
(5) In this section —

'ADR' includes conciliation, mediation, early neutral evaluation, adjudication, expert determination and arbitration, and

'proceedings' includes oral and written proceedings.

It can immediately be seen that the provisions are less detailed than those of the Bahamas, they do not for example specify an arbitral tribunals power in such cases nor do they appoint the arbitral tribunal to appoint anyone to act on behalf of beneficiaries, in fact they require a court to do so. Most problematic is the limitation of the provision to 'claim[s] against a trustee founded on breach of trust'. It is unclear whether this means that only breach of trust actions can be arbitrated or whether, for example, an action to remove a trustee due to their alleged breach of trust would also come within its scope. It is notable that the drafting of the section changed when it was in Bill form as it was originally intended to cover any type of trust dispute.[1] This lack of clarity will inevitably lead to litigation regarding what is and is not covered within the scope of a Guernsey trust arbitration clause, and ultimately means that the provision is stillborn except for clear-cut breach of trust actions. **7.010**

A further problem with the Guernsey provisions is that the desired statutory reform has not been carried out in a joined up way, in particular the relevant arbitration law (The Arbitration (Guernsey) Law 2016) has not been amended. Consequently, individuals affected by a trust arbitration agreement could argue that there was no agreement to arbitrate under the trust, which is a requirement of s 1 of the 2016 Arbitration Law. Any argument about that **7.011**

1 SI Strong and AP Molloy, *Arbitration of Trust Disputes: Issues in National and International Law* (Oxford University Press 2016) para 12.62.

issue by those who wished to enforce the arbitration agreement would have to be based on the common law arguments I noted above. Parties could challenge the substantive jurisdiction of the tribunal under s 62 for the same reason, and the same applies with regard to the enforcement of foreign trust arbitration awards under ss 85–89 of the Law. It seems odd for the legislature to have taken the time and trouble to address the matter of trust arbitration and yet not have made any of the necessary amendments to the Arbitration Law, leaving the whole matter on the same common law basis as before.

7.012 A last problem, noted by commentators,[2] is that the provision provides as a condition for enforcement of a trust arbitration clause that 'the ADR results in a settlement of the claim which is recorded in a document signed by or on behalf of all parties'. However, trust (and indeed all) arbitration awards clearly would not be signed by all the parties. In consequence, it would seem that the Act contains a fatal contradiction as arbitral awards would only come within its scope if they resulted in a 'settlement' (which by definition arbitral awards are not, unless they are consent awards) and said 'settlement' would have to be signed. As such requirements could only potentially be met in the context of consent awards, although even then it is difficult to see why individuals other than the arbitrators would sign the award, the legislation would appear to be of no use in the vast majority of cases.

C. NEW ZEALAND

7.013 The relevant New Zealand provisions can be found mainly in the Trusts Act 2019 as follows:

> **142 Definitions for purposes of sections 143 to 148**
> In sections 143 to 148,—
> **ADR process** means an alternative dispute resolution process (for example, mediation or arbitration) designed to facilitate the resolution of a matter
> **ADR settlement**, in relation to a matter,—
>
> (a) means an enforceable agreement reached through an ADR process that resolves the matter; but

2 ibid.

(b) does not include an arbitral award

arbitral award, in relation to a matter that has been referred to arbitration, has the same meaning as award in section 2(1) of the Arbitration Act 1996

arbitration agreement, in relation to a matter that has been referred to arbitration, has the same meaning as in section 2(1) of the Arbitration Act 1996

external matter means a matter to which the parties are a trustee and 1 or more third parties

internal matter means a matter to which the parties are a trustee and 1 or more beneficiaries, or a trustee and 1 or more other trustees, of the trust

matter—

(a) means—
  (i) a legal proceeding brought by or against a trustee in relation to the trust; or
  (ii) a dispute in relation to the trust between a trustee and a beneficiary, or between a trustee and a third party, or between 2 or more trustees, that may give rise to a legal proceeding; but
  (iii) does not include a legal proceeding or a dispute about the validity of all or part of a trust.

143 Power of trustee to refer matter to alternative dispute resolution process

(1) This section applies if there is no provision in the terms of a trust that requires or empowers a trustee to refer a matter to an ADR process.

(2) A trustee may, with the agreement of each party to the matter, refer the matter to an ADR process.

(3) For the purposes of this section, a beneficiary is not a party to an external matter.

144 ADR process for internal matter if trust has beneficiaries who are unascertained or lack capacity

(1) If a trust has any beneficiaries who are unascertained or lack capacity, then, for a matter relating to that trust that is subject to an ADR process,—
  (a) the court must appoint representatives for those beneficiaries; and
  (b) those representatives may agree to an ADR settlement, or agree to be bound by an arbitration agreement and any arbitral award under that agreement, on behalf of the beneficiaries who are unascertained or lack capacity; and
  (c) any ADR settlement must be approved by the court.

(2) If representatives have been appointed under subsection (1) for beneficiaries who are unascertained or lack capacity,—
  (a) the representatives must act in the best interests of the beneficiaries on whose behalf they have been appointed; and
  (b) the court may order that a representative's costs be paid out of the trust property; and
  (c) the court may make any order that it thinks fit regarding the terms of a representative's appointment.

(3) This section applies only to internal matters.

145 Power of court to order ADR process for internal matter

(1) The court may, at the request of a trustee or a beneficiary or on its own motion,—
   (a) enforce any provision in the terms of a trust that requires a matter to be subject to an ADR process; or
   (b) otherwise submit any matter to an ADR process (except if the terms of the trust indicate a contrary intention).

(2) In exercising the power, the court may make any of the following orders:
   (a) an order requiring each party to the matter, or specified parties, to participate in the ADR process in person or by a representative:
   (b) an order that the costs of the ADR process, or a specified portion of those costs, be paid out of the trust property:
   (c) an order appointing a particular person to act as a mediator, an arbitrator, or any other facilitator of the ADR process.

(3) This section applies in relation to internal matters only.

146 Trustee may give undertakings for purposes of ADR settlement or arbitration agreement and any arbitral award

Despite section 33 (duty not to bind or commit trustees to future exercise of discretion), a trustee may, for the purposes of an ADR settlement or arbitration agreement and any arbitral award under that agreement, give binding undertakings in relation to the trustee's future actions as trustee.

147 Trustee's liability in relation to ADR settlement or arbitration agreement and any arbitral award limited

(1) This section applies to a proceeding brought by or on behalf of a beneficiary and arising from or relating to an ADR settlement or arbitration agreement and any arbitral award under that agreement.

(2) An ADR settlement or arbitration agreement and any arbitral award under that agreement is valid and a trustee is not liable in the proceeding unless, in relation to the settlement, agreement, or award, the trustee failed to comply with—
   (a) the trustee's mandatory duty under section 25; or
   (b) any duty specified in the terms of the trust for the purposes of establishing liability under this section.

(3) Despite subsection (2)(a), a trustee is not liable in the proceeding by reason only that the settlement, agreement, or award was not consistent with the terms of the trust.

148 Application of Arbitration Act 1996

If arbitration is the ADR process to which a matter is referred under this Act or under the terms of the trust, the Arbitration Act 1996 applies to the arbitration.

7.014 The Arbitration Act 1996 additionally provides that:

10A Arbitration of trust matters

(1) If an arbitration relates to a trust matter, sections 142 to 148 of the Trusts Act 2019 apply to the arbitration.

(2) In this section, **trust matter** has the same meaning as matter in section 142 of that Act

As with the Bahamas statutory provision it is clear that the New Zealand provision is extremely detailed and well drafted. In particular, it addresses the issue of representing unascertained or legally incapable beneficiaries as well as providing guidelines for how representatives for such beneficiaries should act, permits trust arbitration for all matters except those concerning the validity of the trust, and explicitly grants the court power to enforce a trust arbitration clause. Moreover, it also addresses the issue of trustee liability as regards any proceedings brought by a beneficiary relating to arbitral proceedings and permits trustees to bind their successors with regard to arbitration. However, as with all acts, the provisions have some shortcomings. 7.015

Firstly, the Act states that arbitration agreement has the same meaning as that provided in the Arbitration Act and s 2 of the Arbitration Act states that 'arbitration agreement means an agreement by the parties to submit to arbitration all or certain disputes which have arisen or which may arise between them in respect of a defined legal relationship, whether contractual or not'. The problem is that this does not provide any clarity as to the situation with regard to beneficiaries. They could (and likely will) argue that there is no arbitration agreement as they were not a party who agreed to submit to arbitration all or certain disputes which arose with regard to the trust. The matter is not therefore solved by legislative fiat as was the case in the Bahamas and would presumably have to be resolved by the common law methods discussed above. 7.016

Secondly, the provisions only apply to 'internal matters' and this is defined as 'a matter to which the parties are a trustee and 1 or more beneficiaries, or a trustee and 1 or more other trustees, of the trust'. The problem is that, as the New Zealand legislator should have been perfectly aware given New Zealand's well developed trust ecosystem and its close links with the more 'wacky' trust law of the Cook Islands, there are many sorts of parties that can be involved in an internal trust dispute. These could include protectors and enforcers; even if these are not terms of art outside certain offshore jurisdictions it is not necessarily the case that these officeholders will always be trustees but they may well hold a power to depose the trustees or give the trustees directions. In such cases, it is plainly desirable that such officeholders be caught by a trust arbitration clause, as, if not, arbitration against them will not only be impossible, but it may be necessary to commence arbitral proceedings against the trustees whilst simultaneously pursuing court proceedings against the protectors, enforcers or other such individuals. 7.017

Thirdly, and as with the Guernsey provisions, the provision requires the court to appoint representatives for beneficiaries who are unascertained or 7.018

lack capacity. This would appear to exclude any of the common law possibilities discussed above, such as applying representative actions by analogy or making provision for representatives in the trust deed, and plainly complicates proceedings. It is not entirely clear why such common law possibilities were excluded and there does not seem to be any justification for doing so as long as the processes involved are fair to the beneficiaries. Moreover, given that trusts often involve unascertained or legally incapable beneficiaries, requiring court intervention in such cases significantly undermines the attractiveness of the New Zealand provisions as a whole.

7.019 A fourth issues arises from s 12(1) of the Arbitration Act 1996 which states that 'An arbitration agreement, unless otherwise agreed by the parties, is deemed to provide that an arbitral tribunal – (a) may award any remedy or relief that could have been ordered by the High Court if the dispute had been the subject of civil proceedings in that court ...'. The issue with this provision is that it could raise public policy issues, for example could an arbitral tribunal vary a trust to give a tax advantage to the beneficiaries? New Zealand is not an offshore jurisdiction and it does not take the same laissez faire attitude to taxation that jurisdictions such as the Bahamas or the DIFC do. In consequence, it is likely that this provision was simply a matter of legislative oversight. It is also true that s 34(2)(b)(ii) allows the court to set aside an award if it is in conflict with the public policy of New Zealand and so it may be that issues regarding the variation of trusts for tax reasons would be caught by that provision. However, from the perspective of an individual choosing a law to govern a trust with an arbitration clause the provision is certainly a useful one.

7.020 In conclusion, although the New Zealand provisions are a significant improvement on the Guernsey provisions they are not without their kinks, and anyone considering making use of the provisions is well advised to read them closely and be aware of the advantages, as well as the disadvantages, when compared with other jurisdictions' provisions or the common law.

D. THE DUBAI INTERNATIONAL FINANCIAL CENTRE TRUST LAW

7.021 The DIFC provisions are mainly provided in the 2018 Trust Law, which states:

> **31. Arbitration of trust disputes**
>
> (1) Where a trust instrument provides that any dispute or administration question arising between any of the parties in relation to the trust shall be submitted to

arbitration ('a trust arbitration'), that provision shall, for all purposes under the Arbitration Law have effect as between those parties as if it were an arbitration agreement and as if those parties were parties to that agreement.

(2) Where a trust instrument does not provide that any dispute or administration question arising between any of the parties in relation to the trust shall be submitted to arbitration but the parties to that dispute agree in writing to have it resolved by a trust arbitration, that agreement shall, for all purposes under the Arbitration Law, have effect as between those parties as if it were an arbitration agreement.

(3) The Arbitration Law shall apply to a trust arbitration in accordance with the provisions of Schedule 2.

(4) The Court may make such orders in relation to an arbitration or possible arbitration which supplement or vary the application of Schedule 2 as may in the opinion of the Court be appropriate in the circumstances of the case.

32. Powers of the arbitral tribunal

(1) This Article shall apply except to the extent otherwise provided in the trust instrument.

(2) The arbitral tribunal (hereinafter referred to as 'the tribunal') may, in addition to all other powers of the tribunal, at any stage in a trust arbitration, exercise all the powers of the Court (whether arising by law (including this Law), under the inherent jurisdiction of the Court or otherwise) in relation to the administration, execution or variation of a trust or the exercise of any power arising under a trust.

...

SCHEDULE 2
APPLICATION OF THE ARBITRATION LAW

1. The Arbitration Law shall apply and be construed with respect to a trust arbitration, as stated hereunder.
2. In the Arbitration Law, 'dispute' includes an administration question.
3. Article 12(1) of the Arbitration Law shall apply as if it read -

'The settlor of a trust shall be free to determine (by provision in the trust instrument) how, in relation to a trust, disputes are resolved, subject only to such safeguards as are necessary in the public interest;'.

4. Where in the Arbitration Law reference is made to a matter agreed between the parties to an arbitration agreement (including a matter which may be authorised, chosen, conferred, designated, nominated or vested by the parties) that matter shall (except where no effective provision is made) be determined as provided in the trust instrument.
5. Neither Article 12 of the Arbitration Law nor any rule of law or construction treating an arbitration agreement separate to any agreement of which it is a part shall apply in relation to a trust arbitration.
6. The term 'action' in Article 13 of the Arbitration Law includes an application or other reference to the Court concerning an administration question which the trust instrument requires to be submitted to arbitration and a stay of that application or other reference may be sought by any of the

parties in relation to the trust, whether or not a party to that application or other reference.

7. In any application or other reference to the Court referred to in paragraph 6, the Court may stay the proceedings on its own volition unless all parties in relation to the trust affected by the application are before it or are represented by persons before it.

8. Article 38 of the Arbitration Law shall apply as if it included the following Articles:

> *'(6) Where a person is or has been a party to a trust arbitration in the capacity of trustee he shall, unless the tribunal otherwise orders, be entitled to the costs of the arbitration, in so far as they are not recovered from or paid by any other person, out of the fund held by the trustee; and the tribunal may otherwise order only on the ground that the trustee has in substance acted for his own benefit rather than for the benefit of the trust.*
>
> *(7) Where a person is or has been a party to a trust arbitration in the capacity of trustee and is entitled to be paid his costs out of the fund held by the trustee any doubt as to whether costs were reasonably incurred shall be resolved in favour of the trustee. Costs shall be presumed to have been unreasonably incurred if they were incurred contrary to the duty of the trustee'.*

9. For the purposes of enforcing an arbitral award under Article 41(2)(a)(iii) of the Arbitration Law, the term 'dispute' includes an administration question.

7.022 As an initial point it is worth noting that the DIFC trust arbitration provisions and the Bahamas provisions are very similar, among other things both refer to a second schedule to their respective acts which addresses trust arbitration and the second schedule in both acts is virtually identical. It is unclear whether the DIFC provisions were merely based on the Bahamas provisions or whether there was an overlap in the drafters, in any event the effect of this is that all of the comments above regarding the Bahamas provisions also apply to the DIFC provisions. In consequence, there is no need to discuss the matter further and those choosing between the two laws would likely be more concerned about the differences between the Bahamas and DIFC legal ecosystems than the differences between the two statutes.

E. FLORIDA

7.023 The relevant provisions in Florida can be found in the Probate Code and provide as follows:

> 731.401 Arbitration of disputes.—

(1) A provision in a will or trust requiring the arbitration of disputes, other than disputes of the validity of all or a part of a will or trust, between or among the beneficiaries and a fiduciary under the will or trust, or any combination of such persons or entities, is enforceable.
(2) Unless otherwise specified in the will or trust, a will or trust provision requiring arbitration shall be presumed to require binding arbitration under chapter 682, the Revised Florida Arbitration Code. If an arbitration enforceable under this section is governed under chapter 682, the arbitration provision in the will or trust shall be treated as an agreement for the purposes of applying chapter 682.

Although the provision is succinct it covers a lot of ground, importantly it provides that it will apply not just to disputes between the beneficiaries and trustees but also to disputes between the beneficiaries and any fiduciaries under the trust. This is a useful expansion of the definition of internal trust disputes found in any statutes, for example the New Zealand provisions, as it would encompass any officeholders such as protectors or enforcers who had fiduciary duties. On the other hand, it is true that there might be disputes about whether such individuals were under fiduciary duties or not and thus the provision might lead to further litigation unless the trust deed clearly specified who did or did not have fiduciary duties. Additionally, the provision clarifies that a trust arbitration clause in the trust deed amounts to an arbitration agreement for the purposes of the Florida arbitration law. It therefore resembles the Bahamas provisions in that it uses legislative fiat to create consent to arbitration where there may well be none. **7.024**

On the other hand, the provision does not address the issue of how to ensure that beneficiaries are represented in arbitral proceedings and it also problematically excludes disputes regarding the validity of all or part of a will or trust from its scope. It is not difficult to see that the result of this limitation is that, in appropriate cases, parties who do not wish to arbitrate will simply frame their arguments in such a way as to challenge at least part of the trust (or will in which it is created) and thereby take themselves outside the scope of the Florida trust arbitration provisions. This limitation is not unique to Florida of course, being found in both the Bahamas and DIFC provisions, but it no less problematic and means that the provisions may not be much of an improvement on the common law position. **7.025**

F. ARIZONA

The relevant Arizona provisions can be found in Title 14 of its revised statutes and provides: **7.026**

14-10205. Alternative dispute resolution

A trust instrument may provide mandatory, exclusive and reasonable procedures to resolve issues between the trustee and interested persons or among interested persons with regard to the administration or distribution of the trust.

7.027 The provision is so threadbare that it is difficult to say anything about it, except that it deals with virtually none of the important issues raised by trust arbitration and also imposes a vague requirement that ADR provisions in a trust instrument be 'reasonable'. On the other hand, it is useful that the provision refers to 'interested persons' as coming within the scope of the clause and thus could potentially include protectors, enforcers, beneficiaries, trustees and all other relevant parties. However, given that the provision is so laconic it does nothing more than state that trust arbitration (as part of ADR) is possible in principle. In this respect it is arguably competing with Guernsey for last place in terms of the best trust arbitration statutes currently in existence.

G. NEW HAMPSHIRE

7.028 The relevant New Hampshire provision can be found in Title LVI of the New Hampshire Revised Statutes and provides that:

564-B:1-111A Nonjudicial Dispute Resolution. –

(a) If the terms of the trust require the interested persons to resolve a trust dispute exclusively by reasonable nonjudicial procedures, then those interested persons shall resolve that trust dispute in accordance with the terms of the trust.

(b) An interested person may commence a judicial proceeding to determine whether the nonjudicial procedures are reasonable. To the extent that the terms of the trust purport to prohibit an interested person from commencing a judicial proceeding under this subsection or penalize an interested person for commencing a judicial proceeding under this subsection, those terms of the trust are void.

(c) For purposes of this section, 'interested person' means any person who would be an interested person in a judicial proceeding to resolve the trust dispute.

(d) For purposes of this section, 'trust dispute' means any matter in which a court has subject-matter jurisdiction under RSA 564-B:2-203, excluding (1) a determination of the validity of the trust or (2) a determination of any material purpose of the trust, including a determination of whether any modification, termination, or other action is consistent with a material purpose of the trust.

(e) Unless the director of charitable trust expressly consents to the nonjudicial procedures, those procedures shall not apply to any matter involving a charitable trust. Unless the department of health and human services expressly consents to the nonjudicial procedures, those procedures shall not apply any matter in which that department would be an interested person.

Although the New Hampshire provisions are considerably more detailed than those of Arizona, they are still fraught with problems. Firstly, we again see reference to 'reasonable nonjudicial procedures' which will inevitably lead to litigation and indeed the provisions guarantee this by providing a right for any interested person to have a court determine whether or not the ADR provisions in a trust are a reasonable nonjudicial procedure. Secondly, the provisions exclude decisions regarding the validity of a trust or decisions regarding the consistency of any actions with a material purpose of the trust. The result of these exclusions is that, as with the Arizona provisions, the New Hampshire provisions are likely to be completely neutered whenever a recalcitrant party has any motivation to challenge the validity of the trust or, additionally, the compatibility of any actions taken with a material purpose of the trust. Another problem is that the provisions do not link up with the arbitration law of New Hampshire and it is therefore unclear whether an arbitration clause in a trust deed would appear to an arbitration clause under the applicable statute. The exclusion of trust disputes where the department of health and human services would be an interested person, presumably trusts which involved legally incapable parties, poses further challenges. On the other hand, it is certainly useful that the provisions apply to any interested person but this cannot outweigh the numerous problems posed by the statute's wording. **7.029**

H. MISSOURI

The relevant Missouri provisions can be found in title XXXI of the 2014 Missouri Revised Statutes and provide that: **7.030**

> 456.2-205. 1. Subject to the exception in subsection 2 of this section, a provision in a trust instrument requiring the mediation or arbitration of disputes between or among the beneficiaries, a fiduciary, a person granted nonfiduciary powers under the trust instrument, or any combination of such persons is enforceable.
>
> 2. A provision in a trust instrument requiring the mediation or arbitration of disputes relating to the validity of a trust is not enforceable unless all interested persons with regard to the dispute consent to the mediation or arbitration of the dispute.

It can immediately be seen that what this provision gives with one hand it takes away with another, although it recognises that trust arbitration is possible in principle it also requires that in order for this to be so all interested persons must have consented to arbitration. However, as the primary issue for trust arbitration is exactly that of consent: what is the point of a statute which effectively merely restates the common law rule? It is because of this unhelpful **7.031** provision that Missouri quickly moves to the bottom of the table of potential trust arbitration jurisdictions.

I. SOUTH DAKOTA

7.032 The relevant provisions in South Dakota are found in its codified laws, which provide:

> 55-1-54. Arbitration.
>
> In addition to the trustee's power to submit to an arbitration claim in favor of or against a trust or trustee as set forth in §55-1A-25, a provision in a trust requiring the arbitration of a dispute between or among the beneficiaries, a fiduciary under the will or trust, or any combination of them, is enforceable pursuant to the provisions of chapter 21-25A. Unless otherwise provided in the governing instrument or a court order, the arbitration shall be held in this state. Notwithstanding the foregoing, a challenge to the validity of all or part of the trust is not subject to arbitration. Any proceeding pursuant to this section is subject, upon request by the acting trustee, the trustor, if living, or any beneficiary, to the privacy protections of § 21-22-28. The arbitrator shall grant the request, if made.

7.033 The privacy protections provision states that:

> 21-22-28. Protection of privacy--Sealing and availability of documents.
>
> The privacy of those who have established a court trust or other trust shall be protected in any court proceeding concerning the trust. Upon the filing of any petition, the instrument on which the trust is based, briefs, and the entire court file including a trust's inventory, statement filed by any fiduciary, annual verified report of a fiduciary, final report of a fiduciary, and all petitions relevant to trust administration and all court orders thereon shall be sealed upon filing and may not be made a part of the public record of the proceeding, but are available to the court, to the trustor, to any fiduciary, to any beneficiary, to their attorneys, and to such other interested persons as the court may order upon a showing of the need.

7.034 Taken together the South Dakota provisions are certainly interesting, it goes without saying that the most intriguing provision is that effectively imposing confidentiality upon trust arbitrations and (presumably) upon any court actions made regarding trust arbitrations. As confidentiality may well be one of the primary drivers behind a choice to require trust arbitration this is certainly a welcome provision. Additionally, the trust arbitration provisions cover fiduciaries and not just trustees as with the Florida and other US provisions. Most importantly the provision joins up with the arbitration provisions in Chapter 21-25 of the South Dakota Codified Laws and thereby makes clear that a trust arbitration agreement amounts to an enforceable arbitration agreement. On the other hand, the provision does not address the issue of representing beneficiaries, including vulnerable beneficiaries, in any arbitral proceedings and also excludes any challenges regarding validity of all or part of the trust from its scope. It is clear therefore that the provisions are not perfect, although they are the best US trust arbitration provisions analysed so far.

J. WYOMING

The Wyoming provision can be found in the 2019 Wyoming Statutes and provides: **7.035**

> **4-10-816. Specific powers of trustee.**
> (a) Without limiting the authority conferred by W.S. 4-10-815, a trustee may ...
> (xxiii) Resolve a dispute concerning the interpretation of the trust or its administration by mediation, arbitration, or other procedure for alternative dispute resolution;

In some ways this provision is even more problematic than the Arizona provisions as it is completely unclear what it actually achieves: does it empower trustees to arbitrate trust disputes even without any agreement in the trust deed? This would appear odd as in this case it may well be that no person interested in the trust would even have considered trust arbitration, much less have consented to it. Alternatively, does the provision merely allow trustees to arbitrate non-contentious administrative trust issues? This might appear more likely, but as noted above such questions would not be a dispute and it is therefore difficult to see how they could competently be submitted to arbitration. In any event, as the trust arbitration provisions do not link up with the general arbitration provisions in Wyoming it is unclear how the two would interact. As a result of these uncertainties Wyoming is unfortunately also a State whose trust arbitration provisions are not particularly useful. **7.036**

K. DELAWARE

The relevant Delaware provisions can be found in Title 12 of the Delaware Code, which provides that: **7.037**

> **§ 3325. Specific powers of trustee**
> Without limiting the authority conferred by § 3324 of this title, a trustee may: ...
>
> (24) If all interested beneficiaries also consent, consent to the resolution of a dispute concerning the interpretation of the trust or its administration by mediation, arbitration or other procedure for alternative dispute resolution;

7.038 This provision is very similar to that of Wyoming and therefore shares many of its weaknesses, additionally it also suffers from the disadvantage of the Missouri provision in specifying that consent is required to arbitrate. In conclusion, the provision is not a usable one.

L. OHIO

7.039 The relevant Ohio provision can be found in title 58 of the Ohio Revised Code and provides:

> **5802.05 Provision regarding arbitration of disputes.**
> (A) A provision in the terms of a trust, excluding a testamentary trust, that requires the arbitration of disputes, other than disputes of the validity of all or a part of a trust instrument, between or among the beneficiaries and a fiduciary under the trust, or a combination of those persons or entities, is enforceable.
> (B) Unless otherwise specified in the terms of the trust, a trust provision requiring arbitration as described in division (A) of this section shall be presumed to require binding arbitration under Chapter 2711. of the Revised Code.

7.040 The provision is certainly more detailed than that of Wyoming, Delaware or Arizona and crucially links with the Ohio arbitration law. It also includes all types of fiduciaries and not just trustees within its scope. On the other hand, it again excludes disputes concerning the validity of all or part of the trust instrument from its scope and does not address the issue of how to represent beneficiaries in trust arbitration proceedings.

7.041 In concluding this section, it is possible to say that among Commonwealth jurisdictions there is a three-way split between New Zealand, the Bahamas, and the DIFC as regards the best trust arbitration provisions. In the US context, South Dakota arguably comes ahead due to its unique privacy provisions followed closely by Ohio and New Hampshire. Unfortunately, the provisions of the other jurisdictions discussed above are, for one reason or another, simply not fit for purpose.

8

ENFORCEABILITY OF TRUST ARBITRATION AWARDS UNDER THE NEW YORK CONVENTION AND COMMONWEALTH LAW

A. INTRODUCTION

If a party refuses to voluntarily comply with an arbitral award then, unless there is a means of enforcing it judicially, the award is effectively worthless and thus the issue of the enforceability of trust arbitration awards is, in one sense, the most important issue facing the field of trust arbitration. This chapter will analyse the matter from a dual perspective. Firstly, it will discuss the international plane by looking at the New York Convention (NYC) which is the preeminent legal instrument governing the enforcement of arbitration awards internationally. Secondly, it will analyse the means by which arbitration awards can be enforced through the English and Commonwealth courts, namely 8.001

three statutory procedures, one of which is exclusively for NYC awards, and a common law action on the award.

8.002 Before beginning this section proper it is worth noting that the approach taken to addressing NYC issues will differ substantially from the approach taken elsewhere in this book. This results from the fact that this work has so far focused on the English and Commonwealth law approach to matters, but as the NYC is an international treaty ratified by over 160 states a much broader approach is necessary to address issues under the NYC. However, it is not possible to analyse the case law and practice of such a broad number of jurisdictions and thus this section will look at the *Travaux Préparatoires* where these are relevant, subsequent commentary and declarations by UNCITRAL, and academic commentary in general. Case law will also be considered, but it will take a secondary role, essentially for reasons of practicality. It isn't possible to consider the case law of 160 jurisdictions, and it isn't possible to say where a trust arbitration award will or will not be enforced and filter jurisdictions in that manner. Moreover, in order to properly understand the Convention, it is necessary to put it into its proper context by briefly looking at the historical background of the Convention itself as well as its predecessors.

8.003 Lastly, it is also important to note that as this is a book on trust arbitration and not the NYC, it will not analyse every section of the Convention but rather restrict itself to those which are most likely to pose issues for trust arbitration, as follows:

I. Issues with the requirement for an award to be 'arising out of differences' under Art I(1)
I. Issues with the commercial reservation under Art I(3)
II. Issues with the writing requirement under Art II(1)–(2)
III. Issues with recognition or enforcement of an award where a party was under some incapacity, according to the law applicable to them, under Art V(1)(a)
IV. Issues with recognition or enforcement of an award where a party alleges a lack of notice or that they were otherwise unable to present their case under Art V(1)(b)
V. Arbitrability issues as a bar to recognition or enforcement under Art V(2)(a)
VI. Public policy issues as a bar to recognition or enforcement under Art V(2)(b)

B. THE NEW YORK CONVENTION

The New York Convention is one of the great success stories of transnational commercial and private international law,[1] having been ratified by over 160 states to date[2] and having 'become the foundation upon which the international arbitral process is built'.[3] It succeeded the 1923 Geneva Protocol on Arbitration Clauses and the 1927 Geneva Convention on the Execution of Foreign Arbitral Awards, which were the first international treaties on the subject which focused on private matters. The need for a new convention, what was to become the New York Convention, had long been felt given that both existing Geneva instruments suffered from several shortcomings such as an excessive reference to national laws and a 'double exequatur' requirement.[4] This requirement meant that 'one had to get the courts of the seat to approve the award before it could be exported'.[5] **8.004**

The International Chamber of Commerce led the charge to reform the existing international arbitral system by adopting a proposal that the 1927 Convention should be replaced or reformed at its 1951 Conference in Lisbon[6] and repeated this call at its Vienna Congress two years later alongside a proposed draft arbitration convention.[7] The draft foresaw the creation of 'an international award ... completely independent of national laws',[8] arguing that this was an 'economic requirement',[9] and unsurprisingly this radical proposal resulted in a significant backlash after being presented to the Economic and Social Council of the United Nations (ECOSOC).[10] The draft adopted by ECOSOC ignored the ICC's draft and effectively replicated the existing system under the Geneva Convention.[11] **8.005**

---

1 Emmanuel Gaillard, Domenico Di Pietro and Nanou Leleu-Knobil, *Enforcement of Arbitration Agreements and International Arbitral Awards: The New York Convention in Practice* (Cameron May 2008) 19–21; Herbert Kronke and others (eds), *Recognition and Enforcement of Foreign Arbitral Awards: A Global Commentary on the New York Convention* (Kluwer Law International 2010) 1–2.

2 'Contracting States New York Convention' <http://www.newyorkconvention.org/countries> accessed 22 November 2019.

3 Marike RP Paulsson (ed), *The 1958 New York Convention in Action* (Kluwer Law International 2016) 1.

4 Gaillard, Di Pietro and Leleu-Knobil (n 1) 7–8; Paulsson (n 3) 4.

5 Teresa Cheng, 'Features of Arbitral Practice that Contribute to System-Building' (2012) 106 Proceedings of the Annual Meeting (American Society of International Law) 292, 292.

6 Gaillard, Di Pietro and Leleu-Knobil (n 1) 9.

7 ibid.

8 Paulsson (n 3) 5.

9 ibid.

10 ibid.

11 ibid.

8.006 Although the ECOSOC draft was an improvement on the Geneva regime, it retained that regime's Achilles heel, the requirement for double exequatur, thereby calling into question the entire project of reform. Thankfully for the world of international arbitration, the delegation from the Netherlands presented what came to be known as the 'Dutch Proposal',[12] which radically revised the ECOSOC draft on the purported basis of clarifying it. Crucially, the Dutch Proposal removed the double exequatur requirement,[13] and the proposal was welcomed by the Conference which took the changes forward into the final draft.[14]

8.007 The text of the Convention is not perfect as it 'naturally reflects compromises'[15] but it was, perhaps surprisingly, just as groundbreaking as the ICC draft, although couched in more diplomatic language. Indeed it has been noted that, 'If one compares these texts with those of the ICC five years earlier, one is struck by the fact that if anything the Dutch Proposal was more progressive than the ICC draft'.[16] The acceptance of an even more radical proposal than the rejected ICC draft is likely 'explicable … as a matter of good diplomacy',[17] although it must be accepted that in other regards the NYC did not always go as far as the ICC's proposals. For example, the Convention speaks of 'foreign awards' and not 'international awards' as the drafters rejected the idea of a 'truly international [or delocalised] arbitration'.[18] This can be contrasted with the ICSID Convention 'which contains a self-sufficient legal regime for a truly international arbitration'.[19]

1. Art I(3) – the commercial reservation

8.008 Article I(3) of the NYC provides that 'any State … may also declare that it will apply the Convention only to differences arising out of legal relationships, whether contractual or not, which are considered as commercial under the

12 ibid 6.

13 Gaillard, Di Pietro and Leleu-Knobil (n 1) 18.

14 ibid 18–19.

15 Paulsson (n 3) 6–7.

16 ibid 12.

17 ibid.

18 Albert Jan Van den Berg, 'Recent Enforcement Problems under the New York and ICSID Conventions' (1989) 5 Arbitration International 2, 8–9; cf Frederic Bachand and Stephen Bond (eds), *International Arbitration Court Decisions* (3rd edn, Juris 2011) 1345; to much the same effect albeit with more nuance see Gary Born, *International Commercial Arbitration* (2nd edn, Kluwer Law International 2014) 1688–1689; Fouchard P and Goldman B, *Fouchard, Gaillard, Goldman on International Commercial Arbitration* (Kluwer Law International BV 1999), para 1387.

19 Van den Berg (n 18) 11.

national law of the State making such declaration'. This reservation has been retained to date by over forty countries,[20] which represents approximately one quarter of the total number of states that have ratified the Convention, and thus remains of significant importance in understanding the Convention's scope.

The most problematic issue caused by this reservation is 'the fact that each Contracting State may determine for itself which relationships it deems "commercial" in nature'[21] and this 'has caused some problems in the uniform interpretation and application of the Convention'.[22] Some of the most problematic interpretations have included an Indian case holding that 'technical "know-how"' and 'turn-key' contracts were not commercial,[23] an Argentine case finding that a shipbuilding contract signed by a provincial authority was not commercial,[24] and a Tunisian case stating that 'architectural and urbanization public works were not commercial'.[25] On the other hand, the prevailing approach of courts globally has been to adopt a broad interpretation of the term 'commercial' so that it covers 'all relationships involving an economic exchange where one (or both) parties contemplate realizing a profit or other benefit'.[26] On occasion, an even broader interpretation, including all 'disputes relating to any pecuniary or economic interest' is adopted.[27] **8.009**

It is clear that the commercial reservation poses special problems for trusts, although this is not the case for 'commercial trusts', such as those used as a form of security, to finance consumer debt or pension funds.[28] On the other hand, the situation is much more complex for 'personal' trusts. Notwithstanding this, it might be possible to hold such trusts to be a commercial relationship in jurisdictions which have an extremely broad definition of commercial disputes as 'relating to any pecuniary or economic interest'.[29] Equally, in the case of offshore, and other complex trusts, it is unlikely that the trustee will be acting **8.010**

20 'Contracting States New York Convention' (n 2).

21 Kronke and others (n 1) 33.

22 ibid.

23 ibid.

24 ibid 35.

25 ibid 34–35.

26 SI Strong and AP Molloy, *Arbitration of Trust Disputes: Issues in National and International Law* (Oxford University Press 2016) para 21.07.

27 ibid.

28 Strong and Molloy (n 26) para 21.10.

29 ibid 21.13; this would appear to be the case in the USA, see David Horton, 'The Federal Arbitration Act and Testamentary Instruments' (2011) 90 NCL Rev. 1027, 1068–1073.

gratuitously. Instead, it is likely that he will be charging a fee[30] and it is also likely that he will be part of a company engaged in the business of making a profit, in other words, a corporate trustee.[31]

8.011 As the relationship between the trustee and the beneficiaries forms the foundation of the trust, it might be possible to argue that this relationship is commercial and not gratuitous in nature, thereby bringing such trusts within the scope of the Convention notwithstanding the commercial reservation. However, this argument is not certain, and the safest way to guarantee that the commercial reservation will not pose a problem is to ensure that trust assets are maintained in jurisdictions which either do not have the commercial reservation, or have interpreted it in a broad manner. This should not be particularly difficult, as most well-known trust jurisdictions, including the UK and its various dependencies, have not availed themselves of the commercial reservation.

2. Art I(1) – the 'arising out of differences' requirement

8.012 Article I(1) of the NYC provides that 'This Convention shall apply to the recognition and enforcement of arbitral awards made in the territory of a State other than the State where the recognition and enforcement of such awards are sought, and arising out of differences between persons, whether physical or legal …'.

8.013 In consequence, the article establishes as a gateway requirement that awards must result out of a genuine difference between parties in order to come within the scope of the Convention. Although this might seem obvious, the issue is of particular relevance in the context of consent awards. The issue of whether consent awards come within the scope of the NYC or not does not appear to have been dealt with yet by the courts and scholars are divided on the matter.[32] On the one hand, it has been stated that where the tribunal simply records the terms of the parties' dispute this is unlikely to be enforceable as, in such a case, 'there is no "difference" between the parties to resolve; the parties have already settled the dispute', and such a difference 'is a necessary precondition of an

---

30 See generally Michael Heyworth, 'The Hidden Cost of Some Trustees–Trustee Commissions' (2007) 13 Trusts & Trustees 37.

31 'The Use of Private Trust Companies | Ogier' (16 September 2010) <https://www.ogier.com/publications/the-use-of-private-trust-companies> accessed 22 November 2019; but see Christopher McKenzie, 'Private Trust Companies: The Best of All Worlds' (2008) 14 Trusts & Trustees 99.

32 See generally Y Kryvoi and D Davydenko, 'Consent Awards in International Arbitration: From Settlement to Enforcement' (2015) 40 Brooklyn Journal of International Law 827.

"award" in the sense of the New York Convention'.[33] On the other hand, Born states that 'Parties are fully entitled to settle their claims, including in arbitration, and if they do so in the form of a consent award, after having previously presented their respective positions in an adversarial process, that award should be fully binding and enforceable on the parties to the arbitration'.[34] Moreover, the UNCITRAL Model Law itself states in Art 30(2) that 'Such an award has the same status and effect as any other award on the merits of the case', with the result that countries which adopted the model law, or were influenced by it, should enforce consent awards in the ordinary manner.[35]

In the context of trust arbitration, as has already been discussed above, the issue arises where a party seeks to bring non-contentious matters before the tribunal, for example if the trustees approach the arbitral tribunal for a non-contentious interpretation of the trust instrument, for a Beddoe order or some other non-contentious relief. This situation should be distinguished from that of consent awards issued after some dispute has arisen, as in this case no dispute ever arose. It would seem that in such a situation any award issued by the tribunal granting such relief would not be enforceable as, 'An arbitral tribunal has the authority to make a consent award only if the parties commenced an arbitration regarding an actual dispute'[36] and in such a case not only has no arbitration commenced, but there is no dispute upon which to start one. **8.014**

It could be argued that in cases regarding interpretation of the trust deed there was a potential academic 'difference of opinion' or perhaps a difference of opinion between the trustees, but it is doubtful whether that would suffice to bring the matter within the scope of the NYC. One of the few cases interpreting the wording 'arising out of differences between' considered the term synonymous with 'dispute',[37] and it seems doubtful whether a mere academic difference or friendly difference of opinion would amount to a dispute. In consequence, it seems unlikely that requests for non-contentious relief in a trust arbitration would be enforceable under the NYC. **8.015**

---

33 ibid 854.

34 Born (n 18) 3026.

35 Fouchard and Goldman (n 18) para 1366.

36 Born (n 18) 3023.

37 *Resort Condominiums International Inc v Ray Bolwell and Resort Condominiums, Pty Ltd* (1993) XX Yearbook Commercial Arbitration 1995 628.

3. Art II(1)–(2) – the writing requirement

8.016 Art II(1)–(2) of the Convention provides that 'Each Contracting State shall recognize an agreement in writing .... The term "agreement in writing" shall include an arbitral clause in a contract or an arbitration agreement, signed by the parties or contained in an exchange of letters or telegrams.'

8.017 This article establishes as a threshold requirement that in order to benefit from the NYC, an arbitration agreement must be in writing. Although it might be thought that this would be a self-evident and non-controversial matter, in actual fact, it has proven to be one of the most problematic articles of the NYC.[38] The essential problem is that the plain wording of the article has failed to keep up with technological advances as well as trade practices which involve neither 'signature' nor 'exchange'.[39] In this regard, the article's reference to 'telegrams' is completely outmoded.[40] The bigger issue has been whether contracts concluded by email, and to a lesser extent fax, can be considered to come within the scope of the NYC.

8.018 In practice, the majority of courts have adopted a 'functional equivalence' test so that 'the references to "letters" and "telegrams" must be interpreted in the light of developing technology'[41] and thus emails, faxes, text messages and so on all come within the scope of the NYC. However, this approach is not universal and at least one court refused to uphold an arbitration contract concluded by email.[42] Although it is clear that this decision is an outlier, it highlights the fact that, to some extent, one must rely on a benevolent attitude on the part of the court in order to prevent this article from causing issues. In consequence, the uniformity intended under the NYC 'has not been attained with respect to the proper application of the "in writing" requirement'.[43]

8.019 Another, and arguably more significant, issue is the requirement for a signature or an exchange of documents as there are many common situations in modern commercial practice which would not meet either requirement:

I. Written offers accepted by performance or conduct or tacitly or orally, e.g. clickwrap contracts;

---

38 Kronke and others (n 1) 75.

39 ibid; Gaillard, Di Pietro and Leleu-Knobil (n 1) 192.

40 Gaillard, Di Pietro and Leleu-Knobil (n 1) 192.

41 ibid 193.

42 ibid.

43 Kronke and others (n 1) 75.

II. Oral offers which are accepted in writing;
III. Contracts incorporated by reference;
IV. Negotiable instruments[44]

In consequence, commentators have catalogued numerous war stories where a literal or overly strict interpretation of the above two requirements led to an inability to compel arbitration or a refusal of recognition or enforcement.[45] Ultimately this resulted in significant consideration by UNCITRAL as to how these issues could be overcome. This eventually led to a 2006 recommendation by them on how the provision should be interpreted.[46] This recommendation was twofold, as follows: **8.020**

> That article II, paragraph 2, of the Convention ... be applied in recognizing that the circumstances described therein are not exhaustive .... That article VII, paragraph 1, of the Convention ... should be applied to allow any interested party to avail itself of rights it may have, under the law or treaties of the country where an arbitration agreement is sought to be relied upon, to seek recognition of the validity of such an arbitration agreement.[47]

The aim of the first recommendation is straightforward, to undermine overly strict interpretations of the writing requirement which consider that an arbitration agreement must either be contained in a document signed by the parties or an exchange of letters or telegrams. According to the recommendation, these situations are only illustrative, and thus a range of other means might suffice to meet the requirements of the Convention.[48] **8.021**

The aim of the second recommendation is slightly more complex. Essentially it aims to allow parties to benefit from 'a domestic (or other treaty) regime with less strict requirements than that of the Convention'.[49] This had long since been the practice of the French courts, which bypassed the form requirements of Art II NYC by interpreting Art VII as allowing them to rely on their less strict domestic law[50] and thus the approach was not without precedent. However, the second recommendation also goes further than this in that it aimed to encourage member states to adopt the less strict form requirements **8.022**

44 Gaillard, Di Pietro and Leleu-Knobil (n 1) 194–199.

45 ibid 202–219.

46 ibid 219; Kronke and others (n 1) 76.

47 Recommendation regarding the interpretation of article II, paragraph 2, and article VII, paragraph 1, of the Convention on the Recognition and Enforcement of Foreign Arbitral Awards 2006.

48 Gaillard, Di Pietro and Leleu-Knobil (n 1) 244–247.

49 ibid 253.

50 ibid 251.

of Art 7 of the Model Law, as revised in 2006, into their domestic laws.[51] Furthermore, it has been suggested that even where a state does not adopt the Model Law its courts can, and should, align their interpretation of the Convention with Art 7. It is also clear that 'UNCITRAL was in favor of the broadest possible interpretation of Art II(2)'.[52]

8.023 Although the UNCITRAL recommendation is likely effective as a matter of Public International Law,[53] its effectiveness ultimately depends on how receptive domestic courts and legislators are and thus it might be argued that a straightforward modification of Art II(2) of the Convention would have been preferable. On the other hand, at the time it was generally felt that as the Convention as a whole works, the idiom 'if it ain't broke don't fix it' applied, particularly as modification might undermine existing liberal interpretations of form requirements by implying these were not previously possible and in any event could risk a 'patch-work' in the world of arbitration.[54]

8.024 Unfortunately, notwithstanding the UNCITRAL recommendations and the revision of the model law (only just over twenty countries have adopted the latter),[55] the writing requirement continues to pose problems for the enforcement of arbitration agreements,[56] and the situation is even more complex as regards trust arbitration agreements. The issue is that in a trust generally 'only one side ... the settlor or possibly the trustee ... signed the agreement while the other side ... the beneficiary, only agreed orally or tacitly'[57] and this is one of the fundamental interpretative disagreements regarding the Convention generally.[58] As a result, in many jurisdictions such a situation would not be considered to fulfil the requirements of Art II(2) of the Convention, resulting in non-enforcement of the arbitration agreement or award.[59] In consequence, one could consider that one of the primary purported advantages of trust arbitration over litigation fails to materialise and thus, the entire scheme of trust arbitration is called into question.

---

51 Kronke and others (n 1) 78.

52 ibid 78–79.

53 Gaillard, Di Pietro and Leleu-Knobil (n 1) 239–244; Strong and Molloy (n 26) para 21.49.

54 Gaillard, Di Pietro and Leleu-Knobil (n 1) 232.

55 'Status: UNCITRAL Model Law on International Commercial Arbitration (1985), with Amendments as Adopted in 2006 | United Nations Commission On International Trade Law' <https://uncitral.un.org/en/texts/arbitration/modellaw/commercial_arbitration/status> accessed 23 November 2019.

56 See the examples in *UNCITRAL Secretariat Guide on the Convention on the Recognition and Enforcement of Foreign Arbitral Awards (New York, 1958)* (United Nations 2016) 51–57.

57 Strong and Molloy (n 26) para 21.47.

58 ibid.

59 Strong and Molloy (n 26) para 21.47.

On the other hand, there are means by which the writing requirement could be fulfilled even in its strictest form in trust arbitration cases, for example where there is a condition precedent in the trust requiring beneficiaries to return a signed document consenting to arbitration which could be jointly subscribed to by all parties under the trust. Equally, leading wealth management jurisdictions such as Switzerland,[60] the Bahamas,[61] the British Virgin Islands,[62] Guernsey[63] and the Cayman Islands[64] all have liberalised form requirements, as does England.[65] In consequence, as long as the settlor settles the assets in one of these jurisdictions, and perhaps limits the power of trustees to move assets to other jurisdictions or change the choice of law clause, form requirements under the NYC should not pose any problems. This is, of course, not a foolproof solution as certain assets might have to be held outside the jurisdiction (immovable property for example), or property might be taken out of the jurisdiction in breach of trust, but, in general, the problem of form does not loom as large in trust arbitration cases as might seem to be the case. **8.025**

4. Article II(1) – the arbitrability requirement

Art II(1) limits contracting states' obligations to recognise arbitration agreements, *inter alia*, to those which concern 'a subject matter capable of settlement by arbitration'. Although this was discussed above, this was in the English context, and the issue here is the approach of other courts to arbitrability under the provisions of the NYC. Alas, despite the fact that 'the nonarbitrability doctrine has deep roots and a reasonably well-defined character',[66] there is no definition under the NYC, let alone a general one, and the types of claims that are inarbitrable differ from state to state.[67] In consequence, the best this section can hope to do is to briefly outline some broad statements of principle and some of the most common situations where the doctrine may come into play. **8.026**

As a preliminary point, it is worth noting that inarbitrability is treated differently in the domestic and the international context so that courts will apply **8.027**

60 Born (n 18) 702–704.

61 'Status: UNCITRAL Model Law on International Commercial Arbitration (1985), with Amendments as Adopted in 2006 | United Nations Commission On International Trade Law'.

62 ibid.

63 The Arbitration (Guernsey) Law 2016 s 1 (2).

64 The Arbitration Law 2012 s 4 (3).

65 Born (n 18) 704–705.

66 ibid 944.

67 ibid 945.

a narrower view of inarbitrability under the New York Convention.[68] In consequence, courts will generally require a clear 'statement of legislative intent' before holding that a particular matter is inarbitrable under the NYC.[69] One justification for the distinction between domestic and international inarbitrability is that international 'arbitral tribunals should not be considered as organs of a particular legal order, and, therefore, they should determine arbitrability on the basis of a genuinely international policy rather than by looking at a set of legal provisions of a given domestic law'.[70]

8.028 It is also the case that, although there is no one definition of inarbitrability, the general approach of arbitration statutes globally is to treat it as a narrow exception 'based upon a clear statement of legislative intention, with particular reserve being utilized in international cases'.[71] It is notable that the UNCITRAL model law provides no definition of arbitrability and although many civil law jurisdictions provide some sort of guidance on the matter most recent legislative instruments do so in very broad terms.[72] Particular examples of disputes which are regarded as inarbitrable include bankruptcy, employment, consumer and natural resource disputes, although the approach varies substantially from state to state.[73]

8.029 Although it is unclear what law should be applied under Art II in order to determine whether a particular dispute is arbitrable or not, it is generally accepted that the *lex fori* should be applied. Another approach is to apply the law applicable to the arbitration agreement, likely the law chosen by the parties in the contract or the arbitration clause. The latter approach would have the advantage that 'the validity of the arbitration clause should be determined in all respects on the basis of the same law, whether the issue is one of arbitrability or whether it is an issue of validity of the parties consent'.[74] However, in practice this is unlikely to lead to a difference as to whether the award is recognised or enforced as the court before which such recognition or enforcement is sought could still refuse it on the basis of inarbitrability under its own law as per Art V(2)(a).

---

68 ibid 957–958.

69 ibid 958–959.

70 Loukas A Mistelis, *Arbitrability: International & Comparative Perspectives* (Alphen aan den Rijn, The Netherlands; Frederick, USA: Kluwer Law International, 2009) Art II, para 5-22.

71 Born (n 18) 959.

72 ibid 960.

73 ibid 995–1027.

74 Mistelis (see 70) para 5-21.

In the context of trust arbitration, the issue of inarbitrability in England and the Commonwealth has already been dealt with while the US is even more permissive of trust arbitration,[75] so the only matter remaining would appear to be the approach of civilian legal systems to trust arbitration. In this regard, the fundamental question is, how do systems which do not know the institution of the trust assess its arbitrability according to their own law? The issue also arises with regards to public policy: how do systems which do not know the institution of the trust assess its compatibility with their public policy? The answer to both questions is substantially the same, and thus it makes sense to deal with both together. **8.030**

As a first point, it is worth noting that several civil law jurisdictions are member states of the Hague Trust Convention and are thus obliged to recognise and give effect to certain consequences of the trust relationship. In these states it cannot be argued that the mere fact that an arbitration clause or arbitral award is dealing with the trust and this institution is unknown to the enforcing state's legal system, means that the dispute is inarbitrable or the award contrary to public policy. Moreover, as noted above, the general approach of civilian legal systems has been to homologate the trust with its closest analogues in their legal system rather than hold it void altogether, and thus, assuming that these analogues are susceptible to arbitration, no special problems of arbitrability or public policy should arise. **8.031**

5. Art V(1)(a) – refusal of recognition or enforcement where a party was under some incapacity

This article provides that a court can refuse recognition or enforcement of an award, at the request of a party, where 'the parties to the agreement referred to in article II were, under the law applicable to them, under some incapacity …'. Although originally this provision derived from a provision regarding improper legal representation in the 1927 Geneva Convention and was thus a due process issue,[76] in its current form it refers to the question as to whether a 'party may submit to arbitration or whether the party has power to contract'.[77] **8.032**

As the Convention does not define 'capacity' and as it is ambiguous regarding the law applicable to determine this, Art V(1)(a) raises a significant number **8.033**

---

75 SI Strong, 'Arbitration of Internal Trust Disputes: The Next Frontier for International Commercial Arbitration?' (2019) 20 ICCA Congress Series 33–36.

76 Gaillard, Di Pietro and Leleu-Knobil (n 1) 616–620; Kronke and others (n 1) 216–217.

77 Kronke and others (n 1) 218.

of interpretative problems.[78] However, it would appear that incapacity in the sense of the Convention, and in comparative law, is 'a general restriction on persons who are not deemed fit to administer their own rights, or as a prohibition that prevents certain persons lacking capacity from entering into some specific legal relationships'.[79] The scope of this section is potentially very wide and could include claims by a party that, 'it was the "weaker party" and thus at a disadvantage in entering the contract negotiations … [or] evidence of oppression, high-pressure tactics or misrepresentation might justify a finding of incapacity'.[80] Most obviously, however, it would appear that the provision would apply where 'an insane person enters into an arbitration agreement'.[81] The same would presumably also apply for minors, children and other legally incapable parties under a trust.[82] It also includes legal entities such as companies as well as states and other governmental entities.[83]

8.034 The Convention does not expressly state the point in time at which the relevant incapacity need have arisen, and there are several different possibilities in this regard; for example, it could arise at the time the arbitration clause was concluded or during all or some of the arbitral proceedings. There is conflicting case law from the US as regards the capacity of bankrupt companies regarding this, and it does not appear that the matter has been subsequently clarified so that it remains a live issue.[84] The better view would appear to be 'that what matters for the purposes of the Convention is whether a certain party had the requisite capacity at the time of execution of the agreement'.[85]

8.035 The problem with the alternative view can easily be illustrated. Suppose for example that a party signs an arbitration agreement and then a dispute arises several months or even years later, but the individual becomes insane several weeks into the arbitral hearings. This introduces considerable legal uncertainty into the effect of the clause. Equally, what happens if the person subsequently regains their sanity at some point during the hearings or has moments of lucidity, should the award nevertheless still be refused recognition or enforcement? A fundamental principle in all civilised legal systems is *pacta sunt servanda*, and it is unclear why someone should be able to escape the binding effects of their

78 Gaillard, Di Pietro and Leleu-Knobil (n 1) 615.

79 ibid 621.

80 Kronke and others (n 1) 219.

81 Gaillard, Di Pietro and Leleu-Knobil (n 1) 621.

82 Strong and Molloy (n 26) para 21.55.

83 Gaillard, Di Pietro and Leleu-Knobil (n 1) 622–627.

84 ibid 631–632.

85 ibid 632.

will, when sane, merely by subsequent insanity. Moreover, any issues as regards due process could still be dealt with under other provisions of the Convention, for example, the right to be heard under Art V(1)(b) rather than attempting to shoehorn it into this section.

Another fundamental issue with this article is that it is unclear what law governs the incapacity defence as the article merely provides that this is governed by 'the law applicable to [the parties]'. There are two options in this regard, firstly that the matter is governed by a party's so-called 'personal law' and secondly that the law of the forum governs the matter. As regards the first approach, a party's 'personal law' would be determined, in the case of them being a natural person, by their nationality, domicile or residence and in the case of a juridical person by the law of their place of incorporation or seat of administration.[86] Although this approach would appear to be supported by the *Travaux Préparatoires* of the Convention, it results in difficulties where a jurisdiction does not have a specific rule governing the capacity to contract or where the issue is controverted.[87] **8.036**

The second approach considers that the relevant law is 'whichever law determines the capacity of the parties pursuant to the applicable rules of the forum, whether that be the "personal law" or not'.[88] The benefit of this approach is that it avoids the situation where the personal law does not govern the matter or where the rules of that law are controversial, and thus it can be said to be more inclusive of the 'diversity of legal systems that have adhered to the Convention and more in line with the aspiration of universality that inspired its creation'.[89] **8.037**

In general, the incapacity defence has rarely arisen in practice and thus is not one of the more problematic parts of the Convention for arbitration as a whole. One example of a situation in which it did arise, albeit via the alternative public policy defence, is a dispute concerning an Indian share purchase and share subscription agreement in the pharmaceutical sector which led to court decisions in both Singapore and India. The genesis of the dispute arose from alleged fraudulent concealment of regulatory investigations in the US concerning the company whose shares were being sold 'so as to induce the Buyer to buy the Shares at a price that did not reflect their true value'.[90] For reasons which are **8.038**

86 ibid 633.
87 ibid 633–634.
88 ibid 634.
89 ibid.
90 *BAZ v BBA & Ors* [2018] SGHC 275 [12].

not entirely clear, the parents of some of the sellers entered into contracts on behalf of their minor children, acting as agents for them, and the arbitral award which was subsequently rendered held the children jointly and severally liable for over US$ 530,000,000 in damages.

8.039 The Delhi High Court held that:

> It is clear that protection of the minor is a fundamental policy of Indian law. It is a sub-stratal principle on which Indian law is founded. Hence, a minor cannot be guilty of having perpetuated a fraud either himself or through any agent. If the natural guardian commits the fraud he cannot bind the minor or the estate of the minor with any penalty or adverse consequences that would result on account of the fraud played by the natural guardian. Any such transaction cannot bind the minor.[91]

8.040 The Court therefore refused to allow enforcement of the arbitral award as against the minor respondents, but did allow it as against the other respondents. Similarly, when considering the same facts, the Singapore High Court stated that:

> The effect of the Award on the Minors is to enforce the SPSSA [Share Purchase and Share Subscription Agreement], which is not a contract falling under any of the exceptions to the general position that contracts do not bind minors. This violates the protection given to minors in contractual relationships under Singapore law. The Award finds them jointly and severally liable for the fraudulent misrepresentation that induced the counterparty to enter the SPSSA. This liability is imposed on the Minors for the fraudulent misrepresentation of their guardian or principal on matters which the Minors had no knowledge of. This has the effect of violating the protection given to a minor under s 35(7) of the Civil Law Act. As stated above, the provision protects a minor even where the minor made a misrepresentation personally. All in all, such an award against the Minors that saddles them with legal liability for an amount exceeding S$720 million shocks the conscience, and it violates Singapore's most basic notion of justice to find the Minors liable under a contract that was entered into when they were only between three to eight years old at the material time. At the time of the arbitration, they were only between eight and twelve years old.[92]

8.041 One might therefore consider that the above two decisions pose problems for the enforceability of trust arbitration awards, as these will often include minor beneficiaries. However, it is important to emphasise that it is rarely the case that arbitral awards will be sought to be enforced against a minor beneficiary. Enforcement of trust arbitration awards would more likely be by the minor beneficiary against the (adult) trustee or the (adult) protector. Moreover, such

91 *Daiichi Sankyo Company Limited v Malvinder Mohan Singh and Ors*, on 15 October, 2020, in the High Court of Delhi at New Delhi, Reserved on: 25.09.2020, Date of Decision: 15.10.2020 [134–135].

92 *BAZ v BBA & Ors* (n 90) para 180.

enforcement would be for the benefit of the beneficiary and as noted by the Indian Court 'under the Hindu Minority and Guardianship Act a natural guardian can do such acts which are necessary and reasonable and appropriate for the benefit of the minor or for the realization, protection and benefit of the minor's estate'.[93] Even if this legislation is unique to India it is arguable that the principles behind it hold good for many jurisdictions given that, as discussed at para. 3.120, parents can decide on the forum (such as arbitration) in which they will prosecute such a claim and this arguably binds the minor beneficiary in question. Although this does not yet appear to have been tested before the courts it is unlikely that they will refuse to enforce awards which are in the interests of the minors in question as this would mean the court was acting contrary to their best interests.

Another important note to make is that even although the matter is dealt with separately to the general public policy by the New York Convention neither the Indian nor the Singaporean courts treated it separately, both subsumed the incapacity defence into the public policy defence. It's unclear as to why this was done given that both the Singaporean and Indian arbitration acts do in fact provide for the incapacity defence in s 31(2)(a) and s 34(2)(a)(i) respectively. It may be that this is because no party pled the incapacity defence as relevant; for example, in the Indian litigation the Court stated that the respondent invoked the lack of proper notice or inability to present their case and public policy exceptions to enforcement.[94] Similarly, in the Singaporean litigation the parties against whom enforcement was sought did not invoke the incapacity defence but rather the principles of natural justice, time limitation and public policy.[95] The courts may also have felt more familiar with the public policy rather than the incapacity defence and decided to opt for the path of least resistance. One could also argue that the incapacity defence represents a sub-set of public policy, but this would appear to be contrary to the intent of the drafters of the New York Convention and the legislators who provided for the defences to be addressed separately in national arbitration legislation. In any event, whether rightly or wrongly, parties enforcing or resisting enforcement of a trust arbitration award which involves minors should be aware that a court may be far more concerned (or indeed only concerned) about the public policy defence as opposed to the incapacity defence. **8.042**

93 *Daiichi Sankyo Company Limited v Malvinder Mohan Singh and Ors* (n 91) para 132.

94 *Daiichi Sankyo Company Limited vs Malvinder Mohan Singh and Ors* (n 91) para 30.

95 *BAZ v BBA & Ors* (n 90) para 23.

8.043 In any event, it is clear that although such cases are relatively uncommon in commercial situations, they are (as discussed above) likely to be common in trust arbitration situations whether because of minor, unborn, incapable or unascertained beneficiaries. [96] The issue which arises is fundamentally one of national law – how can such parties be bound to an arbitration clause – and as a result has already been dealt with elsewhere in this work, so it would make little sense to dwell upon the point again here. The important point to make is that settlors need to consider how the law they choose to govern the trust, and the likely jurisdictions where enforcement will be sought, will address the matter. This is because public policy is fundamentally a national matter as noted by the Singapore High Court's refusal to consider the minor's habitual residence when deciding on the public policy objection. The court stated that 'I reject this contention as it potentially brings into consideration concepts of public policy of foreign states which may be different from the public policy concepts of Singapore'.[97]

8.044 In conclusion, although the incapacity defence is a serious issue for trust arbitration, at least as regards those which involve minor, unborn, unascertained or incapable parties, it is certainly not an insurmountable problem and can be overcome with careful drafting and sensible placement of assets in trust-arbitration-friendly jurisdictions.

6. Art V(1)(b) – refusal of recognition or enforcement where a party did not receive due notice or was otherwise unable to present his case

8.045 This article provides that a court can refuse to recognise or enforce an award where 'The party against whom the award is invoked was not given proper notice of the appointment of the arbitrator or of the arbitration proceedings or was otherwise unable to present his case'. It can be considered the 'due process charter' of the Convention and is the most important of all the grounds in Art V NYC for a court to refuse to recognise or enforce an arbitral award.[98]

8.046 As is unfortunately often the case, no common definition of due process has been adopted by member state courts,[99] and thus what amounts to a violation

96 Strong and Molloy (n 26) para 21.55.

97 *BAZ v BBA & Ors* (n 90) para 181.

98 Gaillard, Di Pietro and Leleu-Knobil (n 1) 681.

99 ibid 683.

of due process varies from state to state.[100] However, in general the term has been interpreted narrowly[101] so that one can speak of a refusal to recognise or enforce an award on the basis of 'grave procedural unfairness in the arbitral proceedings',[102] as opposed to any procedural unfairness, no matter how *de minimis*. It is also important to note that Article V(1)(b) is mandatory so that even where parties consent to 'fundamentally unfair arbitral procedures', a court could refuse to recognise a resulting award on the basis of a violation of Art V(1)(b).[103]

The article itself can be split into two. The first limb deals with failures to give 'proper notice' and the second limb deals with other failures which resulted in a party being unable to present his case. The first issue is not particularly problematic. Examples of a lack of proper notice would be where the notice did not include the names of the arbitrators so that the parties could not evaluate whether there were any impartiality issues or where a party was given a very short time limit in which to present his defence.[104] In general, courts will apply the notice provisions found in the arbitration clause or the relevant rules, although they are unlikely to rely on strict notice formalities if it is clear that a party has in fact been notified of the proceedings.[105] Moreover, courts will usually require that it be shown that the late or otherwise imperfect notice would have affected the result of the arbitration in order to refuse recognition or enforcement.[106] **8.047**

The second limb is, as is evident from its wording, significantly broader in scope than the first as it covers all situations where a party 'was otherwise unable to present his case', and thus an analysis of this section is significantly more complex. As an initial and common-sense point it is worth noting that if a party refuses to appear at the hearings or negligently or wilfully fails to do so, it is unlikely that a court would hold that Art V(1)(b) had been violated.[107] The same would appear to apply to situations where a party failed to take advantage of an opportunity given to it to present its case.[108] Situations where a party could argue that it had been unable to present its case include a denial **8.048**

---

100 ibid 683–687.

101 ibid 687–689.

102 Born (n 18) 3494.

103 ibid 3497–3498.

104 Kronke and others (n 1) 241.

105 ibid 242–244.

106 ibid 245; Paulsson (n 3) 186.

107 Gaillard, Di Pietro and Leleu-Knobil (n 1).

108 ibid 712.

of the opportunity to comment on evidence or arguments, a denial of the right of reply, surprise decisions, unfair evidentiary decisions, a refusal to permit examination or cross-examination and *ex proprio motu* factual investigations.[109] As can be seen from these examples, the potential scope of application of this provision is extremely broad, and it is therefore plainly impossible to consider every possibility in depth. Instead, some basic principles will be laid out.

8.049 Firstly, in order to be able to present its case, a 'party must have [the] opportunity to reply to allegations and evidence of [the] other side'.[110] Thus there would be a clear violation of due process if an arbitral tribunal decides a dispute on the basis of facts and evidence to which a party has not had the opportunity to object.[111] Equally, a party's right to present its case would be violated 'if the arbitral tribunal authorized the last-minute introduction of an entirely new claim or defense, without affording the respondent an adequate and equal opportunity to respond'.[112] It should be noted, however, that 'in practice, most national courts considering this issue … have allowed arbitrators substantial discretion in permitting or excluding the introduction of new claims and defenses'.[113]

8.050 Secondly, as is the case with the due notice requirement, this limb is only concerned with 'serious procedural unfairness' and does not deal with *de minimis* situations.[114] In this vein, some commentators have suggested that the procedural violation in question must actually have affected the arbitral proceedings, although they admit that most courts approach this requirement in an extremely liberal fashion.[115]

8.051 Thirdly, objections under Art V(1)(b) are capable of being waived by a party and will usually be considered waived where a party has continued to participate in arbitral proceedings without objecting to an alleged breach of due process.[116] In a similar vein, some jurisdictions hold that failure to challenge procedural conduct of the arbitration in annulment or set aside proceedings at

109 Born (n 18) 3515–3530.

110 Kronke and others (n 1) 246.

111 ibid 247.

112 Born (n 18) 3524.

113 ibid 3524–3525.

114 ibid 3532.

115 Gary Born, 'Chapter 6: Nonarbitrability and International Arbitration Agreements', in *International Commercial Arbitration* (2nd edn, Kluwer Law International 2014) 3535–3537; Kronke and others (n 1) 252–253.

116 G. Born, *International Commercial Arbitration* (2nd edn, Kluwer Law International 2014) 3537–3539; Kronke and others (n 1) 253–255.

the seat will bar an attempt to refuse recognition or enforcement on those same procedural grounds.[117]

Fourthly, an arbitral tribunal is under no obligation to consider all the evidence a party wishes to present or indeed to permit the submission of all the evidence such a party wishes to present.[118] This means that evidential rules which apply to state courts, for example a requirement to consider all evidence presented to the court, will not necessarily apply to an arbitral tribunal, and even if they do apply the courts will generally defer to the decision of the arbitral tribunal.[119] **8.052**

In general, it should be noted that although 'the "due process exception" to enforcement proves to be one of the most popular claims to avoid enforcement'[120] it is rarely successful in practice, with one commentator noting that a 2006 survey showed that it was rejected by courts in 90% of the cases analysed.[121] Moreover, in the context of trust arbitration, this ground is most likely to be invoked in the same situation as the incapacity defence, where a minor, incapable, unborn or unascertained beneficiary has been involved, and thus it turns around the same issue of whether representation provisions for them are likely to be accepted by the courts or not. Another issue which has been discussed above is the possibility that a party is impecunious and therefore unable to present his case. It would appear that this ground does not attract much sympathy in the world of international arbitration,[122] although, as noted above, there are possible human rights concerns which could lead to a refusal of recognition or enforcement. **8.053**

7. Art V(2)(a) – refusal of recognition or enforcement on the basis of inarbitrability

Art V(2)(a) provides that 'Recognition and enforcement of an arbitral award may also be refused if the competent authority in the country where recognition and enforcement is sought finds that … (a) the subject matter of the difference is not capable of settlement by arbitration under the law of that country'. The wording of this provision implies a key difference from the grounds of refusal of enforcement or recognition considered so far, namely that this ground does not need to be invoked by a party but rather can be invoked *ex proprio motu* **8.054**

117 Born (n 116) 3539–3541.

118 Kronke and others (n 1) 248.

119 ibid 249–250.

120 ibid 233.

121 Gaillard, Di Pietro and Leleu-Knobil (n 1) 727–728.

122 ibid 715.

by the courts. In consequence, whereas, in the absence of a disputing party, defects under Art V(1) would not result in a refusal of recognition or enforcement, under Art V(2) a court could still refuse to recognise or enforce an award even if there is no dispute between the parties.[123]

8.055 As arbitrability has been considered both under national law, specifically English and Commonwealth law, and in the context of Art II(1) of the Convention, it is unnecessary to elaborate further on the point here. This is particularly the case as the two articles apply similar standards and answer essentially the same question. In consequence, there are relatively few decisions addressing the point under Art V(2)(a) as it is usually dealt with under Art II(1).[124]

8. Art V(2)(b) – refusal of recognition or enforcement due to a violation of public policy

8.056 Article V(2)(b) provides that 'Recognition and enforcement of an arbitral award may also be refused if the competent authority in the country where recognition and enforcement is sought finds that: ... (b) the recognition or enforcement of the award would be contrary to the public policy of that country'. This ground of refusal is closely related to the arbitrability provision addressed immediately above, with some commentators holding that 'arbitrability is part of public policy even if Article V(2) separates in its text one from the other'.[125] Assuming this is true, however, the two are not coextensive, and in considering the Convention, it appears more convenient to adopt the structure of the Convention and separate the two, as has been done in this work.

8.057 The concept of public policy is central to the NYC, as without Art V(2) 'Contracting States would not have accepted the obligations of the Convention',[126] but it is unfortunately not defined in the text of the Convention. Three main alternatives were identified by the Interim International Law Association Report on the topic as follows:

I. A violation of basic norms of morality and justice;
II. International public policy;
III. Transnational or 'truly international' public policy;[127]

---

123 Paulsson (n 3) 217–218.

124 Born (n 116) 3696.

125 Mistelis (n 70) para 5-38.

126 Paulsson (n 3) 217.

127 Audley Sheppard, 'Interim ILA Report on Public Policy as a Bar to Enforcement of International Arbitral Awards' 19 Arbitration International 218–221.

The first alternative emphasises the fact that public policy is an extremely high bar to reach, a common shorthand is that 'enforcement of a foreign arbitral award may be denied on public policy grounds "only where enforcement would violate the forum state's most basic notions of morality and justice"'.[128] **8.058**

The second alternative emphasises the fact that 'a distinction [is] drawn between domestic and international public policy' so that the public policy defence rarely leads to a refusal of enforcement.[129] In certain jurisdictions the requirement for an award to violate international public policy before it can be refused enforcement is provided in statute, whereas in other jurisdictions it has merely been applied by the courts.[130] In general, it is accepted that international public policy is 'confined to violation of really fundamental conceptions of legal order in the country concerned'.[131] **8.059**

The third alternative comprises 'fundamental rules of natural law; principles of universal justice, jus cogens in public international law and the general principles of morality accepted by what are referred to as "civilized nations"'.[132] This concept was pioneered by, *inter alia*, Pierre LaLive who considered that an international arbitrator 'is not the organ of a State; he is not bound by any national system of private international law, while being obliged to follow, or so it would seem, the general principles of private international law …'.[133] In consequence, the arbitrator is obliged to apply transnational public policy even against the international public policy or laws of a state.[134] **8.060**

Of the three possibilities, the first and second are not necessarily exclusive as 'international public policy' could be considered to be only applying to situations which violated 'the most basic notions of morality and justice'. However, the third possibility is a clear alternative as it excludes all public policies except those which are common to several states or part of public international law.[135] The general consensus is that the international public policy approach is the correct one,[136] and this is the approach adopted by the ILA Report on Public **8.061**

128 ibid 219.

129 ibid.

130 ibid 219–220; Gaillard, Di Pietro and Leleu-Knobil (n 1) 789–791.

131 Sheppard (n 127) 220.

132 ibid.

133 LaLive P, 'Transnational (or Truly International) Public Policy and International Arbitration' (1987) 3 Comparative Arbitration Practice and Public Policy in Arbitration 258, para 43.

134 ibid 312–314.

135 See generally LaLive (n 133).

136 Born (n 116) 3655.

Policy as a Bar to Enforcement of International Arbitral Awards.[137] On the other hand, there are several examples of courts applying the domestic public policy or even explicitly rejecting the concept of international public policy.[138] As regards transnational public policy, it has been stated that there are no examples of this being clearly and expressly applied, although some courts appear to have done so indirectly.[139] It can therefore safely be said that this approach is not a mainstream one. In consequence, it seems sensible to focus on international public policy for the remainder of this section.

8.062 International public policy, and indeed public policy generally, can be divided into two parts: (i) procedural public policy; and (ii) substantive public policy.[140] In the international context, the prohibition of abuse of rights is an example of a substantive public policy issue, whereas an example of a procedural public policy issue would be the requirement for tribunals to be impartial.[141] As to the general content of international public policy, it has been stated that it includes:

(i) fundamental principles, pertaining to justice or morality, that the State wishes to protect even when it is not directly concerned;
(ii) rules designed to serve the essential political, social or economic interests of the State, these being known as "lois de police" or "public policy rules"; and
(iii) the duty of the State to respect its obligations towards other States or international organisations.[142]

8.063 It is clear then that international public policy is an extremely narrow category, albeit not as narrow as transnational public policy, and this narrow approach has been reflected in the vast majority of contracting states as well as commentary.[143]

8.064 One last point about public policy in general merits mention: although Art V(2)(b) clearly mandates the application of the *lex fori*'s public policy and not the application of another state's public policy, some state courts will consider the public policy of another state where that state 'has a materially closer con-

137 P Mayer and A Sheppard, 'Final ILA Report on Public Policy as a Bar to Enforcement of International Arbitral Awards' (2003) 19 Arbitration International 249, 250–253.

138 Born (n 116) 3655.

139 Sheppard (n 127) 221.

140 ibid 230.

141 Mayer and Sheppard (n 137) 255–256.

142 ibid 255.

143 Sheppard (n 127) 226–228; Born (n 116) 3655–3658; Paulsson (n 3) 231; Kronke and others (n 1) 366–367.

nection to the matter than the recognition forum',[144] building on the approach in the choice of law context.[145] The ILA Final Report does not approve of this approach,[146] except to a limited extent in the transnational law context,[147] but Born has stated that it is not *per se* contrary to the Convention.[148]

In the context of trust arbitration, it is difficult to see why it would it be held *per se* contrary to public policy. As discussed above in the context of arbitrability, there is little reason for civil law legal systems to do so, and there is no support for this view in common law legal systems either. However, as was noted in the section on the Hague Trust Convention and elsewhere, there may be scenarios in which a court could refuse to recognise or enforce an award, as follows: **8.065**

I. Where the award relates to a trust which violates forced heirship rules[149] in a civil law jurisdiction or, in the English context, the award violates provisions of the Inheritance (Provision for Family and Dependants) Act 1975; or
II. Where an award would have unreasonable adverse tax consequences or would appear to be related to criminal tax avoidance; or
III. Where an English court or other onshore Commonwealth court was asked to recognise or enforce an award relating to immovable property located in the jurisdiction which was held by a trust not subject to a perpetuity period; or
IV. Where the beneficiaries were not properly represented in the proceedings, particularly if they were minor, incapable, unborn or unascertained, or, in the European context, if there was a breach of Art 6(1) ECHR.

All of these situations have been discussed in the appropriate place above, and thus there is no need to expand on them further here. However, it should be stated that in the context of the NYC, the third example is the most contentious. Although the issue discussed there would involve domestic public policy, it is unclear whether it would reach the high bar of international public policy. On the other hand, given that commentary[150] on the Hague Trust Convention, **8.066**

144 Born (n 116) 3666.

145 ibid 3666–3667.

146 Mayer and Sheppard (n 137) 258–259.

147 ibid 259–260.

148 Born (n 116) 3667.

149 See generally Caroline Deneuville, 'Choice of Foreign Law Not Providing for Forced Heirship' (2019) 25 Trusts & Trustees 17; Thomas Wach, 'Forced Heirship and the Common Law Trust – Especially from the Swiss Point of View – Part I' (1996) 2 Trusts & Trustees 15; Thomas Wach, 'Forced Heirship and the Common Law Trust – Especially from the Swiss Point of View – Part II' (1996) 2 Trusts & Trustees 21.

150 Hayton DJ (ed), *The International Trust* (Jordans 2011) para 3.54.

which includes a public policy exception worded in narrower terms than the NYC, suggests that this would be a possibility, it may well meet the high bar of international public policy.

C. ENFORCEMENT UNDER ENGLISH AND COMMONWEALTH LAW

8.067 As an initial point it should be noted that, as elsewhere, while this section focuses on English law, most of what is said will apply *mutatis mutandis* in a number of Commonwealth jurisdictions, as, in general, Commonwealth jurisdictions share similar means of enforcing arbitral awards. In England, these are the summary procedure under s 66 of the Arbitration Act 1996, the special regime for NYC awards provided for in ss 100–104 of the 1996 Act, enforcement at common law by an action on the award and enforcement under the Foreign Judgments (Reciprocal Enforcement) Act 1933. Each of these methods of enforcement will be considered in turn below.

1. Section 66 of the Arbitration Act 1996 and equivalent overseas provisions[151]

8.068 Enforcement under this section is the usual means for enforcing an arbitral award[152] and is a summary procedure which can be used to enforce awards regardless of their seat.[153] Section 66(1) provides that with the court's permission an award can be enforced in the same way as a court judgment, while s 66(2) provides that where the court grants permission, judgment can be entered in terms of the award. It is possible to 'seek leave of the court [so] that the award may be enforced in the same manner as a judgment or order of the court under s.66(1), but not go further and seek judgment in the terms of the award under s.66(2)'.[154] The primary reason why an individual might seek to unlink the two subsections is to prevent enforcement issues abroad where the award has merged with the judgment.[155] As an action under s 66 is summary, it is usually made *ex parte* with merely an arbitration claim form, a witness state-

151 Singapore Arbitration Act s 46; Hong Kong Arbitration Ordinance s 84; Rule 26.20 New Zealand High Court Rules 2016.

152 DStJ Sutton, J Gill and M Gearing, *Russell on Arbitration* (24th edn, Sweet & Maxwell 2015), para 8-003.

153 ibid.

154 ibid.

155 ibid para 8-003; para 8-008.

ment, the arbitration agreement and the arbitral award itself, with translations of the foregoing if necessary.[156]

Although the court will usually give permission to enforce an award under s 66,[157] the court retains a discretion to refuse to do so,[158] and it has been stated that the s 66 procedure should only be used in 'reasonably clear cases'[159] or at least only in cases where an objection to enforcement 'can properly be disposed of without a trial'.[160] Moreover, it is important to note that 'there is no closed list of cases where leave to enforce an award may be refused',[161] with the courts' discretion instead being limited 'in a negative way, i.e. by setting out certain cases where enforcement shall not be ordered'.[162] However, the courts are aware of the fact that refusing enforcement under s 66 and requiring a party to bring an action on the award would 'potentially [waste] time and costs'.[163] They are therefore not favourably disposed to refuse enforcement for essentially formalistic reasons[164] and will allow disputed issues of fact to be decided under a s 66 application rather than requiring a full trial, particularly when the issues are of a type which 'are commonly determined on a s.67 application'.[165] As s 67 addresses the issue of substantive jurisdiction, and it would appear that objections to enforcement under s 66 can also include issues of public policy, arbitrability or defects of form,[166] it must be that situations in which enforcement cannot be sought under s 66 are exceedingly rare. **8.069**

It is important to note that even though s 66 is a summary procedure, the opposing party is still entitled to object to enforcement of the award as well as the award itself, not just on the mandatory s 66(3) ground of lack of substantive jurisdiction, but also on discretionary grounds of, *inter alia*, public policy, arbitrability and defects of form.[167] In consequence, a party who wishes to challenge a decision to enforce an arbitral award 'is likely to try first to set aside **8.070**

---

156 ibid para 8-003.

157 ibid para 8-004.

158 'Report on the English Arbitration Bill' (UK Departmental Advisory Committee on Arbitration Law 1996) para 374; Sutton, Gill and Gearing (n 152) para 8-005.

159 Lord Mustill and Stewart C Boyd QC, *Commercial Arbitration: 2001 Companion* (2nd edn, Butterworths, 2001) 349.

160 ibid 419.

161 'Report on the English Arbitration Bill' (n 158) para 374.

162 ibid.

163 *Sovarex SA v Romero Alvarez SA* [2011] EWHC 1661 (Comm) [46].

164 ibid.

165 ibid 48.

166 Sutton, Gill and Gearing (n 152) para 8-011; Mustill and Stewart (n 159) 349.

167 Sutton, Gill and Gearing (n 152) para 8-011; Mustill and Stewart (n 159) 349.

the decision. Failing that, he may seek leave to appeal the decision to the Court of Appeal.'[168] However, the burden of proof is on the party resisting enforcement, as is also the case under the NYC, s 103 of the Act and the UNCITRAL Model Law.[169] Moreover, as with ss 68–69 of the Act, a party may have lost the right to object under s 66 due to s 73(1), which provides that a person loses the right to object to an arbitral proceeding in which they have taken part unless they timeously raise objections regarding alleged lack of jurisdiction or other irregularities. Furthermore, s 73(2) provides that where a tribunal rules it has substantive jurisdiction and a party does not challenge the award through any available arbitral appeal process or challenge the award timeously, 'he may not object later to the tribunal's substantive jurisdiction on any ground which was the subject of that ruling'.[170] It is clear then that whilst s 66 is not 'an administrative rubber stamping exercise',[171] it is not likely to be easy for a party to successfully challenge an application for enforcement under s 66.

8.071 As regards practical issues of enforcement permission, if an order has not been successfully challenged, nor the award set aside, it can then be enforced in the same way as a court judgment, which can include an injunction or application of the doctrine of issue estoppel,[172] a writ or warrant of control, third party debt or charging order, attachment of earnings and even the appointment of a receiver.[173] Failure to comply with an injunction, either granted by the court or a tribunal, can be rectified via 70.2A of the Civil Procedure Rules (CPR) which provides that the court can direct that the 'act required to be done may, so far as practicable, be done by another person',[174] which could be either the claimant or any other person appointed by the court.[175] The recalcitrant party will have to bear the costs of the act being done,[176] and the court also retains the power under s 39 of the Senior Courts Act 1981[177] to order the execution, or in the case of a negotiable instrument indorsement, of conveyances, contracts or other documents and negotiable instruments. In such a case, the document in

168 Sutton, Gill and Gearing (n 152) para 8-011.

169 *Sovarex S.A v Romero Alvarez S.A* (n 163) para 43.

170 Arbitration Act 1996 s 73(2).

171 *West Tankers Inc v Allianz Spa & Generali Assicurazione Generali Spa* [2012] EWCA Civ 27 [38].

172 Sutton, Gill and Gearing (n 152) para 8-007.

173 See 'PRACTICE DIRECTION 70 – ENFORCEMENT OF JUDGMENTS AND ORDERS – Civil Procedure Rules' <https://www.justice.gov.uk/courts/procedure-rules/civil/rules/part70/pd_part70> accessed 1 February 2020.

174 ibid rule 70.2A(2).

175 ibid.

176 ibid rule 70.2A(3).

177 ibid rule 70.2A(4)(a).

question shall be treated 'as if it had been executed or indorsed by the person originally directed to execute or indorse it'.[178] The court also retains the power to hold the recalcitrant party in contempt of court.[179]

In the context of trust arbitration, there is no reason why enforcement of a trust arbitration award under s 66 should be different than for any other type of award. As all the objections which can be brought against trust arbitration, namely public policy or arbitrability objections, jurisdictional objections and issues of due process and human rights, can be addressed in the s 66 procedure, there does not seem to be any obvious reason why a trust arbitration award could not be enforced under s 66. It should also be noted that where a person has not taken part in the proceedings, something which may be more likely in trust arbitration for example where there is a wide class of beneficiaries, where the beneficiaries couldn't afford to participate or were minors or where the beneficiaries couldn't be located, s 72 of the Act grants them the right to apply for declaratory, injunctive or other relief on certain grounds. The Act states that such persons have the right on application for such relief to question '(a) whether there is a valid arbitration agreement, (b) whether the tribunal is properly constituted, or (c) what matters have been submitted to arbitration …'.[180] Moreover, they also have the right as a party to the proceedings to challenge an arbitral award on any of the grounds listed in ss 67–68 of the Act and do not have to comply with the s 70(2) duty to exhaust arbitral procedures.[181] Although this is not strictly speaking related to s 66, it is clear that s 72 will play a role when enforcement is sought under s 66 against a recalcitrant party who took no part in the proceedings. **8.072**

2. Enforcement via sections 100–104 of the Arbitration Act 1996 and equivalent overseas provisions[182]

These sections are a re-enactment of ss 3–7 of the Arbitration Act 1975,[183] and provide a special regime for the enforcement of NYC awards. As noted above, the regime is not mandatory so that a claimant can choose whether he wishes to enforce under the special regime, s 66 or an action on the award. However, in practice, a claimant will usually enforce under the NYC-specific regime as **8.073**

178 Senior Courts Act 1981 s 39(2).

179 Rule 70.2A(4)(b) 'PRACTICE DIRECTION 70 – ENFORCEMENT OF JUDGMENTS AND ORDERS – Civil Procedure Rules' (n 173).

180 Arbitration Act 1996 s 72(1).

181 ibid 72(2).

182 Australian International Arbitration Act s 8; Singapore International Arbitration Act ss 19, 29.

183 Mustill and Stewart (n 159) 383.

there is no advantage in proceeding via s 66 or an action on the award.[184] As with s 66, enforcement under this procedure is via a summary procedure and is usually made *ex parte*[185] and the documents which a claimant is required to produce under s 102 are also identical to those required under s 66. However, there is one key difference between the two regimes: unlike under s 66, the court has no discretion not to enforce an award, it must recognise or enforce an award unless one of the grounds specified in s 103(2) applies.[186] However, the court does have discretion under s 103(5) to adjourn a decision on recognition or enforcement where an application for setting aside or suspension of the award has been made before a competent authority, i.e. a court at the seat or in the jurisdiction under whose law it was made.[187] As with s 66, the burden of proof is on a party resisting enforcement, not the claimant,[188] and this burden is significant as 'English law recognises an important public policy in the enforcement of arbitral awards, and the courts will only refuse to do so ... in a clear case'.[189]

8.074 Moreover, even where grounds for refusing recognition or enforcement are made out, the court retains discretion to recognise or enforce an award although the case law on the matter is somewhat convoluted.[190] There is a further lack of certainty on the matter as it does not appear that there are any cases in which an English court has enforced an award notwithstanding the existence of one of the grounds in s 103(2), and there are only two cases where it has adjourned a case on the basis of s 103(5).[191] As s 103(2) merely replicates the grounds for refusal of enforcement or recognition provided in Art V of the NYC which have already been discussed above, and the possibility of adjournment on the basis of s 103(5) is outwith the scope of this book, there is no need to analyse either section further.

---

184 ibid 350.

185 Sutton, Gill and Gearing (n 152) paras 8-029–8-030.

186 Arbitration Act 1996 s 103(1)–(4).

187 ibid ss 103(5), (103)(2)(f).

188 Sutton, Gill and Gearing (n 152) para 8-033.

189 AV Dicey, *Dicey, Morris and Collins on the Conflict of Laws* (Sweet & Maxwell/Thomson Reuters 2012) para 16-150; *Honeywell International Middle East Ltd v Meydan Group LLC* [2014] EWHC 1344 (TCC) [67].

190 See Sutton, Gill and Gearing (n 152) para 8-035; *Yukos Oil Co v Dardana Ltd (No 1)* [2002] CLC 1120, 1128; *Dallah Real Estate and Tourism Holding Company v The Ministry of Religious Affairs, Government of Pakistan* [2010] UKSC 46 paras 67–70, 126–131.

191 Sutton, Gill and Gearing (n 152) para 8–035.

3. Action on the award

This is a substantially more cumbersome process as it requires the claimant to prove not only the existence of a valid arbitration agreement covering the relevant dispute, but also that an arbitral award was made on the basis of the agreement and that it has not been complied with.[192] In other words, unlike under the s 66 procedure, the burden of proof is on the party enforcing the award and not the party resisting its enforcement. This is undoubtedly one of the most important differences between the two procedures. All the same grounds of objection are open to a defendant in both procedures, except that a party bringing an action on an award cannot plead serious irregularity as a defence[193] and as they cannot set aside an award via a counterclaim[194] in such a case they would have to make a separate application to have the award set aside.[195] It would also appear that the practical means of executing the judgment resulting from an action on the award are the same as those discussed above in the context of section 66.[196] **8.075**

It is unsurprising that given the more burdensome nature of an action on the award as opposed to a s 66 proceeding, such proceedings are only likely to occur where, for some reason, the award does not come within the scope of the Act. One example would be where the arbitral proceedings arose out of an oral arbitration agreement which was not evidenced in writing and thus fell outwith the scope of s 5 of the Arbitration Act 1996. Given that the writing requirement under s 5 is extremely expansive, as discussed above, such cases are likely to arise only rarely. An example of a case where an award had to proceed via an action on the award as opposed to a s 66 action is *Goldstein v Conley*.[197] In that case, possibly due to clumsy drafting and subsequent amendments, although awards from the Lands Tribunal generally were treated as arbitral awards and came within the scope of the fact, awards of costs did not. In consequence, the award of costs was only enforceable at common law by an action on the award and not via the expedited s 66 procedure. **8.076**

It is difficult to see how the possibility of an action on the award has any relevance in the context of trust arbitration, given that, as with arbitration **8.077**

---

192 ibid para 8-020.

193 *Scrimaglio v Thornett and Fehr* [1924] All ER Rep 802; Sutton, Gill and Gearing (n 152) para 8-021.

194 *Birtley District Co-Operative Society Ltd v Windy Nook and District Industrial Co-Operative Society* (1959) 1 WLR 142.

195 Sutton, Gill and Gearing (n 152) para 8-021.

196 ibid para 8-023.

197 *Goldstein v Conley* [2001] EWCA Civ 637.

in general, it would be simpler to enforce a trust arbitration award via s 66 and there are no advantages to doing so via an action on the award instead. Moreover, the primary issue for trust arbitration awards is whether there was an agreement between the parties not whether there was an agreement in writing, given that, as discussed above, the writing requirement in English law is extremely widely construed. In consequence, as an arbitration agreement is a necessary precondition to a successful action on the award, just as with the s 66 procedure, there seems to be no reason to enforce via the former.

4. Enforcement Under the Foreign Judgments (Reciprocal Enforcement) Act 1933 and equivalent Acts

8.078 As an initial point it should be noted that although this section only refers to the English Act in the interest of conciseness, it has been replicated in numerous Commonwealth jurisdictions and thus it can be applied to the equivalent overseas Acts *mutatis mutandis.*[198] The main purpose of this Act is to 'facilitate the enforcement of commercial judgments abroad by making reciprocity easier'. It also establishes a registration system for judgments of countries to whom the Act has been applied.[199] The registration system set up by the Act is mandatory and exclusive so that no other proceedings, including common law actions, can be brought before UK courts as regards registrable judgments.[200] Its importance in the context of arbitration arises from the fact that s 10A of the Act states that, 'The provisions of this Act, except sections 1(5) and 6, shall apply, as they apply to a judgment, in relation to an award in proceedings on an arbitration which has, in pursuance of the law in force in the place where it was made, become enforceable in the same manner as a judgment given by a court in that place'. This means that where a foreign court grants leave to enforce in an equivalent fashion to that set out in s 66(1) of the Arbitration Act 1996, the award can be enforced under the 1933 Act. If the foreign court has given judgment in terms of the award, then the judgment itself will be enforceable under the 1933 Act.[201]

8.079 The procedure set out for the registration of judgments in the Act is straightforward, requiring merely an application 'supported by a verified or certified

---

198 Hong Kong Foreign Judgments (Reciprocal Enforcement) Ordinance; New Zealand Reciprocal Enforcement of Judgments Act 1934; Queensland Reciprocal Enforcement of Judgments Act 1959; Singapore Reciprocal Enforcement of Foreign Judgments Act.

199 For a list of those countries and discussion of the Act's relevance in the present day see Dicey (n 189) para 14-014.

200 *New Cap Reinsurance Corporation Ltd ((in Liquidation)) v Grant; Rubin v Eurofinance SA* [2012] UKSC 46 para 170; Dicey (n 189) para 14-014.

201 Dicey (n 189) para 16-168 fn 474.

or otherwise duly authenticated copy of the judgment, and by a certified translation thereof, as well as by a witness statement or affidavit stating that the applicant believes himself entitled to enforce the judgment and that registration is not liable to be set aside'.[202] Moreover, an application can be made *ex parte*, and although the order granting permission to register the judgment must be served on the defendant, service can be done without permission.[203] These aspects of the scheme are comparable to the procedures available under s 66 and ss 102–103 of the Arbitration Act, but the grounds on which an award can be set aside are somewhat broader. Section 4(1)(a) requires an award to be set aside on a variety of jurisdictional grounds, breach of due process, namely that the defendant was not served in sufficient time to allow him to defend the proceedings and did not appear, fraud, public policy or lack of *locus standi*. Section 4(1)(b) sets out a discretionary ground of set aside where there is an issue of *res judicata*. Assuming that an award is not set aside, the effect of registration is that it can be executed in the same way as a judgment of the High Court of England and Wales.[204]

It is important to note that, contrary to what is stated in *Mustill & Boyd*,[205] whether by the passage of time or mere error, enforcement under the 1933 Act is not mandatory or exclusive for arbitral awards. This results from the fact that s 6 of the Act, which requires registrable judgments to be enforced only under the Act, does not apply to arbitral awards and thus it is possible to enforce such awards under s 66 or ss 102–103 of the 1996 Act or by an action on the award.[206] As the procedure is archaic, and a claimant does not benefit from the presumption of validity or reversed burden of proof,[207] as under s 66 and ss 102–103, it is unclear why enforcement would ever be sought under this procedure as opposed to the alternatives. One tentative suggestion, as laid out in Dicey, is to circumvent the requirement for notice when seeking enforcement of an award in jurisdiction B by obtaining executory force for an award before the courts of jurisdiction A, whose law does not require such notice, and then registering the award for enforcement *ex parte* in jurisdiction B.[208] As with s 66 and ss. 102–103 of the Arbitration Act, no special issues appear to arise in the context of trust arbitration awards. **8.080**

202 ibid para 14-188.
203 ibid.
204 ibid para 14-189.
205 Mustill and Stewart (n 159) 422–423.
206 Dicey (n 189) para 16-169.
207 ibid para 16-168.
208 ibid para 16-171.

9

ISSUES TO CONSIDER WHEN DRAFTING A TRUST ARBITRATION CLAUSE

A. INTRODUCTION

9.001 The aim of this relatively short but nevertheless important section is to review some of the key drafting issues discussed above. It is not meant to be a drafting checklist, nor, for obvious reasons, can it provide any legal advice, but it can highlight the critical things which settlors and their legal advisors must take into account when considering whether and how to draw up a trust arbitration clause.

B. WHERE, WHICH, WHAT AND WHO?

9.002 These are really the fundamental issues for any trust:

I. *Where:* Will the trust be based onshore or offshore? A trust isn't a legal person so what this question really means is, where will the trust assets be placed? And where will the trustees, beneficiaries, and other parties be based? This is a crucial issue with regards to the question of public policy, the potential application of forced heirship and familial provision rules, taxation and so on.

II. *Which:* What law will govern the trust? In particular, does the law governing the trust explicitly recognise trust arbitration or will the trust deed instead be relying on the common law and general arbitration statutes to validate its use of trust arbitration?

III. *What:* Will the trust be a discretionary trust? Will it even be a 'black hole trust' with almost unlimited discretion? Or a bare trust? Or even an interest in possession trust? This question is closely related to the question of which law will govern the trust, as certain trusts can only be created in particular jurisdictions (such as the Cayman Islands STAR trust, the BVI VISTA trust, or private purpose trusts generally, which are not permitted in England and more mainstream trust jurisdictions).

IV. *Who:* Are the beneficiaries all adults with full capacity or are some of them children or otherwise mentally incapable? Will the beneficiaries be able, and willing, to explicitly consent to the trust arbitration clauses or will one of the mechanisms discussed in this paper have to be used to prove such consent? Alternatively, does the chosen law recognise trust arbitration so that there is no need to be overly concerned about the issue of consent. If there are any children or mentally incapable parties, how will their consent to trust arbitration be obtained: can the parents or guardian consent on their behalf or can the court ratify their consent? If not, does their interest have to be deferred until a certain age in order to obtain their consent as an adult or does someone have to be appointed to consent on their behalf?

Although we might wish that it were otherwise, it goes without saying that trust arbitration clauses are not the most important part of a trust (although they are not an unimportant part, given how crucial they are when any conflict arises) and thus the answers to many of the above questions may already have been determined by decisions made about other parts of the trust deed. However, it is still important for there to be joined up thinking regarding the dispute resolution clause (in this case a trust arbitration clause) and the rest of the trust deed: as is well known, the dispute resolution clause is often the last clause to be considered in contracts or other agreements[1] and this causes a whole host of problems.[2] Moreover, given that the drafting of trust deeds, **9.003**

---

1 Jane Parsons, 'Don't Be a Midnight Cowboy: Avoiding Common Pitfalls When Drafting and Negotiating Arbitration Clauses' (*Arbitration Blog*, 1 November 2018) <http://arbitrationblog.practicallaw.com/dont-be-a-midnight-cowboy-avoiding-common-pitfalls-when-drafting-and-negotiating-arbitration-clauses/> accessed 4 July 2021; 'The Conundrum of the Arbitration vs. Litigation Decision' <https://www.americanbar.org/groups/business_law/publications/blt/2015/12/07_veasey/> accessed 4 July 2021; Edna Sussman and Victoria A Kummer, 'Drafting the Arbitration Clause: A Primer on the Opportunities and the Pitfalls' (2012) 67 Dispute Resolution Journal 30.

2 This includes conflicting arbitration and litigation clauses; see in the Singapore context 'Interpreting and Enforcing Conflicting Jurisdiction and Arbitration Clauses in the Singapore Courts' (2021) e-First Singapore Academy of Law Journal. The most infamous problem in the arbitration context is that of pathological arbitration clauses, for a classic example see Stefan Michael Kroll and Loukas A Mistelis (eds),

outside of commercial contexts, generally lacks the same urgency as the drafting of contractual arbitration clauses (where one may be in constant last-minute negotiation with the other side) there is really no excuse for rushing the dispute resolution clause or the trust deed generally.

C. MAKING THE TRUST ARBITRATION CLAUSE STICK: HOW WILL BENEFICIARIES AND OTHER PARTIES BE BOUND?

9.004 As has been discussed repeatedly in the literature, this is one of the crucial challenges faced by trust arbitration, particularly when minor or otherwise legally incapable beneficiaries are involved. To recap, the possibilities for binding beneficiaries and other parties are as follows:

I. Explicit consent;
II. Condition precedent;
III. Condition subsequent in the form of a forfeiture clause;
IV. Statutory provisions.

9.005 The first option, that of explicit consent, is usually only viable for the trustee and the settlor as, *inter* alia, the beneficiaries may change over time, they may not exist at the time of the creation of the trust, they may not be able to consent, or they may refuse to consent (at least explicitly). On the other hand, the option of conditions precedent or subsequent only applies to beneficiaries and not to the trustee or the settlor (at least in so far as they are trustee or settlor, they could also be beneficiaries under the trust). Although conditions precedent and subsequent are different, the fundamental question which a settlor must ask himself is the same in both cases: does he want a beneficiary to be unable to benefit from the trust or forfeit their interest in it if they do not consent to arbitration? Is the need to have any disputes which arise under the trust settled by arbitration really that important to him?

9.006 Although the likelihood of a beneficiary giving up their benefits under a trust purely out of a refusal to arbitrate must be thought to be low, it nevertheless remains a risk that the settlor must consider. It is also important that the settlor consider what legal systems are in play, as the use of forfeiture clauses may cause problems in legal systems with familial provision statutes such as Canada and in any event regardless of whether the settlor uses a condition precedent or a forfeiture clause: the courts in certain jurisdictions may override these

---

International Arbitration and International Commercial Law: Synergy, Convergence and Evolution (Kluwer Law International 2011) 123–139.

clauses due to the existence of a familial provision statute or forced heirship provisions. That issue, however, is really one to be dealt with by 'where' above: if the trustees and the trust assets are in jurisdictions which do not have familial provision or forced heirship rules, and even more so if they have so-called 'firewall' provisions preventing the enforcement of such claims, such issues may not arise. The same applies, *mutatis mutandis*, regarding the law chosen to govern the trust relationship.

The last option, that of benefiting from statutory provisions which validate trust arbitration, applies to all parties involved in the trust relationship and is subject to the limitations regarding international enforcement that were discussed above. This, again, goes back to the issues of where and which above: if the trust assets and the trustees are based in jurisdictions with trust arbitration provisions and if a law is chosen to govern the trust which recognises trust arbitration, the lack of international enforcement may not be an issue. **9.007**

D. DUE PROCESS ISSUES

This, again, is a key issue for trust arbitration. The fundamental question is, how can the beneficiaries' consent be obtained in a way that is compliant with due process and how can it be ensured that the dispute resolution process as a whole is fair to them. The main issues are as follows: **9.008**

I. If the ECHR applies, how can it be ensured that all the relevant parties give a valid waiver of their ECHR rights?
II. How can the beneficiaries' right to be heard be protected in the arbitral proceedings? This is a particular issue for minor or otherwise legally incapable beneficiaries, as well as those who are impecunious.
III. Do the provisions for the appointment for arbitrators, or other parts of the dispute resolution clause, violate the rule against no man being a judge in their own cause?

As with many of the above issues, the answers to the above questions will often depend on where and which: for example, if the trust assets and parties to the trust relationship are not in a country where the ECHR applies, nor is a law chosen which is subject to the ECHR, then there is no need to consider the issue of waiver of ECHR rights. Similarly, jurisdictions which have statutory provisions for trust arbitration may well address the issue of how to represent beneficiaries in arbitral proceedings. Moreover it stands to reason that in trusts where the beneficiaries have no enforceable rights but instead must rely on an **9.009** enforcer or the like (for example under a Cayman Islands STAR trust) the issue of due process for beneficiaries need not be at the forefront of your mind.

9.010 In general, as long as one has chosen to apply the law of an arbitration-friendly jurisdiction and as long as the trust assets and trustees are in arbitration-friendly jurisdictions, one need not necessarily be concerned about technicalities: instead, one should consider whether a particular provision is fair or not to the beneficiaries or other parties. Although the settlor may be motivated by a desire to minimise the possibility of recalcitrant beneficiaries causing any problems, he presumably does not want actually legitimate claims to be stifled (for example where the trustee is in cahoots with a particular beneficiary or class of beneficiaries and completely ignores the legitimate rights of other beneficiaries, or where the trustee is completely negligent and the value of the trust fund is significantly reduced as a result, or where the trustee actually defalcates the trust fund) and thus the settlor should not focus on a desire to minimise legal proceedings to the exclusion of all else. Moreover, having fair due process provisions will minimise the risk of legal challenges and may even demotivate beneficiaries from bringing challenges as they will not feel hard done by. That said, it is possible to briefly review some of the specific issues which should be considered for the above questions, and this will be done below.

1. Waiver of ECHR rights

9.011 As a reminder, the ECtHR has held that in order for a waiver of an ECHR right to be valid it must be:

I. Free;
II. Unequivocal;
III. Permissible; and
IV. Attended by minimum safeguards commensurate to its importance.

9.012 It isn't possible or desirable to discuss all the various complexities of each requirement here but it is important to note that the ECtHR does accept implied waiver of rights so that, in general, as long as the beneficiary takes some benefit under a trust with a trust arbitration clause (which they know about) no issues should arise. In any event, it is worth noting that the author isn't aware of any arbitral awards which were refused enforcement due to a violation of the ECHR, and, in any event, even where the ECtHR holds that an individual's rights were violated by arbitration this can be a pyrrhic victory as the legal costs often dwarf any remedy granted by the court. For example, in the case of *Mutu and Pechstein v Switzerland* Claudia Pechstein claimed almost € 4,000,000 but was only awarded € 8,000 by the court, despite it finding that her right to a public hearing had been violated.[3] It must be the case that this paltry sum was far exceeded by the claimant's legal costs. Similarly, in the more recent case of *BEG S.P.A. v Italy* the successful claimant requested that the court award it over € 2,000,000 in damages under various categories and € 350,000 in legal costs, in addition to ordering the Italian state to have the proceedings reheard. However, the court only awarded it € 15,000 in damages and € 30,000 in costs, as well as declining to order Italy to have the proceedings reheard as it lacked the power to do so.[4]

The conclusion of the above is that, while it is theoretically very interesting, in practice the ECHR does not have a great deal of practical importance when it comes to trust arbitration or even arbitration generally. **9.013**

2. Right to be heard

The primary issues here are as follows: **9.014**

I. How can beneficiaries, and in particular minor or legally incapable beneficiaries, be represented in trust arbitration proceedings?
II. How can provision be made for legally impecunious beneficiaries so that they can protect their rights?

Both of these issues will be addressed in turn below.

(a) Representation of beneficiaries

As discussed above, there are effectively three means of representing beneficiaries, including minor and legally incapable beneficiaries, in trust arbitration proceedings: **9.015**

I. The first option is to have litigation friends or the like appointed by the arbitral tribunal, the court or some other means;
II. The second option is to provide for virtual representation provisions in the trust deed;
III. The third and last option is to provide for provisions analogous to representative actions in litigation in the trust deed.

It isn't necessary to address each of these options in detail as that has already been done above, but broadly speaking the first option is suitable for trusts where there are only a few clearly identified beneficiaries and where there are **9.016**

3 *Mutu and Pechstein v Switzerland* [2018] Application nos 40575/10 and 67474/10, para 192.
4 *BEG SPA v Italy* [2021] Application no 5312/11 [156–165].

minor or legally incapable beneficiaries, whereas the latter two options are suitable for trusts where there are different classes of beneficiaries. The reason for this is that while it is practical to appoint a litigation friend or the like to represent individual beneficiaries in trusts with a low number of beneficiaries, this becomes more difficult in trusts with broadly drawn clauses and dozens or hundreds of beneficiaries. In the latter situation rather than representing each individual beneficiary it is more practical to represent different classes of beneficiaries as a whole, while allowing individual beneficiaries to represent themselves if they wish.

9.017 As already discussed, the choice of which representation mechanism to provide for in the trust deed depends on which legal system is chosen to govern the trust (among other reasons because certain states may have enacted representation provisions for trust arbitrations), and the settlor's appetite for risk. The latter issue arises because the doctrine of virtual representation is recognised in the US but not in England, and therefore a settlor with less appetite for risk may opt for the idea of representative actions instead. In any event, the key takeaway is that settlors do need to consider the issue of representation for beneficiaries and should provide clauses in their trust deeds that address the matter. Not doing so could have serious consequences, not only because of the rules of natural justice but also because many of those jurisdictions which do statutorily recognise trust arbitration require that beneficiaries be represented in trust arbitration proceedings.

(b) Making provision for impecunious beneficiaries

9.018 As the apocryphal case of *Jarndyce v Jarndyce* has shown millions of readers throughout the world, trust litigation used to be automatically funded from the trust fund, however this is no longer the case[5] (indeed, even if it was still the case this would not necessarily be the case in trust arbitration) and thus the possibility arises that a beneficiary might have a legitimate claim but be unable to bring it due to a lack of financial means. It is highly unlikely that such claims would be funded by legal aid and they may therefore be complete stifled. Although the common law generally took a 'tough luck' approach to such situations, as discussed above, there is a risk that a failure to provide such beneficiaries could breach the ECHR or violate provisions in the applicable law which require the beneficiaries to be represented in the arbitral proceedings. It is true that representatives could be appointed for impecunious

5 'Costs in Trusts Litigation | STEP' <https://www.step.org/tqr/tqr-february-2010/costs-trusts-litigation> accessed 5 July 2021.

beneficiaries, or indeed that impecunious beneficiaries could simply represent themselves, and it is also true that in many jurisdictions contingency fee, 'no win, no fee' or third party funding arrangements might be available depending on the nature of the dispute and the size of the trust fund. Notwithstanding this, it is nevertheless prudent for the settlor and his legal advisors to consider whether he should include provisions for impecunious beneficiaries in the trust deed in order to avoid any issues. This does not mean that he need necessarily include such beneficiaries, he may take the view that the size of the trust fund does not justify such provisions or that *pro bono* or other funding arrangements can be reached with lawyers and therefore decide not to include them.

It goes without saying that there is always a risk of provisions which are **9.019** intended for impecunious beneficiaries being abused by those who want to litigate hopeless or frivolous claims or who simply don't want to pay their own legal fees. It is therefore important that such provisions are carefully drafted, as provisions which simply give carte blanche to an individual who feels they are impecunious to draw from the trust fund run the risk of causing a *Jarndyce v Jarndyce* situation and exhausting the trust fund.

3. Issues regarding the appointment of arbitrators

The fundamental issue here is, once again, that the provisions for appointing **9.020** arbitrators should be fair. It goes without saying that this excludes only allowing one party to appoint arbitrators or requiring the appointment of biased arbitrators, but it also raises more nuanced issues where there is multi-party arbitration (as will often be the case for trust arbitration) so that different group of beneficiaries with conflicting interests are not forced into selecting the same arbitrator. As discussed above, in such cases arbitral institutions may well require that the entire arbitral tribunal be appointed by them in order to avoid any procedural unfairness, and thus selecting an arbitral institution may well take care of this situation. Indeed, if one selects the ICC for example it would probably be better not to include any provisions regarding arbitrator appointment in multi-party situations as the relevant part of the ICC rules may well be held mandatory and one may consequently face a situation where the ICC refuses to allow the arbitration to proceed under the ICC rules.

Another issue concerns imposing requirements for arbitrators, which might **9.021** well be sensible in certain circumstances (for example, requiring arbitrators to have trust law experience), in that it is important not to select individuals or categories of individuals who might have conflicts of interest with parties involved in the proceedings. For example, it goes without saying that you cannot nominate the trustees as arbitrators (at least, if there are claims against them or which involve them) or other beneficiaries, nor would it be sensible to have them select the arbitrators in the same circumstances.

BIBLIOGRAPHY

JOURNAL ARTICLES

Aall J, 'Waiver of Human Rights' (2010) 28 Nordic Journal of Human Rights 300

Aall J, 'Waiver of Human Rights' (2011) 29 Nordic Journal of Human Rights 206

Aall J, 'Waiver of Human Rights' (2011) 29 Nordic Journal of Human Rights 56

Alexander D and Robins S, 'Settlor Insolvency and Fraudulent Dispositions: England and Wales' (2011) 17 Trusts & Trustees 132

Ambrose C, 'Arbitration and the Human Rights Act' [2000] Lloyd's Maritime and Commercial Law Quarterly 468

Angoura S, 'Arbitrator's Impartiality Under Article V(1)(D) of the New York Convention' (2019) 15 Asian International Arbitration Journal 29

Bamforth N, 'The Application of the Human Rights Act 1998 to Public Authorities and Private Bodies' (1999) 58 The Cambridge Law Journal 159

Besson S, 'Arbitration and Human Rights' (2006) 24 ASA Bulletin 394

Blattmachr J, 'Reducing Estate and Trust Litigation Through Disclosure, In Terrorem Clauses, Mediation and Arbitration' (2008) 9 Cardozo Journal of Conflict Resolution 237

Böckstiegel K-H, 'Public Policy and Arbitrability' (1987) Comparative Arbitration Practice and Public Policy in Arbitration, Volume 3 ICCA Congress Series 177

Boesch BW, 'The ICC Initiative' (2012) 18 Trusts & Trustees 316

Bosques-Hernández GJ, 'Arbitration Clauses in Trusts' [2008] InDret

Bove AA, 'Another Look at Trust Decanting' (2018) 24 Trusts & Trustees 338

Bratza MJ and Padfield A, 'Exhaustion of Domestic Remedies under the European Convention on Human Rights' (1998) 3 Judicial Review 220

Brazier L, 'The Arbitrability of Investor-State Taxation Disputes in International Commercial Arbitration' (2015) 32 Journal of International Arbitration 1

Brekoulakis S, 'The Historical Treatment of Arbitration under English Law and the Development of the Policy Favouring Arbitration' (2019) 39 Oxford Journal of Legal Studies 124

Cheng T, 'Features of Arbitral Practice that Contribute to System-Building' (2012) 106 Proceedings of the Annual Meeting (American Society of International Law) 292

Chia HY, 'Keeping Trusts Out of Court: Toward Arbitrating Trust Disputes in Singapore' (2014) 27 New York International Law Review 1

Chung RKL, 'The Rules of Natural Justice in Arbitration' (2011) 77 Arbitration 167

Clark R and Lange DG, 'Recent Changes in English Arbitration Practice Widen Opportunities for More Effective International Arbitrations' (1980) 35 The Business Lawyer 1621

Clover Alcolea L, 'Trust Arbitration and the European Convention on Human Rights' (2018) 24 Trusts & Trustees 976

Cohen L and Poole J, 'Trust Arbitration – Is It Desirable and Does It Work?' (2012) 18 Trusts & Trustees 324

Cohen L and Staff M, 'The Arbitration of Trust Disputes' (1999) 7 Journal of International Trust and Corporate Planning 203

'Common Law Trusts in Civil Law Courts' (1954) 67 Harvard Law Review 1030

Conaglen M, 'The Enforceability of Arbitration Clauses in Trusts' (2015) 74 The Cambridge Law Journal 450

'Costs in Trusts Litigation | STEP' accessed 5 July 2021

Dainow J, 'Restricted Testation in New Zealand, Australia and Canada' (1938) 36 Michigan Law Review 1107

Davenport K and Nelson T, 'The Court's Role in Assisting Trustees: *Re Beddoe* Orders and Other Directions' (2017) 23(3) Trusts & Trustees 343

Davern R, 'Does the Virgin Islands Special Trusts Act Achieve Anything Special?' (2010) 16 Trusts & Trustees 750

Davies S and Ellis J, 'HMRC Wades in Offshore: Gresh v RBC Trust Company (Guernsey) Ltd & HM Revenue and Customs, Court of Appeal of Guernsey, 16 September 2009' (2010) 16 Trusts & Trustees 331

Deneuville C, 'Choice of Foreign Law Not Providing for Forced Heirship' (2019) 25 Trusts & Trustees 17

De Schutter O, 'Waiver of Rights and State Paternalism under the European Convention on Human Rights' (2000) 51 Northern Ireland Legal Quarterly 481

Douglas M and Loadsman N, 'The Impact of the Hague Principles on Choice of Law in International Commercial Contracts' (2018) 19 Melbourne Journal of International Law 1

Dunmore M, 'What to Expect from the Review of Arbitral Awards by Courts at the Seat' (2015) 33 ASA Bulletin 293Ellenbogen G, 'English Arbitration Practice' (1952) 17 Law and Contemporary Problems 656

Elliott M, 'Beyond the European Convention: Human Rights and the Common Law' (2015) 68 Current Legal Problems 85

Emberland M, 'The Usefulness of Applying Human Rights Arguments in International Commercial Arbitration' (2003) 20 J. Int'l Arb. 355

Fox D, 'Non-Excludable Trustee Duties' (2011) 17 Trusts & Trustees 17

Frolik LA, 'Trust Protectors: Why They Have Become "The Next Big Thing"' (2015) 50 Real Property, Trust and Estate Law Journal 267

Furness M and Scott T, 'In the Post-Pitt World …' (2014) 20 Trusts & Trustees 871

Gaillard E and Trautman DT, 'Trusts in Non-Trust Countries: Conflict of Laws and the Hague Convention on Trusts' (1987) 35 The American Journal of Comparative Law 307

Goode R, 'The Role of the Lex Loci Arbitri in International Commercial Arbitration' (2001) 17 Arbitration International 19

Goode R, 'Arbitration – Should the Courts Get Involved?' (2002) 2 Judicial Studies Institute Journal 33

Goudkamp J, 'The Rule Against Bias and the Doctrine of Waiver' [2007] Civil Justice Quarterly 310

Goudkamp J, 'Facing up to Actual Bias' (2008) 27 Civil Justice Quarterly 32

Graham T, 'The Problems with Compulsory Arbitration of Trust Disputes' (2014) 20 Trusts & Trustees 20

Groves M, 'The Rule Against Bias' [2009] Monash University Law Research Series 485

Groves M, 'Exclusion of the Rules of Natural Justice' (2013) 39 Monash University Law Review 285

Groves M, 'Waiver of Natural Justice' (2019) 40 Adelaide Law Review 641

Hacking, Lord, 'The Story of the Arbitration Act 1979' (2010) 76 Arbitration 125

Hale B, 'Argentoratum Locutum: Is Strasbourg or the Supreme Court Supreme?' (2012) 12 Human Rights Law Review 65

Hartwig HJ, 'Infants' Contracts in English Law: With Commonwealth and European Comparisons' (1966) 15 The International and Comparative Law Quarterly 780

Hayton D, 'The Hague Convention on the Law Applicable to Trusts and on Their Recognition' (1987) 36 International & Comparative Law Quarterly 260

Hayton D, 'Trusts and Forced Heirship Problems' (1993) 4 King's College Law Journal 12

Hayton D, 'Problems in Attaining Binding Determinations of Trust Issues by Alternative Dispute Resolution' (Kluwer Law International 2001)

Hayton D, 'The Strength of Beneficiaries' Rights under English Law and the Laws of Caribbean States' (Transcontinental Trust Conference, Geneva, 19 June 2013)

Hayton D, 'Reflections on The Hague Trusts Convention after 30 Years' (2016) 12 Journal of Private International Law 1

Heyworth M, 'The Hidden Cost of Some Trustees – Trustee Commissions' (2007) 13 Trusts & Trustees 37

Holden A, 'The Arbitration of Trust Disputes: Theoretical Problems and Practical Possibilities' (2015) 21 Trusts & Trustees 546

Horton D, 'The Federal Arbitration Act and Testamentary Instruments' (2011) 90 NCL Rev. 1027

Horwitz H and Oldham J, 'John Locke, Lord Mansfield, and Arbitration During the Eighteenth Century' (1993) 36 The Historical Journal 137

Hughes M, 'More Good News than Bad for Bond Trustees' (2004) 8 Journal of International Banking and Finance Law 310

'Interpreting and Enforcing Conflicting Jurisdiction and Arbitration Clauses in the Singapore Courts' (2021) e-First Singapore Academy of Law Journal

Jackson N, 'Certainty of Beneficiaries in Jersey and the First Principles of Trust Law' [2015] The Jersey & Guernsey Law Review 236

Jeremy A, 'Pacta Sunt Servanda the Influence of Canon Law upon the Development of Contractual Obligations' (2000) 144 Law & Justice – The Christian Law Review 4

Jones G, 'Trusts on Tour: Jurisdiction Clauses in Trust Instruments' [2015] The Jersey & Guernsey Law Review 309

Kennett W, 'It's Arbitration, But Not As We Know It: Reflections on Family Law Dispute Resolution' (2016) 30 International Journal of Law, Policy and the Family 1

Kerr M, 'Arbitration and the Courts: The UNCITRAL Model Law' (1985) 34 International and Comparative Law Quarterly 1

Kryvoi Y and Davydenko D, 'Consent Awards in International Arbitration: From Settlement to Enforcement' (2015) 40 Brooklyn Journal of International Law 827

LaLive P, 'Transnational (or Truly International) Public Policy and International Arbitration' (1987) 3 Comparative Arbitration Practice and Public Policy in Arbitration 258

Langbein JH, 'Mandatory Rules in the Law of Trusts' (2004) 98 Northwestern University Law Review 1105

Lawson PG, 'The Rule Against "In Terrorem" Conditions: What Is It? Where Did It Come from? Do We Really Need It?' (2005) 25 Estates, Trusts & Pensions Journal 71

Le Poidevin N, 'Going Bust: Insolvency and Trusts' (2010) 16 Trusts & Trustees 299

Le Poidevin, N, 'Arbitration and Trusts: Can It Be Done?' (2012) 18 Trusts & Trustees 307

Logstrom BA, 'Arbitration in Estate and Trust Disputes: Friend or Foe' (2004) 30 ACTEC J. 266

Lorenzen EG, 'Commercial Arbitration. International and Interstate Aspects' (1934) 43 The Yale Law Journal 716

Lucke HK, 'Arbitration Clauses in South Australia' (1975) 5 Adelaide Law Review 244

MacDougall R, 'Courts and ADR: A Symbiotic Relationship' (LEADR & IAMA Conference, Sydney, Australia, 7 September 2015)

Matthews P, 'Remuneration for Professional Trustees' (1995) 9 Trust Law International 50

Matthews P, 'Shooting STAR: The New Special Trusts Regime from the Cayman Islands' (1997) 11 Trust Law International 67

Matthews P, 'Capacity to Create a Trust: The Onshore Problem, and the Offshore Solutions' (2002) 6 Edinburgh Law Review 176

Matthews P, 'What Is a Trust Jurisdiction Clause?' (October 2003) The Jersey Law Review 232

Maurici J, 'The Modern Approach to Bias' (2007) 12 Judicial Review 251

Mayer P and Sheppard A, 'Final ILA Report on Public Policy as a Bar to Enforcement of International Arbitral Awards' (2003) 19 Arbitration International 249

McKenzie C, 'Private Trust Companies: The Best of All Worlds' (2008) 14 Trusts & Trustees 99

Molloy T and Graham T, 'Arbitration of Trust and Estate Disputes' (2012) 18 Trusts & Trustees 279

Niegel J, 'Liechtenstein Trusts: An Overview of the Law and Practice' (2004) 10 Trusts & Trustees 19

Nolan RC, '"The Execution of a Trust Shall Be under the Control of the Court": A Maxim in Modern Times' (2016) 2(2) CJCCL 469

Nottage L and Morrison J, 'Accessing and Assessing Australia's International Arbitration Act' (2017) 34 Journal of International Arbitration accessed 15 May 2021

Ortner H and Schwarz F, 'Chapter III: The Arbitration Procedure – Procedural Ordre Public and the Internationalization of Public Policy in Arbitration' in Gerold Zeiler and Irene Welser (eds), *Austrian Arbitration Yearbook*, vol 2008 (Manz'sche Verlags- und Universitätsbuchhandlung 2008)

Oster J, 'Public Policy and Human Rights' (2015) 11 Journal of Private International Law 542

Penner JE, 'The (True) Nature of a Beneficiary's Equitable Proprietary Interest under a Trust' (2014) 27 Canadian Journal of Law & Jurisprudence 473

'Resolution of Tax Disputes in International Arbitration' (2017) 4 McGill Journal of Dispute Resolution 86

Rigozzi A, 'Challenging Awards of the Court of Arbitration for Sport' (2010) 1 Journal of International Dispute Settlement 217

Robinson W, 'The Effects of the Human Rights Act 1998 on Arbitration' (2002) 42 Amicus Curiae 24

Robinson W and Kasolowsky B, 'Will the United Kingdom's Human Rights Act Further Protect Parties to Arbitration Proceedings?' (2002) 18 Arbitration International 453

Rotman LI, 'The Vulnerable Position of Fiduciary Doctrine in the Supreme Court of Canada' (1996) 24 Manitoba Law Journal 60

Samuel A, 'Arbitration, Alternative Dispute Resolution Generally and the European Convention on Human Rights' (2004) 21 Journal of International Arbitration 413

Schaul-Yoder R, 'British Inheritance Legislation: Discretionary Distribution at Death' (1985) 8 Boston College International and Comparative Law Review 205

Shauer FF, 'English Natural Justice and American Due Process: An Analytical Comparison' (1976) 18 William & Mary Law Review 47

Smith, L, 'Give the People What They Want? The Onshoring of the Offshore' (2018) 103 Iowa Law Review 2155

Sheppard A, 'Interim ILA Report on Public Policy as a Bar to Enforcement of International Arbitral Awards' (2003) 19(2) Arbitration International 217

Sheppard A, 'Chapter 10: Third Party Non-Signatories in English Arbitration Law' (2016) 37 The Evolution and Future of International Arbitration, International Arbitration Law Library 183

Sheppard A and Chaston MJ, 'Third-Party Rights under the English Arbitration Act 1996' (2004) 6 Asian Dispute Review 43

Smith, Lionel, 'Unravelling Proprietary Restitution' (2004) 40 The Canadian Business Law Journal 317

Steyn J, 'Arbitration and the Courts: Arbitration Systems in England and Wales' (1980) 35 Arbitration Journal 9

Stone O, 'Recent Developments in Family Law in British Common Law Jurisdictions' (1967) 67 Columbia Law Review 1241

Strong SI, 'Arbitration of Internal Trust Disputes: The Next Frontier for International Commercial Arbitration?' (February 22, 2018). To be published in final form in ICCA Congress Series No. 20, *Evolution and Adaptation: The Future of International Arbitration* (Wolters Kluwer, 2019 forthcoming)

Sussman E and Kummer VA, 'Drafting the Arbitration Clause: A Primer on the Opportunities and the Pitfalls' (2012) 67 Dispute Resolution Journal 30

'The Conundrum of the Arbitration vs. Litigation Decision' accessed 4 July 2021

Tweeddale A and Tweeddale K, 'Scott v Avery Clauses: O'er Judges' Fingers, Who Straight Dream on Fees' (2011) 77 Arbitration International 423

Ugarte R and Bevilacqua T, 'Ensuring Party Equality in the Process of Designating Arbitrators in Multiparty Arbitration: An Update on the Governing Provisions' (2010) 27 Journal of International Arbitration 9

Van den Berg AJ, 'Recent Enforcement Problems under the New York and ICSID Conventions' (1989) 5 Arbitration International 2

von Segesser G, 'Arbitration of Trust Disputes' (2017) 35 ASA Bulletin 10

Wach T, 'Forced Heirship and the Common Law Trust – Especially from the Swiss Point of View – Part I' (1996) 2 Trusts & Trustees 15

Wach T, 'Forced Heirship and the Common Law Trust – Especially from the Swiss Point of View – Part II' (1996) 2 Trusts & Trustees 21

Young S, 'The Evolution of Bias: Spectrums, Species and the Weary Lay Observer' (2017) 41 Melbourne University Law Review 928

MONOGRAPHS AND BOOK CHAPTERS

Arsanjani MH and others (eds), *Looking to the Future: Essays on International Law in Honor of W. Michael Reisman* (Brill Nijhoff 2011) accessed 8 November 2019

Bachand F and Bond S (eds), *International Arbitration Court Decisions* (3rd edn, Juris 2011)

Bar C von and others (eds), *Principles, Definitions and Model Rules of European Private Law: Draft Common Frame of Reference (DCFR)* (Full edn, Sellier European Law Publishers 2009)

Bates E, *The Convention of 1950 and Key Features of its Subsequent Evolution* (Oxford University Press 2010) accessed 2 November 2019

Blackaby N and others, *Redfern and Hunter on International Arbitration* (5th edn, Oxford University Press 2009)

Born G, 'Chapter 6: Nonarbitrability and International Arbitration Agreements' in *International Commercial Arbitration* (2nd edn, Kluwer Law International 2014)

Born G, *International Commercial Arbitration* (2nd edn, Kluwer Law International 2014)

Brekoulakis S, Lew J and Mistelis L (eds), *The Evolution and Future of International Arbitration* (Wolters Kluwer 2016)

Cane P, *Administrative Law* (Oxford University Press 2011)

Carlevaris A, 'The Bounds of Party Autonomy in Institutional Arbitration' in A Carlevaris and others (eds), *International Arbitration Under Review: Essays in Honour of John Beechey* (ICC 2105).

Chitty J, *Chitty on Contracts* (Sweet & Maxwell 2012)

Collins S, *International Trust Disputes* (Oxford University Press 2012)

De Groot JK and Nickel BW, *Family Provision in Australia* (4th edn, LexisNexis Butterworths 2012)

Dew Richard, Marine Olya and Bedworth Georgia, *Trust and Estate Practitioners' Guide to Mental Capacity* (LexisNexis/Butterworths 2007)

Dicey AV, *Dicey, Morris and Collins on the Conflict of Laws* (Sweet & Maxwell/ Thomson Reuters 2012)

Elliott S, Birke H and Mitchell C, *Restitution of Overpaid Tax* (Hart Publishing 2013)

Fouchard P and Goldman B, *Fouchard, Gaillard, Goldman on International Commercial Arbitration* (Kluwer Law International BV 1999)

Gaillard E, *Legal Theory of International Arbitration* (Martinus Nijhoff Publishers 2010)

Gaillard E, Di Pietro D and Leleu-Knobil N, *Enforcement of Arbitration Agreements and International Arbitral Awards: The New York Convention in Practice* (Cameron May 2008)

Gold AS and Miller PB (eds), *Philosophical Foundations of Fiduciary Law* (Oxford University Press 2014) accessed 3 June 2020

Graziadei M and others, *Commercial Trusts in European Private Law* (Cambridge University Press 2005) accessed 20 November 2019

Greenberg D, Greenberg Y and Stroud F, *Stroud's Judicial Dictionary of Words and Phrases* (Sweet & Maxwell 2016)

Grierson J and van Hooft A, *Arbitrating under the 2012 ICC Rules* (Kluwer Law International 2012)

Harris DJ and others, *Law of the European Convention on Human Rights* (4th edn, Oxford University Press 2018)

Harris JM, *The Hague Trusts Convention: Scope, Application and Preliminary Issues* (Hart 2002)

Hayton DJ (ed), *The International Trust* (Jordans 2011)

Hayton DJ, *Law Relating to Trusts and Trustees* (LexisNexis, 2016).

Hayton DJ and others (eds), *Underhill and Hayton. Law of Trusts and Trustees* (19th edn, LexisNexis 2016)

Horvath GJ and Wilske S (eds), *Guerrilla Tactics in International Arbitration* (Kluwer Law International 2013)

Jaksic A, *Arbitration and Human Rights* (P Lang 2002)

Kessler J, *Drafting Trusts and Will Trusts: A Modern Approach* (Sweet & Maxwell, 2017)

Kroll SM and Mistelis LA (eds), *International Arbitration and International Commercial Law: Synergy, Convergence and Evolution* (Kluwer Law International 2011)

Kronke H and others (eds), *Recognition and Enforcement of Foreign Arbitral Awards: A Global Commentary on the New York Convention* (Kluwer Law International 2010)

Lau MW, *The Economic Structure of Trusts: Towards a Property-Based Approach* (Oxford University Press 2011)

Lew JDM and others (eds), *Arbitration in England: With Chapters on Scotland and Ireland* (Kluwer Law International 2013)

Mann F, '"Lex Facit Arbitrum", in P Sanders (ed), *International Arbitration. Liber Amicorum for Martin Domke* (The Hague, Nijhoff 1967) [Reprinted under the title 'The UNCITRAL Model Law – Lex Facit Arbitrum' (1986) 2 Arbitration International 241]

Maitland FW, *Equity, Also the Forms of Action at Common Law: Two Courses of Lectures* (Cambridge University Press 1910)

Marchisio G, *The Notion of Award in International Commercial Arbitration: A Comparative Analysis of French Law, English Law, and the UNCITRAL Model Law*, vol 44 (Kluwer Law International 2017)

Marin M, *The Family Lawyer and the Court of Protection* (Family Law 2010)

Martyn JR, *Williams, Mortimer and Sunnucks on Executors, Administrators and Probate* (Sweet & Maxwell/Thomson Reuters, 2013)

Waincymer J, *Procedure and Evidence in International Arbitration* (Kluwer Law International 2012)

Mistelis LA, *Arbitrability: International & Comparative Perspectives*, vol 19 (Kluwer Law International 2009)

Mistelis L and Shore L (eds), *Arbitration Law and Practice in Asia* (Juris 2020)

Mustill MJ, *The Law and Practice of Commercial Arbitration in England* (Butterworths 1989)

Mustill MJ and Boyd, SC, *Commercial Arbitration: 2001 Companion Volume to the Second Edition* (Butterworths, 2001)

'Natural Justice – Oxford Reference' accessed 13 November 2019

Oakley AJ, *Trends in Contemporary Trust Law* (Clarendon Press 1996)

Oosterhoff AH and others, *Oosterhoff on Wills* (8th edn, Thomson Reuters 2016)

Paulsson MRP (ed), *The 1958 New York Convention in Action* (Kluwer Law International 2016)

Peel E and Treitel GH, *The Law of Contract* (13th edn, Sweet & Maxwell 2011)

Pollock F and Maitland FW, *The History of English Law before the Time of Edward I, by Sir Frederick Pollock and Frederic William Maitland* (Cambridge University Press 1898) accessed 4 April 2020

Poudret J-F and others, *Comparative Law of International Arbitration* (2nd edn, Sweet & Maxwell 2007)

Russell F, *A Treatise on the Power and Duty of an Arbitrator, and the Law of Submissions and Awards; with an Appendix of Forms, and of the Statutes Relating to Arbitration* (T & J W Johnson 1849) accessed 28 February 2021

Russell F, *Russell on the Power and Duty of an Arbitrator and the Law of Submission and Awards, with an Appendix of Forms, Precedents and Statutes* (Stevens and Sons 1935)

Santolaya Machetti P and García Roca J, *Europe of Rights: A Compendium on the European Convention of Human Rights* (Martinus Nijhoff Publishers 2012) accessed 2 November 2019

Sheedy JM and Baker SM, *Litigating Trust Disputes in Jersey: Law, Procedure & Remedies* (Hart Publishing 2017)

Smith L (ed), *Re-Imagining the Trust* (Cambridge University Press 2012) accessed 20 November 2019

Stebbings C, *Law Reporting in Britain* (Hambledon Continuum 2003)

Strong SI and Molloy AP, *Arbitration of Trust Disputes: Issues in National and International Law* (Oxford University Press 2016)

Sutton DStJ, Gill J and Gearing M, *Russell on Arbitration* (24th edn, Sweet & Maxwell 2015)

Terrell M, *A Practitioner's Guide to the Court of Protection* (3rd edn, Tottel Publishing 2009)

The Conscience of Europe: 50 Years of the European Court of Human Rights (Third Millennium Publishing Limited 2010)

Tucker L, *Lewin on Trusts* (Sweet & Maxwell 2012)

Tucker L and others, *Lewin on Trusts* (19th edn, Sweet & Maxwell/Thomson Reuters 2015)

UNCITRAL Secretariat Guide on the Convention on the Recognition and Enforcement of Foreign Arbitral Awards (New York, 1958) (United Nations 2016)

Van den Berg AJ, *International Arbitration 2006: Back to Basics?*, ICCA Congress series no 13 (ICCA & Kluwer Law International 2007)

Voser N, 'Multi-Party Disputes and Joinder of Third Parties', in *50 Years of the New York Convention*, ICCA Congress series no 14 (ICCA & Kluwer Law International 2009), 343

Wade W and Forsyth CF, *Administrative Law* (10th edn, Oxford University Press 2009) accessed 12 November 2019

Walton A, *Russell on the Law of Arbitration* (18th edn, Stevens and Sons 1970)

Waters DWM, Gillen MR and Smith LD, *Waters' Law of Trusts in Canada* (4th edn, Carswell 2012)

Wetton E, *Russell on Arbitration* (14th edn, Stevens and Sons 1949)

BLOGPOSTS AND WEBSITES

'About Us' (*GOV.UK*) accessed 16 November 2019

'Asser International Sports Law Blog | The "Victory" of the Court of Arbitration for Sport at the European Court of Human Rights: The End of the Beginning for the CAS' accessed 9 November 2019

Blogger G, 'Mutu and Pechstein v. Switzerland: Strasbourg's Assessment of the Right to a Fair Hearing in Sports Arbitration' (*Strasbourg Observers*, 30 November 2018) accessed 8 November 2019

'Contesting Probate | Contentious Probate' (*Myerson Solicitors*) accessed 11 November 2019

'Contracting States New York Convention' accessed 22 November 2019

'Dispute Resolution – Clarkson Wright & Jakes Solicitors (Orpington, Kent)' (*Clarkson Wright and Jakes Ltd*) accessed 11 November 2019

'Governor Rankin Appoints Two New Justices' (*Bernews*, 9 April 2018) accessed 3 August 2020

'HCCH | #30 – Status Table' accessed 21 November 2019

'HCCH | #40 – Publications' accessed 26 December 2019

'Judiciary' accessed 3 August 2020

'Justices of Appeal' (*Cayman Islands Judicial & Legal Website | An official website of the Cayman Islands Government*) accessed 4 May 2020

King's Road SPP, 'Judge of the Royal Court' (13 September 2011) accessed 3 August 2020

News Unlimited staff and agencies, 'Pinochet Leaves Britain' (*The Guardian*, 2 March 2000) accessed 2 May 2021

Parsons J, 'Don't Be a Midnight Cowboy: Avoiding Common Pitfalls When Drafting and Negotiating Arbitration Clauses' (*Arbitration Blog*, 1 November 2018) accessed 4 July 2021

Ross A, 'Lord Goff 1926–2016' (*Global Arbitration Review*) accessed 3 August 2019

'Sports Arbitration Revisited Pt II: Mutu and Pechstein v Switzerland' (*Keep Calm Talk Law*) accessed 7 November 2019

Staff N, 'Clarke Appointed New Court of Appeal President | The Royal Gazette: Bermuda News' (*The Royal Gazette*) accessed 3 August 2020

'Status: UNCITRAL Model Law on International Commercial Arbitration (1985), with Amendments as Adopted in 2006 | United Nations Commission on International Trade Law' accessed 23 November 2019

'The Use of Private Trust Companies | Ogier' (16 September 2010) accessed 23 November 2019

'Will Disputes Solicitors | George Green | Wolverhampton' (*George Green Solicitors*) accessed 11 November 2019

SPEECHES AND PRESENTATIONS

Bathurst HTF, 'The History of the Law of Commercial Arbitration' (Francis Forbes Society Australian Legal History Tutorials, Woolloomooloo, 18 October 2018)

French CJRS, 'Procedural Fairness – Indispensable to Justice?' (The University of Melbourne Law School 2010)

French CJRS, 'International Commercial Dispute Resolution and the Place of Judicial Power' (International Commercial Law and Arbitration Conference, Sydney, Australia, 22 August 2013)

Mance, Lord, 'Arbitration – a Law unto Itself?' (London 2015).

The Lord Thomas of Cwmgiedd TRHon, 'Developing Commercial Law through the Courts: Rebalancing the Relationship between the Courts and Arbitration' (The Bailii Lecture, London, 9 March 2016)

REPORTS

'2015 International Arbitration Survey: Improvements and Innovations in International Arbitration' (Queen Mary University of London 2015)

'A Guide to the Family Law Arbitration Scheme. An Introductory Guide for Family Arbitrators, Judges and Professional Referrers' (Institute of Family Law Arbitrators) Third Edition

'Report of the United Nations Commission on International Trade Law on the Work of Its Thirty-Ninth Session' (United Nations 2006) A/61/17

'Report on Commercial Arbitration' (Law Reform Commission of New South Wales 1967) 27

'Report on the English Arbitration Bill' (UK Departmental Advisory Committee on Arbitration Law 1996)

'Representative Proceedings' (Law Reform Commission of Western Australia) Final Report 103

'Review of the Law of Trusts. A Trusts Act for New Zealand' (New Zealand Law Commission 2013) 130

'Seen and Heard: Priority for Children in the Legal Process' (Australian Law Reform Commission 1997) 84

Sheppard A, 'Interim ILA Report on Public Policy as a Bar to Enforcement of International Arbitral Awards' (2003) 19(2) Arbitration International 217

'Traditional Rights and Freedoms – Encroachments by Commonwealth Laws Final Report' (Australian Law Reform Commission 2015) 129

'Trust Law: General Proposals' (Law Reform Commission of Ireland 2008) 92

'Trustee Exemption Clauses' (Law Commission of England and Wales 2006) 301

MISCELLANEOUS

Bureau Permanent de la Conference, *Actes et Documents de La Quinzieme Session 8 Au 20 Octobre 1984 Proceedings of the Fifteenth Session Tome II Trust – Loi Applicable et Reconnaissance Trusts – Applicable Law and Recognition* (Imprimerie Nationale 1985)

'General Anti-Abuse Rule (GAAR) Guidance' (HM Revenue & Customs 2018)

'Guide on Article 6 of the European Convention on Human Rights – Right to a Fair Trial (Civil Limb)' (European Court of Human Rights 2019)

Hudson A, 'The Trust as an Equitable Response', *Staff seminar paper* (2002)

'ICC Arbitration Clause for Trust Disputes and Explanatory Note' (*ICC – International Chamber of Commerce*) accessed 5 December 2019

'November Meeting Minutes' (Commercial Court User Group 2020)

'Suda v. the Czech Republic' (2010) 134

INDEX